Éilís Ní Dhuibhne:
Perspectives

Rebecca Pelan

Editor

Éilís Ní Dhuibhne:
Perspectives

Arlen
House

ISBN 978–1–903631–48–5, paperback
ISBN 978–1–903631–97–3, hardback

Published in 2009 by
ARLEN HOUSE
(an imprint of Arlen Publications Ltd)
PO Box 222
Galway
Phone/Fax: 353 86 8207617
Email: arlenhouse@gmail.com
www.arlenhouse.ie

Distributed in North America by
SYRACUSE UNIVERSITY PRESS
621 Skytop Road, Suite 110
Syracuse, NY 13244–5290
Phone: 315–443–5534/Fax: 315–443–5545
Email: supress@syr.edu
www.syracuseuniversitypress.syr.edu

Typesetting ¦ Arlen House
Printing ¦ Betaprint

Tá Arlen House buíoch de
Chlár na Leabhar Gaeilge
agus d'Fhoras na Gaeilge

Foras na Gaeilge

CONTENTS

7   *Acknowledgements*

9   Introduction
    Rebecca Pelan

29 Burn, Road, Dance: Éilís Ní Dhuibhne's *Bildungsreise*
    Christine St. Peter

49 The Unwritten Land:
    The Dynamic of Space in Éilís Ní Dhuibhne's *The Bray House*
    Giovanna Tallone

69 'What Matters But the Good of the Story?':
    Femininity and Desire in Éilís Ní Dhuibhne's *'The Inland Ice'*
    and Other Stories
    Anne Fogarty

87 Exile in Éilís Ní Dhuibhne's Short Fiction
    Caitriona Moloney

113 Female Maturation in Éilís Ní Dhuibhne's *Cailíní Beaga*
    Ghleann na mBláth
    Sarah O'Connor

129 'That Embarrassing Phenomenon: The Real Thing':
    Identity and Modernity in Éilís Ní Dhuibhne's Children's Fiction
    Mary Shine Thompson

151 Éilís Ní Dhuibhne's *Hurlamaboc* and the Coming-of-Age of
    Irish Children's Literature
    Anne Markey

171 Éilís Ní Dhuibhne:
    Is Minic Ciúin Athchruthaithe
    Brian Ó Conchubhair

197 'Beidh sé crap':
Bilingualism and Pidginisation in Éilís Ní Dhuibhne's Irish
Language Writings
Pádraig Ó Siadhail

221 Indirection in Éilís Ní Dhuibhne's Re-telling of 'The Search
for the Lost Husband' and 'Midwife to the Fairies'
Jacqueline Fulmer

245 'Ethnografiction':
Irish Relations in the Writing of Éilís Ní Dhuibhne
Helena Wulff

263 With Her Whole Heart:
Éilís Ní Dhuibhne and Irish Folklore
Anne O'Connor

APPENDICES
287 The Man Who Had No Story
Éilís Ní Dhuibhne

301 The Sugar Loaf
Éilís Ní Dhuibhne

319 Luachra
Éilís Ní Dhuibhne

325 Bibliography

340 Publications by Éilís Ní Dhuibhne, 1974–2008: Listed by Genre

344 Éilís Ní Dhuibhne's Major Publications: Listed Chronologically

345 Notes on Contributors

347 Index

ACKNOWLEDGEMENTS

Sincere thanks to all of the contributors to the anthology; it has been a great pleasure to work with you. I am indebted, in particular, to Anne O'Connor, for all her help and guidance in relation to both the Irish language and folkloric aspects of the collection. Her patience and generosity in answering what must have felt like an endless number of questions from me are very much appreciated. Love and thanks also to Frank Mc Guinness for his advice, given with such good humour, over our many cups of tea. To administrative and academic staff in the School of English, Drama and Film, University College Dublin, many thanks for making me feel so much at home. As always, love and thanks to my family for their support. Thanks to Professor Carole Ferrier and the Centre for Research on Women, Gender, Culture and Social Change, the School of English, Media Studies and Art History at the University of Queensland for hosting me during my time in Brisbane.

Introduction

Rebecca Pelan

Recently, I received a request for information from an American man who, during a trip to Ireland in order to visit locations mentioned in James Joyce's *Ulysses*, visited the 'Monto' area of Dublin (once known for its links with prostitution, the 'Monto' appears in *Ulysses* as 'nighttown'). While walking down Railway Street (formerly Mecklenburgh), the man noticed a number of white figurines in apartment windows; these were around ten inches in height, and showed a seated, naked woman, with a drape partially covering her. Over a distance of only two streets, he counted approximately twenty of the statues. Near the General Post Office, the visitor asked a policeman about the significance of the figurines, but the policeman didn't know. The man wondered whether I could provide any answer given that I had recently reviewed a book on Irish prostitution in which I discussed the history of the 'Monto', and he seemed curious to know whether there was some connection between the figurines and the area's background. My response could only have disappointed him. The statues, as far as I knew, were no more than a local phenomenon that took place a couple of years ago when a number of local import shops in the north city area found themselves in the midst of a figurine frenzy. The fad passed soon enough, as fads do, and what remains are a few select streets, mostly in north Dublin city, where the statues continue to take pride of place in the windows.

What struck me as interesting about this, and worthy of mention here, is the complex nature of interpretation and perspective. The interpretation of a text of any kind, whether a statue in a window or a piece of literature, depends as much on the activity of the reader as it does on the designer or author, but depends also on the place a text has in the social and historical forces at work when it is produced *and* consumed: in other words, texts are diachronic as well as synchronic, so that meaning becomes an activity produced as much by the reader as it is by the author. The active nature of texts, then, as well as the role that perspective plays in any interpretation, is evident in the query about the statues in north Dublin: an American visitor, presumably working on or interested in James Joyce, produces a perfectly valid 'reading' of something that isn't there – or is it? The owners of the statues may well have their own reasons for keeping the figures in the windows – but this can only be accessed by those who have the appropriate knowledge; the policeman, an Irish national and member of An Garda Síochána, has no knowledge of the meaning of the figurines, but neither is he familiar with James Joyce's *Ulysses* or the history of that part of Dublin city – none of which is odd, given that Dublin is a very different city now from the days when the Monto was a notoriously 'shady' area, and it is still the case that *Ulysses* is a text taught at tertiary level, mostly in English Departments, so any knowledge of these things will, largely, depend on age and type of education.

You're probably wondering by now what all of this has to do with a critical anthology on the work of Éilís Ní Dhuibhne. Well, one of the things that became apparent to me during the editing of these essays is the way in which Ní Dhuibhne's work is assessed so very differently by scholars, depending on their area of expertise and/or knowledge of things beyond the writing itself and, sometimes, even, on their geographical distance from Ireland, which is where most of Ní Dhuibhne's writing is set. This might seem really obvious – different scholars will, of course, write different essays on the same material depending on their expertise or perspective, but that's not quite what I mean. When I first read Ní Dhuibhne's story 'Midwife to the Fairies' some years ago, for example, I was a long way from Ireland, and even though I had been raised on the island, I knew very little about folklore, Irish or otherwise, at the time. What struck me most about the story was that it was written by a contemporary of mine who was prepared to address, creatively, the issue of infanticide (not to mention some pretty menacing male behaviour) in a way that was very Irish, but it was a way that I couldn't identify: I had a very clear sense of there being a depth of meaning to the story that I didn't have access to. As a feminist, my reading centred on those issues that I knew the most about, and I thought, overall, that the story was brave. Irish folklorists who read that same story around the same time, and who would have been familiar with the original tale, almost certainly produced quite different readings, and bravery probably never even entered the equation.

In alluding to these multiple readings, I'm not referring to the kinds of variations of interpretation we've come to expect in many contemporary anthologies, which, more often than not, mark their differences through diverse theoretical perspectives – Marxist, post-structuralist, postcolonial, feminist, and so on. Not that I'm suggesting this writing would resist a more theoretically-inflected treatment, quite the contrary: Ní Dhuibhne's work lends itself to serious analysis within a number of theoretical frameworks focusing on, for example, identity (gender, class and national) as fluid, unstable and socially-constructed rather than innate and constant; language (Irish/English) as the most important factor in shaping our identity and world; and anti-essentialism (identity and language) to show that constants are fluid and truths relative. Rather, the readings collected here are the result, not only of a diverse set of critical interpretations of the texts themselves, but of an even broader range of knowledge bases and critical perspectives, reflective, I suggest, of the writing that Ní Dhuibhne herself has produced and of her role as creative fíodóir:[1] novels in English and Irish, short stories (predominantly in English), drama (predominantly in Irish), and children's/young adult fiction (in both English and Irish), woven through all of which are threads of folklore, linguistic interplay, and Irish/English literary/cultural history, while, at the same time, confronting the more abstract nature of who we are as people through an interrogation of, amongst other things, families, spiritualism, materialism, love and hate, by means of this same weaving of the same threads. The degree of intertextuality in Ní Dhuibhne's work is worthy of a separate study.

In addition, Ní Dhuibhne's work traverses many of those things that have come to exist as binaries in our lives: literature/folklore, high culture/popular culture, working-class/middle-class, urban/rural, women/men, girls/boys, girls/women, youth/old age, tradition/modernity, old Ireland/Celtic Tiger Ireland, local/international and, perhaps most controversially of all, Irish/English. No doubt there are those who feel that the ways in which Ní Dhuibhne uses language in her fiction is politically questionable, especially in light of arguments that the preservation and promotion of the Irish language must rely on protection from external influences. At the same time, however, there are clearly those who think that what she does is both innovative and worthy as a means of bridging two languages/cultures, as well as helping to bring the Irish language to a broader audience: put simply, I know that there are those, especially outside Ireland, for whom Ní Dhuibhne's fiction is their only knowledge of and contact with the Irish language, and I also know that, for many others, this is not necessarily a good thing. Such polarised views reflect long-standing debates concerning the Irish language that are beyond the scope of this collection, not to mention the capacity of its editor. Nevertheless, as editor, I did have to decide whether or not to follow convention by italicising non-English words within the English language essays. I chose not to italicise Irish, in deference both to Ní Dhuibhne's own bilingualism and to the fact that a good number of the essays use or are concerned with the Irish language. Accordingly, I have worked on the basis that Irish is not a foreign language in this context.

Ní Dhuibhne's creative negotiation of the binaries mentioned can be viewed through a number of lenses, including that of hybridity. Like most really useful concepts, hybridity is a complex term that has become associated with a diverse, and sometimes contradictory, set of political and theoretical aims focusing on identity formation, although it is most often located these days within postcolonial theory to mean the integration of cultural signs and practices between colonising and colonised cultures. Jacqueline Lo outlines at least two opposing applications of the term: first, is its popular use to denote fusion, most often located in cultural activities such as music or cookery. Hybridity in this sense, most often found in eclectic postmodernism, serves as a stabilising function in settling cultural differences and contestations and, more often than not, according to Lo, "celebrates the proliferation of cultural difference to the extent where it can produce a sense of political in-difference to underlying issues of political and economic inequities",[2] hence her ironic use of the term 'happy hybridity' to mark the lack of tension, conflict or contradiction involved in this application when applied to inter- and/or cross-cultural encounters. Lo's second application tends to operate most prominently in the area of cultural and postcolonial studies, where the term 'hybridity' retains its potential to unsettle and dismantle hegemonic relations through a focus on the process of negotiation and contestation between cultures.

While Homi Bhabha suggests that hybridity is the construction of a political object that is new, "neither the One nor the Other but something else in-between",[3] Mikhail Bakhtin, who was principally concerned with language, sees hybridity as:

> a mixture of two social languages within the limits of a single utterance, an encounter within the arena of an utterance, between two different linguistic consciousnesses, separated from one another by an epoch, by social differentiation, or by some other factor.[4]

Bakhtin identifies two types of hybridity: organic (unconscious) and intentional. While there is fusion in organic hybridity, for Bakhtin, "the mixture remains mute and opaque, never making use of the conscious contrasts and oppositions" even though it is "pregnant with potential for new world views".[5] By contrast, intentional hybridity is an "artistically organized system for bringing different languages in contact with one another, a system having as its goal the illumination of one language by means of another",[6] which, when transferred to a broader cultural context is usually taken to mean that the latter has more potential for political intervention. This second definition is the most useful application of hybridity in terms of the politically-orientated work of, for instance, Gloria Anzaldúa whose fundamental concern in her work – poetry, fiction, memoirs, as well as literary and cultural criticism (all, on occasion, within the one text) – is the articulation of what she calls a new consciousness: an identity characterised by hybridity, flexibility, and plurality, centred on the life experiences of Chicana (Mexican American) women, but especially *mestizas* (Chicana and Mexican women who have mixed Native American and Spanish heritage).[7] But I think both of Bakhtin's definitions hold potential for deciphering the ways in which Ní Dhuibhne, a literary iconoclast, brings cultural binaries – including Irish and English – together in so much of her work in order to interrogate both. Whether she does this as part of a deliberate 'political' agenda (intentional hybridity) or not (organic hybridity) has not been an issue of great importance for most of her readers and critics to date, but it is easy to see how it will almost certainly become more important over time.

Despite the admiration for Ní Dhuibhne's work evident in this collection, it is intended to be, above all else, a critical anthology and not simply a tribute to a complex and interesting writer. As such, the notoriously uneasy relationship between creativity and criticism is evident at the level of critique and, also, in attempts at classification. Most writers retain a dislike of categorisation, yet it is an inherent part of literary criticism that an author's work be 'placed' – either within her or his existing *oeuvre*, or, more commonly, within a broader generic classification. This process is made even more difficult when dealing with a living author, like Ní Dhuibhne, whose work to date suggests generic and narrative experimentation, as well as a restlessness of spirit indicative of an on-going search for suitable formal modes to carry her creative voices – and I use the plural deliberately. Ní Dhuibhne makes classification difficult, not only because her work is generically diverse, but because it is the product of different authorial positionings, used for different purposes. Just as she has been able to exploit folklore, literary history, and her knowledge of English and Irish, so Ní Dhuibhne has exploited multiple creative identities: Elizabeth Dean in her earliest published work, Éilís Ní Dhuibhne for her fiction and drama (first used on publication of her story, 'Blood and Water' in 1983), Éilís Ní Dhuibhne-Almqvist (her married name) for much of her folkloric work, and Elizabeth O'Hara for her children's books (Elizabeth is the English version of Éilís, and O'Hara was her grandmother's surname). In relation to the earliest pseudonym, Elizabeth Dean, Éilís has said that she used it when she first started publishing her work, at age 18 or 19, because of a certain shyness about being a writer generally, and because of a concern over people finding out that she was writing about sexual feelings. The intensity of these feelings in her work only became obvious to Ní Dhuibhne when she saw her first short story, 'Green Fuse' in print, following its inclusion by editor David Marcus in his anthology *The Irish Eros*. The name, Elizabeth Dean, is close to the English version of Ní Dhuibhne's name, Elizabeth Deeney, which, interestingly, she has never used in print. Ní Dhuibhne did not reveal her real name to David Marcus until the 1980s when she started publishing poetry.[8] In terms of the later pseudonym, Elizabeth O'Hara, Ní Dhuibhne has said that there were two reasons for adopting this hybrid pseudonym: the first was to "distinguish her children's books from her adult ones", and the second was to "use a name that readers might be able to pronounce".[9]

Yet even here there is an anomaly: Ní Dhuibhne's novel *Singles*,[10] published in 1994 by Basement Press (the general publishing division of Attic), was published under the name Elizabeth O'Hara, but cannot comfortably be classified as either children's or young adult fiction. Having at its centre a quirky young (twenty-something) Dublin woman who is on a mission to find love, and who isn't averse to a bit of sex along the way (at one point, with two different men, though separately), the novel represents Ní Dhuibhne's first venture into the world of popular fiction, and stands as an early example of Irish 'chick-lit'. Though published in the 1990s, the novel is set in the '70s and, as such, also represents a retrospective glance at nascent Irish feminism. The central character, Nuala, develops throughout the novel from a young, insecure woman whose identity is intricately bound to a man, to one who is able to leave both the men in her life to take up an academic scholarship in Denmark, largely achieved through her discovery of the women's movement. Viewed in the context of Ní Dhuibhne's *oeuvre*, *Singles* is perhaps best assessed as a transitional work that seems to have vanished into relative obscurity, overtaken perhaps by novels like Emma Donoghue's *Stir Fry*, also published in 1994, and which deals with much the same material, but from a lesbian perspective. In addition, the appearance of writers such as Marian Keyes, who published her first Irish 'chick-lit' novel, *Watermelon*, in 1995, marked the birth of a separate category of Irish women's fiction, one that has its own prolific and committed authors who tend not to cross genre lines in the way Ní Dhuibhne does.

Ní Dhuibhne's latest English language novel, *Fox, Swallow, Scarecrow* (2007),[11] once again brings the word 'brave' to mind through its appropriation of Tolstoy's architecture in *Anna Karenina*[12] to say something about contemporary Ireland and, like Tolstoy in relation to his Russia, what Ní Dhuibhne has to say is not complimentary: the east (principally Dublin and Bray) is filled with banalities, literary launches, gossip, multi-million Euro deals, and extra-marital affairs. The west (Kerry),[13] by contrast, is the haven of all that is stereotypically Irish (though diminishing as a result of internal migration and property development): it is ostensibly quieter, more neighbourly, healthier, and more spiritual in a very Bord Fáilte (Irish Tourist Board) way – there are fairy clouds of mist and mysticism – but there is also a sinister other-worldliness, as well as an unappealing drabness and parochialism. Like

Tolstoy, then, Ní Dhuibhne draws a contrast between the decadence of modern urban society, and the peace and wholesomeness of the rural lifestyle, though, in Ní Dhuibhne's case, the contrast is ironically drawn since both Irelands, ultimately, are exposed as vacuous and false. In keeping with much of Ní Dhuibhne's writing, *Fox, Swallow, Scarecrow*, appropriates a model from the past in order to say something about the present.

The similarities between *Fox, Swallow, Scarecrow* and *Anna Karenina* are plentiful, not least in both authors' criticism of the excesses that abound in their respective societies, the interweaving of real and fictional events, as well as in characters' names and the roles they play in the overall plot: Kate/Kitty, Vronsky/Vincy, Alexei/Alex, and, of course, Anna/Anna and Levin/Leo (Levin is considered by many to be the most autobiographical character in Tolstoy's novel, and Leo is Tolstoy's first name in English); both novels are narrated in the third-person; there is a brother who has an affair with the nanny, followed by reconciliation with his wife, instigated by Anna; Anna's pregnancy to her lover and ultimate rejection of the new daughter, Annie in Tolstoy, Apple in Ní Dhuibhne – references to apples (red and green) and apple trees appear throughout the novel, but, specifically in relation to the child – Japan/nature/apple blossom, as suggested by Anna herself (320), 'apple of my eye', Garden of Eden or, in a popular reading, Chris Martin and Gwyneth Paltrow's daughter!; characters in both novels discuss current socio-political events and issues; in common also is Levin/Leo's awkwardness and rural retreat as an attempt at escape and to rid life of falseness, as is an echoing of Tolstoy's representation of the difficulty of being true to oneself when the rest of society is so false.

But there are major differences between the novels as well, not least in Ní Dhuibhne's use of humour in place of Tolstoy's drama: Leo, who is a publisher of Irish language poetry, is hopeful that his latest 'find' will bring him success at last:

> This would have to be his unique selling point. An old shocking story [about child abuse in orphanages] in an old beautiful language (Irish) and a new beautiful medium (the poetry of this

woman, which he would insist was beautiful). She was beautiful herself, which helped. And black. The first black Irish language woman poet, he was almost certain, in the world. (142)

Similarly, Ní Dhuibhne plays with Tolstoy's opening line in *Anna Karenina*: "Happy families are all alike; every unhappy family is unhappy in its own way" (*AK* 1) by opening Chapter 17 of *Fox, Swallow, Scarecrow* (almost exactly half-way through the novel) with the words: "All happy families are happy in different ways, and unhappy families are also unhappy in different ways" (201). While death occurs in Ní Dhuibhne's novel, it isn't the death of Anna, but Leo's wife, Kate, although Anna does undergo a metaphoric death (through break-down) and resurrection, one that is prophetic of a new life as a woman and as a writer. Ní Dhuibhne transposes Tolstoy's clairvoyant to the figures of the fox (with broken leg), the swallow (with damaged wing) and the scarecrow (in the figure of shape-shifter Charlene whose mind is damaged) using folklore – or at least the suggestion of folklore – to create a novel of two parts, as was its model.

The folklore of *Fox, Swallow, Scarecrow* is most closely associated with the Leo/Kate relationship, in particular during their new life in Kerry, as might be expected, given Ní Dhuibhne's ironic handling of the rural theme. The three words of the title act as a symbol of Kate's new life in the west, but are also death omens for her, though ones that she has no ability to read:

A swallow, a fox, a scarecrow.

What a strange homecoming it had been! The fairy clouds of mist, then the bird and now the fox, and the scarecrow, had welcomed her, or warned her, as she came to this new place. Were they telling her something about her life here? What would it be like?

The excitement of starting on a new path exhilarated her but it was frightening as well. She was heading into a mist. (308)

Here, Ní Dhuibhne mixes up many different representations of foxes, swallows and scarecrows drawing on ancient myths and folklore, as well as on an English literary tradition, especially in relation to the figure of the fox. Foxes have long been central characters associated with the supernatural in a number of cultures, including Native American and Scandinavian, for instance. The fox also has, of course, a long literary association via the bible, Aesop's Fables, the Canterbury Tales and children's stories, such as 'The Gingerbread Man', 'Chicken Licken', 'The Sly Red Fox and the Little Red Hen', and 'Fantastic Mr. Fox',[14] as well as with more modern writing within the English literary canon, such as D. H. Lawrence's 'The Fox' in which, when one of the central characters, March, first sees the fox, she becomes "spellbound ... So he looked into her eyes and her soul failed her":[15] in Ní Dhuibhne, "he ... [Kate] assumed it was male" had a colour unlike anything she had ever seen "an unearthly colour ... The fox's eyes were piercing. Sharp, focused. She shivered." (307). Equally, references to swallows and scarecrows abound in myths and folklore from many different countries and cultures and, in the case of the latter, can also be read as a Jungian archetype and spiritual symbol most commonly referred to as 'the shadow', representing monstrous emotions and thoughts:

> The [Jungian] Shadow is the personification of that part of human, psychic possibility that we deny in ourselves and project onto others. The goal of personality integration is to integrate the rejected, inferior side of our life into our total experience and to take responsibility for it".[16]

For me, however, the most interesting connection between the two novels is Ní Dhuibhne's borrowing of Tolstoy's use of trains as a literary motif. Trains appear in many nineteenth-century novels in English as symbols of progress and technological advancement. In some literatures, however, including Russian, they are often represented more negatively as an insidious symbol of western imperialism, which have a detrimental effect on indigenous life and its communities, which was Tolstoy's view. Accordingly, most of the references to trains in *Anna Karenina* carry negative connotations, while the speed of trains is used as a metaphor, not of progress and movement, but of destruction and harm. Tolstoy's Anna first meets Vronsky in a train station, after which she witnesses the death of a worker in the railyard, a bad omen related to Anna herself since she commits suicide by throwing herself under a train.

In *Fox, Swallow, Scarecrow*, there are several dreams/ nightmares involving trains and death, but it is Anna and Leo who are most closely connected with them: Anna, who does drive, uses, for convenience, the modern, urban (Dublin) LUAS (the word 'luas' in Irish means speed) – described in the opening to be "like a slow Victorian roller coaster" (1), and she is ultimately knocked down by one, 'dreaming' that her lover, Vincy, is beheaded in the same accident, and leading her to take a new path in life, as a woman and as a writer; while Leo, who does not drive, is more often associated with the older, somewhat archaic intercity trains that transport him between Dublin and Kerry in an irritatingly slow manner:

> But as he settled into a seat by a window that had not been cleaned in months, irritating memories of train journeys he had undertaken in other countries kept popping into his head. The TGV from Paris to Bordeaux: two and a half hours. Seville to Madrid: two and a half hours. Stockholm to Gothenburg: three hours. Dublin to Tralee: four hours and forty minutes. (55)

Leo is the connecting figure between the polarised representations of Ireland. A non-medicated manic-depressive whose parents died in a road accident when he was a young man, he has become evangelical about stopping deaths on Irish roads. Ostensibly at least, Leo undergoes a metamorphosis when he moves from east to west after his parents are killed: he sells their/his house in Dublin (Dundrum – the same place where Anna goes for the ultimate shopping experience) and buys a rural retreat in Kerry: "a beautiful house. Nestling in a niche that had been dug out of a hill overlooking the Atlantic" (60); he makes a decision not to be a manic-depressive and stops taking his medication (300); he changes from someone who hates vegetables (in Dublin) to one who becomes a vegetarian (in Kerry). What he perhaps doesn't choose is his role in the death of others, including his new wife, through his alter-ego in the form of illiterate, Irish-speaking Charlene, the scarecrow, shape-shifter (and banshee?). Both Anna and Leo have portentous figures associated with their characters and respective identities: for Anna it is the homeless man who reads the classics (a reversal of this character in Tolstoy who is connected with Levin rather than Anna), while for Leo it is the scarecrow, which manifests itself in the figure of Charlene.

There are clues from quite early on in the novel that Leo is not a well man, and much of his illness is associated with trains or train stations. His and our introduction to Charlene takes place during a train journey from Heuston Station (Dublin) to Tralee, when she sits opposite him:

> He glanced at her over the rim of his book, gradually taking in her unusual, her weird, appearance. Her hair was long, black and dry, like burnt straw. She had exceptionally pink cheeks and a wide red mouth. She did not look like an Irish speaker. Or an English speaker. He could not put his finger on it, but something about her looked extraordinary, as if she had possibly come, not just from another country, but from another planet. (57–8)

As she gets up to leave the train, Leo notices that Charlene is wearing a very short pink coat, and black lacy stockings with pink, high-heeled shoes: "Everything about her looked dotty. On the one hand, she reminded him of a character from a television series he had liked as a child, all about scarecrows (59). Later, looking at Connolly Station, Leo:

> ... did not see James Connolly, strapped into a chair to be executed in front of another grey wall in the stone breakers' yard or whatever they called the execution ground in Kilmainham (was he mixing it up with Calvary? People did). He saw crowds of soldiers on their way to the Great War. There in front of his eyes he could see them, lines of marching men in their khaki uniforms, heading to Flanders or the Somme. And among the ranks someone odd marched, a woman who looked like a scarecrow, with black straw for hair and a wide red smile. On her head was a black straw hat with a red rose in the brim, a hat only a scarecrow would wear. (171)

The reference to Calvary here connects with the real source of Leo's pain and mental illness:

> Hardly anyone was killed instantly. Most died in agony. Terrible agony. He mother and father had ... someone had revealed the truth to him some time after the funeral. A nurse from the hospital, who had not known who he was. She told him his father had lived for two hours, and his mother for four. "It is like a crucifixion," she said. "It's often like that." They didn't tell you that on the news. (272)

Charlene is consistently described as 'scarecrow-like' (205, 208), and her disappearance from the house and re-appearance in the field once Kate is installed as the new wife (308), followed by her coming to life in another field in an unsuccessful effort to forewarn Kate of danger (or cause her death?), suggest that Ní Dhuibhne's novel, ostensibly straightforwardly realist, moves subtly – arguably too subtly, since it is easily missed – in the direction of magic realism as it progresses.

Magic or magical realism is characterised by two conflicting perspectives: a rational view of reality and, at the same time, an acceptance of the supernatural as equally real. The use of the supernatural in literature has a long history, of course, and is most often used by writers to investigate oppositions (such as good v evil), and to probe hidden fears and desires, at both the individual and societal level. As a literary mode distinct from fantasy, for example, magic realism is marked by being set in an identifiable, realist world and often fuses the real and the fantastic in order to say something about disharmony between binaries: the old world and the new, rural and urban, western and indigenous. It is also, interestingly, closely linked to the concept of literary hybridity, most notably in the work of those authors who seek to represent or expose a clash of ideologies or cultures. Angela Carter, for instance, is considered to be one of the finest exponents of the style, using it most often to creatively articulate her feminist and post-modernist views on the undermining of the old orders of western patriarchy. Carter was adept at injecting her realism with fantasy elements that incorporated both the supernatural and the Gothic. Similarly, in *One Hundred Years of Solitude (1970)*, Gabriel García Marquez,[17] incorporates many supernatural elements as well as characters with supernatural powers within what is, substantially, a realist narrative, in order to represent those 'unbelievable' phenomena obliterated by European realism, but which continued to be entirely real and believable for many non-western cultures. The supernatural is also, of course, central to the Irish folk tradition.

In *Fox, Swallow, Scarecrow* Ní Dhuibhne makes use of magic realism in the shadowy figures most closely associated with

Anna and Leo. Anna's homeless intellectual is a male alter-ego of her self, as writer and reader, while the female character of Charlene/scarecrow is the alter-ego of Leo, the manic-depressive. This use of the characterised alter-ego appears also in several contemporary Irish plays, most notably Brian Friel's *Translations*, in which Jimmy Jack dreams of marrying Athene from antiquity, and has an extensive knowledge of the ancient world exhibited through his quotations from classical texts. Like Ní Dhuibhne's homeless man, Jimmy Jack uses literary texts as a means of crossing between two worlds, and just as Jimmy Jack, temporally and spatially, carries knowledge from antiquity into a nineteenth-century Irish hedge-school, so Ní Dhuibhne's homeless man carries Tolstoy's world, textually, into contemporary Dublin, also echoing Hugh's view in *Translations* that, "it can happen that a civilization can be imprisoned in a linguistic contour that no longer matches the landscape of fact".[18] The figure of the alter-ego has also been used recently and to great effect by Marina Carr in *Woman and Scarecrow* (2006),[19] in which the inner-self of the main character rises up in protest against a life of repression, unhappiness and denial of her main self. Damaged in a variety of ways, all of these characters live their lives as lies – loveless marriages, repression, denial, mental illness – until the damage demands to be dealt with. The effect is a refusal to allow the reader a passive or comfortable (realist) reading position from which to make sense of what is going on. More than one of the essays in this collection discusses Ní Dhuibhne's use of such 'supernatural' elements as a means of destabilising readers' expectations by introducing ambiguous moments of disruption, thus encouraging the possibility of alternative, non-realist, readings.

The ending of *Fox, Swallow, Scarecrow* is inconclusive – we never meet Leo again after we are told that he has settled, somewhat uncomfortably, into his new domestic life and that Kate is making plans to change his beloved house, but there is enough ambiguity throughout the text to show Leo's decline and movement towards self-destruction: his denial of his illness, his falling in love with a woman who has also spent time in an institution (which he finds distasteful), his vacuous attempts to keep reality at bay, and his increasing lethargy – he becomes used very quickly to being driven in Kate's car, and has seemingly lost interest in the 'Killing Roads' project – suggest that Leo is steadily descending into an abyss. But, distinct from Tolstoy's novel, Ní Dhuibhne's Anna survives her physical encounter with a train, survives the loss of her lover, chooses to put a distance between herself and her false life, and is introduced to us, albeit concussed and disoriented, as a woman who is finding her way back to her/self:

> Art.
>
> Peace and tranquility and art.
>
> The gabled house, yellow ochre, the smiling windows [of Annaghmakerrig].
>
> I need that.
>
> Tranquility and peace.
>
> I need to see what art is, what artists do …
>
> No talk of advances, bestsellers, pricing your book.
>
> I want to write what I have not yet written, something deep inside me, not yet seen, nor yet felt, not yet known, to me. Myself. I want to write. Real, I want to write, and unreal. (352)

Linguistically, Anna, in particular, comes complete with all kinds of playfulness and resonances: Anna Karenina/ Annaghmakerrig,[20] the writer's retreat, where Ní Dhuibhne's Anna finally "lets the words" (355) flow in a linguistic bloodletting, which, we assume, will lead her to find and write her/self rather than continuing to pursue some kind of a charade as a writer. In addition, the colour red is associated throughout the novel with both Anna/Vincy and Leo/Kate, in different ways, but consistently as a symbol of otherworldliness or the supernatural,[21] not least in the title of the novel: foxes are red, swallows have red wings (said to come from the fact that they brought fire to earth), and Ní Dhuibhne's scarecrow always has a flash of red somewhere on her being (lips, flower). However, for Kate/Leo the symbols of red foretell of death and destruction while, for Anna, they represent at least the hope and potential of liberation from false life in the novel's conclusion. In this sense, Ní Dhuibhne reverses the overall 'message' of Tolstoy's novel, in which his Anna's tragedy is most commonly interpreted as being based on her inability to be completely honest or completely false – an inner torment that eventually drives her to suicide. Tolstoy's Levin wins the love of Kitty only when he allows himself to be himself. In Ní Dhuibhne, however, it is Leo who is lost, while Anna, at least potentially, finds herself in the end.

My reason for including, however briefly, these glances at *Singles* and *Fox, Swallow, Scarecrow* is because neither novel is discussed in any of the anthology's essays, yet they reveal something about the trajectory of Ní Dhuibhne's work. In terms of her adult novels, *Singles* stands, chronologically, between *The Bray House* (1990) and *The Dancers Dancing* (1999), which are, I suggest, novels of arrival rather than of transition. It remains to be seen whether *Fox, Swallow, Scarecrow* will, ultimately, be assessed as a work of transition or arrival, but, either way, I have no doubt that it will play a part in contributing to an understanding of contemporary Irish fiction as being both innovative and engaged.

As a result of the breadth of the writings and readings covered in this collection, one of the great pleasures of my job as editor has been to see, if not the whole picture (if such a thing exists), then certainly a much greater spectrum than has previously been available in one place in relation to a writer who has attracted a serious level of interest from readers and scholars in Ireland as well as from those in many other geographic locations and with diverse areas of expertise. Hopefully, the anthology reflects that level of interest and range through the inclusion of essays by Irish scholars (writing in both English and Irish), as well as by others from America, Canada, Italy, and Sweden. Christine St. Peter opens the collection by placing *The Dancers Dancing* (1999) within the tradition of the *Bildungsroman*, or, more particularly, the *Bildungsreise*, which involves an educational trip or journey, to show how Ní Dhuibhne interweaves the motifs of burn, road, and dance to create a renewed version of the coming-of-age tale; Giovanna Tallone's examination of mapping and space in *The Bray House* (1990) shows how Ní Dhuibhne uses the device of science fiction to look at contemporary Ireland, thus intertwining interest with the local and concern with global ecological matters; Anne Fogarty concentrates on Ní Dhuibhne's short story collection, 'The Inland Ice' and Other Stories, in order to examine the ways in which Ní Dhuibhne remodels and reconstructs traditional tales and isolates overarching themes that interconnect the traditional, 'ritualised' tale with the modern/postmodern short story; Caitriona Moloney analyses the effect of exile on Irish identity, by looking specifically at the intersection of exile, Irishness, and women's sexuality as represented in a number of Ní Dhuibhne's short stories; Sarah O'Connor examines the motif of female maturation in Ní Dhuibhne's second Irish language novel, *Cailíní Beaga Ghleann na mBláth* (2003), to show how the author changed elements from Elizabeth Bowen's *The Little Girls* (1964) in order to investigate Irish female identity, decolonising childhood and, more specifically, the Irish female childhood. Two of the essays examine Ní Dhuibhne as a writer of children's or young adult fiction: Mary Shine Thompson explores the representation of modernity, especially in the content and form of Ní Dhuibhne's trilogy for young adults, *The Hiring Fair* (1993), *Blaeberry Sunday* (1994), and *Penny-farthing Sally* (1996), while Anne Markey examines the way *Hurlamaboc* (2006) probes the boundaries of writing for young readers in Ireland in the twenty-first century in terms of its target audience, its use of vernacular Irish, and its subject matter and style. Brian Ó Conchubhair, writing in Irish, places Ní Dhuibhne's writing in the context of the 're-writing' of familiar narratives, most often associated with both feminist and postcolonial writing practices, in which the 'new' story gives voice to a previously marginalised or silenced perspective. Pádraig Ó Siadhail's essay examines bilingualism and pidginisation in Ní Dhuibhne's Irish language work and asks a number of inter-related questions concerning her use of the Irish language, including whether her use of English and pidgin Irish is an example of deliberately catering to a readership that is unable to deal with 'literary Irish'. The final section of the collection concerns the intertextual influence of folklore in Ní Dhuibhne's work: Jacqueline Fulmer examines Ní Dhuibhne's re-telling of two traditional tales, 'The

Search for the Lost Husband' and 'Midwife to the Fairies', within a framework of indirection to show how, in an apparent contradiction, Ní Dhuibhne's fiction brings together an offbeat postmodern feminist sensibility with an Irish oral tradition; Helena Wulff, whose own background is in anthropology and ethnology, examines Ní Dhuibhne's awareness of ethnographic detail, and argues that this awareness makes her portraits of people and their relations revealing of human life beyond the specific contexts of her fiction. The collection concludes with Anne O'Connor's tracing of Ní Dhuibhne's background in folklore, and discusses its on-going influence in her writing to suggest, ultimately, that Ní Dhuibhne's literary work both embodies and manifests a new, and a revival of, interest in the 'Irish tradition'. In keeping with the complexities of the writing itself, these essays cross a number of critical borders: there are essays in English on Ní Dhuibhne's Irish language work, in Irish on her English language work, essays that examine her Irish language and English language fiction, *about* being young and Irish, and those that examine this work *for* those who are young and Irish, and there are those that ask us serious questions about our own critical reading practices and assumptions. All in all, I think this is a fine body of critical work that enhances our understanding of a fine contemporary writer.

NOTES

1   Fíodóir means 'weaver' in Irish and is often used to refer to a 'weaver of tales'. I'm deliberately using the term here to mark the interplay between literature, language and folklore evident in so much of Ní Dhuibhne's writing.

2   Jacqueline Lo, 'Beyond Happy Hybridity: Performing Asian-Australian Identities' in *Alter/Asians*. Ien Ang, Sharon Chambers, Lisa Law and Mandy Thomas, eds. (London: Pluto Press, 2000: 152–168), 152–53.

3   Homi Bhabha, *The Location of Culture* (London: Routledge, 1994), 25.

4   Mikhail Bakhtin, *The Dialogic Imagination: Four Essays*. Trans. Caryl Emerson and Michael Holquist. (Austin: University of Texas Press, 1981), 358.

5   *ibid*. 360.

6   *ibid*. 361.

7   Gloria Anzaldúa, *Borderlands/La Frontera: The New Mestiza* (San Francisco: Aunt Lute Books, 1987).

8   Personal correspondence, January 2009.

9   Nicola Warwick, 'Interview with Éilís Ní Dhuibhne.' *One Woman's Writing Retreat* http://www.prairieden.com/front_porch/visiting_authors/dhuibhne.html (2001).

10 Elizabeth O'Hara, *Singles* (Dublin: Basement Press, 1994).

11 Ní Dhuibhne, *Fox, Swallow, Scarecrow* (Belfast: Blackstaff Press, 2007). Further references to *FSS* are in parentheses in the text.

12 Leo Tolstoy, *Anna Karenina* (London: Oxford University Press, 1998). Further references to *AK* are in parentheses in the text.

13 Kerry is not strictly in the west, being geographically south-west. 'The west', in most discussions of politically-, linguistically-, and culturally-polarised Ireland, traditionally, would be represented by Galway. However, I think Ní Dhuibhne is using Kerry in *Fox, Swallow, Scarecrow* to *connote* 'the west' and all that is authentically 'Irish' in contemporary Ireland, perhaps in a way that Galway was, but isn't any longer.

14 http://www.thefoxwebsite.org/attitudes/folklore.html

15 D. H. Lawrence, 'The Fox' in *Four Short Novels of D.H. Lawrence* (New York: Viking Press, 1965), 32.

16 http://www.iloveulove.com/psychology/jung/jungarchetypes.htm – for information on the scarecrow as Jungian archetype, see www.supernatural.tv/reviews/legends/scarecrow.htm

17 Gabriel Garcia Marquez, *One Hundred Years of Solitude* (London: Harper Collins, 1997).

18 Brian Friel, *Translations* (London: Faber and Faber, 1981), 43.

19 Marina Carr, *Woman and Scarecrow* (Loughcrew: Gallery Press, 2006).

20 'Annaghmakerrig' (anglicised from the Irish 'Eanach Mhic Dheirg' – 'the marsh of Mac Deirg' (Dearg's son (patronymic) or Mac Deirg (surname) (An Brainse Logainmneacha/ Place Names Commission, Dublin) – is part of the Tyrone Guthrie Centre in Newbliss, County Monaghan. For further information, see http://www.tyroneguthrie.ie The Irish word 'dearg' also means 'red'.

21 The colour red represents the supernatural in folklore. As with her use of 'the west', I think Ní Dhuibhne uses red throughout the novel, explicitly and connotatively, to suggest other-worldly elements.

Burn, Road, Dance:
Éilís Ní Dhuibhne's *Bildungsreise*

CHRISTINE ST PETER

The body is a source. Nothing more.
There is a time for it. There is a certainty
About the way it seeks its own dissolution.
Consider rivers.[1]

Where they died, there the road ended
and ends still and when I take down
the map of this island, it is never so …[2]

Rivers run through them, the works of literature, not least
those of Ireland.[3] Eavan Boland's and James Joyce's Liffey
recalls Jordan and Styx, the Congo, the sweet Thames, the
Rhine and its maidens, the mighty Amazon. Rivers are, by their
nature, richly symbolic. Their meanderings trouble the false
certainties of human, especially political, geography. Their
instability challenges the fixities of printed maps. Their
silt carries and sometimes covers the sins of the past; as
Heraclitus already understood, they represent change. Their
water is salvific and destructive, creating tunnels, waterfalls,
fishing pools, places for hiding or for finding treasure. Éilís Ní
Dhuibhne, folklorist *par excellence*, had such associations in
mind when she made a small Donegal river, here just a 'burn',
the symbolic centre and structural spine of her novel *The
Dancer's Dancing*.[4] This is an author who knows the old stories
of world myth and legend, appreciates their value, and puts

them to use as "counterpoint" in her own stories, making the "contemporary" a "never never or always always", and placing them "in an international context".[5]

The Dancers Dancing insistently draws the burn – so aptly oxymoronic in this tale of female coming-of-age – to the reader's attention. It first appears in the opening epigraph, a kind of *envoi* that sets the novel in motion via the quotation from Gerard Manley Hopkins's 'Inversnaid', which eulogises a "darksome burn ... roaring down" (iv). The burn, specific to the novel, first appears innocuously in the second chapter, entitled 'Washing', but the burn's next appearance, which signals the beginning of Orla Crilly's river travel, occurs after fourteen chapters, in a section entitled 'The Burn Scene One', with four more such 'burn scenes' carefully positioned among the remaining chapters of the novel. These five burn scenes, a five-part play threaded among the chapters of the larger novel, trace an educational journey that young Orla, the novel's protagonist, will follow as her rite of passage into womanhood. But the novel also weaves other challenges for Orla during this summer of 1972 at an Irish College in the Gaeltacht. While she must attend to the lessons of the burn, she must also travel the "road to the shore" (114), as well as learn to understand the antithetical patterns of the céilí and the Fairyland Ballroom: three difficult paths to necessary knowledge in this *Bildungsroman* or, more accurately, *Bildungsreise*.[6] These three motifs – burn, road, dance – interweave in this novel to form a particularly evocative version of one of the world's most ubiquitous stories, the coming-of-age tale.[7]

But journeys into unknown experiences require maps. If others have preceded the traveller into this place, maps might exist, but they could be inaccurate, even dangerously misleading. "Maps are too important to be left to cartographers", writes cultural geographer, J.B. Harley, who challenges cartographers to learn to "subvert the apparent naturalness and innocence of the world shown in maps both past and present".[8] Maps represent, as well as occlude, cultural and political systems, constructing a story that supports the map-makers' version of their world. This kind of critical cartography informs the opening chapter of *The Dancers Dancing*, entitled 'The Map', in which an omniscient narrator challenges the reader to consider the problem of colonial mappings. Naming some great map-makers of medieval and Tudor times, as well as Richard Bartlett, a seventeenth-century British military surveyor of Ireland, the first chapter of this novel calls into question the maps and stories of Ireland that we carry in our imaginations and in our travel kits. The opening line of the novel urges us to "[I]magine that you are in an airplane, flying at twenty thousand feet", while the next conjures up an image of the landscape below, the Irish landscape, as a "chequered tablecloth thrown across a languid [female] body" (1). This languid body, we are told, is what "the early map-makers" with their "outrageous ambition" imagined. Their:

> minds' eyes flew hundreds of thousands of feet above the earth, then, when the eyes descended, brought back 'diminished, distorted images from their imagined flight' all the while insisting with their maps that this is 'the earth, the place you live in. This is what it looks like really! See you! Look!' (1)

Such maps, with their "superior angle" (2), are documents whereby the world is "normalized, disciplined, appropriated and controlled",[9] even as they fail to convey the complex dynamics of "class, gender, race, ideology, power and knowledge, myth and ritual".[10] As Catherine Nash has argued, the function of such mapping, which relies on a controlling viewpoint, is to fix the 'other', neutralising the threat of difference by the apparent stability of the map's coherence.[11] But even the most authoritative maps – and the military maps of Ireland were certainly that – cannot guarantee that control, however hard they work to cover over "alternative spatial configurations, which indicate both the plurality of possible perspectives on, and the inadequacy of, any single model of the world".[12]

Ní Dhuibhne's omniscient narrator does not deny that a "superior angle" allows one to "see plenty", but such an angle does not allow a vision "inside", or "behind, or below, before or after" (2). The view of the burn promoted by the old map-makers, and by contemporary "holiday agents", will not be able to follow the stream on its "endless journey", nor see the figures along the burn:

> on their little journeys, back and forth and up and down and in and out, until they move out of the picture altogether, over the edge, into the infinity of after the story. (2)

The opening chapter closes with the following incantation by a narrator who can make a poem of simple daily details before that voice gives way in the final statement to the demotic rhetoric of a speaker, aged thirteen and a half, both of the voices guiding the reader into the story-map of the novel:

> What you can't see is what it is better not to see: the sap and the clay and the weeds and the mess. The chthonic puddle and muddle of brain and heart and kitchen and sewer and vein and sinew and ink and stamp and sugar and stew and cloth and stitch and swill and beer and lemonade and tea and soap and nerve and memory and energy and pine and weep and laugh and sneer and say nothing and say something and in between, in between, in between, that is the truth and that is the story … The rest of the story is hidden in the mud. Clear as muddy old mud. (2–3)

The second chapter, 'Washing', shifts from the macro-vision of hegemonic mapping to a proleptic focus on four girls sitting on "rocks in the middle of the stream" (4), before they have actually started the journeys from their homes, which occurs in Chapter 4. This scene, the prologue to the five-part drama on this same stream that occurs later in the novel, underscores its symbolic centrality, as well as introducing the theme of girls on the cusp of womanhood wondering about their future. The timelessness, and possible ubiquity, of the scene give it a folkloric quality. The four girls, Dubliners Orla and Aisling, with fourteen-year-old Pauline and Jacqueline from Derry, are washing their clothes in the "brown, boggy water" of the burn, and singing "*Che sera sera.* What will be will be!" (3). This shift into a self-consciously discursive frame reminds us of the fictionality of the text, but also of the need they (and the readers) have to compose a life. This is reinforced in the chapter's final statement: "But by now their future is their past, an open book, a closed chapter, water under the bridge" (5).

The summer of the Irish College in 1972 is already in the past by the time we read the novel, and the girls somewhere in the "infinity of after the story" (2). As we shall see, each of the five subsequent burn scenes will move (will have moved) Orla, the drama's protagonist, one step closer to crucial understandings of female embodiment and sexuality, her own and that of the women who came to that stream before her, leaving behind clues to secret knowledge buried "in the mud" that the reader was promised in the first chapter of the novel. At the beginning of this tale, the stream seems tame enough as it runs through an old garden rich with rambling roses, fat onions and blackberry bushes, almost a Garden of Eden in fact, or at least a version of what Orla thinks of as Eden, "an English Country Ga-a-arden" (43). Only the barbed wire fence along one side suggests the dangers ahead.[13]

But Orla must also retrace another path, a familiar one, on another difficult journey, based not so much on the psychosexual as on the social dimension of her life and the social structures that shape her. This one begins back in Dublin, at her school, where the children board the bus that will take them from Dublin to Tubber, County Donegal. *En route* they cross the border into Northern Ireland during the violent summer of 'Operation Motorman', but this means nothing to Orla and her Dublin schoolmates, except the possibility of Mars bars, not then available in the Republic, a youthful insouciance wittily captured in the chapter's title, 'The Unchronicled Jouissance of Summer Bus Journeys When You're Young' (7). Onto that bus in Dublin pile all the old social divisions of gender and class (ethnic homogeneity being the rule here), and the ways these will affect the children's potential *jouissance*, in all its possible connotations. Nothing can be left behind, but to what extent must these old tales continue to define Orla? This road of her journey continues on foot once the bus arrives in Tubber, and plays out narratively and symbolically along the "Road to the Shore" (144), from the Irish College and Orla's host farm, past her Aunt Annie Crilly's cottage where she and her family have come in the past for summer holidays. This voyage Orla must pursue, if only because it leads to the beach

33

where the children play after lessons. But Orla dreads it, and spends most of the summer avoiding it (and swimming, her favourite activity), because she fears that her Aunt Annie, "not quite the full shilling", will insist on publicly claiming Orla as her relative in front of the teachers and the other scholars. Not bad enough that Aunt Annie wears funny clothes, has a jerking face and a squeaking voice, but – even worse – Annie and Orla share some physical resemblance. Aunt Annie, waving from the gate of the ancient cottage, demanding Orla's attention, will reveal Orla's connection to this rural world and to her working-class father's origins in this poor little farm, so far from the middle-class Dublin that Orla and her mother aspire to, and which Orla's Gaeltacht roommate, Aisling, inhabits with the effortless grace that so often accompanies class privilege. With the revelation of this 'culchie'[14] origin, other secrets might emerge: that Orla's mother has made their home into a boarding house in order to pay Orla's school expenses, or that "everything about them is too shameful" (129).[15] In a Tubber without Aunt Annie, Orla experiences (falsely, of course) the Irish College as a place of "equality that isn't possible in Dublin, land of 'What Does Your Father Do?' This is the Gaeltacht, a land of the child. What matters is the length of your hair and your skirt, the sweetness of your smile and your voice and your Irish … the ability to make friends" (136). Orla fears, not without cause, that a loss of her carefully crafted urban identity will result in the loss of her friends. The narration captures the brutal snobbery and meanness of young adolescence, but, more importantly, the way class position will shape one's experience, one's way of knowing, even one's body, something I will return to later.

The value of the traditional Ireland, represented by Aunt Annie and her cottage in the novel, is so important to the narrator that it must be rescued from Orla and her adolescent self-loathing, and one of the tests Orla must pass, on her *Bildungsreise,* will be her acceptance of her deep connections to this Gaeltacht world. In a distinctly pedagogical turn midway through the novel, the omniscient narrator delivers a paean to the miracle of the Tubber farm:

Crilly men have built the house: they have been masons and carpenters for centuries. Almost every chair and bed and table in it was made by their hands. The old clothes that fill the wardrobes were made by the women: Orla's grandmother, great-grandmother. With wool from their own sheep they spun and wove, dyed and sewed. The house is full of history, it is full of the history of work and creation (138).[16]

Anyone failing to appreciate these achievements cannot be fully mature.

Whatever its history, however, in 1972 this is Aunt Annie's house, and Orla devoutly wishes that Aunt Annie would "not exist" (140). Indeed, when Orla can no longer escape the necessity of delivering gifts from her mother to her aunt and finds her slumped in the barn, possibly dying, Orla creeps away to leave her to her fate (183–192). In an interview, Ní Dhuibhne says that Orla's willingness to let her Gaeltacht aunt die symbolises the attitude of "Irish people in general" who would be pleased to break the link with their Irish and Gaelic past, although they would not take responsibility for making that break nor for killing the Irish language.[17] But another danger also exists, a false cultural nostalgia,[18] and the omniscient narrator moves uneasily between these two currents, offering a lengthy digression about another Tubber farm that is so beautiful it will be moved stone by stone to Derry, where it will function as an open air museum; the only farm in that Catholic valley that is run on the principles and practices of Ulster Protestant farmers, learned by the elderly Catholic owners when they were sent as impoverished children to hiring fairs and shipped out to Tyrone to work on Protestant farms (186–189).[19] The narrator's treatment suggests a love for this idiosyncratic farm, but the romance is punctured immediately with the satiric comment that *this* farm is the emblem of "rural idyll, real Ireland" (188).[20] As an examination of the final chapter will show, the novel celebrates the lost traditions of the Gaeltacht even as it laments the public relations quality of its contemporary renaissance. But young Orla, at least, is allowed to redeem herself by being pleased that her aunt survived, although only when she discovers, late in the novel, that other people, folklorists in fact, value Annie Crilly and what she represents.

All this makes Orla sound very venal, but, of course, she is not. Intensely bright and self-aware, she condemns herself even as she persists in creating the story that she is not two people, Orla, "the niece of Aunt Annie" as well as Orla "the schoolgirl from Dublin" (30). But Orla "knows the score" (29) so she opts for the face-saving lie: "If her friends got wind of [the inferiority of Orla's family] she'd be done for. It's friends or family and she is thirteen and a half. She needs friends" (30).

She also needs guidance and, like the other young Irish scholars, does not look to the teachers to provide it. At such a distance from her mother, her usual guide, she relies on other, internalised maps in the form of books. Orla is a reader, and, like other precocious book-lovers of her age, reads a wide variety of texts according to her emotional and intellectual needs. In serious trouble and in need of comfort, she allows herself the secret pleasure of *Heidi,* the favourite reading of her earlier years, and a book fraught with the dangers of childhood travel (179). When she is feeling a bit more jaunty, and thirteen, she plays a fantasy role, adopting the language of Darrell Rivers, hero of Enid Blyton's 'Malory Towers' novels. Darrell is the stuff of daydreams, a girl who refuses the frippery of femininity, wears a shirt and tie and no make-up, will be a surgeon when she grows up, is always "noble, fair and kind" – and is a character "with whom Orla has always identified absolutely" (27). So deeply imbued is young Orla with the virtues of this English paragon and her redefinition of gender scripts that Darrell even inhabits her dream life. One such dream, which presages crucial landmarks of Orla's educational journey along the burn, shows Darrell/Orla fearlessly diving into a pool "with dark rocks jutting around the edges" but, here, the dream pool is quite unlike the burn's black pool; instead it is a "huge expanse of blue" in the "clean air" of an English landscape, and the language of the dream-girls is "English as she should be spoke …. Life as it should be lived" (28). True, Orla, herself, is afraid to dive in her waking moments, but "only horrible people did not dive, Orla knew" and she "believed she would be brave enough soon, given the right circumstances" (28).

Those circumstances emerge in novel's five burn scenes, which provide the crucial educational journey. At this point, the importance of the poem that prefaces the novel emerges; Hopkins' 'Inversnaid' with its eulogy of the "wildness" of the "darksome burn, horseback brown / His rollback highroad roaring down" (iv). The poem sets the tone for the whole novel, in which the young Irish scholars (some more than others, to be sure), on the brink of adulthood, take desperate chances, experiment with sex, alcohol and cigarettes, and, like the burn, roar down the path to knowledge, flooding over the banks that would contain them. "O let them be left, wildness and wet" prays the poem, and Ní Dhuibhne gives her young characters their heads. Of course, visits to this burn are strictly forbidden by the teachers, as it has "deep treacherous pools and strong currents" (208), but the map the Headmaster carries "in his head" with "every pupil carefully spotted on it", with its apparent stability and coherence, begins to crack by the second week of the scholars' arrival, and "through the cracks the insects start to creep" (67).

In 'The Burn Scene Two', Orla's version of creeping takes her over the boundary of the barbed-wire fence and onto the burn itself, leaping from stone to stone, her "feet going … as if they have a life of their own" as she follows the burn's journey deeper and deeper into the forbidden territory. Her courage is rewarded when she discovers a "verdant tunnel" through which she crawls, finding herself in a "hidden green cathedral … a completely enclosed, completely private place" (70–71). The sacredness of nature here enchants her, but the birthing and sexual resonances of the experience do not escape Orla who suddenly awakens to new dangers. She does not fear drowning – a real possibility – but, rather, a more recondite and complex sexual threat from fairies and otters, a fear born of stories from Celtic (and Norse) folklore where otters and salmon are associated. 'Dobharchú', the Irish word for otter, is, in Celtic folklore, the "father of all otters and king of the lakes", with a snout so "powerful it can break through a rock" as well as a figure that can "kill people and animals and drink their blood".[21] So, Orla's enchanted "glaucous cavern" frightens her even as it remains the most "magically seductive" place she has ever seen (71), no doubt *precisely* because it elicits so many resonances from the symbols and tales she carries in her head, her physical experience being constructed discursively through story. Not yet ready to venture into that kind of experience, she retreats back along the burn, although not before she discovers "crimson raspberries", which confirm for her the promise of a "jewel-studded world that awaits exploration … sometime soon, when she grows up" (72).

At the beginning of the next chapter, the magic of the burn scene continues into Orla's social life, filling her with courage. "Something has happened to her, there in the chestnut water, in the green tunnel … Orla belonged with the river. She was nothing there … and completely herself. Orla Herself" (73). Such moments of integral wholeness are rare in any life and transient in all. Orla's courage, which extends even to the thought of telling her friends about her relatives – no longer shameful now that she has "found her own place" (73) – fades as the topic of 'what does your father do?' arises among the girls at teatime. The moment in the burn and that perfect communion with nature recedes, and Orla is pinned back onto a social map, unable to say her father is a bricklayer. "Not now. Not ever" (77).

But Orla seeks out the burn again, unwilling to lose its seductive magic. On her next foray into the secret territory in 'The Burn Scene Three', Orla invites the daring Pauline to accompany her. Pauline is brave enough to jump off the waterfall they discover – an experience Orla actually finds orgasmic (116), although when Pauline dares Orla to jump after her, she balks. While she loves to look at the "dark, black pool, to find stepping stones across it", she can't jump, "can't cope with that sensation of free falling, being out of control" (117).

By 'The Burn Scene Four' some days later, however, much is changing for Orla. This time, she follows the burn as it runs alongside her Aunt Annie's house, "wide and quiet here, a sweet thoughtful river, not a burn any longer, although they still call it the burn anyway" (193). Here, instead of creeping through the secret entrance into a cavern, Orla stands upon a bridge from which she sees Micheál, the son of the family in whose house she is living. This is a boy who has been despised by the other girls because he is a farm boy, a "weed" (39), although Orla has been watching him, and he her for some weeks (93). At this moment, Micheál is revealed to Orla's newly sexualised vision as "the most beautiful boy she has ever seen" (194). As he stands fishing at a distance in the burn, Orla notices his physical grace and strength (and otter-like feet), but also sees him through the lenses of myth, legend and literature: he looks like the "playboy of the western world, the hero of some historical romance about Ireland" (194). When he raises his eyes from the salmon he is stalking, Orla greets him with a fractional wave, her first acknowledgement of this boy she has known for years. He does not yet respond, intent on his quarry, but then a "miracle" happens, almost unthinkable: he catches the salmon in his bare arms "as it leaps" (194). When, finally, the salmon dies in his arms, the two greet each other with full waves, Micheál and Orla, otter and salmon shape-shifting in a new dance of sexual recognition.[22]

'The Burn Scene Five' follows quickly. Here, the body-knowledge gained by the solitary Orla is joined to that of other girls and women who – as she discovers – have preceded her into this secret place on their own transgressive journeys, using the burn to hide their shame. Pauline, "anarchy personified" (52), has been embarking on her own journey, falling in love/lust with Gerry, the College's "star boy" (51), stealing out in the night to meet him by the sea. Orla's transgression takes a different turn as she seizes an opportunity to creep off alone to the burn. "I'm alone", she says, "I can do anything I want to!" (200). Her first use of this new freedom is linguistic, not surprising for this bookish girl who already knows "languages: tongues – or at least myriad dialects" (34). She "tries out all the taboo words she knows" but had never before said aloud (201). As she shouts curses and imprecations, she listens as never before to her own voice, which gets "louder and louder, clearer and clearer", getting used to uttering the language used by "uncivilised men" (and by Jaqueline and Pauline). But this outlaw mood passes quickly as the "green dampness of the burn seems to be seeping into her stomach, pressing upon it ... It is as if something is dragging her whole body down into the water" (202). As she moves to climb out of the burn, she quotes Hopkins' poem: "This darksome burn, horseback brown / His rollrock highroad roaring down", and now the wild natural energy, so clearly masculinised, is no longer a source of delight, but a weight that drains her energy (202). As she climbs from a slippery stone in the river onto the bank, her feet sink first into the "wet greenery", then into "soggy clay". On her third step "her foot strikes something very hard" and what she discovers in the mud are a "dozen skulls and tiny skeletons" (202), babies killed by their desperate, unwed or unwilling mothers. Oddly, Orla recognises immediately what it is she has found, and experiences not horror, but curiosity (202), although she is horrified when, later that evening, it appears that Headmaster Joe knows what she has been doing and what she has found: "He knows about the skulls. He knows I am connected to the skulls, although I don't know how, myself" (207). When it turns out that all he knows is that she plays by the burn, Orla is reassured: "Obviously he knows nothing, not a single thing" (209). Not a single thing that Orla is discovering, perhaps, although he has profound knowledge of the dangers of pre-marital sex, and his "most urgent task is to prevent [among his scholars] any sexual disaster. Pregnancy" (52). The next two chapters telescope discoveries Orla will need a lifetime to decipher and negotiate, but with the revelation of the dead babies, the narration circles back to the beginning of the novel, where we were promised a subversive map, "in between, in between, in between, that is the truth and that is the story ... The rest of the story is hidden in the mud" (3).

In the chapter following the fifth burn scene, 'Blood', Orla has her first period, much to her relief: "Unlikely as it seemed, she is going to be a normal woman" (204). And, yet, the only guides she inherits to read this epochal physical change are the murmurings of her classmates and her mother's statement that "the very worst thing that could happen to any family was that their unmarried daughter would get a baby" without ever "explaining how this phenomenon would occur" (203). The following chapter, 'The Workhouse', with its echoes of punitive nineteenth-century Ireland, makes clear the effects of such sexual and social transgression in an economical narrative that layers historical infanticide – Orla's dream of an ancestor executed for infanticide – with her bewildered sense that this is a story she already knows. In her dream, Orla "sees words, printed or written, people, places, moving through narratives that her sleeping self invents. But the people, the places, the words, come from where she has been awake. Can it be like that?" (210). It can; a subterranean river of desire and fear passed on from generation to generation, emerging, for example, in her mother's veiled threat that sexual transgression will result in death. This literary technique of layering events in modern Ireland with old stories of infanticide in Irish history and Irish folklore is one Ní Dhuibhne has described as "negotiating the boundaries of different worlds" where the buried, taboo past erupts in the present.[23] In this dream sequence, the lovely, liberatory promise of the "dark, black pool", into which Pauline had jumped with such abandon in 'The Burn Scene Three', is transformed in Orla's dream; here, she "enters the tunnel of foliage" with an infant, only this time she is watched sadly by a "boy that looks like Micheál" who watches as she drops it over the waterfall, the baby smiling at her as he falls "like a stone into the black skin of water" (211).

Earlier, I claimed that one needs maps when embarking on an educational journey. The guides Orla and her friends have inherited are neither natural nor innocent, as they attempt to contain the girls within particularly strict limits of gender, sexuality and class, marking them as 'other'. But it is not just freedom of movement and thought that is curtailed; the human body itself is actually constructed via these kinds of discipline and, thus, one needs to use one's body, as Orla has on her burn voyage, to achieve a deeper level of knowledge than the one on offer. Ní Dhuihne brilliantly captures this phenomenon in her use of the trope of shapeshifting. But one might also offer a theoretical framework for this idea. Just as post-structuralist thought has problematised the Enlightenment belief in the self-present, coherent, human subject, so, too, are contemporary theorists of the body arguing that the "unitary and stable condition of the body itself needs to be questioned".[24] According to this theory, a body is not a self-contained, biologically determined 'being' but, rather, a "variable boundary, a surface whose permeability is politically regulated, a signifying practice with a cultural field of gender hierarchy and compulsory heterosexuality" [among other "fields"], which will take different forms in different times and places and is always discursively constructed.[25] Elizabeth Grosz articulates this more succinctly: "It is not simply that the body is represented in a variety of ways according to historical, social and cultural exigencies while it remains basically the same; these factors actively produce the body as a body of a determinate type".[26] This 'body' theory does not pretend to banish the reality of materiality, nor does it argue for an Orwellian determinism, but it does refuse the idea of body as physical essence. This malleability of the body offers hopeful possibilities whereby the "process of securing the body's boundaries is never complete or certain [and thus] this lack of an essential corpus opens up the possibility, even the inevitability of transgression".[27] And with that, one might add, comes the possibility of change.

The discipline of the human body within particular parameters occurs in every culture, to be sure, but the control of women's bodies and the use of the body as a politically-regulated signifier has a long and particular tradition in Ireland as generations of colonial and postcolonial politicians and artists have represented the territory of Ireland as a woman's body.[28] If such inherited orthodoxies are inculcated in young people, it will take the physical use of the body to form different possibilities and truths. Thus, Ní Dhuibhne's deployment of body-maps is symbolically important, both in representing the traditional social order her text challenges *and* in narrating the discoveries her characters achieve as they traverse the inherited definitions of the 'territory'. By providing a variety of different responses among the different girls (and boys) in Tubber, Ní Dhuibhne also demonstrates how their experiences, their knowledge, and their very bodies are being constructed discursively.

Of course, this means that the individual body is also, and importantly, part of a larger social weave. The promise of the *Bildungsroman* and its sub-genres, with their humanistic belief in the notion of individual agency, comes up against the social discipline that requires that everybody be tailored into the social fabric.[29] And this disciplinary force is wonderfully evoked in this novel through the different uses of the symbol of the dance, which shapes experiences of embodiment. In their nightly céilís, the young scholars are relentlessly trained in a "system that works with great efficiency" (47) to reproduce patterns of movement and gendered interaction as formulaic and as ancient as the "swirls cut into the stones at Newgrange" (48). Although at the beginning of the summer the students have difficulty following the orders of Headmaster Joe, who is training his scholars into these patterns, by the final céilí mór, on the night before they return to their respective homes, the students have learned their lessons thoroughly and become one with (and in) the dance:

> [I]t's Carrickmacross lace, it's the river running, it's the salmon leaping, it's the ploughman ploughing, it's the spinner spinning, the boatman sailing, the fellow fishing, the fire flaming. It's the dancers dancing. (236)

But dancing takes many forms and even the order of the céilí can be disrupted by the outlaw presence of Pauline and Jacqueline who can light a corner of the schoolroom with the danger of "charm, sexuality, fashion" (50). Older characters find their way to Tubber's Fairyland Ballroom where alcohol and individual sexual contact erupt into the carefully constructed social patterns that should hold everybody in their place. Sava, the daughter of the Gaeltacht family hosting the girls, has spent her summer in that unsettling dance hall, just as Pauline has been creeping out to the seashore at night with Gerry. At the end of the Irish college summer, both these girls are possibly pregnant, but Orla's caution in the face of temptation creates a different set of options for her. She has ventured deep enough into secret places to learn important lessons, not least the value of risking the exploration; she has also realised the need to read the territory carefully, using her own understanding to map her way. She learns, too, that unless she is very careful – an adroit reader and a careful chooser of pathways – the tragic stories she discovers might become the story of her own maturing body. On the edge of jumping, Orla pulls back, unlike the reckless Pauline and Sava, but she has the imagination to see the possibilities, unlike her middle-class friend Aisling, or the fourth lodger, Jacqueline, a Bogside Catholic who is engulfed in panic about her father imprisoned in Long Kesh and her burnt-out neighbourhood in this violent summer of 'Operation Motorman'.

The Ireland of the Gaeltacht College for these adolescents has a small compass; the Dubliners do not know or care about the war in the north, for example, a blinkered response satirised by the narrator. The indifference to the politics of the north among these self-engrossed young Dubs rings true, as does Pauline's attitude, whose privileged class position in the north protects her from "bombs, shootings, hunger strikes …. For Pauline, as for [Orla and Aisling], all this happens only on the news" (99). But if Orla's geographic compass is small, it is deep, as she travels to the edge of the waterfall of sexual release, before she pulls back, instructed by the bodies in the mud. She learns caution and the need to save her body/life for a future as a "Lady Driver" (81), that is, an educated career woman whose body will be able to follow different, freer trajectories than those inherited from her mother and her teachers. And this caution continues even when she returns to Tubber with her family in the following summer and continues her relationship with Micheál, into the Fairyland Ballroom and onto the "burn bank", but not into the river, where they [only] kissed and kissed and kissed (240).

While we are never free of the social structures in which we live, the possibility of resistance always exists. To recall the statements quoted earlier from Shildrick and Price, the "process of securing the body's boundaries is never complete or certain", therefore, "the lack of an essential *corpus* opens up the possibility, even the inevitability of transgression" (234). A different Ireland, and different kinds of Irish bodies, emerged after 1972, with costs and benefits that the novel suggests. The class divisions, for example, became deeper than ever, even if the Celtic Tiger allowed more people – including Orla – into the middle-class. In the final chapter of the novel, entitled 'Now' (239), the adult Orla returns on holiday with her husband and children to the valley where Tubber had existed. For the first time, the narrative voice is both in the present tense and in the first-person as Orla reports that the village and her father's Irish dialect have disappeared. The "green cathedral" of the burn, where young Orla gained such important body-knowledge, has been replaced by a sleek Heritage Centre, "vast as a cathedral", the "Gaeltacht triumphant – not a bit like Tubber" (239). The novel ends with a Joycean echo, reshaped to capture the reality of a *woman* artist, as Orla in the 'Now' catches a glimpse of Micheál standing knee-deep in the waves of the shore with his small daughter (239). Although he is a man still "in my dreams, in my body" (240), marriage to a man with no education, no prospects, was "out of the question" (241) to the girl who had loved him, but who chose instead a life in a society that had changed enough so that some women, at least, had more expansive possibilities than those available to Sava, her mother, and Orla's mother. Surprised by the sight of him, Orla does not address him immediately, something she later regrets as she would have liked to "find out everything. Learn his story" (241).

Ní Dhuibhne deploys maps as metaphors in this novel to call into question the standard cartographies presented to these Irish girls. Their educational journeys have not resulted in freedom from sex/gender disciplines or from class/ethnic divisions. But the coherence and stability of the maps that would fix the girls as 'other' have been cracked open and the novel itself functions as a challenge to the idea of cartographic orthodoxies. Maps and social mores are coercive and a young woman wishing to challenge these must focus carefully on creating successful forms of resistance to the coercions. *The*

Dancers Dancing celebrates journeys of exploration and self-formation even as it models, through the character of young Orla and the ironic, thoughtful voice of the narrator, the importance of intense self-critical awareness as one engages in the various dances that shape bodies, lives and societies. By these means, it actively engages in the politics of cultural representation.

NOTES

1   Eavan Boland, 'Anna Liffey' in *A Time of Violence* (Manchester: Carcanet, 1994), 46.

2   Eavan Boland, 'That the Science of Cartography is Limited' in *ibid.*, 5.

3   Many thanks are owed to Ní Dhuibhne who has generously responded to my requests for information and insight. I am also indebted to the careful editorial attentions of Pádraig Ó Siadhail and John Tucker, and have benefited in my reading from the work of women's studies students at the University of Victoria, particularly Lindsay Cuff, Michelle Da Silva, Masae Day, Julie Grassmuck, Stephanie Howdle, Lauren Warbuck, Jennifer Scowcroft and Drew Williams. The mistakes, of course, remain my own.

4   Ní Dhuibhne, *The Dancers Dancing* (Belfast: Blackstaff Press, 1999). Further references to *DD* are in parentheses in the main text. Blackstaff reissued the novel in 2000 and again in 2007. In an appendix to the 2007 edition, entitled 'Éilís Ní Dhuibhne on Writing *The Dancers Dancing*', the author describes her lifelong fascination with rivers and, particularly, the Donegal river of her childhood, which is represented in this novel (287–9).

5   Christine St. Peter, 'Negotiating the Boundaries: Interview with Éilís Ní Dhuibhne'. *Canadian Journal of Irish Studies*, 32.1 (Spring 2006: 68–75), 70.

6   Declan Kiberd states that this novel is "literally without precedent ... probably the first fully achieved female *Bildungsroman* in Irish writing". Declan Kiberd, 'Excavating the Present: Irish Writing Now'. Lecture Transcript (Dublin: Irish Writers' Centre and the James Joyce Centre, 2001: 1–23), 12. Kiberd's generic classification certainly informs my own reading, although in my evocation of the *Bildungsreise* I am arguing for a specific type of the larger genre.

7   Ní Dhuibhne has also written another version of the Gaeltacht summer in an Irish-language novel, *Cailíní Beaga Ghleann na mBláth* (Baile Átha Cliath: Cois Life, 2003).

8   J.B. Harley, 'Deconstructing the Map' in *Writing Worlds: Discourse, Text and Metaphor in the Representation of Landscape*. Trevor L. Barns and James S. Duncan, eds. (London: Routledge, 1992: 231–247), 232.

9   Catherine Nash, 'Remapping and Renaming: New Cartographies of Identity, Gender and Landscape in Ireland'. *Feminist Review*, 44 (Summer 1993: 39–57), 49.

10   Harley, 'Deconstructing the Map', 231–2.

11   Nash, 'Remapping and Renaming, 50.

12   *ibid.*

13   This essay does not consider another remarkable aspect of this novel: its brilliant exploration of dialects and registers of English and Irish as spoken in different places and among different groups within Ireland. See the essay by Pádraig Ó Siadhail in this collection for an example of this approach to this novel and other writings of Ní Dhuibhne.

14   'Culchie' is a colloquial name for someone from the Irish countryside. When used by Dubliners, in particular, it is highly derogatory. A version of this part of the novel appeared earlier in a short story, 'Blood and Water' from Ní Dhuibhne's first volume of stories, *Blood and Water* (Dublin: Attic Press, 1988): 109–121.

15   The narrative reiterates this struggle throughout the novel. One example occurs in a chapter chronicling the "surprising history" of Orla's parents, where her father realises that British working-class people have much more in common with working class Irish than with their own more privileged countrymen (*DD* 126). Another occurs when Pauline reflects that the important difference between her Northern Irish grandmothers was not that one was Catholic and the other Protestant, but that one was rich and one was poor (*DD* 106).

16   This short description of what Ní Dhuibhne calls the 'medieval' life of such a farm is superbly developed in her recent story, 'The Makers' in *The Pale Gold of Alaska* (Belfast: Blackstaff Press, 2000: 115–28).

17   Caitriona Moloney and Helen Thompson, eds. *Irish Women Writers Speak Out: Voices from the Field* (New York: Syracuse University Press, 1003: 101–115), 104.

18   In another interview, the author comments on John McGahern's treatment of the "romance of rural Ireland" saying, "there's a danger in succumbing to this romantic fallacy because it takes you from the way life in Ireland is right now, which is very poor".

Donna Perry, 'Éilís Ní Dhuibhne' in *Backtalk: Women Writers Speak Out* (New Brunswick: Rutgers University Press, 1993: 246–260), 24.

19 Ní Dhuibhne, using the *nom de plume* Elizabeth O'Hara, has produced a fictional version of this rural Irish history in a trilogy of novels, written for young adults: *The Hiring Fair* (1993), *Blaeberry Sunday* (1994), and *Penny-Farthing Sally* (1996).

20 Ní Dhuibhne complains that Orla is not alone in this class-shame about traditional roots. The Irish, she says, only value their dying language if "an outsider, a foreigner, the European Union suggests that Irish is a valuable cultural commodity". Moloney and Thompson, *Irish Women Writers Speak Out*, 104.

21 'Dobharchú'. *A Dictionary of Celtic Mythology*. James McKillop, ed. (Oxford University Press, 1998). Oxford Reference Online. (Oxford University Press. University of Victoria). Accessed: 20 June 2007. http://www.oxfordreference.com.ezproxy.library.uvic.ca/views/EN TRY.html?subview=Main&entry=t70.e1513

22 Ní Dhuibhne combines here, as elsewhere in her creative and scholarly work, the evocative intersections of folklore and human psychology. In an interview, she discusses her use of 'shapeshifting', a frequent trope in folklore, as a device that reveals the "tendency of people to change bodies, personalities, moods". Perry, 'Éilís Ní Dhuibhne', 254. Ní Dhuibhne also uses a mixture of infanticide in folklore and contemporary Ireland in her story 'Midwife to the Fairies', first published in *Blood and Water* and reprinted in *Midwife to the Fairies: New and Selected Stories* (Cork: Attic Press, 2003): 22–30.

23 Ní Dhuibhne, 'Why Would Anyone Write in Irish?' in Ciarán Mac Murchaidh, ed., *'Who Needs Irish': Reflections on the Importance of the Irish Language Today* (Dublin: Veritas Publications, 2004), 80.

24 Margrit Shildrick and Janet Price, eds. *Vital Signs: Feminist Reconfigurations of the Bio/logical Body* (Edinburgh: Edinburgh University Press, 1998), 233.

25 Judith Butler, *Gender Trouble* (New York: Routledge, 1990), 419.

26 Elizabeth Grosz, *Volatile Bodies: Toward a Corporeal Feminism* (Bloomington: Indiana University Press, 1994), x.

27 Shildrick and Price, *Vital Signs*, 234.

28 Gerardine Meaney, *Sex and Nation: Women in Irish Culture and Politics* (Dublin: Attic Press, 1991).

29 For a heuristic discussion of the female *Bildungsroman* and the "complicating factor of social class" in the politics of feminist optimism, see Susan Midalia, 'The Contemporary Female *Bildungsroman*: Gender, Genre and the Politics of Optimism'. *Westerly*, 41.1 (Autumn 1996: 89–104), 92.

The Unwritten Land:
The Dynamic of Space in Éilís Ní Dhuibhne's *The Bray House*

GIOVANNA TALLONE

Every story is a travel story – a spatial practice.[1]

The spaces of Éilís Ní Dhuibhne's fiction range from the local perspective of Irish towns and villages to the wider prospects of European cities and American resorts. The shift between the local and the international is a recurring pattern in her collections of short stories from *Blood and Water* (1988) onwards, so that areas of Dublin, like Rathmines or Killiney, or locations in Ireland, such as Wicklow, Dún Laoghaire, Donegal or Kerry, alternate with Birmingham, Bath, France, Sweden, Klondike and Delaware. The variety of settings underlying both stories and novels corresponds to the "variety of concerns" with contemporary Ireland,[2] a place where individuals of all ages and social classes, but often "professional women",[3] look for personal identity and, in the process, face loss of one kind or another. Schoolgirls and servants, mothers and daughters, young and mature women, all strive to find a place of their own in the maps of their own lives, so that space and self can cohere.

In Ní Dhuibhne's female *Bildungsroman*, *The Dancers Dancing*,[4] the concern with space is at the heart of the protagonist's disorientation and rootlessness. Young Orla's first experience of Irish college in Donegal raises questions of "bifurcation of identity",[5] as she feels split between "Orla of the city and the country, Orla who belongs in both places and belongs in neither" (*DD* 29). Orla's perception of self is a perception of space, and her need to make order in her personal spaces is the need to reconcile "the maps that Orla has held in her head since babyhood", the map of Dublin and the map of the village of Tubber (6). Private and public maps intersect in the aerial view of the landscape opening the novel, as a picture from above is a response to "what the early map-makers imagined" and "a two-dimensional surface of wood or parchment or vellum or paper" (1) gives shape in writing to what is imagined. Claire Connolly exploits the opening of *The Dancers Dancing* to introduce a discussion of Irish Studies in *Theorizing Ireland*, eliciting questions on Irishness and identity from the "controlled, domesticated" image of Ireland where "hedges and fields become the squares of a tablecloth".[6] In Ní Dhuibhne's simile of landscape spread "like a chequered tablecloth over a languid body" (1), landscape and map are one, as the tablecloth itself is an allomorph for a map containing and defining space.

Concern with mapping is also at the root of Ní Dhuibhne's early novel *The Bray House*,[7] in which an archetypal voyage by sea enhances the polarity of space and the otherness of the unknown country of destination. Issues of mapping and writing come to the fore since the voyage out implies the need to read maps, but also to write new maps or rewrite existing ones. The voyage itself is perceived as an act of writing, as the ship traces a pattern on the sea surface. Early in the novel the first-person narrator mentions the crew's motivations in metaphorical terms as "a clean slate ... an open road" (*BH* 6), so that the sense of novelty implied in the expedition to Ireland interlaces the movement of the journey with the movement of writing.

In a futuristic setting, a group of Swedish archaeologists, Karen, Karl and Jenny, led by "ambitious and arrogant" Robin Lagerlof,[8] set out on a journey of exploration to Ireland, a wasteland after the nuclear disaster of Ballylumford. The objective of the expedition is to "excavate sites buried under mountains of nuclear ash" (8) looking for "the debris of the

Irish way of life" (70). The search centres on a house in the former town of Bray (the Bray House), which becomes the object of scientific scrutiny and, as a consequence, the object of further maps, catalogues and acts of writing at large.

The Bray House is a multifaceted and provocative novel in its use of diverse issues, as the ecological message of the world's annihilation is set alongside the exploration of power, feminism, intertextuality, metafiction and geographical and cultural borders. A study of the dynamic of space in the novel interlaces with the *topoi* of reading and writing as a *fil rouge* sustaining the novel, shedding light on the journey of exploration as a textual journey.

The Bray House exploits the device of science fiction to look at contemporary Ireland, thus intertwining interest with the local and concern with global ecological matters. In fact, the subtext of pollution, the global impact of the greenhouse effect, the possibility of annihilation,[9] and "environmentalism itself" concern "the human experience of space".[10] The composition of the novel predates Chernobyl and in some ways anticipates it. Awareness "of the dangers of nuclear power" and "proximity to Sellafield, and motherhood" were personal sources for the novel,[11] which became "more ecological" when Ní Dhuibhne's revised it after Chernobyl.[12]   Published in 1990, *The Bray House* escapes the trend of realist fiction featuring the 'New Dublin' of Roddy Doyle, Dermot Bolger and Joseph O'Connor in the late 1980s.[13] The unreal space of an Ireland devastated by nuclear disaster is a background and a descriptive element having symbolic functions, since the voyage to a new land is a voyage into the undiscovered world of the self, a map of the interior. Concern with space is at the core of the novel in different respects. The frame of the science fiction genre *per se* implies the exploration of unknown spaces. However, in *The Bray House*, the unknown country used to be known and the protagonist, Robin, used to be familiar with Ireland, having lived there with her Irish husband, Michael. This provides her with the insight and authority to be the only one capable, not only of 'reading' Ireland, but also interpreting it and, therefore, writing about it.

The novel follows the steps of the apocalyptic vision of a

"globally destructive nuclear war" first explored by H.G. Wells in *The World Set Free* in 1914[14] and, as such, deals with the science fiction *topos* of "a post holocaust world".[15] Likewise, *The Bray House* also features the encounter with alien creatures, basically the "encounter with difference".[16] Maggie Byrne, the only survivor of the 'Ballylumford Incident' is, in a way, the alien that the group encounter. As a single survivor, she is a witness to the holocaust, a key figure highlighting the "survivalist" body of science fiction,[17] the theme of the last man and the "*fin de globe* story".[18] However, if in science fiction since the 1960s "aliens have been abducting humans for experimental purposes",[19] then alien abduction is reversed in *The Bray House* since Maggie Byrne, as an object of study, is taken away from the unknown space of Ireland to the known space of Sweden.

The novel contains a reversal of the traditional pattern of Utopian voyages. The land of destination is not a *locus amoenus*, but a "desolate desert" (85), a place of destruction. In an anti-Utopian journey, the characters move from the Utopia of post-nuclear Sweden to the extinct society of Ireland, so, in a future setting, the voyage moves "backwards from the Present … to the Past".[20] The journey is, thus, ambiguous in its objectives and the parameters of travel literature are reversed. "Space that is unmapped and unnamed is chaotic and dangerous"[21] and yet this is a known and once-mapped space that has become empty and alien, a *terra incognita* and a *terra nullius*. A new map has to be re-written or re-drawn to negotiate the chaos and dangers caused by the disaster and to bridge the gap between the known and the unknown.

The novel also clearly bears characteristic features of travel literature, where "the sea itself is the finest symbol of the uncertainty of travel".[22] First-person narration imitates or reproduces the official writing of the log and, as such, is a form of autobiography, "a genre closely aligned to travel literature".[23] The purposes of the geographical and scientific exploration underlie a process of "territorial surveillance",[24] so that the leader of the expedition, Robin, is not unlike an imperialist traveller assuming to be able to understand the country and its culture "by looking at it"[25] or, in this case, by looking at what remains of it.

Critical approaches to *The Bray House* have taken into account a variety of perspectives. While Carol Morris identifies a feminist strand in matters of power and gender reversal, Gerry Smyth reads the novel as a portrait of the Irish obsession with land, and Derek Hand focuses on the metanarrative construction of the novel, whose core is "a narrative about narrative", where "writing, reading and interpretation" are expressions of power.[26] In fact, Robin's report interprets the data of the Bray House "subjectively"[27] bearing in mind standards of cultural homogenisation in which the inhabitants of the house have "some specifically Irish, and thus rare, traits", but are, at the same time, "part of the global society … not essentially different from … anyone in Sweden, France, Germany or any other developed country" (165).

The novel shares with many of Ní Dhuibhne's short stories a preoccupation and experimentation with form and storytelling, since first-person narration interweaves with scientific and journalistic prose, and the "conscious literariness"[28] of the novel highlights its intertextuality. The expedition starts in April and the novel opens with a statement of space and time: "We embarked at Gothenburg just before dawn on 28 April" (5). In April, the Ballylumford explosion takes place, as is reiterated in Robin's account with an obsessive emphasis on dates: "On 20 April, 20—"; "The first I heard of this was on 23 April"; "On 24 April, three thousand people were evacuated"; "On the night of the 24 April … the main reactor at Ballylumford reached meltdown stage" (63–64). This recalls both the Prologue of Chaucer's *Canterbury Tales* and T.S. Eliot's "cruellest month" in *The Waste Land*. Chaucer's "sweet showers" find an allomorph in the "acid rain" (7) to which Karen's hair is compared early in the novel. As a matter of fact, Ireland is now nothing but a waste land, as the cruelty of a paradoxical moment in time is the giver of both life and death. Thomas Mann's *The Magic Mountain*, Daniel Defoe's *Robinson Crusoe*, Herman Melville's *Moby Dick*, the novels of Swedish author Selma Lagerlof, and Samuel Richardson's

Pamela, are a conscious literary presence, and generic echoes resonate throughout the novel, exploiting features of science fiction, travel writing, scientific prose and traditional storytelling. Ní Dhuibhne's decision to give the archaeologist at the centre of *The Bray House* the surname of Lagerlof – the same as that of the first woman writer and Swede to win the Nobel prize for literature – emphasises the intertextual construction of the novel and highlights the protagonist as both a reader and a writer.

Such variety of texts and intertextual references sheds light on *The Bray House* as a conscious literary construction. The beginning of the journey at the centre of the narrative marks the beginning of a textual journey and coincides with Robin's beginning to read Thomas Mann's *The Magic Mountain*, a novel whose slow pace (17) highlights the difficulty of the journey. Notably, Mann's novel is introduced simply as "a novel, in German" (16) and, later, as "a long and heavy account of the adventures ... of a diseased man, which was supposed to be an allegory for a diseased, twentieth century society" (17). Only when Robin decides to switch to reading *Robinson Crusoe* does she mention its title:

> I was bored with Thomas Mann and could not bring myself to read any more of *The Magic Mountain*, which looked as if it would never end, and moved its mountains of difficult language and interminable sentences at snail's pace across long packed pages. (100)

This marks a significant turning point in the narrative. Once the sea voyage is over, arrival in Ireland requires a different kind of text, or subtext. The "snail's pace" of the journey, underlined by the slow reading, is counterbalanced by the fast pace required by action on land, where exploration and excavation is soon to begin. A Robinson Crusoe figure, in the form of Robin as feminine alter ego, sets about discovering her own desert island.

If *The Magic Mountain* and *Robinson Crusoe* have a direct influence on the writing of *The Bray House*, other texts are also more or less present. When first tackling Thomas Mann, Robin also mentions other books – "Chaucer, Boccaccio or ... the

Icelandic sagas" (17) – all of them having some sort of journey at the core. The survival of Sweden as the consequence of wise environmental policies is commented on with an open reference to Richardson's *Pamela*: "Virtue was rewarded" (23). *Middlemarch* is fleetingly mentioned when describing the coast of East Anglia as "a certain stereotype of an English lady" (36), while the name of the British Prime Minister at the time of the 'Ballylumford Incident', Elizabeth Bennet, casts a glance at Jane Austen's *Pride and Prejudice*, whose name returns, along with Charles Dickens's, at a later stage (41). Selma Lagerlof is made fun of, as her name is mistaken for the title of the novel Karl is reading to Jenny, "something old-fashioned and sentimental, like *Selma Lagerlof*" (101). The voyage by sea and its association with *Moby Dick* is enhanced by the reference to the custom of the *grindadráb*, the whale slaughter in the Faroe Islands, which is to be the subject of Michael's abortive PhD thesis. Texts from popular songs such as 'Yankee Doodle' and Bob Dylan's 'Mr. Tambourine Man' are juxtaposed with extracts from limericks and children's poems. A stretch from a poem Karen mistakenly thinks is by Yeats is quoted at length and dismissed as "something I learned at school" (215). The poem is, in fact, Robert Louis Stevenson's 'The House Beautiful' from the collection *Underwood,* and its presence in the novel is significant because of the parallelisms and connections it establishes with the space of the Bray House. The opening, "A naked house, a naked moor" is a coreferent to the house that has been scanned and excavated; its garden is "bare of flowers and fruit", it is "bleak without and bare within", which enhances the bleakness and bareness of the landscape of Ireland.

The tradition of fairytales comes to the fore in Robin's reference to herself as a witch (197), and to her mother as "the Little Match Girl" (144), in her devotion to the match factory she worked in. Jenny's long ponytail makes her look like Rapunzel (93), which anticipates her role of storyteller at the end of the novel. In the fairytale, Rapunzel is imprisoned in a tower, so her relationship with space is of domination and subjection, which are the same issues at stake in the Ireland expedition – to dominate the land and subject it to scrutiny.

Interestingly, when the excavation is over, Robin resumes her reading of *The Magic Mountain* having "nothing else to read": "I'd got through about half of *Robinson Crusoe*, but I didn't feel like finishing it" (212). The active reading of *Robinson Crusoe* covers the active part of the expedition, as well as being Robin's reading about her own exploration of space. So the relationship with a page to be read is also the relationship with space, something Robin has acknowledged early in the novel when drawing a parallelism between the space of the ship and the setting of *The Magic Mountain*: "I sat ... thinking how dull sanatoria were and how, in some ways they resembled ships" (35).

The polarity of space – sanatoria-ship, Sweden-Ireland, destroyed land and land that has survived – underlies the construction of the novel. The pattern of "ecocriticism"[29] and the voyage between Sweden and Ireland gradually enhance geographical and cultural distance. While Sweden survived because it chose "denuclearisation and a policy of environmental protection", Ireland "opted for environmental suicide" (22) and, by doing so, has become a non-place. Likewise, all the spaces related to the expedition are deprived of identity and specificity, or are claustrophobically-enclosed spaces. The sense of claustrophobia is conveyed early in the novel by the image of protective clothing that keeps the protagonists "encased" in "restrictive suits", "closely woven" that "did not allow the skin to breathe" (6). The novel opens with the movement of the ship out of Gothenburg harbour. By nature, this is a closed and open space at the same time; it is a place of encounters, a nowhere that is also an everywhere, the centre of the world, some sort of *omphalos*, a point of departure and of return. The place of landing in Ireland has similar features, since Robin and her crew anchor "in a sheltered rocky cove, close to the foot of Bray Head" (35). The cove, too, is a liminal space, both closed and open at the same time. Likewise, the ship is a multiple and ambiguous space, a movable and moving self-contained space bordering with a non-place. Like the ships in *Robinson Crusoe* and *Moby Dick*, it is a space of alterity, a "heterotopic"[30] space whose "physical constraints"

(180) make it a claustrophobic container, calling back the enclosed space of the shelters used during the fall-out. The open space of the sea is closed, too, in its ambiguous description as a container. In fact, the "grey empty water which looked dismally dead but was certainly vibrant with radioactivity" (6) anticipates the lifeless landscape of Ireland, defined as a "desert" (68), "like the moon" (70), "a skeletal landscape" (91) that hides mysterious inner spaces, one of which, the Bray House, is brought back to surface.

The novel can be divided into three parts, roughly corresponding to the movements of departure, exploration and return, each of them having specific textual strategies. The first-person authorial narrator in part one, the voyage out, leaves room to the textual space of the exploration and Robin's scientific report, in part two, between Chapters 12 and 15, where third-person narration enhances factual and objective analysis, while first-person narration is resumed in the third part, the voyage back. In the background, it is possible to identify Caren Kaplan's description of space as "a substance that is relatively immune to the workings of time unless culture perpetrates its crimes against space by spoiling, crowding, polluting and *inscribing* its presence onto and into that blank expanse".[31] The landscape of post-nuclear Ireland is the prototype of such 'inscription' so that the ecological message is part of the dynamic of space. Namely, the metaphor of writing is embedded in the destruction of physical space:

> … these stations blew up, destroying vast areas surrounding them, until within a short space of time most of Britain and all of Ireland had been wiped out. (64)

The process of annihilation and obliteration of space is juxtaposed with the process of writing, as "wiped out" recalls the "clean slate" at the opening of the novel. After all, you cancel what is written, and the 'inscription' of Ireland as space is cancelled, thus requiring new processes of writing.

So, if the process of reading is relevant in the novel, so is the process of writing. The core of the novel is Robin's report about the Bray House; it is a text-within-a-text,[32] embedded in subjective narrative and supported by further microtexts in the form of written documents, such as newspaper articles, or personal and official letters. At one stage, the narrative is suspended and attention is drawn to the text and its fictional structure:

> At this juncture, in my account of the Ireland Expedition, I feel it is opportune to present the reader with my full report and Analysis of the Bray House, before proceeding with the narrative of my adventures. (115)

In this self-conscious reflection, the capitalisation of the words 'Report' and 'Analysis' creates a textual limbo between the conscious narrative and the official report, anticipating the titles of the report, divided into 'Report on the Bray House' (Chapter 12), 'Documents from the Bray House' (Chapters 13 and 14), and 'Analysis of Report' (Chapter 15). Likewise, the same kind of self-conscious attention characterises the textual lull at the opening of Chapter 16, where the narrative is resumed in the first-person:

> My report and analysis have now been presented. It would be easy to assume on account of their neat logic and easy flow that the excavation they describe followed a similarly systematic and untwisting path. But unfortunately this was not so. (169)

The use of narrative and commentative verbs, namely Simple Past ("followed", "was") and Simple Present ("describe"),[33] enhances the double position of the report as a text-within-a-text, both inside and outside the narrative. Robin, too, positions herself both inside and outside the report, referring to herself as "the writer of this report" (115), so that the deictic *this* is a word of contention, both inside and outside the text. In a more subjective stance, Robin refers to "our report" as "our magnum opus" (203), once again inside the story, but also having a life of its own. Furthermore, when resuming her own narrative, Robin appreciatively praises the "neat logic and easy flow" of her writing, so that writing turns out to be a sort of obsession and a form of power. The scientific need to "make a permanent record of the physical state of this section of Ireland" (88) is highlighted by the constant presence of the log, the official record that will provide a basis for the report and will give permanence to the experience of space. Expressions like, "I spent the rest of the evening working at my log and making notes for my report of the excavation" or "I wrote in my cabin" (108), are juxtaposed with the fatigue of writing. In fact, during the storm, "when I tried to write, I found my microcomputer slipping about the table" (99). Writing gives form and validity to space and yet it is not steady but, like mapping, it seems to be constantly slippery.[34] Paradoxically, writing fixes by movement – the movement of hand and pen on a page – and, as such, it can be deceiving. Early in the novel, the first reference to writing is seen as a lie, or as an object of bargain or barter, as real coffee had been presented to Robin in return for "a glowing review of a book which had little to recommend it" (7). The written word is, in some way, a form of conquest, which is reiterated in Robin's appropriation of Michael's PhD thesis and, later, Karl's notebook containing Maggie Byrne's story. Just as she will later 'open' the Bray House, Robin "opened his filing cabinet", a closed and secret space, "and began to browse through his notes" (79). Robin's obituary, which closes the novel, sheds light on her academic career, mentioning only one title: "She published several books in her field, the best known of which is *The Whale Race: A Study of the Faroe Islanders*" (255).

Robin's life story closes on stolen words, and not on the written words of the protagonists of the Ireland expedition. Supported by photographs, maps, drawings, blue-prints (85, 118, 120), all forms of writing, the written report gives form to a wasteland, where the constant presence of ash and cinder draws attention to the land as a desert: "We had landed in a desert, of a particularly featureless and gloomy aspect" (68–9). What they see is "a desolate desert, greyish sand, mounds of various sizes dotting it" (85), the soil is made of "the crisp, cindery substance which crunched under our feet everywhere we went" (85), and the perception of the landscape as a desert is enhanced by "dusty dunes, created by the wind" (96).

As a matter of fact, the desert is a structural element. What Robin is doing is not simply writing about the desert, but writing THE desert. The desert is, by definition, empty and shapeless, it is a void. Writing gives form to the void. And, in order to write and describe what is shapeless, the writer/narrator has to give shape to the shapeless, to fill the page/void with written signs. The archetypal emptiness of the space of the desert is, thus, counterpointed by the "fullness" of the written page,[35] which gives the desert form and reality.

The place of absence in *The Bray House*, the wasteland of Ireland, is, thus, a potential text, and images of writing, erasing, rewriting and mapping are embedded in the landscape. When approaching Ireland, the Wicklow Hills are seen as "blue elevations *traced* on a *papery* sky" (50, emphasis added), thus mingling the jotting down of a map with the artistic creation of drawing and the creativity of writing. The sea itself is a blank page, "grey as lead, with little dark *scribbles scrawled* on its even surface at irregular intervals" (113, emphasis added). Space is, thus, not only written about, but written. The signified space turns into signifying space, and the space designed by the text turns into the space of the text.

The inner space of the ship is accurately mapped out. Chapter 3 opens with the geography of the spatial order of "cabin arrangements", of the control room and the galley:

> Jenny and Karl shared quarters in the stern of the launch. Karen had an extremely small cabin next to theirs, amidship, and just opposite hers, mine, the main cabin, lay. To the fore were the galley, the control room, and the deck ... the galley ... was quite a spacious room, serving not only as a kitchen but as a space for relaxation: it was furnished with some soft seats, a television, compact disc players, an exercise bicycle, as well as other aids to leisure. (26)

This detailed map of the ship and its objects anticipates the order and the precision with which the Bray House is mapped out room by room. Its contents are accurately listed, and the report is largely a collection of lists, of furniture, paintings and watercolours, kitchen equipment, books, magazines, and documents of all sorts, such as bills, letters, shopping lists, diary entries, so that the Bray House seems to take shape and life from such process of listing. The written word is, thus, a way to take possession of the space of the house, make order in it and control it, and the report is the written evidence of other written evidence.

Throughout the novel, an organisational pattern recurs interlacing space and time, so the extended map of the Bray House also calls back a static moment in history. A notable example occurs in the building of the house "bearing the date '1887' on a quartz stone over the hall-door" (120). The house speaks of its own past through written words outside and inside and is, by nature, a container for time. The interior of the house, both physically and metaphorically, speaks of spaces and times beyond its own. On the other hand, description or introduction of a new location is an occasion for subjective anachronisms on the part of the first-person narrator, an evocation of things past which makes *The Bray House* a recurrent analepses. At the very opening of the novel, the ship leaves the protective environment of the harbour and crosses "the bar to the open sea" (5), which allows crossing a time border, indulging in the space of the recent past while, at the same time, providing background information.

Space is, thus, a container for time, and the horizontal, synchronic crossing of geographical spaces interlaces with the vertical, diachronic movement into the past. If this is true for the objective of the expedition – the unearthing of Ireland's past in the physical excavation of the Bray House – it is also a recurring narrative strategy that weaves together the present of the narration with flashbacks from the past that come to the surface and provide a glimpse into Robin Lagerlof's traumatic childhood and bitter experiences.

The approach to Britain is expressed in a verb-less and, therefore, lifeless sentence: "The English coast" (36), so that the first glimpse of England is something that does not exist, a nowhere: "England had vanished, it simply no longer existed" (40). There is no description for the "scene of general devastation" (89), because the place is no longer there. Only names have survived, as signifiers whose signified have gone. Likewise, the glimpse of the Irish coast mingles Michael's biography with the places that belonged to him: Dublin,

Portadown, Kerry, the Blasket Islands. And the coastline where Bray used to lie is easily recognisable through the mountains that have survived the blast: "Bray Head, the Little Sugarloaf, the Big Sugarloaf, Lugnaquilla, the Three Rock Mountain" (54). Once again, the process of listing marks the encounter with space, as the list of placenames bridges the gap between the unknown space of the wasteland and the familiar landscape of the past.

In Ní Dhuibhne's *The Dancers Dancing*, the landscape is perceived as a body, marked by "varicose vein[s] in the smooth skin of the land" (*DD* 1). *The Bray House* anticipates this with its "rounded haunches", "pointed breasts", "humps. Lumps. Tumours" (*BH* 54); corporeal images of deformity recalling the corpse England had evoked when approaching its coastline (40). Likewise, the first image of Bray has the double quality of life in death: "I knew, as soon as I saw that landscape, the humps of Bray riding like camels across a desert, that that was it. Bray" (55). A semantic linker – "I had been here before" (55) – fills the ellipses of Robin's life in Ireland with Michael. This is a recurring procedure, often marked by a graphic blank or by the repetition of the geographical name giving rise to a private space of memory in subjective analepses. For example, Karl's mentioning Copenhagen allows Robin to go back to her first meeting with Michael – "Copenhagen. Wonderful wonderful" (32) – and to indulge in memories.

Chapter 17 of *The Bray House*, in particular, closes on a geographical and descriptive space, a physical and symbolic void that is, in fact, a blank page, to be filled by the writing of Robin's past memories. Propped up against a radioactive rock (186), Robin overhears the crew sharply gossiping about her, pointing out her selfishness and ruthlessness and recalling episodes from her university years. She starts walking on the beach, without destination, escaping from words. However, she soon reaches a stop:

> The tide was low, so I continued on the strand for a few miles, until I reached a crevice in the rocks that I could not cross. I stood there, gazing into the black depths of the small canyon. My mind was filled with memories. (188)

The narrow opening is a figurative space for a personal niche, a textual space to be filled with memories in the following chapter. The textual canyon is a private space, the only private space that belongs to Robin. This crack in the rock is an allomorph of corners, as described by Bachelard, in which corners are the germs of a room or a house providing the shelter of silence and meditation.³⁶ However, here in Ní Dhuibhne's Irish wasteland, shelter and peace do not seem to be possible. Halfway between inside and outside, partly a wall and partly a door (160), a corner is a place in-between. The crevice in *The Bray House* is both a liminal place and a textual corner, as it closes Chapter 17 and opens Chapter 18, recounting the most significant and traumatic part of Robin's autobiography, shedding light on the events that led to the break-up of her family.

As a matter of fact, there is no space the protagonist can identify with. Unlike the other characters, whether the other members of the expedition or the fleeting figures from her past, Robin does not have a place or a space that she can claim as her own. Each of the characters, in turn, seems to belong somewhere, from the father's garden, to the mother's wandering around the world (190), from Lena the childminder's care-centre to the hammock where Robin discovers her father's betrayal, to the University of Uppsala. This is an ambivalent space; it is a place of development for young Robin where "she found a niche" in her mentor's protection (186) – again, a small, self-contained place, half-way between inside and outside – but also a place of frustration, when she is refused a permanent position. After the break-up of her family and her move out of Lulea to Uppsala, Robin does not have a home any more: "'Home'? After that, I ceased to have a home ... (Did I ever have one again?)" (195).

Unable to find a place she can call home, Robin finds another home in the object of her archaeological dig. So, just as Lena used to be a sort of substitute mother, the Bray House is a substitute home. The space of the past, the home in Lulea, was "clinical in atmosphere", "never a comfortable place", "ordinary", "all empty spaces" (42), "bare" (43). The emptiness of her childhood home and the landscape of cinder and ash are the objective correlative of her lack of affections. The wasteland of Ireland, described as a "desolate landscape" (85) is a coreferent to the "desolate events ... of childhood" (92), and it is probably the only space Robin can identify with. In a world of total annihilation, the process of exploring and digging the house in Bray has the power of metamorphosis, so that, when leaving Ireland, Robin admits she "had come to appreciate this barren place ... to love it" (215). Paradoxically, it is precisely what had made it dismal that enhances its attractiveness:

> Perfect design. Contours clearly outlined against a pure sky. Shape of the earth, plain at last. Uncluttered by the frippery of flora and fauna which masquerades under the name of nature ... I saw its perfection. (215)

Such desert is, thus, a mirror; its lifeless state acquires a life of its own, since "the greyish landscape seemed to borrow colour and texture from my own memories and ideas" (212).

The ambivalent and ambiguous quality of the ghost landscape recurs in the archaeological site of the Bray House, necessarily enclosed and secluded, "an area covering few square kilometres" (88). Maps and photographs anticipate the objective research, just as the scientific report objectively describes the contents of the house. While Robin's home was bare and empty, the Bray House is full of furniture and objects, each of them described and catalogued. And, just as the voyage to Ireland is the reversal of a utopian journey, the unearthing of the Bray House is an upside-down process. Excavating, like mining, is both an act of destruction and construction, in order to reveal the "fully intact house ... that was emerging from the dust" (112); earth and dust have to be moved, the landscape has to be destroyed in order to reveal the construction of the building. Likewise, the vertical character of a house[37] is reversed, as the Bray House is 'built' from top to bottom.

Robin takes possession of the space of the house by writing her report on it and interpreting contents and documents. She indulges, particularly, in the books that fill the Bray House, most of which "concern Irish and international law" and "parliamentary papers"; others are "literary works by Gaelic or Anglo-Irish authors" (126). Exercise books and scrapbooks (130) are the coreferent inside the house to notes and drawings on the part of the archaeologists, while a typewriter (131) and a filocomputer (137) are witnesses to the activity of creative writing of one of the inhabitants, Elinor. The variety of written documents reveals the life of the Bray House as a double image of Robin's childhood. Like Robin's, the family in Bray is dysfunctional and is about to disintegrate at the time of the explosion. Her report is the textual result of the process of digging that uncovers and unearths the house and its contents as well as the buried stories of the Bray House inhabitants. Other buried stories are dug out: Maggie Byrne's account of the fall-out and her survival, Ireland before Ballylumford, Robin's life in Lulea, her life with Michael, her bitter childhood experiences. The house is, thus, a receptacle for private time.

Space, too, is turned upside down in the Bray of pre-Ballylumford, where an impression of claustrophobia is given by the railings that "seemed to cordon off the sea and make it a public park" (67). Space is overturned – what is open becomes closed, what is inside becomes outside; the land and the sea invert their role and position. If this were the past, where "there was no beach" (67), now Bray has become an endless beach, a "hostile-looking landscape" (68), again suffocating and claustrophobic in its openness.

Closed spaces await Robin on her return to Sweden, the hospital "to be quarantined" (250) first, and then the State Prison once she is "under arrest", charged with the murder of Karl Larsson (251). Once again, Karl's death is caused by Robin's thirst for power, primarily the power of the written word, since she accidentally kills Karl trying to steal his precious notebook. This is an alternative text to Robin's report and, as such, is a potentially dangerous one, capable of subverting Robin's writing, since it contains the account of Karl's expedition with Jenny into the interior, the void from where they came back with Maggie Byrne.

Robin is soon disillusioned. She realises that the hope of an exhibition that will bring her success is just an illusion. In an ironic *dénouement*, "there would be nothing, because there was no interest" (253), the whole enterprise is exposed as pointless. Unlike Columbus, whose name is once obliquely (5) and once openly mentioned (172), who gave the world a 'new world', Robin's journey has turned into a void; the journey, the exploration, the excavation have led nowhere. What remains to map out the experience is Robin's posthumous book in the form of, as Carol Morris suggests, the novel *The Bray House* "in its entirety", not just the report.[38] Maybe this, too, is a textual void, a desert that has remained empty in spite of the words written to give it shape. In this metanarrative and transtextual reflection, Robin's mentioning of "the story I'll write" (248) is a link to her obituary closing the novel, both outside and inside the story of the Ireland expedition, a narrative space beyond time. In her textual journey to an undiscovered country, Éilís Ní Dhuibhne has told a story of space, confirming her view that the aim of "fiction is to take you to a place that you don't already know".[39]

NOTES

1   Michel de Certau, *The Practice of Everyday Life* [1974] Trans. Steven Randall. (Berkeley: University of California Press, 1988), 115.

2   Derek Hand, 'Being Ordinary. Ireland from Elsewhere: A Reading of Éilís Ní Dhuibhne's *The Bray House*'. *Irish University Review*, (Spring/Summer 2000: 103–16), 103.

3   Christina Hunt Mahony, *Contemporary Irish Literature: Transforming Tradition* (London: Macmillan, 1998), 261.

4   Ní Dhuibhne, *The Dancers Dancing* (Belfast: Blackstaff Press, 2000). Further references to *DD* are in parentheses in the text.

5   Caitriona Moloney and Helen Thompson, eds. *Irish Women Speak Out: Voices from the Field* (New York: Syracuse University Press, 2003), 103.

6   Claire Connolly, *Theorizing Ireland* (Basingstoke: Palgrave Macmillan, 2003), 1.

7   Ní Dhuibhne, *The Bray House* (Dublin: Attic Press, 1990). Further references to *BH* are in parentheses in the text.

8   Gerry Smyth, *The Novel and the Nation: Studies in the New Irish Fiction* (London: Pluto Press, 1997), 167.

9   Carol Morris, '*The Bray House*: An Irish Critical Utopia. Éilís Ní Dhuibhne'. *Études Irlandaises*, 21–1 (Printemps 1996: 127–140), 132.

10   Gerry Smyth, *Space and the Irish Cultural Imagination* (Basingstoke: Palgrave, 2001), 7.

11   Shirley Kelly, 'Fiction is to Take You to Places You Didn't Know'. *Books Ireland*, No. 236 (Dec. 2000), 349.

12   Donna Perry, 'Éilís Ní Dhuibhne' in *Backtalk. Women Writers Speak Out* (New Jersey: Rutgers University Press, 1993: 245–60), 252.

13   Anthony Roche, 'Introduction: Contemporary Irish Fiction'. *Irish University Review*,(Spring/Summer 2000: VII–XI), VIII.

14   Roger Luckhurst, *Science Fiction* (Cambridge: Polity Press, 2005), 81.

15   Leon Stover, *Science Fiction from Wells to Heinlein* (North Carolina: McFarland, 2002), 155.

16   Adam Roberts, *Science Fiction* (London: Routledge, 2000), 8.

17   Roz Kaveney, 'The Science Fictiveness of Women's Science Fiction' in Helen Carr, ed., *From my Guy to Sci-Fi. Genre and Women's Writing in the Postmodern World* (London: Pandora, 1989: 78–97), 81.

18   Stover, *Science Fiction from Wells to Heinlein*, 41, 155.

19   Luckhurst, *Science Fiction*, 233.

20   Morris, '*The Bray House*', 129.

21   Smyth, *The Novel and the Nation*, 42.

22   Peter Hulme, 'Travelling to Write (1940–2000)' in Peter Hulme and Tim Youngs, eds., *The Cambridge Companion to Travel Writing* (Cambridge: Cambridge University Press, 2002: 87–101), 96.

23   Kristi Siegel, ed., *Issues in Travel Writing: Empire, Spectacle and Displacement* (New York: Peter Lang, 2002), 3.

24   Roy Bridges, 'Exploration and Travel outside Europe' in Hulme and Youngs, eds., *The Cambridge Companion to Travel Writing*, 57.

25   Siegel, *Issues in Travel Writing*, 2.

26   Hand, 'Being Ordinary', 104.

27   Smyth, *The Novel and the Nation*, 167.

28   Morris, '*The Bray House*', 136.

29   Smyth, *Space and the Irish Cultural Imagination*, 7.

30   Michel Foucault, 'Of Other Spaces'. *Diacritics*, 16 (Spring 1986: 22–7).

31   Caren Kaplan, *Questions of Travel, Postmodern Discourses of Displacement* (Durham: Duke University Press, 1996), 147. Emphasis added.

32   Morris, '*The Bray House*', 131.

33   Harald Tempus Weinrich, *Besprochene und erzählte Welt* (Stuttgart: Kohlhammer, 1964); Italian translation, Tempus. *Le funzioni dei tempi nel testo*, (Bologna: Il Mulino, [1978], 2004).

34 Richard Phillips, 'Writing Travel and Mapping Sexuality. Richard Burton's Sotadic Zone' in James Duncan and Derek Gregory, eds., *Writes of Passage. Reading Travel Writing* (London: Routledge, 1999), 71.

35 Véronique Magri-Mourgues, 'Écrire le Désert' in Gérard Laverge, ed., *Création de l'Espace et Narration Littéraire*. Colloque International Nice-Séville, 6–7–8–mars 1997, (Cahier de Narratologie N. 8, 1997: 249–61), 249.

36 Gaston Bachelard, *La Poétique de l'Espace*, 1957; *La Poetica dello Spazio*, Italian Transl. Ettore Catalano. (Bari: Dedalo, 1975, 1999), 159.

37 *ibid.*, 45.

38 Morris, '*The Bray House*', 136.

39 Kelly, 'Fiction is to Take You to Places You Didn't Know', 349.

'What Matters But the Good of the Story?':
Femininity and Desire in Éilís Ní Dhuibhne's
'The Inland Ice' And Other Stories

ANNE FOGARTY

The success of her novel, *The Dancers Dancing*, and the recent publication of *Fox, Swallow, Scarecrow* (2007), have, to a degree, eclipsed Éilís Ní Dhuibhne's achievement as a short story writer. Moreover, the protean nature of her highly prolific literary output, which spans two languages, Irish and English, and encompasses numerous genres, including the novel, children's writing, short fiction, and drama, makes it difficult to assert a particular proclivity in one area above another. However, it is noteworthy that collections of short stories have punctuated Ní Dhuibhne's career to date and that she continues to return periodically to this genre. Her first volume of short stories, *Blood and Water*, was published by Attic Press in 1988. Thereafter, she produced three further significant collections, *Eating Women is Not Recommended* (1991), *'The Inland Ice' and Other Stories* (1997), and *The Pale Gold of Alaska* (2000). *Midwife to the Fairies*, containing new and selected stories, was published under the Attic imprint by Cork University Press in 2003.

In the Anglophone tradition, it is not unwonted for fiction writers to alternate between the composition of novels and short stories. But, in general, proficiency in one mode rather than the other is pursued. In Ireland, however, given its peculiar status in the canon of twentieth-century literature, mastery of the short story is still seen as a totem of literary accomplishment. Indeed, the production of a volume of short stories is a frequent prerequisite for staking one's claims as a novelist. John McGahern and John Banville, for example, both published collections of short stories early in their writing careers.[1] It is also common for established Irish novelists to have recourse to the short story in mid-career in order further to test and extend their command of fictional form. Both Roddy Doyle's *The Deportees* and Colm Tóibín's *Mothers and Sons* have been hailed as original and distinctive contributions to the genre of the short story.[2] Éilís Ní Dhuibhne, however, is unusual because of the consistency with which she has practised the art of the short story while simultaneously creating a profile as an original and compelling novelist.

With a view to investigating the particular manner in which she has refashioned and made her own the genre of the short story, this essay will concentrate on Ní Dhuibhne's third major collection, 'The Inland Ice' and Other Stories.[3] This volume is singular, not just because of the degree to which it foregrounds issues of sexuality, the problem of female desire, and the clash between male and female apprehensions of the world, but also because of its structure. Fourteen highly formulaic installments of a traditional Irish folktale, 'The Search for the Lost Husband', are interwoven with thirteen postmodern stories, most of which are set in contemporary Ireland or in other European countries, including Sweden, Italy, and Greenland. Two of the tales, however, 'Gweedore Girl' and 'Summer Pudding', have historical settings. Thus, the reader is confronted with shifting spaces and timeframes in the successive stories, while being periodically regaled, in the interstices between the modern fictions, with a further segment of the folktale, which is relayed piecemeal and with leisurely elaboration.[4]

The peculiar architecture of the collection seems to posit a radical opposition between the traditional and the modern. The indirection, emotional turmoil, and disjunctions of the contemporary narratives contrast with the honed simplicity, stark truths, and linearity of the folktale that is threaded through the volume. An initial reading might conclude that Ní Dhuibhne, in pointing up these two types of narration and fictional world, and in so designedly counterposing them, is exemplifyng the way in which the cohesiveness and essential wisdom of the folktale have been irrevocably lost to modernity. The organisation of the text appears to bear out Walter Benjamin's oft-cited account of the demise of the oral storytelling tradition, which, in his eyes, was triggered by a shrinking sense of community at the advent of the modern era and a diminution in the communicablility of experience.[5] Benjamin further held that contemporary narratives had lost the ability to relay the universal insights and practical wisdom that had been the mainstay of the traditional tale. This essay will argue that, contrary to the definitive rupture upon which Benjamin insists, the lost world of oral storytelling, with its practical and philosophic dimensions, is actually reanimated by the postmodern stories in Ní Duhibhne's collection. In 'The Inland Ice' and Other Stories, both modes of narration cross-contaminate and subtly inform each other. The folktale is not a nostalgic recreation of an oral text; nor can it be viewed as a romantic embellishment or a consolatory diversion from the ramifying emotional dilemmas of modern existence. Rather, the two forms of narration supplement, counterpoint, and overlay each other. The dual perspectives, which the reader is invited to entertain, provide the impetus for a volume that underscores the subtle layerings of experience and reality wherein past and present are ineluctably intertwined and the personal is inevitably part of a universal pattern. As will be demonstrated in this essay, the bipartite structure of the collection represents not only the difference between the verities and communality of oral culture and the psychic unease and troubling internality of modernity, but also the possibility of exchange and dialogue across these modalities. Consequently, the seemingly archaic and settled pieties of the folktale are radically rethought, while the restless stories of modern discontent are revealed to have an elemental resonance and mythic underpinnings.

With a view to exploring the narrative dynamics of 'The Inland Ice' and Other Stories, this essay will first examine the traditional tale, which Ní Dhuibhne remodels and reconstructs, and consider the import of the changes that she has made to this inherited story that is now enshrined, and to a degree embalmed, in the archive of Irish folklore. It will, then, seek to isolate the overarching themes that interconnect this ritualised text with the modern stories in the volume. Therafter, I shall examine how these interlocking symbolic patterns and archetypal personal quests are treated in the individual texts and probe the manner in which the narrative devices deployed by Ní Dhuibhne, such as repetition, tone, irony, intertextuality, elision, and point of view, create unsettling effects. Additionally, I will explore how these techniques establish points of contact between past and present and the oral and the written and constantly hint at the unconscious substrata that determine the way in which the characters we encounter make sense of themselves and experience the world.

Ní Dhuibhne's 'The Search for the Lost Husband' tells of a young woman's hopeless but unflagging love for a white goat who, at her specific behest, becomes her consort at night by turning into a man. Stories about animal husbands have an ancient pedigree. Re-tellings of this archetypal plot are widespread and may be encountered in numerous cultures under many different guises. Well-known variants are the legend of Cupid and Psyche and the fairytale 'Beauty and the Beast'. Many versions of the story were gathered by folklorists in Ireland where it appears to have enjoyed unusual popularity. The particular rendition of this tale that Ní Dhuibhne uses as a source and template was recounted under the title, 'The Story of the Little White Goat' by Máire Ruiséal to the folklorist, Seosamh Ó Dálaigh, who recorded it in Dún Chaoin in County Kerry on 5 September 1936. In her chapter on oral traditions for The Field Day Anthology of Irish Writing: Irish Women's Writing and Traditions, Volume IV, Ní Dhuibhne includes her own redaction and translation of Ruiséal's vivid and lengthy story. In the accompanying editorial essay, she reviews the role played by female storytellers in Ireland, and considers the degree to which gender constraints might have dictated the kinds of narrative that they related. Ní Dhuibhne takes issue with James H. Delargy's influential but dismissive view that women were prohibited from telling hero-tales and that they specialised in less complex forms, such as the legend and fairytale, destined for domestic or more private contexts. By contrast, Ní Dhuibhne argues that women could range widely in their material and that they did not feel bound simply to tell stories that coincided with stereotypical views of a putative feminine perspective. The Irish female storytelling tradition that she asserts is robust, variegated, and inventive; amplitude and creative resourcefulness are amongst its many hallmarks. In the essay, Ní Dhuibhne lauds Máire Ruiséal's artistry in moulding the tale of the animal groom, and particularly commends her playful foregrounding of the undeviating and frankly enunciated passion of her heroine. The Kerry seanchaí had learnt the story from her father. Hence, her rendering of the inherited tale is a female appropriation of a key symbolic narrative that has deep-seated cultural import.

Ruiséal's account of the travails of her lovelorn heroine in the 'The Story of the Little White Goat' may be briefly summarised as follows: a farmer's daughter who has fallen in love with a white goat, bears him three sons, each of whom, in turn, is taken away from her at birth by her goat husband who warns her that she is not to grieve over their disappearance or she will lose him forever. When she sheds a tear at the removal of her third child, the white goat fulfills his threat and deserts her. She, however, pledges to pursue him and follows after him through the roughest of terrain with grim determination. She tracks him down on three successive occasions and each time is urged by him to seek shelter for the night in a cottage where hospitality is extended to her and she acquires magic gifts: a comb that makes hair wondrously beautiful, scissors that turn rags into splendid garments, and a tablecloth that miraculously conjures up a feast of food and drink. The goat finally disappears into the ground, but the girl, undaunted, pursues him to his subterranean country. Here, she discovers that the goat, his deformed sister Scabby Crow, and another three sisters, have all been placed under a spell by an old 'mother' hag/witch who lives in a nearby castle. With the help of an old couple, the girl bribes Scabby Crow with the gifts that she has received and contrives to fix things so that she can sleep with the white goat. The hag, however, spoils the plan by drugging the goat so that he does not respond to his wife. On the third night, he manages to spill the sleep-inducing potion and is finally reunited with his faithful lover. With the help of Scabby Crow, they discover how to kill the hag and to reverse the effects of her pernicous spell. He is turned back into a man, while his sister loses her deformity. Once the three children have been restored, the resolute young woman lives happily ever after with her consort who has now been returned to human form.

Ní Dhuibhne's version of the story is faithful to its structure, detail, and quirkiness. It, above all, replicates the waywardness of the heroine and her defiant and unabashed pursuit of sexual desire. Nonetheless, it executes a number of crucial alterations. In retitling the tale, 'The Search for the Lost Husband', Ní Dhuibhne explicitly foregrounds the determination and resourcefulness of the young woman. A female quest now becomes the key focus of the narrative. The redesignation of the white goat as a lost husband in the title further reconfigures the central concerns of the story and allows it to acquire a modern purchase and resonance. This shift in wording redirects attention from the traditional theme of virtue rewarded to less easily negotiated problems, including deficiencies in marital relationships, the seemingly fateful and self-destructive nature of female desire, patriarchal power, and the abusive aspects of erotic love. In her recounting of the tale, Ní Dhuibhne retains many of the facets of oral storytelling, including repetition and the reliance on formulaic markers such as, "That's how it was" (43), to achieve narrative progress. However, she modernises the tale by drawing out its embedded psychological insights and conflicts through the addition of dialogue. In an argument with the white goat, for example, the young woman makes it clear that she sees herself as emotionally bound to him when she declares that, "you are my man" (104). Implicit in this assertion is an irrational surrender to her lover, which seemingly foils her desire for independence and control. However, at the end of the tale, the heroine exhibits a forthrightness that is more obliquely rendered or even suppressed in the original folktale, by directly confronting the white goat and demanding an explanation for his cruel actions: "Why did you take my children away from me?" (237).

The most striking and consequential change that Ní Dhuibhne effects is her re-writing of the happy ending of her source text. In her re-alignment of the plot, after she is reunited with her children, the heroine rejects her lover and declares that, "it's time for me to try another kind of love. I'm tired of all that fairytale stuff" (262). Eluding her apparently inalienable destiny to be bound to her inexplicably sadistic husband, we are told that she returns to her father's house, marries a young famer who is ready to accept her children, and thereby achieves happiness. Notably, this new ending retains an essential facet of animal husband stories, which, unlike those about animal brides, invariably end positively. As Boria Sax notes, narratives about animal consorts are always tragic romances that confront the problem of the encounter with difference.[6] Yet, despite such concerns, animal groom stories such as 'The Frog Prince' by the Brothers Grimm or Jeanne-Marie Leprince de Beaumont's 'Beauty and the Beast', culminate with a reconciliation of the lovers.[7] Generally, too, the animal husband turns out to be a human who was enchanted and, hence, does not properly belong to the untamed realm of nature. Consequently, as Sax argues, such stories seem to evince a greater faith in the human sphere.[8] But, despite this retention of the fundamental trajectory of such mythic stories, Ní Dhuibhne's ending remains equivocal. Her heroine appears to renegotiate happiness on her own terms and exhibits a healthy self-interest by definitively repudiating what may be seen as an abusive relationship, unlike her counterpart in Máire Ruiséal's version. However, her choice of a pragmatic love over the doomed desire of "all that fairytale stuff" is not necessarily a guarantee of satisfaction as other female fates in the volume indicate. Indeed, the impossibility of counterbalancing happiness and desire, or in reconciling the need for security with the draw of *jouissance*, as I will later argue, may be seen as the irresolvable dilemmas reflected upon by all of the narratives in the volume, including the reworked folktale. The final comments of the narrator remind us of the fabricated nature of this ending even as it tries to depart from the artifical conclusions of fairytales:

> That is my story. And if there is a lie in it, it was not I who made it up. All I got for my story was butter boots and paper hats. And a white dog came and ate the boots and tore the hats. But what matter? What matters but the good of the story? (262)

The overdetermined accumulation of the markers of closure in an oral narrative alerts us to their essential artificiality and the contrivances on which they depend. The story is declared ultimately to be driven by ineluctable principles that are beyond the command of the narrator, who only here makes her presence known. The "good of the story" lies in its indeterminacy and in the arbitrariness and constructedness of its design. An ending that appears to have moral weight or to intimate how female predicaments might be resolved, as in the case of 'The Search for the Lost Husband', is as much a product of the illusory effects of storytelling as the satisfying conclusion achieved by the fairytale.

Moreover, the crossover structure of *'The Inland Ice' and Other Stories* allows for a trafficking of themes and symbolic moments between the folktale and the postmodern stories in the volume, which complicates our apprehension of both. The issues of female desire, violence and sexuality, and of marital conflict, which are foregrounded in the folktale, are also treated in the stories. Indeed, Ní Dhuibhne constructs the volume as a series of mirror effects. Emotional scenarios repeat themselves in these fictions and the heroine in the successive narratives finds herself facing similarly knotted emotional impasses that have complex psychic and cultural roots. In particular, the female protagonists grapple with the problem of fathoming their own desire and are invariably caught in tension-ridden marriages or trapped in love affairs that have become increasingly undermining and dissatisfying. Like in 'The Search for the Lost Husband', most of these figures, too, struggle to come to terms with gendered patterns of domination and oppression in sexual relations that assign agency and autonomy to the male partner and enforce female passivity and victimisation. The selflessness of the young woman in 'The Search for the Lost Husband' is revealed in more modern configurations to border on a masochistic compulsiveness that is ultimately self-destructive. Despite such dark reflections, however, female desire is primarily represented as an anarchic excess in these narratives that refuses to be contained and is not easily subject to rational scrutiny or social control. Suspended endings, gaps, or surprise twists in the plots are often deployed in order to capture the waywardness of passion and the degree to which expectations are always foiled by the drives and needs of the heroine.

An analysis of the initial two stories in the collection, 'Gweedore Girl' and 'Love, Hate, and Friendship', will provide an insight into how these themes are established and the ways in which the female quest for love is scrutinised. 'Gweedore Girl' relays the tale of Bridget, a young woman from Gweedore, County Donegal, who takes up a post as servant in a Derry household. Her difference is underlined throughout; her rural, Irish-speaking background, her standing as maid, her defamiliarised perspective on the customs of the *bourgeois* household in which she lives, and her cumbersome physicality are amongst the several indicators of her status as outsider. She is pursued thoughout the story by two men: her employer who fondles and molests her covertly, and Elliot, the butcher boy, who seduces her and with whom she falls in love. She passively endures and, even, initially enjoys the overtures of the former, but through the latter, in particular, she is introduced not only to the joys of physical pleasure but also to the pain of a self-immolating love:

> ... and there was never enough time, for kissing Elliot, for feeling his body, hot and sweet and pounding, press into mine. I always left him with huge reluctance, unable to believe that I could exist away from his arms and his mouth.

When I came home from these evenings, I was dishevelled, with
my stockings torn as often as not, and inside I felt strange. Ripped.
I was with him, wrapped up in every way, and then I was ripped
away from him, so that I felt torn like an apple that has been
broken in two. (17)

For Jacques Lacan, all human longing may be conceived of as
the "desire of the Other": we discern the desire of those who
have power over us, especially of parents and, above all, of the
father, and model our wishes on theirs.[9] Thus, desire is
borrowed and secondhand. Additionally, Lacan's formulation
of desire construes it as the yearning at once to be the object of
another's affection and to attain recognition by another. Bridget
experiences love in just this manner; her obsession with Elliot is
fed by his ardent courting of her. Her desire for him mimics his
seeming passion for her. Eventually, he persuades her to marry
him and she agrees, but the plan turns out to be a ploy to con
her out of her money as Elliot is actually already married. Akin
to the young girl in 'The Search for the Lost Husband', Bridget,
however, refuses to accept the role of victim, despite losing her
savings and being sacked from her job as a servant. She sues
Elliot, successfully, takes up a fresh career as a shop assistant,
and also finds a new boyfriend, Seamus, whose reliability and
kindness are a counterweight to her former lover's treachery.
Yet, surprisingly, she confesses at the end of the story that,
even though she now enjoys the genuine prospect of marriage
and future contentment, this liasion will not be based on love
as she still remains attached to Elliot. His deceit and
abandonment of her merely increased her investment in the
fantasy of love that he awakened.

In this manner, 'Gweedore Girl' restages and heightens the
conflict at the core of 'The Search for the Lost Husband' and
gives it further psychological dimensions without ever
removing its mystery. Female desire is motivated neither by
security nor the dictates of happiness. Rather, it is defined by a
troubling fusion of eros, pain, and voluntary submissiveness.
The abusive object of desire is always inherently bound up
with its nurturing opposite. Hence, the pragmatic choice that
the heroine exercises at the end of the story is undermined by

her blunt and disarming disclosure that her love for the man who has deserted and humiliated her continues unabated and in defiance of her attempts at self-preservation. Yet, her clear-eyed and clipped enunciation of the conflicted and darkly perverse nature of female desire is registered with a cold but precise objectivity at the end of the narrative: "It is amazing that I know that Seamus is good and kind and honest and will never mistreat me; also I will never love him". This insight into female sexuality is proffered like the details in the folktale as an unfathomable aspect of things; it can be circumscribed but not fully rationalised or teased apart. However, there is a sense that Bridget retains ownership of her feelings, even if they defy easy explanation. Female *jouissance*, in its admixture of pleasure and pain, is an excess that overspills all of the moral and social structures that are set up to contain it and pushes against the boundaries of the narratives that purport to pin it down.[10]

Such alternating moments of insight and bafflement also characterise 'Love, Hate, and Friendship', which meditates on similar themes and presents a woman who likewise battles an emotional deadlock in which she feels trapped. Fiona has decided to go to a short conference in Bordeaux in order to take stock of a painful affair from which she feels unable to wrest herself. Edward, her lover, like the white goat and many of the male figures in the other stories, is typified by his initial forcefulness and mastery:

> It is hard to resist men like Edward, men who overwhelm you initially with the intensity of their need for you. It is hard to resist them even if you know from experience that such men will, and must, cool off just as abruptly, and almost as emphatically, and there will be nothing you can do about it. Because there was nothing you did in the first place, either, to start the whole thing off. Except acquiesce. (37)

The waning of his ardour leaves Fiona in a painful condition of dependency that she feels unable to terminate, despite her recognition of its fundamentally debilitating and masochistic nature. As she concludes, her lover's "absence was more powerful than his presence" (38). Like Bridget in 'Gweedore Girl', Fiona is troubled by a nightmare that concretises her sense of powerlessness. She dreams that a huge tidal wave on an Irish beach pursues her and threatens to drown her. Her experience of the otherness of the French landscape allows her a temporary respite from this sense of entrapment and permits her to attain sufficient clarity about the deleterious effects of her hopeless love for a man whose neglect and indifference have become abusive. The ironised introspection of the story, however, does not issue in closure or nudge the heroine in the direction of a life-changing decision. Instead, the ending is equivocal, hinting at her continued state of conflict and irresolution. Fiona makes do with a paddle in a lake close to her conference centre, as she has forgotten to bring a swimsuit: "So she keeps paddling around, letting her toes have a holiday" (42). Pleasure irrepressibly breaks through here in this final moment. But the partial nature of her immersion intimates that she is not yet ready to free herself of the self-defeating love affair in which she has got ensnared.

Similarly playful indeterminacies that simultaneously circle the emotional blockages of Ní Dhuibhne's heroines are used to punctuate the other stories. The predicaments of all these figures echo each other, as they are either caught in marriages that have turned out to be unsatisfactory or fixated on lovers who are uncaring and casually sadistic. The repetition of these scenarios not alone suggests a continuing and quintessential kinship between these contemporary women and the archetypal heroine in 'The Search for the Lost Husband', but also indicates that gendered patterns of behaviour, which enforce and license male dominance and female subservience, are inculcated by social laws and cultural dictates that cannot easily be extirpated or altered. One of the stories that deviates from this pattern, 'Bill's New Wife', tracks a reversal of gender roles, in which the positions of husband and wife are swopped around merely to prove that, even when exchanged, they remain fixed.

The female protagonists of the other tales enact variants of a joint but dispersed narrative that reproduces and re-envisages the elemental quest of the young woman who tries to maintain and defend her love for an animal husband who persists in thwarting and rejecting her. In 'Lili Marlene', the unnamed heroine wonders whether her heart is "a block of white, hard ice which never thaws" (79). She has an extra-marital affair as an adult with John, a man with whom she once fell hopelessly in love while working in a hotel in Dublin as a young girl. She eventually breaks off the liaison, both because John continues to prove himself to be uncaring and indifferent and because she wants to protect her loveless but sustaining marriage with Cyril, who has given her freedom and security. This seemingly rational choice only underlines the turmoil of her emotions. The spiralling abyss of desire reminds her forcefully of the compromises involved in the salvationary but mundane relationship that she has chosen for herself:

> What I think is that life is like Doctor Zhivago up to a point – more like it than some would admit. People can have a great passionate love. I have. Probably you have. But it doesn't seem to survive. One way or another it gets done in, either because you stay together or you don't. (102)

In 'Hot Earth', Bernadette is also faced with devastating insights into the disturbing and potentially deadlocked nature of desire during a visit to the Etruscan museum in Volterra with her practical and unromantic husband. The absence of the prize exhibit in the collection, a funerary monument that depicts an elderly married couple reclining in seeming harmony on their tomb, becomes emblematic of the entanglements and impasses defining her existence. She makes the radical decision not only to jettison her lover, who refuses to make a commitment to her, but also to leave her husband from whom she has grown apart. She takes up a job teaching English in Perugia, leading a precarious existence akin to a "governess of slender means in a novel by Henry James" (120). The assumption of a quasi-literary role hints that she has not exchanged delusion for sanity or fantasy for reality. The fragility of Bernadette's new life reminds us that her sudden decision has not cancelled out the lack that defines desire or the inveterate conflict between the abusive but captivating lover and the sustaining but unappealing husband. In 'Swiss Cheese', Clíona similarly struggles with her devotion to her engineer husband, Martin, and her daughter, Afric, and her tempestuous affair with a government minister, Paddy. The latter casts her in the role of a beatific Madonna who can selflessly put up with the constant experience of rebuff and disappointment when he fails to show up for pre-arranged rendezvous. Even though she harbours murderous feelings towards her careless and exploitative lover, she still agrees to see him when he calls her after another missed appointment, which he fails even to register. At the end of the story, she looks forward to the moment when she will shake off her current abasement to her lover and discover a means of egress from the treacherous emotional terrain in which she finds herself stranded. But this *denouement* is one that can only be sketched in a shadowy fashion, not actually realised: "But for some reason she can't begin the journey back as yet. Not quite yet" (162).

Clare Hansen has usefully outlined the differences between the formal designs of traditional tales and of the modernist story, inaugurated by Edgar Allen Poe, Anton Chekhov, James Joyce, and Katherine Mansfield, amongst many others. She contends that, whereas oral narratives place an emphasis on plot and events and on the universal aspects of human interaction, modern short fictions tend to probe the vagaries of individual behaviour, but to be plotless and without a precisely contoured design.[11] Discrete moments of truth, hence, may be uncovered by the latter narratives, but the trajectories they trace are jagged and formless and rarely permit a sense of definitive ending. Ní Dhuibhne's contemporary tales, even though they shadow the symbolic scenarios and end-determined design of the folktale, may be categorised as plotless stories that delve into the complexities of female desire, but necessarily leave things vague, unresolved, or deliberately suspended. Thus, in 'Estonia', Emily horrifyingly discovers that Olaf, a man with whom she had a brief affair, has drowned in the cataclysmic sinking of the Swedish car ferry, the 'Herald of Free Enterprise'. The story, however, seems deliberately to evade this recognition and its repercussions and affective aftermath. Instead, it lingers on

Emily's joyous reunion with her husband, who is reporting on the incident, and on an appended counter-narrative that tells in false journalistic mode of a young couple miraculously rescued from the ferry. The fragmented shape of this disjointed text, in which everything appears to be out of kilter, more closely captures the conflicting and wildly veering emotions of guilt, grief, and amoral pleasure that are gestured at than any linear story would be capable of achieving.[12] Understatement and gaps within the narrative, like the reticence and lack of psychologisation of the oral tale, become a means of outlining the mysterious and abysmal depths of human behaviour.

Yet, even as they make use of the plotless form of the modernist story to convey their ambiguous and teasing accounts of heroines who are apparently engaged on a quest for self-knowledge and control over their personal lives, Ní Dhuibhne's stories also subtly trace the mythic dimensions of experience. In 'The Inland Ice', Polly, who feels estranged from her dying husband and let down by a marriage and career as a librarian that have failed to fulfill her, is moved by a visit to an icecap in Greenland that, initially, looks dirty and banal but which, on closer inspection, is revealed to contain shapes like stalagmites: "and when you peer under you see that they are blue and turquoise, silver, jade, and other subtle, shining, winking colours for which you have no name" (217). This sudden upsurge of pleasure and the recognition of the hidden depths of existence, do not change the disaffected heroine, but, in a suspended moment of insight, it hints at chthonic designs that knit things together. In a similar manner, Bronwyn in 'How Lovely the Slopes Are', is distracted from her bickering relationship with her Swedish husband and their arguments as they get lost on the way to IKEA in Uppsala, when she recalls a passage in Njal's Saga. The mundane tensions of a twentieth-century marriage are juxtaposed with the bloody conflicts of heroic saga. Irony, however, is held at bay as Ní Dhuibhne's heroine derives comfort from a vivid and involuntarily recalled passage in the Icelandic tale:

They rode down to the Markar river, on their way to the ship. Gunnar's horse stumbled, and he had to dismount. He glanced up the hill to his home.

"How lovely the slopes are!" he said. "More lovely than they have ever appeared to me before. Golden cornfields and new-mown hay. I am going back home and I will not go away." (258)

No resolution is suggested nor metacommentary offered. Rather, this moment of intertextuality hints at points of convergence between traditional and modern stories and at the archetypal designs that might help to make sense of the splinterings and randomness of contemporary existence.

Marina Warner has argued that modern versions of the 'Beauty and the Beast' tale concentrate on the affinities between the woman and her barbaric consort rather than solely on their differences. Beastliness, in its modern forms, is seen as part of human nature and not something that is clearly demarcated or comes from without.[13] In similar fashion, Ní Dhuibhne's protagonists are forced to admit their affinity with their beastly lovers. They also find themselves caught in several interlocking patterns. Despite their modernity, they are drawn into atavistic gender divisions in which oppressive roles are foisted upon them, and with which they compulsively and disturbingly collude. Simultaneously, they have to recognise the untamable and amoral nature of their desire, even though, unlike the reordered ending of 'The Search for the Lost Husband', no pragmatic solution to such insights presents itself. Above all, Ní Dhuibhne's playful and ironic tales succeed in tracking the impossible and unspeakable excesses of a female *jouissance*. The plotless narratives of *'The Inland Ice' and Other Stories*, eschew the commonsensical wisdom of the traditional folktale, but, with their unexpected epiphanies and sudden reversals that constantly waylay the reader, they deliver sharply realised critical and imaginative accounts of the trials of modern relationships and the deep-seated and intractable problem of desire for the contemporary heroine.

1   John McGahern, *Nightlines* (London: Faber and Faber, 1970) and *Getting Through* (London: Faber and Faber, 1978); John Banville, *Long Lankin* (London: Secker and Warburg, 1970).

2   Roddy Doyle, *'The Deportees' and Other Stories* (London: Jonathan Cape, 2007); Colm Tóibín, *Mothers and Sons* (London: Picador, 2006).

3   Unless otherwise noted, all stories discussed in this essay are from *'The Inland Ice' and Other Stories* (Belfast: Blackstaff Press, 1997). Page numbers are provided in parentheses in the main text.

4   For an incisive and perceptive interpretation of *'The Inland Ice' and Other Stories*, to which this essay is much indebted, see Elke D'hoker, 'The Postmodern Folktales of Éilís Ní Dhuibhne'. *ABEI Journal (The Brazilian Journal of Irish Studies)* 6 (June 2004): 129–39.

5   Walter Benjamin, 'The Storyteller: Observations on the Works of Nikolai Leskov' in *Walter Benjamin Selected Writings: Volume 3 1935– 1938*, trans. Edmund Jephcott, Howard Eiland *et al.*, eds. Howard Eiland and Michael W. Jennings (Cambridge, Mass.: The Belknap Press of Harvard University Press, 2002), 143–66.

6   See Boria Sax, *The Serpent and the Swan: The Animal Bride in Folklore and Literature* (Virginia: The McDonald and Woodward, 1998), 21–2.

7   For the texts of these stories and a commentary on their plots, see *The Classic Fairy Tales*, ed. Maria Tatar (New York: Norton, 1999), 25–72.

8   Sax, 76–9.

9   See Jacques Lacan, 'The Subversion of the Subject and the Dialectic of Desire in the Freudian Unconscious' in *Écrits: A Selection*, trans. Alan Sheridan (London: Tavistock Publications, 1977), 292–325; and Bruce Fink, 'The Dialectic of Desire' in *A Clinical Introduction to Lacanian Psychoanalysis: Theory and Technique* (Cambridge, Mass.: Harvard University Press, 2000), 50–71.

10   For a discussion of the Lacanian concept of female *jouissance*, seen as a sexual pleasure peculiar to women that eludes and escapes the phallic function, see Rosalind Minsky, ed. *Psychoanalysis and Gender: An Introductory Reader* (London: Routledge, 1996), 164–76.

11   Clare Hanson, *Short Stories and Short Fictions, 1880–1980* (London: Macmillan, 1985), 1–9.

12   For an analysis of the use of obliquity in Ní Dhuibhne's work, see Jacqueline Fulmer, *Folk Women and Indirection in Morrison, Ní Dhuibhne, Hurston, and Lavin* (Aldershot: Ashgate, 2007).

13   Marina Warner, *From the Beast to the Blonde: On Fairy Tales and Their Tellers* (London: Vintage, 1995).

Exile in Éilís Ní Dhuibhne's Short Fiction[1]

CAITRIONA MOLONEY

Éilís Ní Dhuibhne's short fiction develops the theme of exile in terms of gender identity, female sexuality, and the urban-rural dichotomy. Generally, the relationship between exile and emigration depends on how the terms are defined, and those definitions range between extremes, with the plethora of terminology used in the discussions reflecting the complexity of the issues. Literary critics have talked about those leaving Ireland as emigrants, expatriates, and refugees; emigration has been called banishment, flight, and exile.[2] Attempts to classify emigration as 'voluntary' and 'involuntary' encounter similar difficulties in definition. On one end of the spectrum, Van Morrison called his production company *Exile Productions Ltd.*, although his wealth and status make his exile seem voluntary. Salman Rushdie, on the other hand, has been in exile for several decades under a very reasonable fear of death. James Joyce is frequently cited as an example of a voluntary exile/emigrant, however, Joyce himself genuinely feared he would be killed or maimed in Ireland. Oddly, on one of his very few visits to Ireland, he was on a train that was attacked by the Irish Republican Army (IRA); although some would say he was paranoid, Joyce took it personally. We see the same contradictions and tensions in the debate over asylum seekers in Ireland today; they claim they will be tortured and killed if forced to return to their homeland, but opponents disagree. Some emigrants see emigration as the only alternative to starvation and death, but the degree to which they are correct is always relative. The extent to which an individual is coerced into leaving Ireland – that survival depends upon departure – is impossible to measure objectively. Some individuals would say that an inability to practice their art, or live openly as gay or lesbian is a form of torture, even a sort of death.

This polarisation of opinion on migration is exemplified by Mary Robinson, on the one hand, valorising emigration as an achievement and offering to cherish and represent "the 70 million people living on this globe who claim Irish descent".[3] Joe Cleary, on the other hand, considers Irish emigration as being "sustained, thoroughgoing, and culturally traumatic experiences" criminally enforced on the Irish poor by the British and the Irish political elite.[4] For women, the questions are more difficult because they have largely been absent from the discussion, an absence Gerardine Meaney views as "women's exile from historical agency and their subjection to history".[5] Jim Maclaughlin also notes the neglect of women in emigration accounts by suggesting that "Irish women are hidden from the history of recent Irish emigration".[6] Ní Dhuibhne's fiction captures many of the nuances of these debates.

This essay will analyse the effect of exile on Irish identity, complicated by gender, looking specifically at the intersection of exile, Irishness, and women's sexuality in Ní Dhuibhne's short fiction. The stories examined here illustrate the extent to which the concept of woman as Mother Ireland – pure, virginal, sacrificing, nurturing – structures representations of real women. They show how the concept of woman as body politic represses women's sexuality; this embodiment seems to be even stronger for the exile, in some relationships becoming an abusive possessiveness, as in Ní Dhuibhne's 'The Pale Gold of Alaska', in which, just as the exiled Irish man is considered inferior by Native Americans and less recently-arrived migrants, so the Irish woman becomes a scapegoat, or the "other of the ex-other".[7] Ní Dhuibhne's 'Sex in the Context of Ireland', which charts the history of church and state's exploitation of women's sexuality, is used to discuss yet another type of exile. Shipment to America (England or Australia) was a form of emigration for babies deemed 'orphans' by the Catholic clergy after being removed, sometimes forcibly, from their mothers. Like women who went to England seeking abortions, this form of migration has, until recently, been invisible and silent. Lastly, the essay considers internal migration, specifically the move from rural Donegal to urban Dublin. Ní Dhuibhne's 'Blood and Water' shows the trauma of such internal migration and its effect on family relationships and gendered Irish identity while, at the same time, examining the ambivalent position of the Gaeltacht's traditional Irish language, music, and folklore to Celtic Tiger Dublin.

Ní Dhuibhne's story, 'The Pale Gold of Alaska',[8] set in the late 1890s at the time of the Yukon Gold Rush, dramatises how women can become both a portable symbol of Ireland and an ethnostalgic memory of home. It also reveals the cost women pay for that role. Because of the attitudes of other characters towards her, the protagonist, Sophie, comes to represent the fundamental contradiction of emigration – the presence and absence of home in the mind of the exile. 'The Pale Gold of Alaska' illustrates how displaced abjection produces hatred, both of the gendered other, women, and the ethnic other, the 'Redskin.'[9] Laurie Sucher's insight on racism is also evident in this story:

> Certainly racism, that is, the hatred, devaluation and utilization of darker peoples by lighter ones, is always connected to obsessive sexual notions: fear of 'miscegenation,' the ostensible elevation of some women to the status of totemic untouchables, and the degradation of others. Racism is always associated with fascism and exaggerated patriarchism: women are objects to be fought over, 'protected,' or raped.[10]

As Janet Nolan demonstrates, between 1885 and 1920, women emigrated in greater numbers than men, often alone or with a sister.[11] In Ní Dhuibhne's story, Sophie and her sister leave Ireland's poverty in the late 1890s and move to New York, financed by a loan from an older sister who is already working there. In doing so, Sophie seems also to move towards prosperity, marriage, a job in a textile mill, owning her own cabin in Montana, being a full-time housewife, and becoming wealthy when her husband discovers gold in Alaska. Superficially, it appears that Sophie has climbed up the social scale by continually moving west but, in reality, she has lost her sense of self and identity and, ultimately, her sanity. The story deconstructs Sophie's ostensible success by detailing her degenerating psychological state. The further she moves west from Ireland, the less she is 'herself'.

The price Sophie pays for her status as a married woman, as well as superiority to her sisters, who are both unmarried domestic servants, is her husband Ned's violent possessiveness. He simultaneously approves and disapproves of her sexuality and attractiveness. Sophie pays a price for having a job and her own money by having to live in a one-room tenement in Philadelphia with Ned and two other men, thereby gaining a reputation for sexual promiscuity, which only increases Ned's violence. She pays a price for having her own cabin in Montana, beyond the isolation and back-breaking work of survival in a primitive frontier town, that of Ned's continual psychological abuse. She lives in fear of his temper; he continually calls her 'stupid' and tells her she can't do anything right. Sophie questions whether she has made the right decision in choosing Ned over the relative comfort of her sisters' lives in Philadelphia:

> It seemed that her life had become a balancing act as she moved from east to west, choosing the lesser of two evils all the time. Ned was better than Sheila and housework in Philadelphia. Being alone in a cabin in Montana was better than working in a factory in Philadelphia. Now going to the Klondike with Ned was supposed to be better than staying in the cabin here. But her judgment was faltering. She could no longer weigh up one choice against another and see, quickly, which was the best. ('Pale' 32–33)

Women generally become emblematic of Ireland for Irish migrant men, and Sophie becomes a fetish-like symbol of Ireland for Ned. The trope of the Irish nation as woman – Cathleen Ní Houlihan, Dark Rosaleen, the Shan Von Vocht, the Poor Old Woman – has been extensively described by scholars.

Rebecca Pelan argues that, although nationalism valorised ancient Irish goddesses like Mebd, "sexuality ... as represented by powerful female figures, was simply written out of an Irish history that had no place for active heroines",[12] while Breda Gray and Louise Ryan write that, "the purity of Irishness was symbolized by the purity of 'Irishwoman'... In constructing symbols of Irish womanhood, the Catholic Church, the State and the Press threatened to render real women invisible".[13] The ambivalence of feelings towards women parallels the male emigrant's ambivalent feelings towards the mother country, which has rejected him, but is still idealised in his mind as being the best country in the world. Ned's feelings towards Sophie illustrate the virgin/whore paradox familiar in feminist theory. On the one hand, woman as mother figure emerges as vulnerable and needing protection, "innocent, pure, unsexed, self-sacrificing motherhood",[14] and, on the other hand, the 'virgin's' counterpart in the syndrome is the 'whore', or the sexualised woman. Kathryn Conrad explains how a feminised Ireland – defeated by colonisers – is metaphorised as a 'whore', who let the invaders into her four green fields.[15] Ned constructs Sophie as both virgin and whore.

Because emigrants tend to be more conservative than those who stay home, the virgin/whore syndrome intensifies in exile.[16] 'The Pale Gold of Alaska' demonstrates this dynamic through the character of Ned and the behaviour of other Irish emigrant men in America. Ned says many decades of the rosary to the Virgin Mary every night, and Sophie equates the words he utters in lovemaking to his saying the rosary: "it was as if they hardly applied to her at all, as if they were just words he said, the way women in Donegal say prayers. The same words over and over again, uttered in a sleepy singsong voice, uttered so often that the speakers do not even know what they are saying" (6). Ned conflates Sophie with the Virgin Mary, but he also beats and rapes her when he discovers that other men find her attractive. The more attention she receives from men, the more he denigrates her. Sophie fails to live up to Ned's impossible icon of woman as virginal and maternal. But the contradictory virgin mother stands in for another significant absent presence – Ireland, or home. Ned's character demonstrates one of Gray's 'narratives' of emigration, whereby the emigrant is only "spiritually at home" in Ireland. Ned always wants to return to Ireland, although he does not do so. Sophie, on the other hand, feels that America is much better than Ireland, and does not want to return. Ned's devotion to impossible versions of female sexuality corresponds to his contradictory feelings about Ireland as the best – but most impossible – place to live.

The themes of race and gender intersect when Sophie falls in love with a Native American named North Wind. Left alone for long periods while Ned is mining, Sophie and North Wind become friends and then lovers. Ailbhe Smyth's term for postcolonial women, 'the other of the ex-other', operates exponentially in this story: the 'Redskins' are the other of the other of the ex-other. Seen as both very dangerous and completely powerless, the 'Redskin' is contradictorily endowed with threatening power and complete abjection. They are lower on the migrants' social scale than women, so the women displace their abjection onto them. "'They'd eat anything', Mrs. Sullivan said disdainfully. 'They're not like us. They have no sense of cleanliness. Ugh.' All the women in Greenough hated the Indians" (20).

When Ned plans to move to the Yukon, Sophie and North Wind fake a 'Redskin' kidnapping. It fails and Ned and the other emigrants 'rescue' Sophie. In fact, all the men in camp unite to rescue her:

> Ned and Mick Sullivan, Mossie Fitzgerald and Miley Gallagher, Fritz Zumpfe and Jon Johannsen, and several others, converged on the camp. They carried shotguns, pikes, shovels, axes, anything they had available. 'Fucking savages.' Ned's voice was heard above the others. 'I'll rip them apart. Fuckers'. (37)

The Irish emigrants' desire to control the American territory and to subdue 'redskins', parallels what Geraldine Moane calls nationalism's "obsession with controlling women's bodies".[17] That Sophie and North Wind were lovers was unimaginable to the emigrants; revenging the honor of an Irish woman unites them as a new community.[18]

Women's sexuality is also problematic in Ní Dhuibhne's story 'Sex in the Context of Ireland', where sexuality and Irish identity collide around the issue of "sexual immorality".[19] The censorious sexual immorality discourse of the new Irish Republic produced several invisible forms of emigration: 'unwanted' infants sent to adoptive parents in America, women seeking abortions, women seeking to have their babies adopted, prostitutes unable to work in Ireland, women who escaped from Magdalen asylums, women the Magdalens sent abroad, and unmarried women seeking to keep and raise their own children.

'Sex in the Context of Ireland' exposes the church and state's exploitation of women's sexuality. The Catholic Church and the Irish Free State criminalised female sexuality, and two profitable businesses emerged out of this collusion: the Magdalen laundries and American adoption schemes. Shipment to America (or England or Australia) was a form of emigration for babies deemed 'orphans' by the Catholic clergy after being removed, sometimes forcibly, from their mothers. Until recently, this form of migration was invisible and silent; as it is for women who travel to England seeking abortions, the historical record is blank or distorted.[20]Although these types of journeys were primarily undocumented, sociologists deduce their existence from other evidence. Frances Finnegan's research scrutinised the Registers of the Good Shepherd institutions in Cork and Limerick, and Maria Luddy analysed records of the nineteenth-century rescue movement.[21] Finnegan quotes clerical advice to send 'fallen' women to America, as well as examples of individual women being sent to England and America by their families or by the Good Shepherd nuns.[22] Luddy quotes Catholic Aid societies in England complaining about the number of pregnant indigent Irish women arriving there.[23]

Following the establishment of the Free State in 1922, the State, together with the Irish Catholic Church, criminalised female sexuality to conform to the newly-independent, nascent Irish nationalism that conceptualised Irish women as pure, self-sacrificing, maternal and non-sexual. In conflating crime and sexuality, the state and clergy constructed "a fiction of Irish cultural purity upon which the national imaginary depended".[24] The Magdalen laundries and the American Adoption schemes illustrate the nature of that partnership. The Irish Free State profited by shirking its financial responsibility to care for marginalised members of society by allowing the church to export them. Moira Maguire writes that, "thousands of healthy Irish children were sent to the United States for adoption simply because they were illegitimate and thus unwanted at home" which "relieved local authorities of the financial burden of maintaining them".[25] The church's laundries made a profit, which was invested in their other establishments. According to Finnegan, "accounts from the Good Shepherd Convent in Cork show an average profit on the laundry operation of the equivalent in today's money of 100,000 pounds", and that the "nuns spent much of this on themselves".[26] Ní Dhuibhne's 'Sex in the Context of Ireland'[27] realistically portrays many aspects of this controversy.

When the story opens, a prostitute, Molly Malone, is dying of venereal disease. Naming her character Molly Malone, Ní Dhuibhne comments wryly on Dublin tour guides' favourite downtown statue. Although contemporary discourses of tourism construct her positively and nostalgically, she is known colloquially as 'the tart with the cart', and, in the song that commemorates her, as a prostitute who dies of venereal disease. According to Finnegan, the threat of venereal disease to English military men in port cities of England and Ireland precipitated passage of the Communicable Diseases Acts between 1864 to 1869 and, although repealed in England in 1889, these Acts were enforced extra-legally in Ireland through the Magdalen homes until the 1970s.[28] Ní Dhuibhne's Molly is 'rescued' by a Catholic lay organisation, the Legion of Mary, who say they are taking her to a hospital; instead, however, they take her to a Magdalen home where she delivers a baby girl and dies. Bella of the story remembers childbirth in a Magdalen asylum: "I'd seen girls having babies in the Good Shepherd. It's not something I'd want to see again. Much less put a pal of mine through it" ('Sex' 125). The nuns put the child in one of their orphanages and, later, send her to be adopted by a "good Catholic American couple" (129). This practice was described by the German newspaper *Uhr Blatt* in 1951 as, "a black-market baby ring that sold 'unwanted' Irish children to the highest American bidder".[29] Sending infants to America to be adopted coincides with the evolution of the homes' clientele from prostitutes to pregnant unmarried women, to socially marginalised girls who deviated from socio-sexual standards. This process created an invisible migration of babies sent abroad as valuable commodities.

'Sex in the Context of Ireland' attributes the extra-legal export of Irish babies to the Legion of Mary; their officer, Mr. Murphy, explains that, "the baby has been given up for adoption to an American couple. It's a new project the good sisters have. Good Catholic American couples ... it's the ideal answer to ... well you know the situation" (129). Just as Murphy didn't have to actually name the 'situation', neither did the Irish government. Murphy's explanation for the absence of the babies on any records is plausible: "I had a meeting with a friend of mine in the Department of Foreign Affairs. Thanks, I may say, to my personal intervention, the scheme can function easily. The babies don't even need passports. They are simply let slip quietly out of the country as if they had never existed" (129). Maguire tells us that the requirement that couples promise to raise the infants as Catholic was, in fact, the only prerequisite for adoption. Maguire describes the process as having "no paperwork ... no information about the adopting couple's background, home life, or financial position" and, in contrast with English practices, "no official oversight or regulation".[30]

These events reflect the conflicted nature of the Irish attitudes towards sexuality, which treated female sexuality outside marriage as a crime. Initially, many of the women who were admitted to the Magdalen homes may have been prostitutes seriously ill with venereal disease. Finnegan notes many of the early converts "were at a hopelessly advanced stage" and that "there was no effective treatment for certain types of venereal disease".[31] The Contagious Diseases Acts required hospitalisation of diseased prostitutes, not incarceration. However, in Ireland, prostitutes were sent to the Magdalen homes from the hospitals. After 1889, when the Communicable Diseases Act had been repealed in England, in Ireland, women who were not prostitutes continued to enter the homes. These women were either unmarried, pregnant, orphaned, intellectually impaired, victims of rape or incest, abandoned by their families, or simply were girls considered to be vulnerable to these events. Gray describes the Magdalen penitents as "Irish women who were sexually abused, became pregnant outside of marriage and were consigned to an institution for life".[32] Elizabeth Butler Cullingford characterises them as "socially marginalized people" including "poor children, mentally disturbed adults, and women who were classified as sexual delinquents".[33] They worked as unpaid laundresses for the church's profitable laundry business and their babies became 'unwanted infants' for the profitable adoption trade.

Bella of Ní Dhuibhne's story personalises the 'sexual immorality' debate, and explains prostitution in terms of economics and social class. Ní Dhuibhne takes a risk in the narrative style of the story, primarily first-person singular. Typical of British people in the nineteenth century, Bella indicates her social class as soon as she speaks in a dialect suggestive of turn-of-the-century Dublin working-class poor – a dialect that is difficult for the modern reader to understand. Siobhan Kilfeather comments on this problem as one of "how to represent the (presumably) inarticulate masses, without merely re-presenting stereotypes associated with stage-Irishry and the brogue".[34] Like *patois* in Caribbean literature, or slang in Afro-American, dialect is initially difficult. Ní Dhuibhne addresses that difficulty immediately, having Bella speak directly to the reader about the problem: "I can hear ye sayin now, talk proper, talk so we don't hafta strain our delicate ears to listen and to understand what it is ye're sayin. Well I won't and if yez can't understand it's your loss" (111). The risk pays off and the story rings true as the legitimate voice of the absent Irish woman. Any other point of view would usurp her agency.

While giving voice to the woman's role in sexuality, Ní Dhuibhne's narrative also fleshes out the man's. In some respects, Bella fits the profile of a resident of an orphanage run by the nuns: she is a half-orphan, her mother died and her father abandoned her. Her description of her treatment is consistent with recent exposés of the Magdalen institutions: "The sound. The blow of wood or leather on children's skin. That was the music of the Good Shepherd. The feelin. Hunger. Fear of yer life. Hate of the nuns. Freezin cold. The weak died" (112).[35] Bella's accusations of sexual abuse in the home received corroboration in the Mercy sisters' 2004 settlement of a class action lawsuit for 128 million Euros, contingent on an indemnity against further claims.[36]

Bella's attempts to escape suggest that the inmates of a Magdalen home were not free to leave. Finnegan cites the Cork Register of Penitents 1876, on a small number of young women who "escaped over the wall".[37] Luddy, however, argues that most penitents joined and left "of their own free will".[38] Escape, however, would hardly have been necessary if the girls were free to leave. Later, Bella has a type of escape when her father takes her out of the orphanage when she is nine years old to care for his ever-increasing offspring, but then puts her out to work as a prostitute when she can't find any other job. He tells her to talk to the local madam, "Pussy Catkins" (119). So, Bella's evolution from orphan, to orphanage resident, to domestic worker at the age of nine, to prostitution as an early teenager, is a logical process because she lacks any other options. Her poverty, her lack of education, and her abuse by her father put her in a position where her only alternative to prostitution is to embrace life-long hard labour, silence, and suffering in a Magdalen home. Finnegan describes one Good Shepherd home as operating "with a callous disregard for the unfortunate women in their care" who were "overworked, under-fed and inadequately housed" and sentenced to a lifetime of silence and isolation.[39]

Bella's grim history contrasts radically with the Catholic and lay hierarchy's explanation for prostitution as a product of women's sin. The church attacked 'female fickleness', women's 'love of dress', dancehalls and cinema as causes of prostitution, explanations that ignored economics and male participation. Clerics frequently extolled against these 'vices' and blamed them for unmarried mothers and illegitimate children. James Smith calls this nationalist and Catholic reform enthusiasm, "obsession with the dangers associated with popular amusements, especially the dance hall".[40] Finnegan also notes that "a striking example from the Cork Annals demonstrates that the Sisters too, regarded 'love of dress' as a preliminary to evil".[41] Gray cites one pronouncement from the 'hierarchy' that young women's "frequenting dance-halls would bring them 'to shame' and necessitate their 'retiring' to refuge institutions",[42] while Pelan quotes one liturgical tract detailing the concerns of the Irish Bishops in 1927: "the evil one is forever setting his snares ... chiefly the dance hall, the bad book, the indecent paper, the motion picture, the immodest fashion in female dress".[43]

Ní Dhuibhne's story ironically revises one of the major targets of the reformers, 'love of dress'. It recuperates this symbol of prostitution by illustrating how fine dress was the uniform of the prostitute and a sign of her oppression. In a version of the 'company store' in American factory life, the madam 'gives' the neophyte prostitute a dress, underwear and shoes on credit for ten pounds with one hundred per cent interest. As Bella explains, "the system was that she gave you your first outfit, to get you started, on credit. You would never pay off that debt" (127). Ten pounds was a large sum of money at that time; the daily wage for manual labor was only two shillings. Bella's pimp, Jockser, brutally enforces the madam's monopoly on clothing.

The madams, the pimps, the prostitutes and their customers enjoyed relative impunity under British rule, except for the Contagious Diseases Acts aimed at controlling venereal disease in seaports used by British military. Luddy writes that, "the police seem generally to have turned a blind eye to prostitutes unless they created a public nuisance".[44] 'Sex in the Context of Ireland' shows legislators winking at the illegality of the business and availing themselves of it personally. However, the establishment of the Free State, with the support of the Irish Catholic Church, saw prostitution being prosecuted much more energetically. Smith lists nine laws, investigations, and commissions between 1925 and 1935 aimed at curtailing "sexual immorality".[45] In Ní Dhuibhne's story, the Legion of Mary has the red light district burned down and the whores arrested. The clients escape, but Bella serves six weeks in prison, and is robbed of her considerable savings by the police, after which she decides to go to England where there is no Free State and no Legion of Mary.

Like Bella, a large proportion of Irish emigrants, traditionally, have gone to Britain.[46] The narrator of 'Kingston Ridge'[47] has many family members living in England who visit Ireland regularly – the Birmingham cousins once a year and those from Leeds twice a year. Consistent with research on emigration, none of these relatives returns to Ireland permanently; as Gray writes, "although the telephone, fax, e-mail and air transport now make the leaving of Ireland seem less final ... most of those who leave *do not return* to live".[48]

Gray's theory about Irish emigration 'narratives' is partially born out in 'Kingston Ridge': the expatriates live bodily elsewhere, but are considered to be spiritually at 'home' in Ireland; emigration is regarded as a normal part of Irish life; and emigrants leave Ireland for career advancement and improved social status. In 'Kingston Ridge' the frequent use of the phrase 'coming home' in place of 'visiting' reiterates the idea that expatriates are only temporarily resident abroad: they belong in Ireland. The story's narrator and her family accept a large part of their family living abroad as normal. However, the story both affirms and denies the narrative that the Irish emigrate to escape poverty, get well-paying jobs, and move up in social class.

As a child, the narrator believes this story; as an adult, however, her experiences partially contradict it. The young narrator tells us that English people were automatically much richer than the Irish, but they paid a high price: "dirt and danger. England was a filthy risky place. There was no green grass there (I envisioned fields of concrete). There were no trees. There were no parks. What England did possess, in great abundance, were murderers" ('Kingston' 45). At the end of the story, the narrator has moved up the social scale beyond her English cousins: she is educated, employed as a professional, and engaged to Ross, a quintessentially upper-class Englishman. But, like Sophie in 'The Pale Gold of Alaska', she has paid a high price for affluence.

The cousins in Leeds are the primary expatriates in the story. The narrator is naturally most interested in her same-aged cousin, Diana, whose name reveals her parents' desire to identify with the English. The narrator's father, Mick (whose name echoes the English derogatory slang names for Irishmen, 'Mick' and 'Paddy'), has married Jane, a Londoner. Mick works in a coal-mine in northern England; he has miner's lung and needs an inhaler when he visits Ireland. Mick's career follows that of most emigrants who "occupy the traditional occupations of the emigrant ... one survey in the 1980s found that 76 percent of Irish men in Britain were manual workers".[49] Jane works in a factory, so, with two well-paying jobs, they can afford two vacations a year. However, they are not paid enough to allow them to vacate without availing of free room and board with relatives. The negative consequences of Mick's career in a coal-mine are immediately obvious in his lung disease. The consequences of Jane's employment are less obvious in her daughter's lack of upward social mobility; as a typist, she has moved up, socio-economically, and can afford a vacation in Spain. Not that far up though, since she still works in the same factory as her mother.

On the other hand, the narrator, nameless except when referred to as 'Ducky' by her family, has advanced higher up the social scale. Her college degree is from an élite university, she has a professional career, and her boyfriend hails from Surrey, where English royalty have country homes (55). However, characteristic of the homelessness attributed to many exiles, she feels alienated from all of her environments, past, present and future. Consistent with research on women emigrants, her anxiety may be a result of dislocated class connections rather than emigration itself. Tension in her future marriage to an upper-class Englishman is foreshadowed by his behaviour while visiting her cousins. Ironically, he indicates his discomfort with her Irish family by drinking whiskey immoderately, "three in the course of ten minutes, the length of our visit" (57). This parallels Gray's findings, that "identifying with the larger Irish community in London has the potential to undermine a hard-earned middle-class identity there".[50]

The narrator's mother welcomes English relatives on their Irish vacations many times a year with stereotypical Irish hospitality. We see Diana, like her namesake, being treated as a princess. The narrator finds the experience of standing "in the back garden, under the long dining room window, staring through the glass at Diana as she ate her tea in state at the white-clothed table" inspirational not of jealousy, but of joy, that such a "glamorous" life existed (48). Her mother has done the invisible women's work, as Mary Robinson famously put it, of "cherishing" the "Irish Diaspora".[51] Gray asks rhetorically, "who will do the work of cherishing? ... [as] yet more 'invisible work' is now being carried out by Irish women".[52] 'Kingston Ridge' suggests that this hospitality may not be completely altruistic; the narrator tells us that the generosity of her American relatives had stopped, perhaps because "too many cousins were arriving too regularly" (43). Hospitality and generosity may be traits remaining from ancient tribal kinship ties, when reciprocity was the rule of the land. As the reciprocity became less real, the value of hospitality declined and was relegated to women's invisible work.

Modernity breaks all that, but not comfortably. When the narrator has accomplished her dizzying climb up the social ladder, she is left nonetheless alienated and estranged: "There was no one to whom I could talk, whose language I actually knew" (57). Her feelings resemble what Edward Said calls "the crippling sorrow of estrangement" and, further, his belief that, "to think of exile as beneficial, as a spur to humanism or to creativity, is to belittle its mutilations".[53] On the other hand, Fintan O'Toole sees a new Irish migration where class trumps national origin: "Irish emigrants, for example, a computer graduate who moves from IBM Dublin to Wall Street, are already economically, psychologically and to a large degree culturally, a part of the centre before they leave".[54] In 'Kingston Ridge' psychological, economic and cultural assimilation are not so happily aligned.[55]

For ordinary emigrants, for example Irish people who move to Britain, dislocation and trauma can result from class, cultural, national, and ethnic differences between immigrants and natives. This cannot be said of the Irish who migrate within Ireland even though their dislocation, trauma, and alienation may be equally as serious. In Ní Dhuibhne's fiction, class trumps other factors as the primary source of difference. Ní Dhuibhne's short stories about moving from rural Donegal to urban Dublin usually involve changing and conflicting social status.[56] Even though the virtues of the Gaeltacht – language, music, folklore – are nominally valorised by Celtic Tiger Dublin, the actual people and lifestyles of the Gaeltacht are more often despised. Ní Dhuibhne's 'Blood and Water' shows the trauma of internal migration and its effect on family relationships; it examines the ambivalent position of the Gaeltacht's traditional Irish language, music, and folklore to Celtic Tiger Dublin, and demonstrates the effects of that migration on gendered Irish identity.

'Blood and Water'[57] describes emigration from rural Donegal to urban Dublin in the 1980s as a journey from a 'traditional' to a modern lifestyle. The life of the protagonist, Mary, shows how the trauma of internal migration affects family relationships and Irish identity. The story represents internal migration and transnational migration as, potentially, equally traumatic, but it also suggests more positive qualities to the country left behind and more ambivalence about the superiority of Dublin's modernity than some critics have identified. Christine St. Peter argues that domestic violence against women is a primary cause of "internal/internalized exile, the loss of a sense of integral 'self' within Ireland due to abuses in personal relationships, often reinforced or perpetuated by systemic social structures that put women at risk".[58]

Although 'Blood and Water' represents life in Ballytra, Inishowen as harsh and difficult, it also casts a shadow on life in suburban Dublin. A character constructed to be almost symbolic of the Gaeltacht, Mary's Aunt Annie, shows the advantages and disadvantages of both cultures. Annie owns and operates a small farm in Ballytra. Annie, who would be considered intellectually impaired today, is better off in the less-sophisticated rural village than she would be in a modern city: "Had she been born in the fifties or sixties, my aunt would have been scientifically labeled, given special treatment at a special school, taught special skills and eventually employed in a special workshop to carry out a special job, certainly a much duller job than the one she pursued in reality" ('Blood' 46).

As a child, Mary has dual citizenship in this world so that when she returns to Ballytra for an Irish language course, she is both Dublin cultural tourist and Gaeltacht native. She is, however, ashamed of her rural roots and pretends ignorance of her relations in Ballytra. She is ashamed of all her country relations, but especially Annie, who is 'different', even by Donegal standards: "There was one simple reason for my hatred, so simple that I understood it myself, even when I was eight or nine years old. I resembled my aunt physically" (109–110). As an adult, the protagonist connects that self-image with the shame associated with Annie and Ballytra: "I am still ashamed, you see, of my aunt. I am still ashamed of myself .... Are my wide education, my brilliant husband, my posh accent, just attempts at camouflage?" (118). Having moved up in social class and wealth, Mary still identifies part of herself with a negative stereotype of the west – primitive, isolated, and backward. She fears her Dublin identity is a masquerade.

Ní Dhuibhne uses a "big splodge of a dirty yellow substance in the scullery of Annie's house" as an image of the values of rural Ireland. As a child, Mary cannot identify the butter and is repelled by it. Later, she learns that butter was "daubed on the wall after every churning, for luck" (121). As an adult, Mary's feelings about her rural past, her aunt, and herself are identified with the butter as "some terrible substance, soft and thick and opaque" (121), and she tries to eliminate Ballytra from her identity – like contemporary Dublin, she looks towards Europe and marries a Spaniard who takes students on trips to Spain. But Mary can't forget Ballytra. She and her mother feel a sense of burdensome responsibility for Annie when she becomes ill, but they both shirk that responsibility. Mary has a spinster sister, "a lecturer in Latin at Trinity" (121), who takes on the responsibility to care for Annie. Latin, a 'dead' language, emphasises the archaic quality of the Gaeltacht and its lack of value to contemporary Dublin.[59]

Unlike much naturalist fiction's bleak and hopeless depiction of rural Ireland, 'Blood and Water' transcends its own critique to simultaneously represent the power and beauty of the landscape of rural Ireland. Mary says, "I didn't want to give up the countryside, and the stream, and the clean clear water" (118), and she describes Lough Swilly as inspirational: "it was a brilliant turquoise colour, it looked like a great jewel ... it had a definite benign quality, that water. And I always emerged from it cleansed in both body and soul" (115).

In 'See the Robbers Passing By',[60] the Donegal-Dublin conflict divides a marriage. Without the option of divorce, the protagonist's mother and father simply live apart; she in Dublin, he in Donegal. Previously, the protagonist, Sheila's, parents had moved to Portsalt, Donegal to "change their lifestyle" ('Robbers' 44), but primitive conditions – "no running water, an outdoor toilet, electric lights in some but not all of the rooms. And the isolation" (44) – drove Sheila and her mother back to Dublin. Her husband is supposed to join her there, but he never does. Set in the 1960s, the story reveals that the only job available to married women in Ireland at that time is housework. One mother 'chars' for six households; Sheila's mother becomes a widower's housekeeper (and later inherits the house). Sheila, however, becomes one of the 'New Irish', acquiring a college degree, and a job in the civil service doing something "connected to the EC" (54).[61] Sheila also marries a European, a German who migrates to Ireland. They vacation with his parents in the Friesian Islands, which seem to have the same relationship to Germany as the Aran islands have to mainland Ireland. Jenny Beale describes that relationship in the 1950s as one in which "the people of the west were streaming away, leaving the traditional way of life as fast as they could".[62] Sheila's husband's feelings for the Friesian Islands expresses a fundamental contradiction for emigrants: he doesn't want to visit, he would like to be able to afford a vacation elsewhere, but he will return because, as he says, "this is my home" (57).

Some of Ní Dhuibhne's stories express their themes partially through correspondences with ancient Irish myth. Ní Dhuibhne's mythic method expresses the past through a postmodern narrative technique of intertextualising myth with contemporary stories.[63] Her method goes beyond direct parallels with myth to reiterate the motifs of ancient Irish myth in a contemporary context and to suggest new modes of interpretation for both. For example, myth functions as a palimpsest in Ní Dhuibhne's collection, 'The Inland Ice' and Other Stories, which uses her translation of an old Irish folktale, 'The Search for the Lost Husband', as inter-chapters to unify the short stories.[64] One of the stories in that collection, 'Summer Pudding', suggests the old Deirdre story found in 'The Exile of the Sons of Uislui', the basis of A.E. Russell's and W.B. Yeats's 'Deirdre' plays. Like other stories in Ní Dhuibhne's work, 'Summer Pudding' does not set up simple parallels or influences with legend, but suggests a pattern more consistent with Homi Bhabha's idea that, "the archaic emerges in the midst or margins of modernity as a result of some psychic ambivalence", an idea he associates with Freud's notion of the uncanny.[65] Angela Bourke advocates a similar theory about Irish folkore when she says that, "the essence of fairy-belief is ambivalence ... [about] occasions of transition and ambiguity ... the liminal, the marginal, and the ambiguous, whether in time, in the landscape, or in social relations".[66] Bourke argues elsewhere that fairy legend "allows one thing to be said, while another is meant".[67] We can see that ambivalence in both 'The Exile of the Sons of Uislui' and 'Summer Pudding'.

'The Exile of the Sons of Uislui' claims that a tribal feud and banishment of the losers, recorded in the Tain, began when an unborn female child yelled from her mother's womb, a sign of future catastrophe, marking the girl as bad luck. While it may have been true that the losers of a battle were exiled, the cause was unlikely to have been a cursed young woman. Possibly names, events, and concrete facts in myth are often true, whereas explanations generally stray farther from truth. The outlines of 'The Exile of the Sons of Uislui' suggest the scapegoating of women for intra-tribal hostilities that surround such figures as Helen of Troy and Dervorgilla. The echoes of the saga that we hear in 'Summer Pudding' suggest a similar use of storytelling to cover ambivalent memories of exile.

In 'Summer Pudding',[68] traces of the legend co-exist with other narrative strands: the famine, the girl's *Bildungsroman*, the love story, and the story of Father Toban. Employing repetition with difference, Ní Dhuibhne's story contains elements of the epic tale: exile, adultery, betrayal by a false friend, and an adventurous, visionary, and sexually-assertive woman as the main character. In the tale, the sons of Uislui are forced into exile from Ireland to Scotland because one of them, Naoise, has eloped with Deirdre, a woman belonging to King Conchobar. In 'Summer Pudding' the Irish girls are in Wales, exiled from Ireland as a result of the famine, where they meet a married man named Naoise.

Ní Dhuibhne bases a character in the story on the nineteenth-century anthropologist George Borrow, called Father Toban in 'Summer Pudding'. In his book *Wild Wales*, Borrow admitted to masquerading as a Catholic priest for Irish famine refugees in Wales.[69] Father Toban functions as a false friend to the refugees and suggests the character of Fergus in the Deirdre story.[70] Ní Dhuibhne's Father Toban illustrates both famine memory and its denial. The story's shifting focus captures characters' differing reactions to Toban: Naoise desperately wants to believe in the priest's legitimacy, but the heroine is sceptical. Without Borrow's autobiographical story of his role-playing in Wales, only the suspicions of the protagonist indicate that he is not a priest. However, the strength of her characterisation as a truth-teller, as well as the story's links to the Deirdre story, combines to discredit Father Toban. In the epic and in the plays, Deirdre is a visionary who sees into the future. In 'Summer Pudding' the protagonist also sees clearly, understanding the reality of the famine's destitution, hunger, and disease. She cautions against return, but, like Cassandra, she is not believed.

Both short story and myth describe exile and return. In the ancient story, return spells disaster; King Conchobar is untrustworthy: he kills Naoise and rapes Deirdre. In 'Summer Pudding' the story ends in Wales, as the hero and heroine are just about to return to Ireland and the famine. The presence of Father Toban at the dock strikes an ominous note. The reader logically concludes that returning to Ireland during the famine will not be fortuitous. As in contemporary sociological research, both the old and the new story suggest that the exile can never go home again.

Ní Dhuibhne's respect for history, as well as her awareness of its omissions, allows her to create fiction that re-imagines women's often silent historical record. When a woman's history has been the subject of extreme hostility or neglect, her fragmented story can easily be misrepresented. For example, in classical Greece, in an era when women were treated virtually as chattels, some histories tell us that Helen caused the Trojan War, almost single-handedly. In the stories discussed here, Ní Dhuibhne's heroines Sophie, Bella, Sheila, and the appropriately anonymous women, although oppressed, offer readers a hopeful suggestion of the powerful roles that women may have actually fulfilled in the past and may again fulfill in the future.

NOTES

1   I would like to express my appreciation to the National Endowment for the Humanities, to Professor James I. Porter's Summer Seminar 2008, and to Maureen Roche, storyteller *extraordinaire*.

2   Patrick Walsh's 2004 book, *Exile, Emigration and Irish Writing*, does an admirable job of charting the history and meaning of terms such as those above through Irish literary history. He is correct to note that the (male) literary critics he discusses omit, overlook, or belittle

women. Unfortunately, he himself does the same thing, neglecting to look for women literary critics and authors who write about exile and emigration, such as those mentioned in this article

3   Quoted in Breda Gray, 'Unmasking Irishness: Irish Women, the Irish Nation and the Irish Diaspora' in *Location and Dislocation in Contemporary Irish Society: Emigration and Irish Identities.* Jim MacLaughlin, ed. (Notre Dame, IN: Notre Dame University Press, 1997: 209–235), 221.

4   Joe Cleary, 'Toward a Materialist-Formalist History of Twentieth-Century Irish Literature'. *Boundary*, 2. 31. 1 (2004: 207–241), 209.

5   Gerardine Meaney, 'Territories of the Voice: History, Nationality and Sexuality in Kate O'Brien's Fiction'. *Irish Journal of Feminist Studies*, 2. 2 (Winter 1997: 100–118), 87.

6   Jim MacLaughlin, 'The New Vanishing Irish: Social Characteristics of "New Wave" Irish Emigration' in MacLaughlin, ed. *Location and Dislocation in Contemporary Irish Society*, 153, 154.

7   Ailbhe Smyth, 'The Floozie in the Jacuzzi'. *Feminist Studies*, 17.1 (1991: 6–29), 6.

8   Ní Dhuibhne, 'The Pale Gold of Alaska' in *The Pale Gold of Alaska and Other Stories* (Belfast: Blackstaff Press, 2000: 1–39), 28. Further references to 'Pale' are in parentheses in the text.

9   'Displaced abjection' is a phrase used by Peter Stallybrass and Allon White in *The Politics and Poetics of Transgression* "whereby 'low' social groups turn their figurative and actual power, not against those in authority but against those who are even 'lower' (women, Jews, animals, particularly cats and pigs)". Quoted in Barbara Spackman, '*inter musam et ursam moritur*: Folengo and the Gaping "Other" Mouth' in *Refiguring Woman: Perspectives on Gender and the Italian Renaissance*. Marilyn Migiel and Juliana Schiesari, eds. (Ithaca, NY: Cornell University Press, 1991: 19–34), 23.

10 Laurie Sucher, *The Fiction of Ruth Prawer Jhabvala: The Politics of Passion* (New York: Palgrave Macmillan, 1989), 120.

11 Janet Nolan, *Ourselves Alone: Women's Emigration from Ireland 1885–1920* (Lexington, KY: University Press of Kentucky, 1989), 1–8.

12 Rebecca Pelan, *Two Irelands: Literary Feminisms North and South* (New York: Syracuse University Press, 2005), 26.

13 Breda Gray and Louise Ryan, 'Dislocating "Woman" and Women in Representations of Irish National Identity' in *Women and Irish Society: A Sociological Reader*. Anne Byrne and Madeleine Leonard, eds. (Belfast: Beyond the Pale, 1997: 517–532), 520.

14 *ibid.*, 521.

15 Kathryn Conrad, *Locked in the Family Cell* (Wisconsin: University of Wisconsin Press, 2004), 11.

16   Benedict Anderson, 'Exodus'. *Critical Enquiry*, 20. 2 (1994: 314–327), 327.

17   Geraldine Moane, 'Legacies of Colonialism for Irish Women: Oppressive or Empowering?' *Irish Journal of Feminist Studies*, 1. 1 (1996: 77–92), 108.

18   We also see this dynamic in Ní Dhuibhne's stories, 'Hot Earth' in *Inland Ice and Other Stories* (Belfast: Blackstaff Press, 1997: 105–121), and 'The Day Elvis Presley Died' in *The Pale Gold of Alaska* (Belfast: Blackstaff Press, 2000: 40–86).

19   Smith uses this term to describe a plethora of legal commissions, reports, and tribunals of the early years of the Irish Free State that criminalised women's sexuality. James M. Smith, 'The Politics of Sexual Knowledge: The Origins of Ireland's Containment Culture and the Carrigan Report (1931)'. *Journal of the History of Sexuality*, 13. 2 (2004): 208–233. Maria Luddy describes similar investigations and legislation in the early days of the Free State aimed at controlling female sexuality in 'Moral Rescue and Unmarried Mothers in Ireland in the 1920s'. *Women's Studies*, 30. 6 (2001): 797–818.

20   Department of Foreign Affairs, Department of Justice, and Dublin Diocesan archive files were released in 1997; however, "the Department of Foreign Affairs began keeping statistics only in 1950." Quoted in Moira J. Maguire, "Foreign Adoptions and the Evolution of Irish Adoption Policy, 1945–52". *Journal of Social History*, 36. 2 (2002: 387–404), 388–89.

21   Considerable controversy surrounds Finnegan's book; for example, Luddy's review criticises its research methodology and considers its conclusions simplistic. Maria Luddy, Rev. of *Do Penance or Perish* by Frances Finnegan. *American Historical Review*,(April 2005), 557. Frances Finnegan, *Do Penance or Perish: Magdalen Asylums in Ireland* (Oxford: Oxford University Press, 2001); Maria Luddy, 'Prostitution and Rescue Work in Nineteenth-Century Ireland' in *Women Surviving*. Maria Luddy and Cliona Murphy, eds. (Dublin: Poolbeg, 1990: 51–84).

22   Finnegan, *Do Penance or Perish*, 167n13.

23   Luddy, 'Prostitution and Rescue Work in Nineteenth-Century Ireland', 215n, 22.

24   Luddy, 'Moral Rescue and Unmarried Mothers in Ireland in the 1920s', fn 29 and 30.

25   Maguire, 'Foreign Adoptions and the Evolution of Irish Adoption Policy', 387–88.

26   Finnegan, *Do Penance or Perish*, 202.

27   Ní Dhuibhne, 'Sex in the Context of Ireland' in *The Pale Gold of Alaska* (Belfast: Blackstaff Press, 2000: 109–133). Further references to 'Sex' are in parentheses in the text.

28   *ibid.*, xiii.

29   Quoted in Maguire, 'Foreign Adoptions and the Evolution of Irish Adoption Policy', 395.

30   *ibid.*, 390, 399.

31   Finnegan, *Do Penance or Perish*, 186, fn 48.

32   Gray and Ryan in Byrne and Leonard, eds. 'Dislocating "Woman"', 523.

33   Elizabeth Butler Cullingford, 'Our Nuns Are Not A Nation: Politicizing the Convent in Irish Literature and Film'. *Eire-Ireland*, 41. 1 (2006: 9–39), 12.

34   Siobhan Killfeather, 'Sex and Sensation in the Nineteenth-Century Novel' in *Theorizing Ireland*. Claire Connolly, ed. (New York: Palgrave Macmillan, 2003: 105–113), 105.

35   This view is consistent with Peter Mullan's film *The Magdalene Sisters*, the documentary *Sex in a Cold Climate*, and the segment on *60 Minutes* (CBS television). This version of a Magdalen home is also supported by Finnegan, *Do Penance or Perish* (2001).

36   Patsy McGarry, 'Renogotiation of Deal with State "Not On" Says Nun'. *Irish Times*, 9 July 2004: 11.

37   Finnegan, *Do Penance or Perish*, 179, fn 39.

38   Luddy, Rev. of *Do Penance or Perish*, 557.

39   Finnegan, *Do Penance or Perish*, 228.

40   James M. Smith, 'The Politics of Sexual Knowledge', 221.

41   Finnegan, *Do Penance or Perish*, 193.

42   Gray and Ryan in Byrne and Leonard, eds. 'Dislocating "Woman"', 523.

43   Pelan, *Two Irelands*, 15.

44   Maria Luddy, *Women and Philanthropy in Nineteenth-Century Ireland* (Cambridge: Cambridge University Press, 1995), 102.

45   James M. Smith, 'The Politics of Sexual Knowledge, 208.

46   MacLaughlin, 'The New Vanishing Irish' in MacLaughlin, ed. *Location and Dislocation in Contemporary Irish Society*, 150.

47   Ní Dhuibhne, 'Kingston Ridge' in *Blood and Water* (Dublin: Attic Press, 1988: 43–58). Further references to 'Kingston' are in parentheses in the text.

48   Gray, 'Unmasking Irishness' in MacLaughlin, ed. *Location and Dislocation in Contemporary Irish Society*, 215.

49   MacLaughlin, 'The New Vanishing Irish' in MacLaughlin, ed. *Location and Dislocation in Contemporary Irish Society*, 153.

50   Gray, 'Unmasking Irishness' in MacLaughlin, ed. *Location and Dislocation in Contemporary Irish Society*, 225.

51   Quoted in *ibid.*, 229.

52   *ibid.*, 229–30.

53   Edward Said, 'The Mind of Winter'. *Harpers*, 269 (1984: 49–55), 49–50.

54   Quoted in Gray, 'Unmasking Irishness' in MacLaughlin, ed., *Location and Dislocation in Contemporary Irish Society*, 235.

55   Ní Dhuibhne's story, 'Bright Lights' in *Eating Women is Not Recommended* (Dublin: Attic Press, 1991) also develops this theme.

56   Gerry Smyth argues that "true exile can take place without physical displacement." Gerry Smyth, *The Novel and the Nation* (Chicago: Pluto Press, 1997), 43. Terry Eagleton also acknowledges an "internal or metaphorical émigré ... a misfit, idealist or outsider trapped within a claustrophobic social order." Terry Eagleton, 'Home and Away: Internal Émigrés in the Irish Novel' in *'Crazy John and the Bishop' and Other Essays on Irish Culture* (Notre Dame, IN: Notre Dame University Press, 1998: 212–247), 215.

57   Ní Dhuibhne, 'Blood and Water' in *Blood and Water* (Dublin: Attic Press, 1988: 109–121). Further references to 'Blood' are in parentheses in the text.

58   Christine St Peter, *Changing Ireland: Strategies in Contemporary Irish Women's Fiction* (New York: Palgrave St Martin's, 2000), 46.

59   These themes are also developed in Ní Dhuibhne's stories, 'The Makers' in *The Pale Gold of Alaska* (Belfast: Blackstaff Press, 2000: 134–149), and 'Gweedore Girl' in *Inland Ice and Other Stories* (Belfast: Blackstaff Press, 1997: 2–28), as well as her novel *Dancers Dancing* (Belfast: Blackstaff Press, 1999).

60   Ní Dhuibhne, 'See the Robbers Passing By' in *Eating Women is Not Recommended* (Dublin: Attic Press, 1991: 38–57). Further references to 'Robbers' are in parentheses in the text.

61   The concept of 'the new Irish' is controversial; MacLaughlin argues that the pattern of Irish immigration has not changed much since the nineteenth-century. MacLaughlin, 'The New Vanishing Irish' in MacLaughlin, ed., *Location and Dislocation in Contemporary Irish Society*, 135.

62   Jenny Beale, *Women in Ireland: Voices of Change* (Bloomington, IN: Indiana University Press, 1987).

63   Ní Dhuibhne holds a PhD in Irish Folklore from University College Dublin.

64   Christopher Cairney reports that "the italicized folktale text is translated from the original Irish of a manuscript in the folklore archive at University College Dublin." Christopher Thomas

Cairney, 'Éilís Ní Dhuibhne'. *British and Irish Short-Fiction Writers 1945–2000.* Cheryl Malcolm and David Malcolm, eds. (Farmington Hills MI: Thompson Gale Publishers, 2006: 263–269), 264.

65   Homi K. Bhabha, 'DissemiNation: Time, Narrative, and the Margins of the Modern Nation' in *Narration and Nation.* Homi K. Bhabha, ed. (London: Routledge, 1990: 291–322), 295.

66   Angela Bourke, 'The Virtual Reality of Irish Fairy Legend' in *Theorizing Ireland: Readers in Cultural Criticism.* Claire Connolly, ed. (New York: Plagrave Macmillan, 2003: 27–40), 31.

67   Angela Bourke, *The Burning of Bridget Cleary: A True Story* (New York: Penguin, 1999), 42.

68   Ní Dhuibhne, 'Summer Pudding' in *The Inland Ice and Other Stories* (Belfast: Blackstaff Press, 1997: 44–60). Further references to 'SP' are in parentheses in the text.

69   Caitriona Moloney and Helen Thompson, *Irish Women Writers Speak Out: Voices from the Field* (New York: Syracuse University Press, 2003: 101–115), 109.

70   Controversy surrounds this figure: Yeats saw him as Conochobar's dupe, but Eleanor Hull's translation constructs a more Machiavellian Fergus. Eleanor Hull, 'The Tragical Death of the Sons of Usnach'. *The Cuchullin Saga in Irish Literature: Being a Collection of Stories Relating to the Hero Cuchullin Translated from the Irish by Various Scholars: Compiled and Edited with Introduction and Notes by Eleanor Hull* (London: David Nutt in the Strand, 1898), 21–53.

Female Maturation in Éilís Ní Dhuibhne's
Cailíní Beaga Ghleann na mBláth[1]

SARAH O'CONNOR

Cailíní Beaga Ghleann na mBláth (The Little Girls of Ghleann na mBláth)[2] is Éilís Ní Dhuibhne's second novel in Irish published by Cois Life in 2003. Its subject matter – female maturation – is also the central concern of Ní Dhuibhne's English language novel, *The Dancers Dancing* (1999). But while the earlier novel deals with the passage from teens to womanhood, *Cailíní Beaga* describes an earlier stage in the maturation process, and the novel is structurally and thematically comparable to Elizabeth Bowen's similarly titled *The Little Girls*, published by Jonathan Cape in 1964. [3] This article explores how Ní Dhuibhne changed elements from Bowen's novel to investigate Irish identity, more particularly Irish female identity, decolonising childhood and, more specifically, the Irish female childhood.

The English boarding school tradition, as portrayed in Bowen's *The Little Girls*, has its equivalent in Ní Dhuibhne in the Irish sojourn to the Gaeltacht, which is a central concern in *Cailíní Beaga* and in *The Dancers Dancing*. Many Irish teenagers go to the Gaeltacht each summer, but this influential experience is more or less absent from literature.[4] The Gaeltacht is particularly suitable to the representation of the process of identity formation precisely because it is a site of translation itself. In essence, the Gaeltacht fosters an experience of independence – translation of the self; it facilitates and, perhaps in some cases, initiates an exploration of identity. Ní Dhuibhne, who attended the Gaeltacht herself, has said that, "you discovered you had the power to move from one environment to another, from one language to another, and survive".[5]

Máire, the protagonist of *Cailíní Beaga*, is very young – just nine years old – when she goes to the Gaeltacht. In the course of the novel she learns to speak in many different registers, to her mother, to her peers, in English, and in Irish. These accumulating registers represent to Ní Dhuibhne the complexity of the language girls need to learn as they grow up:

> Girls have to navigate many discourses and juggle a lot to find their identity and develop ... maybe ... women tend to have ... better ways of talking which actually ... transcend language ... Using two languages, negotiating two languages, is a symbol of what they will have to do which is negotiate dozens of modes of expression and discourses as they go through their lives.[6]

Readers, writers, and characters negotiate discourses, languages and registers together in *Cailíní Beaga Ghleann na mBláth*. The uniquely Irish rite of passage that Ní Dhuibhne explores is characterised not only by bilingualism, but by multilingualism. Ní Dhuibhne speaks of the languages she learned in the Gaeltacht as a young girl:

> I notice I have not said anything about the point of it all, Irish. But one learned quite a lot. In our case, a taste of the marginalised dialect, Donegal Irish. Fosta and bomaite and falsa and goitse. And we heard somehow, in the shop and in the air, burn and wean and scon and brae, since this was the Ulster Scots as well as the Ulster Gaelic region. Also Derry English, Belfast English and Monaghan English ... But the most significant language one learned was the one without words, the language of the river and the grass.[7]

Elizabeth Bowen's opening in *The Little Girls* uses a tripartite structure containing a section that takes place in the past, placed between two sections that take place in the present – a type of structural nostalgia to subject both her characters and her readers to the dynamics of nostalgia. Though this structure suggests that readers may simply engage in a nostalgic return along with the characters, Bowen uses it instead to force both her characters and her readers into a conscious examination of both the pleasures and the dangers of summoning up one's childhood fifty years later. Similarly, Ní

Dhuibhne's narrative employs temporal shifts to emphasise the personal excavation taking place. Maintaining a delicate balance between past and present, Ní Dhuibhne allows each to illuminate and inform the other. The novel is a combination of retrospective and present first-person narration told by Máire (as a grown woman).

In Bowen's novel, the little girls in question – Diana Piggott, Clare Burkin-Jones and Sheila Beaker – are day-boarders at St. Agatha's in 'Southstone', on the south-east coast of England before the outbreak of the First World War. Upon learning about Roman remains, the girls bury, within the school grounds, a coffer containing, among other objects, one secret keepsake from each of them. Diana 'Dicey', Clare 'Mumbo', and Sheila 'Sheiki', are separated by the war and meet approximately fifty years later as adults. This reunion is orchestrated by Diana, who now calls herself Dinah, and who is currently engaged in collecting other mementoes in a cave in her garden, an activity that jogs her memory of the treasure buried in her childhood and leads her to contact her former classmates. The adult women unearth the buried coffer, only to find it empty. Though all three are disturbed by this discovery, it sparks a nervous crisis in Dinah who suffers a kind of mental breakdown towards the end of the novel. This breakdown results from an attempt to dig up the past, literally and metaphorically. This personal excavation has both dangerous and healing properties. In *Cailíní Beaga*, by contrast, 'digging up the past', though traumatic, possesses only healing properties. Repression of painful memories manifests itself in a threatening and dangerous silence. This silence is Ní Dhuibhne's coffer, and she weaves issues relating to Irish cultural memory into her narrative giving it local significance and strong cultural currency.

As *Cailíní Beaga* opens, the protagonist, Máire, is a successful journalist with a satisfying career, married to gentle, quiet Muiris, an architect. They have two teenage children, Emma and Dara. Máire is sona, that is she has achieved 'happiness' as defined by the author in a prefatory note. However, this sonas soon turns to upheaval.

Seventeen/eighteen-year-old Emma has grown increasingly despondent, introverted and uncommunicative: she suffers from a disease with no name, and which causes Máire to meditate upon a defining moment in her own life; a sojourn in an Irish college at the age of nine. This Irish college, like her life, had promised perfect happiness, but brought something rather different. There follows a deep excavation of Máire's consciousness, as memories that have been previously suppressed, or lain dormant, are disturbed and awakened. By recovering and repossessing these buried secrets of her own personal history, Máire begins to comprehend her present.

Much has been written about silence as a response to traumatic events.[8] Examining the trope of muteness from an Irish perspective, Angela Bourke observes that:

We have urgent need of stories in Ireland at the moment, as our society comes to terms with painful memories. All at once, it seems, we are trying to cope with the famine of the mid-nineteenth century, when a million people died of fever or starvation and another million emigrated; with twenty five years of violence in Northern Ireland, followed by the sudden possibility of peace, and then more violence; and with the heartbreaking series of revelations about betrayal of trust, about domestic violence, and about cruelties secretly inflicted on women and children. The old narratives will no longer serve, and it is not just politicians and journalists who are struggling to make sense of it all. Religion used to offer answers and explanations, but more and more it is artists who confront the broken certainties that lie all around.[9]

Emma, the protagonist's daughter, is "reoite nó ina codladh" [frozen or asleep] like Sleeping Beauty of the fairytale. Even her bedroom is "an-bhanúil, banphrionsúil fiú amháin" [very feminine, princess-like even], the four poster bed is "díreach cosúil le leaba a bheadh ag banphrionsa i scéal" [exactly like a princess's bed in a story] (CB 17). Emma is like a two-dimensional character in a story, but the reader, of course, is aware that Emma *is* only a character in a story, *Cailíní Beaga*, and so Ní Dhuibhne is playing with the boundaries of the novel itself.

Emma corresponds to what Sara R. Horowitz calls the "figure of muteness" in a study that addresses the trope of muteness and memory in both literary and visual texts about the Holocaust.[10] Horowitz details how writers of Holocaust literature must find a way to give voice to that which is essentially beyond speech; to use language *against* itself. Literary critics can learn much by listening to this silence; muteness itself is a form of communication. By casting Emma in this role, Ní Dhuibhne alerts the reader to the difficulty of saying anything meaningful about a painful Irish past. Silence also represents the elemental nature of that particular traumatic event itself. The painful events to which Angela Bourke alludes to above, are represented by historical narrative, but have remained largely unspoken by the individual subject. On a macrocosmic level, Emma represents the damaged and the wronged of Ireland. Their silence and suffering are hers. *Cailíní Beaga Ghleann na mBláth* is Ní Dhuibhne's attempt to bridge the gap between a traumatic past and a meaningful present.

Máire decides to take a few weeks off work so she can care for her daughter since, in Máire's mind, forgetting puts Emma "i mbaol" [in danger] (52).[11] It is only when Máire remembers and narrates one particularly traumatic event in her past – the night when she ignored her seriously injured friend, Juliet, on the beach, an act that subsequently led to Juliet's drowning – that Máire's daughter is healed. However, Ní Dhuibhne tells this event three times only towards the end of the novel and each telling is slightly different, but incorporates elements from the other versions. Ní Dhuibhne uses many of the same words in order to highlight the re-telling of this incident. However, subtle differences between the versions show the reader that the narrator is trying to remember the event herself and, so, the narrative operates as a form of memory in itself.

Recovery of personal history is bound up with reclamation of social history. In Chapter 13 of the novel, Máire returns to Gleann na mBláth as an adult. The Big House in which the Irish college was located has been converted into a hotel: "Tá sé sin ar fad imithe" [It's all gone], "Ach níl sé imithe ar fad" [but not gone totally] (173). By retracing her pre-adolescent steps, Máire recovers her memory from annihilation *and* recovers an Irish past in which this Big House (reclaimed for a new Irish master-narrative) was used as an Irish college. Máire notices that the history pertaining to the house and its former occupants is, at best, gapped. There is no record of the Irish College. Part of Máire's history, her identity as a person, has been erased. Just as she has been erased from a certain area of social history, she erases certain aspects of her personal memory.

While Bowen's structure does not portray the transformative process between childhood and adulthood, this is central to the investigation of identity in Ní Dhuibhne's novel. Section Two of Bowen's narrative tells of a summer in the lives of the girls as children, however, it is presented as an alternative present rather than part of an historical sequence. *Cailíní Beaga,* balanced between past and present, depicts the maturation process, the *becoming individual* of Máire as an historical progression. Ní Dhuibhne infuses this *becoming* with Irish folktales about swimming to give it relevance in an Irish sphere but, more importantly, in a female one, something that I will discuss in more detail later.

The author establishes a dichotomy between the Irish College, Gleann na mBláth, and the outside world. Life outside Irish college is defined as "saol na ndaoine fásta" [the life of grown ups] (121). On the 'outside', school is compulsory. Corporal punishment is practised on those who disobey the rules, rules which silence the children:

> Níl cead cainte. Bígí i bhur dtost. Empty vessels make most noise. Téann tú ar scoil lán-Ghaelach cun foghlaim conas Gaeilge a labhairt, ach an phríomhaidhm atá ag an scoil ná aon claonadh chun cainte atá ionat a mharú. (77)
> [Talking is forbidden. Be quiet. Empty vessels make most noise. You go to an all-Irish school to learn to speak Irish, but the chief aim of the school is to kill off any inclination towards talking.]

Gleann an mBláth, by contrast, is full of all kinds of talk. Ní Dhuibhne lists all the ways of speaking in order to emphasise the differences and to underline the freedom that the girls have when they are away from the oppressive institutions of home and school:

Cogar cogar cogar. Tá rún á n-insint, scéalta á dtairscint, nuacht ag tarlú. Cogar cogar scige scige scige. Tá Gleann na mBláth lán de sciotaráil. De shiosarnach, de chogar, de chúlchaint, de bhéadán, de ráflaí. Lán suas go béal le caint, caint, caint, agus síorchaint. (79) [Whisper, whisper, whisper. Secrets are being told, stories offered, news is happening. Whisper, whisper, giggle, giggle, giggle. Gleann na mBláth is full of giggling, of hissing, whispering, backbiting, gossip, rumours. Full up with talk, talk, talk, and endless talk.]

In Gleann na mBláth, "Tá a lán tréimhsí saora acu ... Caithfidh tú do rud féin a dhéanamh sna bearnaí" [they have a lot of free time – you have to do your own thing in the breaks] (76). In this institution "Níl siad dáiríre faoi riail ar bith" [They aren't serious about any rules] (77), however, Máire does not feel part of this communication. She is "lasmuigh" [outside] what she perceives as the 'magic circle' (80). She must navigate her way between different discourses and different registers to find her own voice. Her isolation is further underscored by her inability to swim. By contrast, the other girls are "snámhaithe den scoth" [brilliant swimmers] signalling their ability to negotiate various registers and discourses with ease.

A special significance attaches to swimming in Irish folk legend. Nuala Ní Dhomhnaill, a contemporary of Ní Dhuibhne's, is another writer who negotiates the space between languages. Her poem, 'Parthenogenesis', in *Féar Suaithinseach* (1984), uses the well-known storyteller, Peig Sayers' 'Scéal an Bhodaigh', to articulate this same area of experience. Born in 1873 in Dúnchaoin (Dunquin) County Kerry, Peig Sayers spent much of her early life working as a domestic servant. At nineteen she married Pádraig Ó Gaoithín, and went to live with his family on the Great Blasket Island. A renowned storyteller, Peig had a marvelous command of spoken Irish, which was recognised by many distinguished international scholars and students of modern Irish who visited her on the Great Blasket. Peig is most famous for her autobiography *Peig: A Scéal Féin*, which details life on the island (1892–1942) from a woman's perspective.

'Parthenogenesis' is both a biological term meaning reproduction without fertilisation, when the female cell splits down the middle, and a theological term for the doctrine of Mary's virgin birth. The word derives from the Greek *parthenos* meaning 'virgin', and 'genesis' meaning creation. Ní Dhomhnaill draws a parallel between the woman's experience in the Irish legend and the Virgin Mary's experience at the Annunciation. One woman encounters a shadow, while the other is visited by an angel; both are impregnated and both give birth to male children. Linda Revie points out a significant difference between the poem and the Biblical story: "[U]nlike the story related by the Apostle Luke which tells of the resignation with which Mary accepted her fate … the subject of the poem is much more resilient and refuses the catatonic state that seems to be her destiny at the bottom of the sea".[12] Rather than being overwhelmed or drowning in this new element, the subject chooses to survive, to swim. Her return to land demonstrates her ability to negotiate unfamiliar, unstable and sometimes threatening terrain, but her pregnancy marks the transforming consequences this entails.

Peig Sayer's tale, 'Scéal an Bhodaigh', tells of a rich man who wants his only son to marry a girl of good social standing. The son soon finds such a girl and marries her. According to the patrilocal system of marriage, the woman returns to his homeplace to live. The new bride makes a habit of swimming every morning. The couple is childless for fourteen years, which displeases the rich man because he has no heir to whom he may leave his fortune. One autumn evening, his wife is swimming as normal when she imagines she sees the shadow of a man swimming alongside her. She becomes frightened and returns to shore. She dresses and goes home, saying nothing of the day's events to anyone. Nine months later she gives birth to a baby boy.

Though bare, this outline shows a young woman without status, power, or money before marriage. In short, a woman with no independence to whom marriage brings a whole new set of responsibilities, which often conflict with each other. Woman ensured the foundation and continuity of the basic family unit and was guardian of family prosperity. She controlled vital agricultural and economic activities, such as child-rearing, milking, butter-making and tending the young livestock and fowl; milk, butter and eggs being important sources of cash in the domestic economy.[13] Socially, however, she may have been regarded as an interloper, thus remaining an outsider. Lack of children could also cause tension in a household.[14] Peig Sayers's tale tells the story of a young woman as she changes from a young dependent, sexually inexperienced girl to a responsible, sexually mature woman of a household. The elemental opposition between land and water represents the huge change experienced by the young woman after marriage. Her childless state causes anxiety, which is registered in her fear of the scáth fir [man's shadow] that swims beside her. Her lust and desire are also contained within this shadowy image. It is only after swimming that she becomes pregnant and swimming becomes a metaphor for her rite of passage into womanhood, her realisation of her own sexuality. Ní Dhuibhne, a folklorist, is no doubt aware of this tale and of the importance of swimming as a powerful symbol.

The swimming pool in Ní Dhuibhne's Ghleann na mBláth is nothing but a concrete hole in the ground (59). No effort has been made to decorate or beautify it. But to Máire it is a precious jewel, shining like a diamond (89). It is noteworthy that the pool is situated on a grassy platform between the house and the sea, between the area occupied by representatives of authority – the teachers – and an area of wide open, unsupervised and, ultimately, dangerous space. The water-filled concrete hole represents another community in which Máire can have ownership of herself. The pool is relatively free from adult control (the lifeguard reads the paper rather than keeping an eye on the young swimmers), and a diverse set of rules apply to it. Her second-hand swimsuit is "ait" [strange], "áiféiseach" [ridiculous], "mí-oiriúnach" [unsuitable], and "seanaimseartha" [old-fashioned] (60). Máire is a little girl in a grown-up woman's swimsuit from another era, a swimsuit which conjures up images of Marilyn Monroe:

> [T]ugtar faoi deara í. Scrúdaíonn siad go géar í. Tuigeann siad go bhfuil rud éigin ait ag baint leis an gculaith, cé nach dtuigeann siad go beacht an bhrí atá léi mar chulaith. (60)

[She is noticed. They study her carefully. They understand that there is something strange about the swim-suit, even if they don't understand exactly what it says about her.]

In the pool, supported by the water, she is stronger and more adventurous than on land. Juliet, (her friend from home) is annoying and constantly invades her personal space. Máire considers what Úna (the girl with whom she shares a chalet) would do: pretend that Juliet does not exist. Her borrowed strategy works. As she learns to swim, so she is slowly learning how to survive awkward social situations. Plainly, Juliet has no knowledge of rules or limits, as she irritates everyone else in the pool until their only recourse is to leave. Máire is changing:

> ó a bheith ina duine nach bhfuil snámh aici, ina duine a bhfuil snámh aici. Cheana féin tá an t-athrú sin tarlaithe agus cheana féin ní féidir dul ar ais go dtí an staid eile … 'Táim ag foghlaim conas snámh' ní fhéadfaidís tábhacht an ráitis sin a shamhlú. (72)

> [F]rom being a person who cannot swim to a person who can swim. Already the change is apparent and there is no going back to the previous state … 'I am learning how to swim' they could not imagine the importance of that statement.]

Ní Dhuibhne desribes Máire's unusual swimsuit as "greamaithe di mar a bheadh craiceann" [stuck to her like skin] (73). Eventually, she becomes so comfortable in this new element that her swimsuit fits like a second skin. Nevertheless, while walking on the beach with Yvonne and Úna, when they spontaneously decide to go swimming, Máire refuses to enter the water because she has no swimsuit. Her friends strip off and run in, naked. Self-conscious about her body, Máire cannot understand the girls' audacity and confidence. Her swimsuit is her second skin, giving her security when tackling a new social *milieu*, but the sea represents an untamed, uncontrollable force. When Máire has her swimsuit and is in her swimming pool, she retains a measure of control over her environment. The sea is unbounded; the girls are naked in its vastness, but the pool has a rail around it and a partially attentive lifeguard.

Máire receives ill-fitting clothes from her friend Juliet, and declares that she is a 'sight' in them, while her mother announces that she looks like "little orphan Annie" (33). Ní

Dhuibhne alerts the reader to the difficulty Máire experiences in trying to 'fit in' to this pre-pubescent society in Gleann na mBláth. She feels strange, ridiculous, unsuitable and old-fashioned. A suit-case under her bunk is filled with dresses that are all unsuitable according to the narrator because no student at Irish College wears dresses. Máire views her wardrobe as a mark of difference. Her opinions and dress habits expose the subtle nuances attached to growing up, to fitting in. Consequently, the self-conscious Máire lives in her single pair of shorts and two t-shirts, which she washes out in the basin of her chalet from time to time. Looking around Concepta's chalet, Máire notes that Concepta's clothes, indeed everyone's clothes, are nicer than her own.

The Big House genre is an important strand in this narrative. Ní Dhuibhne constructs *Cailíní Beaga* around the history of the Trabolgan Estate in east Cork.[15] Within Big House fiction there are normally two narrative strands: fictional and historical. Oliver MacDonagh, writing about the Big House novel, describes it as coming "as close, perhaps, as it is possible to get in literature to that of the historian".[16] The Big House element is important to the overall narrative because it calls attention to the historicity of the fictional Gleann na mBláth, the historical Trabolgan Estate (and the period when Máire attended Irish college there, in particular), recovering this particular episode of the Irish past, thereby preventing its erasure from memory. As Kreilkamp states, "the endurance of the genre in contemporary fiction suggests the persistence of Irish historical memory".[17]

The Big House novel is a product of Anglo-Irish fiction and, as such, it is descended from a history of conquest and occupation. Such fiction represents an important tradition in Irish writing. Normally set on remote country estates, these novels dramatise the tensions between several social groups: the landed Anglo-Irish Protestant gentry, an increasing Catholic middle-class, and the native, landless, Catholic tenants. Ní Dhuibhne introduces the Big House to the reader as decayed, un-ruled and untidy. Decomposition signals that the once-alien architecture, symbolic of colonial oppression and authoritarian rule, no longer exercises such power. Kreilkamp observes that the physical distance between the Big House and the local village, coupled with the long driveway leading up to the Big House, emphasises the "social isolation" and "defensive self-sufficiency", while also clearly indicating the "spatial barriers" erected by the Anglo-Irish against Catholic Ireland.[18] Ní Dhuibhne uses the same 'spatial barriers' to evoke an un-policed, uncensored space where self-sufficiency is not viewed with suspicion. This edifice now houses and fosters an independence of mind and spirit.

The girls' first glimpse of the house in Gleann na mBláth is the rust-eaten iron gate. Máire notes that the driveway is "cúng" [narrow], and "míshlachtmhar" [untidy], "fásra ag gobadh amach trí na clocha ina lár" [weeds poking out through the stones in the centre]. Máire was expecting "ord agus eagar" [order and organisation]. Máire and her mother have voraciously consumed colonial narratives of order and aristocracy all their lives, robbing them of any individual response to the reality that confronts them. Ní Dhuibhne gives the protagonist the space, time and strength to form her own opinions. Gleann na mBláth offers the girls room to grow and express themselves. Such individuality is registered on arrival, when Juliet and Máire have entirely different opinions of Gleann na mBláth. Máire thinks it is "lovely" (CB 39), whereas Juliet proclaims that it is nothing more than a "dump":

> Ach ar ndóigh ní fheiceann aon bheirt an rud ceannann céanna. Braitheann do bhreithiúnas ar do dhearcadh féin. (39)
>
> [But of course no two people see things the same way. Your judgement depends on your own view.]

Ní Dhuibhne impresses upon the reader that a change in perception is about to take place. As an individual in her own right, Máire's 'reading' or response is valid, but Ní Dhuibhne creates the impression of a society quick to judge those who are self-sufficient in any way. However, the above quotation suggests that this judgement also comes from within, since Máire struggles to gain self-determination, not only within the community of girls, but also within herself. The historical, angst-ridden social background of Anglo-Irish relations provides the perfect setting for the class tensions that run through *Cailíní Beaga*. The representatives of colonial power have been supplanted by an Irish college, an institution devoted to the cultivation of Irish language and culture.

Máire, though inexperienced with regard to class difference at the beginning of the novel, becomes acutely conscious of her position in society by the end of her sojourn in Gleann na mBláth. It is in the Gaeltacht that she learns the phrase 'go maith as' [well-off] when invited to Concepta's chalet. Máire notices immediately that the area where this chalet is situated is different:

> Tá atmaisféar speisialta san áit, áfach. Tá rud éigin rúnda neamhghnách, ag baint leis. Tá sé níos deise mar áit chónaithe ná an tsraith chúng mar a bhfuil an chalet atá ag Máire agus na cailíní eile. Tá rud éigin galánta ag baint leis an bhfaiche agus an spás go léir. (95)
>
> [There is a special atmosphere in the place, however. There is something secret, unusual about it. It is a nicer place to live than the narrow row of chalets where Máire and the other girls live. There is something beautiful about the lawn and the whole space.]

Social stratification occurs equally within this parent-free zone as without. Instead of four bunk-beds, this chalet has two single beds. Such luxury, Concepta announces, is more expensive and only available to those who are 'go maith as'. Concepta manages a bank of sorts in Irish college. Every day at five o'clock the bank is opened for 'business'. Concepta gives orders and the other girls obey. The formality and rules that are attached to this *dráma beag* [little drama] (97), place Concepta in a position of power. The girls call her 'mam' and conform to the conventions laid down by Concepta. The bank deals in currency of a different sort, a currency entirely appropriate to this parent-free zone: the safe contains sweets of all kinds, chocolate and crisps. Social standing dictates the quality and quantity of the sweets one receives. Juliet is disgusted when Babaró's social profile within this community is raised above her own. Furious with her demotion, Juliet breaks the delicate rules and robs the bank, resulting in

Concepta ordering all the girls to ostracise Juliet. This episode relates the fickle and capricious nature of the society in which Máire lives,[19] whereby a delicate balance exists between the various societal forces operating within this social order, and in which upsetting the equilibrium carries serious consequences. *Cailíní Beaga* follows Máire as she picks her way through this hazardous civic terrain. The final insult comes when Juliet reveals the identity of Máire's true benefactor – her own father, Mr. Smith. After the disclosure, Máire is ashamed and feels guilty because she is poor:

> Ní deir Máire faic. Tá náire uirthi fós. Náire seachas fearg. Ise atá ciontach toisc go bhfuil sí bocht, ag brath ar charthanacht athair Juliet. (126)

> [Máire says nothing. She is still embarrassed. Embarrassment, not anger. She is guilty, guilty because she is poor, depending on the charity of Juliet's father.]

Máire is exposed as underprivileged in this world where opportunity is valuable and privilege reigns.

Ní Dhuibhne recovers Irish childhood from the clutches of a destructive and debilitating romanticism prevalent in Irish revival literature. Declan Kiberd discusses this romanticism in relation to William Butler Yeats, by suggesting that the "process of childhood – like Ireland itself – had to be reinvented as a zone of innocence, unsullied and intense, from which would emerge the free Irish protagonist".[20] Clearly, Ní Dhuibhne's 'free Irish protagonist' emerges from quite a different process, one full of experience and guilt, marred, but equally as intense. While texts of the Irish revival, such as Yeats's *Autobiographies*, nourished Irish national feeling, they were, as Kiberd points out, "British in origin, and open to the charge of founding themselves on the imperial strategy of infantilizing the native culture". Childhood in the landscape of early Yeatsian desire was:

> surrounded by a *cordon sanitaire* of nostalgia and escape. It is a world neither of change nor of growth: intense, unpurged feelings for childhood are not submitted to the test of adult life or, for that matter, of childhood itself. What the child actually *is* or *wants*

means nothing in such literature, for this is the landscape of the adult heart's desire.[21]

Ní Dhuibhne's fictional children populate the same geographical space, however, they travel through it as a fearann breac – a speckled, brindled, dappled landscape, where the road signs, like the voices in their heads, speak two languages. They must engage creatively and responsively with their surroundings in order to survive and grow. Nostalgia has no place in Ní Dhuibhne's narrative. Hers is a world characterised by transformation and development. Progress and maturity are registered in the telling and re-telling of the central episode in Gleann na mBláth. Moreover, the same repetitive process of telling and re-telling also occurs *between* the novels, *The Dancers Dancing* and *Cailíní Beaga Ghleann na mBláth*.

NOTES

1   All translations are by the author.

2   Ní Dhuibhne, *Cailíní Beaga Ghleann na mBláth* (Baile Átha Cliath: Cois Life, 2003). Further references to *CB* are in parentheses in the text.

3   Ní Dhuibhne revealed her use of Elizabeth Bowen's *The Little Girls* in e-mail correspondence with Angela Bourke. I owe this idea to a subsequent conversation with Angela Bourke.

4   Nicola Warwick, 'Interview with Éilís Ní Dhuibhne'. *One Woman's Writing Retreat* http://www.prairieden.com/front_porch/visiting_authors/dhuibhne.html (2001).

5   Ní Dhuibhne, 'Learning Language without Words'. *Irish Times*, 5 August 2005: 13.

6   Personal communication with author, 15 August 2005.

7   Ní Dhuibhne, 'Learning Language without Words', 13.

8   Sara R. Horowitz, *Voicing the Void: Muteness and Memory in Holocaust Fiction* (New York: State University Press of New York, 1997), 38.

9   Angela Bourke, 'Language, Stories, Healing' in *Gender and Sexuality in Modern Ireland*, Anthony Bradley and Maryann Gialanella Valiulis, eds. (University of Massachusetts Press/Amherst. Published in co-operation with the American Conference for Irish Studies), 1997), 305.

10   Horowitz, *Voicing the Void*, 33–45.

11   It seems that Máire's heart believes some magic is at work as long as she torments herself with worry. This worry protects Emma from harm. If Máire fails in her duty, if Máire forgets Emma for half an hour, Emma will be in danger (*CB* 52).

12   Linda Revie, 'Nuala Ní Dhomhnaill's "Parthenogenesis": A Bisexual Exchange' in *Poetry in Contemporary Irish Literature*. Micheal Kenneally, ed. (Gerrards Cross: Colin Smythe, 1995), 349.

13   Richard Jenkins, 'Witches and Fairies: Supernatural Aggression and Deviance among the Irish Peasantry'. *Ulster Folklife*, 23 (1977): 50–51.

14   See Conrad M. Arensberg and Solon T. Kimball, 'Family Transition at Marriage' in *Family and Community in Ireland*, (Ennis: Clasp Press, [1968] 2001, 32.

15   Personal communication with author, 15 Aug. 2005.

16   Oliver MacDonagh, cited by Vera Kreilkamp, 'Fiction and History' in *The Anglo-Irish Novel and the Big House* (New York: Syracuse University Press, 1998), 3.

17   *ibid.*, 4.

18   *ibid.*, 9.

19   *Cailíní Beaga Ghleann na mBláth* has similarities with William Golding's *Lord of the Flies*. The societal web is destroyed when a community of young boys, stranded on an island, revert to savagery.

20   Declan Kiberd, 'Childhood and Ireland' in *Inventing Ireland* (London: Vintage, 1995): 101–2.

21   *ibid.*, 103.

'That Embarrassing Phenomenon: The Real Thing': Identity and Modernity in Éilís Ní Dhuibhne's Children's Fiction

MARY SHINE THOMPSON

Éilís Ní Dhuibhne[1] admits to a tendency to be "ambivalent, to prevaricate, to negotiate at least two main cultures and several subcultures".[2] That she writes for children as well as adults in both English and Irish – the latter being a language that limits her markets – supports her own analysis of her situation. One of the reasons she adduces for this refusal to adopt absolute positions is her formative linguistic experience: she was "a bilingual child in Dublin".[3] When she elaborates on her particular family circumstances, what becomes apparent is that neither of the 'two cultures' – the official version of Irish-language culture encompassed by the state ideology and its elite, and the quotidian English – captures the experience of her father, and, by extension, of countless other silent Irish citizens:

> My connections with the Irish language are intricate and deep-rooted, and they are intensely personal. My father was a native speaker who was born and brought up in a Gaeltacht, Glenvar on Lough Swilly in County Donegal. He spoke a dialect of Irish which was rare then and is now almost extinct. My mother, however, did not speak Irish. My father was usually out of the house, pursuing the demanding life of a tradesman in the Ireland of the 1950s and 1960s … occasionally he had to travel away from home to other towns to find work, in the depressed Ireland of my youth, so English was the language of my home and of course the language of my surroundings – Ranelagh, in Dublin. Nevertheless I heard Irish, my father's strange esoteric Irish, from birth, and spoke to him in his own language. [4]

Never, she continues:

did I encounter a teacher or anyone else who spoke Donegal Irish like my father ... I understood from an early age that my father was a problematical entity in the world of school, which was part of the Irish-language community in Dublin. That was not only because he spoke Donegal Irish, the marginalised dialect, [and] came from Donegal, a place nobody from Dublin ever visited, it seemed ... But what was even worse was that my father was a real Gaeltacht man, a carpenter who spoke Irish because that is what his mother spoke, not because he was a member of Conradh na Gaeilge a civil servant or an *aficionado* of the annual Oireachtas dinner-dance ... I sensed that nobody knew what to make of my father, that embarrassing phenomenon: the real thing.[5]

'The real thing', in this instance, is no Yeatsian fisherman, no Playboy of the Western World who seduces with the power of his banter – in short, no cultural icon. 'The real thing' does not serve the nationalist ideology and, particularly, the Gaelic League ideology of Irish Ireland and social mobility. In this instance, he is not a civil servant, but a more lowly tradesman. He does not stand for linguistic law and order: rather his idiom makes him a linguistic rapparee at odds with the cultural jucidiciary for whom *An Caighdeán Oifigiúil* – the set of linguistic norms that include standard orthography and idiom that was published in 1958 after decades of controversy – becomes a measure of cultural conformity. He may be a Gaeltacht man, but his is not the Gaeltacht of Kerry or Connemara made famous by Peig Sayers, George Thompson and Padraig Pearse. His is the Gaeltacht that was once synonymous with shame and inferiority. In 1987, locals in the Strabane area told Colm Tóibín there was "a sort of stigma" attached to it: "There were men who spoke Irish, from an Irish-speaking area, living in Derry and Tyrone; they didn't want anyone to know they spoke Irish, as it would signify that they came in from Donegal to be hired".[6] Donegal writers, and Patrick MacGill in particular, with his focus on abject poverty, child labour and prostitution, were, if anything, an embarrassment to the respectability of the mid-twentieth-century Irish state. Ní Dhuibhne highlights how powerful official constructions of Irishness are, and how they serve to render invisible individuals, groups and regions. Yet these very groups and regions often confronted the challenge of negotiating modernity at social, political and psychological levels while retaining outward signs of tradition. This paper focuses on how Ní Dhuibhne explores modernity especially in the content and form of her fiction trilogy for young adults, *The Hiring Fare* (1993), *Blaeberry Sunday* (1994) and *Penny-farthing Sally* (1996).[7]

A Grand Narrative of Modernity

Underlying much of her fiction for young people is a critique of Irish identity in flux. If her children's fiction is seen as one grand narrative of modernising Ireland, then she offers two possible and conflicting conclusions, one conciliatory and one satirical. The first may be found in her crossover novel about teenagers on an Irish-language programme in a Donegal Gaeltacht, *The Dancers Dancing* (1999), a book that was originally intended for adults, but which garnered a wide young adult readership. In it, Ní Dhuibhne attempts to posit an integrated Irish identity. Of this book, she writes: "Yeats's image of the dancer and the dance is used to convey the ultimate wholeness of the Irish linguistic and cultural experience, and .... instead of viewing Irish and English as separate sides of Irish identity, the heroine, Orla, learns to view them as complementary and enriching".[8] The novel ends with Orla "learning to conform to the path of communal values", as one critic has put it.[9] The creation of a character who can successfully integrate the elements that are mutually exclusive, as Ní Dhuibhne's father's metonymic experience illustrates, may be seen as a case of wish-fulfillment, of literature succeeding in providing plot resolution where life has failed.

An alternative ending to Ní Dhuibhne's grand narrative of Irish identity may be found in *Hurlamaboc* (2006), an Irish language novella for young adults, whose title means chaos or commotion. A mimetic triumph that employs the techniques of multiple perspectives, psychic displacements, and disjunction, it conducts a cool appraisal of contemporary suburban Ireland in a contemporary, sassy idiom. Ní Dhuibhne's young characters are more confident, more mobile, more affluent than those found in Mark O'Sullivan and Siobhan Parkinson's social realist novels with distinctively Irish settings. That *Hurlamaboc*'s story is told in the Irish language underwrites a further success – the coming-of-age of Irish, the fact that it has broken free of its iconic status and can now construct and interrogate postmodern, fluid Ireland with ease. However, the novella's greatest strength derives from its satiric, uncompromising gaze on an Ireland in which the best lack all conviction and the worst are full of passionate intensity. Teens and their parents are equally self-absorbed, and complacency, crass ambition and materialism consume adults.

Ní Dhuibhne's scepticism about affluent Ireland's human values is further underlined in *The Sparkling Rain* (2003). This tale for younger readers contains a storyline that owes much to the genre of fantasy and draws on some of the stock characters of children's fiction, such as greedy, cruel relatives. However, it has a disturbingly Gothic edge, and the Gothic has long been a vehicle for the exploration of complex psychological states, not least in the Anglo-Irish literary context. The book's psychological realism lies in the way it conveys the plight of children at the mercy of unstable and irresponsible, though affluent parents. Was it to this vacuous, even pathological, prosperity that the Gaelic speakers of isolated Donegal aspired? These two works of fiction respond in their conflicting ways to this rhetorical question. It is ironic that Ní Dhuibhne saves her edgiest realism for her children's books while her adult novel (*The Dancers Dancing*) toys with the possibility of reconciling the irreconcilable.

If *Hurlamaboc, The Sparkling Rain* and *The Dancers Dancing* form the *dénouement* of the plot of an extended narrative of engagement with Irish identity, Ní Dhuibhne's trilogy of novels on the experiences of Sally Gallagher from Glenbra in Donegal in the 1890s, *The Hiring Fare, Blaeberry Sunday* and *Penny-farthing Sally,* constitutes its exposition, rising action, and climax. The novels were published in 1993, 1994 and 1996, respectively, in the period of Mary Robinson's presidency

(1990–97), a period of rapid change and economic growth in Ireland. The kinds of events and conditions that led to the present state of Ireland – a state (in two senses of the word) from which her father is forever estranged – form the subject matter of this series of novels for early teens. The trilogy fictionally reshapes and temporally relocates her father's experience: the extended, realist narrative concerns the odyssey of a young girl (rather than of a young man) brought from a secure Donegal Gaeltacht childhood to the brink of urban adulthood, a point at which she contemplates possible futures, all of which see her as part of a rapidly modernising, *bourgeois* Ireland. In the process, it explores "how various notions of Irish identity came to be sanctioned, legitimized, challenged and to gain ascendancy in a nation that had not yet found full political expression".[10] However, the commitment to the principles of realist fiction is not unbridled: Ní Dhuibhne's restrained deployment of its devices and strategies indicates scepticism about the kind of selfhoods it implies.

The Trilogy

The first book of the trilogy, *The Hiring Fare*, set against the backdrop of Parnell's Ireland, sees Sally and her sister leave home to enter into seasonal service with Tyrone farmers. The second, *Blaeberry Sunday*, has Sally return home for a summer period, during which she witnesses death and eviction, falls in love and befriends a 'Visitor' who wants to learn the Irish language. The final tale, *Penny-farthing Sally*, has Sally ensconced in middle-class Dublin and becoming acculturated to its norms. It is a place of rapid change and modernisation, with romance in the foreground and revolution, both cultural and military, on the horizon. In this final tale, we also learn the fate of Sally's sister, who entered into domestic service at the same time as her sister, but who lacks Sally's flexibility. Social stratification is everywhere apparent.

Language and Modernity

The Hiring Fare and *Blaeberry Sunday*, like Brian Friel's play *Translations*, also set in Donegal, are predicated on the conceit that the main protagonists speak primarily in Irish. By the third novel, Irish has become the cultural capital that could ensure security and middle-class respectability. The language was already endangered in the 1890s, when the trilogy is set: the 1891 census reveals that, of a population of over four million, only 38,192 were monolingual Irish speakers. Fluent Irish, ironically, would become the marker of the educated, the factor that would distinguish the emerging body of civil servants and teachers who would become the visible presence of the new Irish state. Sean O'Casey's comment that for certain "fretful popinjays lisping Irish wrongly" (doubtless he had Douglas Hyde, the founder of the Gaelic League, in mind), "the fight for Irish" was associated with "the fight for collars and ties".[11] His remark is applicable to Ní Dhuibhne's character Thomas in the final book of the trilogy, *Penny-farthing Sally*. Thomas courts impoverished Sally, but he is acutely aware that his friends marry the daughters of judges or of their bosses. In time, Irish speakers – Gaeilgeoirí – came to have access to a plethora of grants and scholarships that were exploited as a means of advancement. Irish, therefore, played an important role, not just in cultural life, but in economic production: *The Dancers Dancing*, which pivots round Irish language courses set in an area of isolated Donegal with little other obvious economic assets, is evidence of this. Embodied in the characters of Geraldina Bannister (who first appears in the second book of the trilogy, *Blaeberry Sunday*) and Thomas, is the ideology of the Gaelic League or Conradh na Gaeilge, an apolitical organisation founded by Douglas Hyde in 1893, the year in which *Penny-farthing Sally* is set. It played a significant role in standardising the Irish language, a process that led to the marginalisation of people such as Ní Dhuibhne's father. It did this by artificially regularising it "through a process of accelerated interventionism" as Michael Cronin has put it.[12] One of the effects of its approach was the downgrading of certain canúintí – dialects – and, by extension, certain kinds of lived experience. In its defence, it may be said that the challenge the Gaelic League faced was to create the kind of linguistic infrastructure that included literacy, which not only enabled Irish to survive and avoid the museum, but also to become a positive instrument of modernisation. What Ní Dhuibhne's trilogy underlines is that the process and the effects of modernisation were uneven, and inevitably took their toll; Sally's sister Katie and the evicted family of *Blaeberry Sunday* are stark evidence of this.

It is no accident that, within the trilogy, Geraldina Bannister, the Gaelic League activist and representative of modernity, is the catalyst for narrative action. It is she who progresses the plots of the trilogy's last two novels: it is she who takes Sally out of the bind of the hiring fair and into an arena where choices are possible: choice being central to the *bourgeois* individualism associated with modernity. Furthermore, Geraldina is associated with other emblems of modernity – with trains that run on time, with that new-fangled contraption, the bicycle, and with wide spheres of cultural influence. She places Sally in a cosmopolitan, well-educated family whose mistress is committed to the suffrage movement, and who seems to believe, like W.B. Yeats and other revivalists, that remnants of pure Irish folk culture survive in pockets, such as this isolated Donegal place. Douglas Hyde had claimed that "a little gentle pressure is necessary" for the restoration of the Irish language.[13] The pressure that Geraldina exerts promotes Sally by using a series of posed picture postcards, including one of Sally adopting the role of 'an Irish colleen' wearing tweeds, an uncustomary attire for her generation, and standing beside an ass. Thus, a cultural icon is invented (or, rather, refined, because stage Irishry was nothing new in the 1890s) in order to promote Irish language and culture, and it then becomes a means of boosting the employment prospects of the 'real' person.

Glenbra and Modernity

The process of modernisation is not confined to the metropolis. As Lady Gregory put it in 1898, the "Irish Sancho has given a lead to the English Hodge in the power of adaptation and of organising for a material purpose".[14] The *bourgeoisie* of Glenbra eschew the timeless celebration of Lughnasa on Blaeberry Sunday in favour of lunch parties. Sally's widowed mother remarries. Her new husband is a decent man, but a suggestion lingers in the air that expediency rather than love prompted this union. While Geraldina Bannister, rather like Miss Ivors in James Joyce's story 'The Dead', is a model of female independence, another such model may be found in Glenbra itself. This alternative model is a woman who is single, but does not lack a husband; who earns a comfortable living; whose home contains that most advanced emblem of progress, the bathroom. Miss Lynch, as the local teacher, is the mediator of literacy and, therefore, progressive ideas. Much of *Blaeberry Sunday* is taken up with the kind of subject matter that came to dominate the Abbey Theatre stage in the mid-twentieth century: the grasping ambition of shopkeepers' sons (in this case, in Donegal) and of minor clerks (in Dublin). It is not so much that modernity is taking hold of Glenbra, but that Glenbra is taking modernity to itself, for reasons that include pragmatism, personal gain, and its undoubted attractions. Glenbra's culture is protean and its borders permeable.

Central to the story are mobility and, especially, border crossings and eventual deracination, which are a measure of the modernity of the period under consideration. Exile is an economic necessity. They also facilitate the achievement of a *bourgeois* individualism, essential to a people intent on proving their right to self-government in the 1890s and commemorating it as a *fait accompli* in the 1990s. It seems as if individuals must be dislocated in order for them to be relocated. The corollary of this is self-evident: plots needs must disrupt social stability in order to enact its reunification.

The Hiring Fair

The rupture that constitutes the rising action of the story consists of the sudden death of Sally's father and the subsequent need for her and her sister, still mere children, to find work. They are hired at a fair in a well-documented barbaric practice by which children were bound to farmers in near-slavery for fixed terms, usually through the six months of winter. The girls' experiences conform closely to those in several historical accounts of the practice, including Micí Mac Gabhainn's *Rotha Móra an tSaoil*, Paddy the Cope's *My Story*[15] and, most notably, Patrick MacGill's *Children of the Dead End*, an autobiographical novel published in 1914, in which the narrator, Dermod Flynn, reflects on his experience as a twelve year-old:

> To [Dermod's employer, Joe Bennet] I was not a human being, a boy with an appetite and a soul. I was merely a ware purchased in the market-place, something less valuable than a plough, of no more account than a barrow ... I, to Bennet, represented five pounds ten shillings' worth of goods bought at the market-place, and the buyer wanted, as a business man, to have his money's worth ... I was only an article of exchange, something which represented so much amidst the implements and beasts of the farm; but having a heart and a soul I felt the position acutely.[16]

Bennet's attitude is little different from that of his fictional employer counterparts in Ní Dhuibhne's *The Hiring Fair*. The reality that both novel and autobiography depict is part of the experience of poor Irish children, which was largely ignored until recent times. However, it offers insight into the contexts of the cruelty to children in Irish institutions exposed by historians and sociologists such as Diarmaid Ferriter, Mary Raftery and Eoin O'Sullivan.[17] The stigma attached to the hiring fair further thickened the blanket of silence that surrounded children's experience. Mac Gabhann was born in 1865 and, so, is older than Ní Dhuibhne's protagonists. However, MacGill was born in 1890, the year in which Ní Dhuibhne's novel is set. The enslavement of children, which Ní Dhuibhne's books document, continued long after the 1890s, at least until the Second World War. Colm Tóibín, writing in 1987, offers a first-hand testimony from a woman, Rose McCullough, sold into service by her mother at a hiring fair around 1930 at age thirteen.[18] If anything, Ní Dhuibhne's fiction is less savage than McCullough's account. However, her narrative serves two functions. It enables young contemporary readers to create some common ground with their fellow children of an earlier period in an act of bonding that transcends, or at least contains the impact of, the bondage it describes. Furthermore, it underlines how the trajectory of modernisation is far from linear in Ireland, and how pockets of inhuman practice continued to flourish.

Past into Future

The co-existence of the past in the present is further underlined in the characters of the two grandmothers, Granny Gallagher and Mrs Campbell, who provide a critique of modernity. Coming from two distinct rural cultures, one Catholic and indigenous, one planter, Protestant and loyalist, neither has any truck with modern ways. Mrs Campbell has recourse to folk potions and magic to deal with her adversaries. Granny Gallagher uses a colourful rhetoric. Like the old man in James Joyce's *A Portrait of the Artist as a Young Man* whose red-rimmed horny eyes the young Stephen Dedalus fears, the women sit and smoke and spit. It is with their ilk, it seems, that the young must struggle "all through this night till day come",[19] till either the young or the old lie vanquished, to quote Dedalus. The grandmothers embody not just opposition to the forward-looking east, but the tension between future-oriented *bourgeois* metropolitan living and the present as unchanging past. John Alphonsus Mulrennan, the Celtic Revival folklorist in *A Portrait* also has his counterpart in Ní Dhuibhne's trilogy. Here it is Geraldina Bannister, who adopts the role of collecting and mediating folk culture, which she does with both devastating lack of insight and powerful effect: she facilitates Sally's new future, removing her from the cycle of seasonal migration and placing her in the nationalist metropolitan sphere of influence.

Plot and Personal Agency

Social mutability embodied in the character of Sally is paralleled in the narrative structure of the trilogy. The configuration and the interrelation of the parts of a series narrative are necessarily open, reflecting MacGill's suggestion that, "a story of real life, like real life itself, has no beginning, no end".[20] The narratives of life do not have the tight structure of the novel form; Ní Dhuibhne refuses to be contained by its strictures. The ending of one volume has to allow for new action, conflict, plot, and, especially in the case of a *Bildungsroman*, the growth and evolution of character. Elements of plot that remain unresolved in one volume increase suspense and create a readership for the next. This dynamic underlines how the two conflicting narrative poles, contingency and personal choice, operate. Anything can happen, it seems, but fate (or rather, the ideological, controlling influence of the writer) needs the helping hand of the protagonist's prudent personal agency. The misery of domestic service in Tyrone can, depending on the character, give way to leafy Palmerstown Park, Dublin, or to exile in Anderson, Glasgow, and with it, social exclusion and death. And so the trilogy conforms to the structures of the nineteenth-century series novel, which foregrounded personal development.

As Linda K. Hughes and Michael Lund's *The Victorian Serial*, for example, shows, installment novels plot the progress both of society and of the individual.[21] They suggest that Victorian readers believed in the idea that personal and cultural progress was steady and inescapable. Notwithstanding the contemporary dominance of postmodernist ideology, it may be argued that the recent economic boom and increased cultural awareness in Ireland in the 1990s, when these books were published, have renewed faith in the concept of progress. It is a concept that underlines much educational philosophy, both at a pragmatic level (*vide* the notorious Leaving Certificate points system) and at a philosophical level (as evinced by the social constructivism that underlies the primary education curriculum). It is the ideology that underlies Frank McCourt's memoir, *Angela's Ashes* (1996): it proclaims that personality, self-possession and adaptability can overcome poverty. In Ní Dhuibhne, the form of the trilogy enacts the process of acculturation of young, maturing readers. Underlying it is the quest for selfhood, for knowing oneself. And the trilogy ends with that holy grail, a knowledge of self. Sally comes to know her own mind, but readers do not know it. What we do know is that she will exercise her capacity to make informed choices. Sally has become a *bourgeois* individual, and a member of a class set to wield increasing influence: *petit bourgeois*, indeed, but it is the *petit bourgeois* that will shape the new Ireland of the Free State. The transformation of a rural, isolated, unchanging society into a locus of modernism has been effected.

In many respects, the trilogy obeys the structures of the *Bildungsroman*, in that it plots Sally's growth within a defined social structure. However, that structure changes radically during the story, from restrictive and determining to one that facilitates a search for meaning through personal action.[22] The impetus to Sally's action is, first, the loss of her father, which leads her to move beyond self-absorption and frivolity. Not that maturity is immediately achieved. Rather, the passage towards it is punishing and laborious, and involves separation, loneliness, mental anguish and physical suffering. Central to this trilogy are themes of spurned affection, betrayal of trust and affection and disappointment, the hallmarks of the *Bildungsroman*.

Unlike her sister, Katie, who is less adaptable, Sally learns to accommodate these changes until she comes to a stage where she identifies sufficiently with the dominant social order that she can progress within it. As is the case in other *Bildungsromane*, Sally, the main protagonist, then takes her place within society. But what is that place? As the novel ends, she remains in a liminal space where anything is possible: blue-collar, suburban genteel respectability with Thomas, or a different kind of respectability, life in untrodden ways, among the springs of Glenbra with the equally class-conscious Manus. Or, as seems equally possible, Sally may emulate Isabel Archer, the heroine of Henry James's novel *The Portrait of a Lady*. While the portrayal of Sally is un-Jamesian in the sense that the narrator is reticent about her internal life, Sally, like Isabel, is prey to what James calls "the isolation and loneliness of pride".[23] There are indications, for example, that Sally may not accept either of the men who have proposed to her. Whatever future she embraces outside the parameters of *Penny-farthing's* narrative, an irreparable break with a traditional past has already been signified within it. Where marriage was once a necessary, if insufficient, condition of the successful *dénouement* of a *Bildungsroman* where female protagonists are concerned (Charlotte Bronte's *Jane Eyre* and Jane Austen's *Mansfield Park* are cases in point), this is not the case in the final book of Ní Dhuibhne's trilogy, *Penny-farthing Sally*. This book celebrates the process of self-definition, but this is achieved independently of family and mate. *Penny-farthing Sally* moves towards autonomy and subjectivity rather than inter-subjectivity.

The embedded narrative of Sally's sister Katie provides a perfect foil, a sharp contrast, to Sally's burgeoning individualism. Katie "had a less adaptable character than Sally's and would not have been inclined to accept change in any circumstances" (*PS* 43). Yet, even from the beginning, two things are evident: fate appears to deal Sally a better hand, and Sally is perspicacious enough to see that better hand for herself (43). Not only has Sally more initiative and dynamism, but she is also more reflective, more schooled (she is an avid reader, even joining a lending library when in domestic service) and more independent, and her ability to identify and evaluate options and choices is rewarded. Katie's bad judgement leads her to industrialised and impoverished Glasgow, Sally's ambition to comfortable and progressive Dublin. Impercipience leads Katie to a premature and ill-advised alliance with labourer Michael. Notwithstanding the narrator's reticence, it becomes clear that Michael is unreliable and, if not downright untruthful, he is tight-lipped and uncommunicative, to the detriment of sound sense. The couple indulges in drinking bouts and inhabits insanitary and unwholesome surroundings. The wages of their sin are not only Michael's death, but their baby's, and Katie's ill-health, which forces her to return to her family. Katie does not outgrow the mode of border crossing implicit in the seasonal service with which the book begins. Her exile does not lead to a renewed reconstruction of home, or to an affiliative rather than a filiative response to it. As the narrator of *The Hiring Fair* comments, because of their experiences, "Sally had grown up and Katie had reverted to childishness. She couldn't help it. She just couldn't bear being away from home" (96). The story ends with Katie back home in Glenbra, where the local community treats her with suspicion: its support for victims is limited. Her bleak future consists of telling her story rather than reshaping and playing a key role in it. And so the trilogy recounts two dialectical relationships, between the characters' active (Sally's) and passive (Katie's) temperaments, and between tradition and modernity. It also appears to pass judgement on numerous other historical Katies. One such is the real person on whom Norah Ryan is based in Patrick MacGill's tale, *The Rat Pit*,[24] a woman whose fate closely parallels Katie's: Norah ends up in disease-ridden Glasgow, indigent and on the streets, literally and figuratively.

Progress and Disruption

However, the trilogy does not confine itself to dirty realism, to socially verifiable realities. It is scrupulous in documenting alternative, liminal experiences. When Sally falls in love in *Blaeberry Sunday*, the experience does not so much slow down the narrative as disrupt it, taking the reader out of historical reality and into a Hardyesque celebration of nubility. This episode is told in the continuous present tense and takes place in hazel-wooded countryside and seashore – timeless, mythological places. It is tempting to interpret the episode as an instance of the eruptive, extreme pleasure that is associated with the term *jouissance*. The reality of passion, it implies, requires a radically different mode of representation. However, the spell is soon broken, and we are abruptly catapulted back to reality. Love, it seems, is not sustainable for extended periods. Another irruption of 'otherness' is the exotic Olaf, who follows his own rules and is content to live under the stars – even though his father, a shepherd, died from exposure. Olaf's way is to eschew plans and progress. He is "a breath of fresh air" to Sally – but no more than that. "He had no effect on her" (*BS* 146). Then there is Sally's 'Rosicrucian' experience in Dublin in *Penny-farthing Sally*. Does Sally see a ghost or does she just imagine it in the highly-charged spiritualist company she was keeping? On balance, it seems that the latter case is more likely. And so a pattern has evolved, of recognising the lure of the imagination, but of settling for sound sense. Looking at the trilogy from this perspective may prompt an interpretation of the Liam O'Flaherty-like story of an elemental love between a mare and a foal, which is inserted into *Penny-farthing Sally*. The narrator returns to this tale at the end of the book, when Sally's future is uncertain. In it, the foal breaks free of his bondage at the call of the mare, and together they plunge to death in the black lake. Will Sally accept unreliable Manus's hand in marriage and plunge into darkness with him, or will sound sense again prevail?

The trilogy's open-endedness underlines the possibility of choice for the characters. But that does not mean that the narrator (he or she?) empathises with the protagonist – or, indeed, with the version of selfhood she embodies. Occasionally, and subtly, the narrator's point of view comes through: s/he is complicit in dismissing others. When Sally's family is admiring postcards sent from Dublin in which Sally is posed beside a donkey, for instance, we are told that, "Everyone agreed that Sally looked lovely in the picture. Granny said it was the work of the devil and they should have no part in it" (*PS* 152). Granny and those she stands for, it seems, are excluded from the category of 'everyone'. Mostly, the omniscient narrator stops short of identification with any one individual or group, often remaining reticent and uncommitted, and the plot, especially, of *Penny-farthing Sally*, is loose and open. In this respect, the novel may be closely identified with other modern Irish fictions that fail to conform to expectations. "If there is a recurrent motif in discussions of narrative forms in Irish culture," writes Luke Gibbons, "it is that 'closure' and 'strict emplotment' are, to say the very least, rare achievements indeed".[25] The trilogy defies the normative thrust of realist fiction, not only in this, but in many other respects also.

As it eschews tight narrative structure, so the trilogy diverges from historical accuracy. For example, *Penny-farthing Sally* – set in 1893 – includes reference to a performance of W.B. Yeats's play, *The Countess Kathleen*. Although the play was published in book form in the previous year,[26] it was not staged until 1899, six years or so after the action of the story. The story rearranges fragments of history in an attempt to suit the exigencies of plot. It is not bound by the landscape of fact, to borrow Brian Friel's phrase.[27] Furthermore, Ní Dhuibhne's trilogy does not purport to be a psychological narrative. Characters' motivations and dilemmas are not explored in any significant or extended detail. Rather, they are hinted at. Sally's opinion about being an 'Irish colleen', for example, is not recorded; her mother's motivations in re-marrying are obliquely conveyed and we do not hear her side of the story.

This narratorial distance may be seen as an act of resistance to assumptions about *bourgeois* identity and to the novel form as a vehicle of mimesis. The critic Frederic Jameson, for example, is highly critical of the focus on private consciousness in the novels of Henry James. He sees it as evidence of a repressive political ideology, because it conceals the social and historical reality that, in fact, constitutes social identity.[28] Jameson is not alone in seeing the limitations of fiction that appears to approve and to encourage readers imaginatively to enter into a fictional character's feelings. Garrett Stewart observes that the act of empathising with a character produced by particular modes of novel-reading is inherently different from the modes of understanding of real people in real societies, and may, therefore, lead to alienation.[29] Ní Dhuibhne presents plausible characters in a plausible narrative, but then she and her narrator stand back from them. That embarrassing phenomenon, the real thing, is an instance of history, of what Frederic Jameson might call 'an absent cause'. As such, it is reconceptualised through history's prior textualisation. It is inaccessible except in textual form.[30] Ní Dhuibhne's narrativisation of it within the genre of the children's novel acknowledges the impossibility of retrieving the historical or psychological past. It also concedes the limitations of her readership. Nonetheless, it creates a narrow bridge of accessibility.

Afterword

Ní Dhuibhne's trilogy was written in the 1990s, and is set in a period exactly a century earlier. The bulk of this essay, written 11–14 years after the publication of the trilogy, has concentrated so far on how the novels dialogue with the period in which they are set. However, the question may legitimately be asked: where does the trilogy fit in the pattern of production and reception of Irish fiction, and, in particular, of children's fiction, since the 1990s? *Blaeberry Sunday* was awarded the 1994–95 Bisto Book of the Year, the premier prize for children's books, and *The Hiring Fair* won a Bisto Merit Award the previous year. Critic Robert Dunbar nominated *The Hiring Fair* as one of his top ten Irish Children's novels.[31] Fellow critic Celia Keenan cites the trilogy in her review of children's historical novels in 1996.[32] Ní Dhuibhne's most recent book, *Hurlamaboc*, was short-listed for the 2007 Bisto Awards, and for the 2006 Oireachtas na Gaeilge Gradam Uí Shúilleabháin. The literary worth of Ní Dhuibhne's works for young people, therefore, has been accorded some recognition. However, until relatively recently, children's literature itself attracted little attention within the academy in general in Ireland, and within Irish studies in particular.[33] Young people's literature was as invisible as Ní Dhuibhne's father at an Oireachtas function. The absence of any substantial criticism on Ní Dhuibhne's children's writing, therefore, says more about critical domains than about Ní Dhuibhne herself.

Yet the 1990s was a boom period for Irish publishing, and a period during which, in Anthony Roche's words, a "quantum leap in standards" of novel writing took place.[34] Despite this, the contemporary novel – as opposed to novels of earlier periods – attracted relatively little significant critical attention in Ireland. Where new Irish novels did come in for critical scrutiny, they were perceived primarily as vehicles for socio-historical explorations of identity. Jameson's imperative, "always historicize"[35] was widely applied as critical approaches took account of postcolonial critical theories to varying degrees. Liam Harte and Michael Parker's edition of essays, *Contemporary Irish Fiction: Themes, Tropes, Theories*[36] is indicative of the critical preoccupations of the period. This collection, according to Bernard O'Donoghue, addresses how the new world and the old manage to negotiate a shared territory,[37] as does Ní Dhuibhne's trilogy. Jennifer Jeffers' analysis of sixteen works of fiction, which sets out to help "reformulate the Irish identity as a complex and indeterminable entity",[38] could be addressing the texts in question here. Critic Eve Patten and fellow critic, Gerry Smyth perceive fiction's content as reflecting – and dissenting from – a culturally and politically evolving Ireland:

> In the publishing boom of the 1990s, the Irish novel repeatedly highlighted the institutional and ideological failings of the country, tracing the halting progress of Ireland's cultural, sexual and economic evolution, and foregrounding its voices of dissent. The works categorised by critic Gerry Smyth as the 'New Irish Fiction' were distinguished by a sociological purpose … Smyth [wrote]: 'the new Irish novelist is concerned to narrate the nation as it has been and is, rather than how it should be or might have been'.[39]

This brief survey of recent criticism of Irish adult fiction demonstrates the close parallels between Ní Dhuibhne's trilogy and contemporary adult Irish fiction and, by extension, the contemporaneity of her work.

The focus of another recent critic of the adult novel in the Irish context, a 2004 book-length study by Linden Peach, has been on narrative responses to psychological tensions, such as mimicry and modernisation versus silence; absences versus mothering; authority versus subversion and transgression. In particular, Peach attends to the 'divided temporality' that is an implicit feature of Ní Dhuibne's trilogy. What 'divided temporality' means for Peach is a time frame "where the previously accepted past and present are undone by the interruption of what has been hitherto silenced or marginalized, in turn complicated by the levels of secrecy in which it was located".[40] It may be argued that Ní Dhuibne's trilogy continues the 'undoing' of the accepted version of past Irish childhood, and does so in a form or genre "in which social, political and historical change could be accommodated", as Gerry Smyth put it in 1997.[41] Ní Dhuibne's commitment to the discourse of realism is restrained, often resisting temptation to elaborate on the characters' inner lives. As I have pointed out, her narrative avoids the kinds of enticements to collusion that might compromise a reader's ability to read subversively.

Although the trilogy does not directly address the 'new world' of the 1990s, there is a sense in which it does show how the cultural nationalism of the 1890s, which was predicated upon a particular kind of social and cultural ideal, laid the basis for the 'halting progress' of contemporary Ireland. Ní Dhuibhne's narrative, in Peach's terms quoted above, is disrupted by "what has been hitherto silenced or marginalized, in turn complicated by ... secrecy": Katie's story, the silent codes of the Donegal people and the narratorial stance, which works to avoid a complacent acceptance of the emerging model of individuality, are evidence of this.

Much has happened in the last decade to impel us to re-evaluate attitudes to exile, immigration, ruptured lives, nomadism and ethnicity. Viewed from the present moment, Ní Dhuibne's neo-Robinsonade enjoys new resonances.[42] As a tale of child labour, of displacement and migration, as an interrogation of *bourgeois* self-reliance, it explores contemporary Irish identities, avoiding any definitive icon of modern Irish identity. That 'real thing', if it ever existed, remains elusive.

NOTES

1   Although Ní Dhuibhne's first two children's books, *Hugo and the Sunshine Girl* (1991) and *The Uncommon Cormorant* (1990), were published under her own name, she has since used the pseudonym Elizabeth O'Hara when publishing children's books in English, including *The Sparkling Rain* (2003), *The Hiring Fair* (1993), *Blaeberry Sunday* (1994), and *Penny-farthing Sally* (1996), all of which are published by Poolbeg, Dublin.

2   Ní Dhuibhne, 'Why Would Anyone Write in Irish?' in Ciarán Mac Murchaidh, ed., *'Who Needs Irish': Reflections on the Importance of the Irish Language Today* (Dublin: Veritas Publications, 2004), 76.

3   *ibid.*

4   *ibid.*, 73–4.

5   *ibid.*

6   Colm Tóibín, *Walking Along the Border* (London: MacDonald Queen Anne Press, 1987), 25.

7   Further references to *The Hiring Fair* (*HF*), *Blaeberry Sunday* (*BS*) and *Penny-farthing Sally* (*PS*) are in parentheses in the text.

8   Nicola Warwick, 'Interview with Éilís Ní Dhuibhne'. *One Woman's Writing Retreat* http://www.prairieden.com/front_porch/ visiting_ authors/dhuibhne.html (2001).

9   Jeanette Roberts Schumake, 'Accepting the Grotesque Body: *Bildungs* by Claire Boylan and Eilís Ní Dhuibhne'. *Estudios irlandeses*, 1 (2006: 103–11), 110.

10   P.J. Mathews, *Revival: The Abbey Theatre, Sinn Féin, The Gaelic League and the Co-operative Movement* (Cork: Cork University Press in assoc. with Field Day, 2003), 11.

11   Sean O'Casey, *Drums under the Window* (London: Macmillan, 1945), 73, cited in Mathews, *Revival*, 131. I am indebted to Mathews for my understanding of the historical issues addressed in this paragraph.

12   Michael Cronin, *Translating Ireland* (Cork: Cork University Press, 1996), 155, cited in Mathews, *Revival*, 133.

13   Pádraig Ó Fearaíl, Conradh na Gaeilge History, Chapter 10, http://irish-nationalism.net/forum/showthread.php?t=846.

14   Augusta Gregory, 'Ireland Real and Ideal'. *Nineteenth Century*, 44 (Nov. 1898), 775.

15   Micí Mac Gabhann, [eag. Proinsias Ó Conluain] *Rotha Mór an tSaoil* (Indreabhán: Cló Iar-Chonnachta, 1959/1996); Paddy the Cope [Patrick Gallagher], *My Story*, Intro. Peadar O'Donnell. John Throne writes of his grandmother's experience in *The Donegal Woman* (Derry: Drumkeen Press, 2006). See also Ruth Russell, *What's the Matter with Ireland?* (New York: Devin-Adair, [c1920]). Other accounts of seasonal migration and emigration of children include

Fionn Mac Cumhaill, *Na Rosa go Bráthach* (Baile Átha Cliath: Oifig an tSoláthair, 1939); Pádraig Ua Cháimhsí *Róise Rua I* 1988; Séamus Ó Grianna, *Caisleáin Óir* (Baile Átha Cliath: Preas Dún Dealgan, 1924); *Nuair a Bhí Mé Óg* (Corcaigh/ Baile Átha Cliath: Cló Mercier, 1942/1979); *Rann na Feirste* (Baile Átha Cliath: Oifig an tSoláthair, no date); Pádraig Ua Cnáimhsí, *Róise Rua* (Baile Átha Cliath: Sáirséal Ó Marcaigh, 1988). I am grateful to Máirín Nic Eoin for her assistance in this matter. A more exhaustive list of sources and articles may be found in a literary anthology on emigration edited by Aisling Ní Dhonnchadha and Máirín Nic Eoin, *Ar an gCoigríoch: Díolaim Litríochta ar Scéal na hImirce* (Indreabhán: Cló Iar-Chonnachta, 2008).

16 Patrick MacGill, *Children of the Dead End*. B. D. Osborne, ed. (Edinburgh: Birlinn, 1999), 39.

17 Diarmaid Ferriter, *The Transformation of Ireland 1900–2000* (London: Profile, 2004); Mary Raftery and Eoin O'Sullivan, *Suffer the Little Children: The Inside Story of Ireland's Industrial Schools* (Dublin: New Island, 1999).

18 Tóibín, *Walking Along the Border*, 25–28. See also 22.

19 James Joyce, *A Portrait of the Artist as a Young Man*. Chester G. Anderson, ed. (Harmondsworth: Penguin, 1982), 252.

20 MacGill, *Children of the Dead End*, 120–21.

21 Linda K. Hughes and Michael Lund, *The Victorian Serial* (Charlottesville; London: University Press of Virginia, 1991).

22 Marianne Hirsch 'The Novel of Formation as Genre: Between *Great Expectations* and *Lost Illusions*'. *Genre XII*, 3 (1978: 293–311), 298.

23 Henry James, *The Portrait of a Lady* (Harmondsworth: Penguin, 1986), 164.

24 Patrick MacGill, *The Rat-Pit* (London: Jenkins, 1915).

25 Luke Gibbons, 'Dialogue Without the Other? A Response to Francis Mulhern'. *Radical Philosophy*, 67 (1994), 29.

26 W.B. Yeats, *The Countess Kathleen: And Various Legends and Lyrics* (London: T. Fisher Unwin, 1892).

27 The character Hugh in Brian Friel's *Translations* says, "civilization can be imprisoned in a linguistic contour that no longer matches the landscape of fact", 351.

28 Frederic Jameson, *The Political Unconscious: Narrative as a Socially Symbolic Act* (London: Routledge, 1986), 221–2.

29 Garrett Stewart, 'Dear Reader' in *The Novel*. Dorothy J. Hale, ed. (Oxford: Blackwell, 2006: 792–802), 793–4.

30 Jameson, *The Political Unconscious*, 35.

31 Robert Dunbar, 'My Top Fifty Irish Children's Novels'. *Inis* 10 (Winter 2004): 24–28.

32   Celia Keenan, 'Irish Historical Fiction' in *The Big Guide to Irish Children's Books* (Dublin: Irish Children's Book Trust, 1996: 68–80), 73. See also Celia Keenan, 'Reflecting a New Confidence: Irish Historical Fiction for Children'. *The Lion and the Unicorn*, 21.3 (1997: 369–378), 375.

33   The first book of essays produced in Ireland on children's literature addressed to the academy is C. Keenan and Mary Shine Thompson, eds. *Studies in Children's Literature* (Dublin: Four Courts Press, 2004).

34   Anthony Roche, 'Introduction: Contemporary Irish Fiction'. *Irish University Review*, 30, 1 Spring/Summer (2001: vii–xi), vii.

35   Jameson, *The Political Unconscious*, 7.

36   Liam Harte and Michael Parker, eds., *Contemporary Irish Fiction: Themes, Tropes, Theories* (Basingstoke: Macmillan, 2000).

37   http://www.word-power.co.uk/catalogue/0333683811

38   Jennifer M. Jeffers, *The Irish Novel at the End of the Twentieth Century: Gender, Bodies, and Power* (New York: Palgrave, 2002), 7.

39   Eve Patten, *The Cambridge Companion to the Irish Novel* 14 *Contemporary Irish Fiction*, http://cco.cambridge.org/extract?id=cco l0521861918_CCOL0521861918A015

40   Linden Peach, *The Contemporary Irish Novel: Critical Readings* (London: Palgrave Macmillan, 2004), 178.

41   Smyth, *The Novel and the Nation*, 6.

42   I use the term 'Robinsonade' to draw attention to Sally Gallagher's narrative of *bourgeois* self-reliance, overlaid with the connotations of the era of Mary Robinson's presidency. The term is usually associated with Daniel Defoe's *The Life and Strange Surprising Adventures of Robinson Crusoe* (1719), a book that "inspired innovative imitations well into the nineteenth century, which became known generically as 'Robinsonades'. These included *The Adventures of Phillip Quarll* by 'Edward Dorrington' (1727); *The Life and Adventures of Peter Wilkins, a Cornishman* by Robert Paltock (1751) and *The Swiss Family Robinson* by Johann Rudolf Wyss. Each depicts "man's ability to subdue, bend and surmount the obstacles of nature to his own ends while at the same time maintaining (or gaining) reason and moral integrity," cited in Kate Hebblethwaite, 'Creating Wildmen in One's Own Image: Maroons, Darwin and the Question of Humanity' in Mary Shine Thompson and C. Keenan, eds., *Treasure Islands: Studies in Children's Literature* (Dublin: Four Courts Press, 2006: 24–32), 26.

Éilís Ní Dhuibhne's *Hurlamaboc* and the Coming-of-Age
of Irish Children's Literature[1]

ANNE MARKEY

Writing in both English and Irish, Éilís Ní Dhuibhne is an
accomplished, award-winning author of fiction for children
and adults.[2] The often painful, frequently chaotic, process of
maturation is a recurring theme in her various works of
fiction.[3] Her Irish language novel, *Hurlamaboc* (2006), represents
a departure for Ní Dhuibhne because it explores this theme in a
work primarily addressed to young readers who are
themselves on the brink of adulthood; it is a coming-of-age
novel for the coming-of-age reader. A glance at the winners
and shortlists for the Children's Books Ireland Bisto Awards of
recent years shows that older teenagers are not particularly
well served by authors writing in either English or Irish.[4]
Nevertheless, this market is an expanding one whose needs are
not met by either fiction addressed to younger children or
older adult readers, or by young adult fiction written by non-
Irish authors. The Irish word 'hurlamaboc' translates into
English as 'commotion' or 'uproar', and Ní Dhuibhne's novel
lives up to its title by relating the interweaving stories of three
contemporary young Dubliners who negotiate various
personal upheavals and disasters during the period leading up
to, and just after, the Leaving Certificate examination, the
assessment that marks the culmination of the Irish secondary
school programme. This essay explores the ways in which
Hurlamaboc probes the boundaries of writing for young readers

in Ireland in the twenty-first century in terms of its target readership, use of vernacular Irish, subject matter and style.

Acknowledging that his inability to read Irish limited his critique, Robert Dunbar surveyed approximately nine hundred English-language works for young Irish readers, ranging from nineteenth-century material to titles published up to July 2004, to come up with a list of his top fifty Irish children's novels. Dunbar noted that books addressed to young readers often emit an off-putting whiff of the classroom and called for more humour, irreverence and subversion in the genre. In Dunbar's view, works of fantasy for young readers display an over-reliance on indigenous myth and legend as starting points for fictions that often follow very predictable and stereotypical paths. Acknowledging the abundance of Irish historical novels for young readers, Dunbar deplored the dearth of fiction for older teenagers, which tries to confront honestly the realities of growing up in the Ireland of the late-twentieth/early-twenty-first century. Bearing all these factors in mind, Dunbar stressed the need to encourage the production of local novels for teenage readers that, while not issue driven, grapple with contemporary social realities in stories that illuminate the experiences of credible characters as they attempt to cope with their lives.[5]

Hurlamaboc is exactly the type of novel that Dunbar wanted. With its striking one-word title and eye-catching cover depicting three white cutout figures against a split background of blue and gold, the first edition of the book looks far too modern and attractive to belong in a school bag.[6] Ní Dhuibhne's astute, and often humorous, social observation enables her to cast a keen and scathing eye on serious issues in modern Ireland, including social disadvantage and prejudice, familial disharmony, alcoholism, and the drawbacks of a narrowly-focused, exam-based educational system. The characters, though not always likeable, are consistently credible and the plot is both convincing and unpredictable. The novel combines contemporary realism with timeless fantasy as it refracts folkloric themes and motifs, most noticeably in its focus on the maturation of young characters in pursuit of true love and worldly success.

Despite its evident potential appeal to young adult readers and critics of children's literature alike, however, *Hurlamaboc* might seem likely to be restricted to a readership of older teenagers and critics with reasonable fluency in the Irish language. However, its appeal may not be as limited as it first appears because the book is written in sufficiently simple Irish to be accessible to those whose knowledge of the language is roughly equivalent to that achieved by secondary school students preparing for the Leaving Certificate examination. Because of its topicality, particularly its exploration of the pressures that attach to that examination, the novel will undoubtedly appeal to students currently completing their second-level studies in Ireland. Because of its exploration of such timeless themes as the challenges of growing up and the compensations of friendship, the novel will also appeal to older readers who studied Irish during their own, more distant schooldays. It may also find an international readership amongst those enrolled on Irish Studies courses outside Ireland and amongst the growing on-line community studying the Irish language. *Hurlamaboc* was written as a result of a commission for a book for teenage readers from Bord na Leabhar Gaeilge, a state agency that aims to assist writers and publishers in supplying accessible material to encourage the development of Irish language reading amongst the general public. It seems that Ní Dhuibhne's commission was an inspired one since the novel received a prize in the Fiction for Young People section of the Oireachtas Literary Awards in 2006, and won a Bisto honours award in 2007, demonstrating that its appeal and merit have been recognised within and beyond the confines of exclusively Irish-language literary circles.

Nevertheless, the book's appeal and marketability is undoubtedly limited by Ní Dhuibhne's decision to write it in Irish rather than English. However, as Ní Dhuibhne has argued elsewhere, there are compensations and challenges in choosing to write in a minority language.[7] Accordingly, her decision to write *Hurlamaboc* in Irish seems driven by a desire to produce a work that would be challenging to compose and enjoyable to read, particularly by young adults. Ironically, because of the dearth of topical Irish language fiction for such readers, *Hurlamaboc*, which finds much to criticise in Ireland's exam-focused education system, may well find itself being studied in Irish-language classes in preparation for the Leaving Certificate examination. With approximately forty five thousand students taking Irish in the Leaving Certificate each year, this development would lead to the type of large readership and high sales figures enjoyed by few Irish language publications.[8]

Ní Dhuibhne's use of the Irish language in the novel represents an imaginative intermingling of tradition and innovation, as she employs a contemporary idiom that deviates considerably from *An Caighdeán Oifigiúil* [Official Standard]. The Irish in *Hurlamaboc* is Dublin Irish, which bears some resemblance to dialects spoken in Gaeltacht areas, but which also reflects the syntax and vocabulary of young people educated in the Gael Scoil [Irish School] system. This system, set up in the early 1970s and catering for over 34,000 pupils in 2007, aims to instruct young people through the medium of the Irish language and has done much to arrest the decline of that language in recent years.[9] The modern Irish in *Hurlamaboc* incorporates English words and phrases, particularly colloquial expressions and slang used by Dublin teenagers. At the beginning of the twentieth century, proponents of the creation of a modern literature in the Irish language differed on the related issues of replicating colloquial speech and the desirability of using folklore as a model for contemporary fiction. Some, including Richard Henebry, insisted that modern Irish literature should eschew vernacular speech in favour of more classical standards and maintained that folklore should provide narrative templates for a revival of Gaelic fiction. Others, including Patrick Pearse, believed that writers should use modern, colloquial Irish and draw on both national and international narrative traditions and models.[10] More recently, Máirín Nic Eoin has argued that, as the millennium drew to a close, prose writing in the Irish language could be seen to be evolving in two distinct directions: a predominantly fabulist art literature addressed to a highly-educated audience and a more popular social realist strand directed at a younger, less academic readership.[11] Written at the beginning of the twenty-first century, *Hurlamaboc* blends folklore with contemporary realism in present-day, vernacular Irish. Ní Dhuibhne's decision to write the novel in Irish suggests that while the aspirations of the revivalists of the early-twentieth century were not fully realised, the language has survived, through adaptation, and remains a viable aesthetic medium one hundred years later. The novel represents an act of faith both in the Irish language and in the young Irish people to whom it is primarily addressed.

Hurlamaboc is a groundbreaking work of fiction whose originality lies not only in Ní Dhuibhne's use of a contemporary Irish-language idiom, but also in her approach to the perennial, universal theme of growing up. Critics agree that although the novel of maturation, or *Bildungsroman*, dates from the eighteenth century, the emergence of young adult literature as a distinct category, written for and marketed to adolescents and concerned with conflict between teenagers and society, is a late twentieth-century phenomenon, ushered in by novels such as J. D. Salinger's *The Catcher in the Rye* (1951).[12] This recent, and still developing, literary category unites the traditional *Bildungsroman* focus on self-development with an investigation of how the individual exists within modern society. In *Hurlamaboc*, Ní Dhuibhne adapts an Irish literary tradition to produce a novel that belongs within the modern, international category of young adult fiction. The title of her first chapter, 'Fiche bliain faoi bhláth' ['Twenty years in bloom'], recalls Muiris Ó Súilleabháin's autobiographical *Fiche Bliain ag Fás [Twenty years a growing]*, first published in 1933.[13] The title of Ó Súilleabháin's memoir prepares the reader for an account of his early childhood in Dingle, through to his youth on the Great Blasket Island, and on to his departure for Dublin as a young man. Ó Súilleabháin's focus is as much on a traditional way of life and a vanishing community as it is on the slow process of his own growth from child to adult. Ní

Dhuibhne's focus is on a modern society, where adolescence constitutes a protracted transitional stage between childhood and adulthood, and on the accelerated maturation of three young people when unforeseen catastrophes befall them. As the first chapter progresses, it becomes clear that this novel is less concerned with fulfilling expectations of what an Irish-language coming-of-age narrative should be than with adapting the genre for the twenty-first century reader.

The setting of *Hurlamaboc*[14] is not an impoverished Gaeltacht region on the western seaboard, far removed from the comforts of modernity, where God-fearing inhabitants battle for survival against the elements. Instead, the first chapter immerses the reader in the affluent, secular, fictional Dublin suburb of Rathmichael, whose amenities include wine bars and facilities for the hire of electrical appliances, and which is inhabited by successful grey-haired male householders and their blonde, fashionably-dressed wives. Property is expensive there, so it has remained largely untouched by immigration and its values and aspirations are predominantly middle-class. Lisín, the first character to whom the reader is introduced, devotes herself to her family and divides what is left of her time between voluntary work for the poor, interior design and landscape gardening classes, and various cultural activities including a book club, theatre and cinema attendance, and the study of local history and foreign languages (*H* 6–10). Although one reviewer has suggested that she resembles a character from the popular American television series *Desperate Housewives*, self-satisfied, complacent Lisín embodies much that is recognisable and fatuous in contemporary Irish society.[15] The narrative voice in the opening chapter is less in sympathy with her or with her husband, Pól, than with their eighteen-year old son, Ruán, who finds his perfect, beautiful mother vaguely dispiriting and who discerns a hollowness behind the façade of affluence that enthrals his parents and their peers. By the end of the first chapter, the reader realises that this coming-of-age novel will cast a cold eye on post-independence, 'Celtic Tiger' Ireland. Over the next few chapters, that reader is introduced to the other two principal young characters, Emma and Colm. Through the depiction of the differing family and social backgrounds of these three characters, and the intrusion of laconic and irreverent but non-judgemental observations, Ní Dhuibhne provides an astute insight into Irish society in the twenty-first century.

Though Ruán's family is comfortably middle-class, Ruán himself is surrounded by pressures on all sides, the most immediate of which is to do well enough in the Leaving Certificate to satisfy his mother's ambitions by gaining entry to a prestigious business course in Trinity College Dublin. Lisín likes to appear cultured, but does nothing to encourage Ruán in his ambition to become an artist (10–12). She loves her son but is too materialistic to allow him to follow his dream, and too selfish to see him as an individual with needs that are not necessarily compatible with her own desire for social status. Ruán is also subject to peer pressure: he has to appear cool to his friends and this involves talking to the right people, drinking, and pretending not to study. Emma lives on the same road, Ashtree Avenue, as Ruán, with her unmarried mother, Eibhlín, who has a good job in the Civil Service, although her neighbours, including Lisín, believe that she is an unskilled office clerk (68). Emma has a close relationship with her father, an Irish-language poet who scrapes a living from an Arts Council grant and by giving creative writing workshops (76). Emma wants to be a writer and is already an astute observer; she knows that her neighbours look down on Eibhlín, not because she is a single mother – that can be seen as fashionable – but because she has a younger lover, Greg, whom Emma despises (69). Emma is not particularly bothered by her neighbours, but she is disturbed by Greg's presence in the house and retreats to her room to escape him. Emma's family background may be unconventional by the standards of Ashtree Avenue, but her mother's well-paying job means that she is not economically disadvantaged. Colm lives in a Council housing estate and works part-time in the local grocery store and off-licence. He gives most of his earnings to his mother to eke out what she makes as a childminder, caring for a little boy from Ashtree Avenue. Colm's father is an aggressive alcoholic who drinks when he has money and causes havoc at home when his pockets are empty. When there is a domestic dispute in which Colm intervenes to protect his mother, the police believe that he, not his father, is the violent one and Colm runs away, ending up in Bangor, Wales.

The focus on these three young characters enables Ní Dhuibhne to paint an often humorous, but far from flattering, portrait of life in contemporary suburban Dublin. A picture emerges of a complacently competitive, class-ridden society, where those who have money flaunt it and want more, and those who have nothing, get nothing, while all the time tuppence looks down on three ha'pence. Ruán, Emma and Colm all live near each other but inhabit different worlds. The County Council housing estate lies to the north of Rathmichael; private estates of three-bedroomed semi-detached houses lie to the south; large, grand houses surrounded by walls and protected by gates lie to the west in the foothills of the mountains, while more modest detached houses line streets, like Ashtree Avenue, to the east. People who live in the east and the south intermingle, but avoid those who live in the north, while those rich enough to live in the west do not mix, even amongst themselves (46–47). Ruán and Colm know each other because they attended the same primary school, but this turns out to have been an accident rather than the result of enlightened social planning. The two local Catholic schools were full when Colm's mother tried to enrol him, but there was a vacancy in the Protestant one so Colm found himself going to the school deemed most fashionable by local, liberal Catholics. By the time the main action of the novel unfolds, the social order has been restored as Ruán is attending a private secondary school on the DART[16] line and Colm is attending the local comprehensive school (47–48). Ruán's friends look down on Emma, who attends a convent school. She is quick to criticise their arrogance, but she, in turn, pities the child from Ashtree Avenue who is minded by a 'knacker' in 'scobieville', her contemptuous name for the Council estate. One of the reasons that she dislikes Greg, her mother's 'toyboy', is that she suspects that he is not middle-class at all, but a 'scobie' with notions above his station (71–72). Being her father's daughter, she wants to be a writer, but she craves the financial success and social acclaim that have eluded him. Even at the end of the novel, when she realises that Colm's father is abusive and aggressive, she pulls a face, observing that "domestic violence" and all that "crap" are boring (146). Snobbery and complacency are endemic in Ashtree Avenue, where nothing succeeds like success, and 'survival of the fittest' is not simply the only way to get a seat in a DART carriage (17) but also, more generally, the order of the day.

Success encourages laziness, smugness and selfish insularity, characteristics that writers other than Ní Dhuibhne have attributed to the Irish. Emma, noting that her neighbours on Ashtree Avenue see everything and miss nothing, believes that Irish society still resembles that depicted in Brinsley MacNamara's *The Valley of the Squinting Windows* (71). Published in 1918, this novel, set in the fictional village of Garradrimna in County Westmeath, is a scathing assault on romantic notions of rural Ireland. MacNamara's novel satirises the narrow-minded self-interest of the inhabitants of an insular, prying, sanctimonious community who relish the misfortunes of others, and who insist on the importance of appearances in maintaining the hierarchical social order. Ní Dhuibhne's novel shows that intolerant self-righteousness is alive and well in twenty-first-century suburban Dublin, particularly amongst well-heeled women with time on their hands. As early as 1918, Pádraic Ó Conaire had written of the empty life of the Dublin housewife in a story called 'M'Fhile Caol Dubh' [My Dark, Slender Poet]:

> Tá na céadta agus na céadta againn de mhná saibhre agus saol suairc suarach á chaitheamh acu – ag siopadóireacht sa tráthnóna, tae agus cáineadh na gcomharsan agus na gcarad ina dhiaidh.[17]

> [There are hundreds and hundreds of us rich women, passing agreeable but trivial existences, what with shopping expeditions in the afternoon, and tea later, spent criticising neighbours and friends.]

Emma's observations on her female neighbours reveal that suburban housewives still lead shallow, unsatisfying lives and are as disparaging as their predecessors. The Avenue women work part-time or job-share while their children are young and cared for by less well-off women in other parts of Rathmichael. Then, they take a career break when the children start school, because they have earned a "sos deas" [nice rest] for themselves. Before long, these erstwhile "career girls" are "stay at home housewives" who prefer to attend creative writing classes and wine appreciation courses than to go to work (71–73). These women set themselves above judgement, but are quite willing to criticise others who do not enjoy their affluent lifestyle, regarding those who live in the Council housing estate as feckless and unwilling to work. Lisín does not ask Emma's mother to the party to celebrate the twentieth anniversary of her marriage to Pól, because a single mother with a lowly job and a young lover would do little to raise the social profile of the occasion. More tellingly, Lisín has not asked her own mother to the party, for much the same reason. Delighted that her richest neighbours have come, Lisín remains blissfully unaware that some of her guests are less interested in toasting a successful marriage than in indulging in a discreet extra-marital dalliance (25–26). Through the depiction of Ruán's family and their neighbours on Ashtree Avenue, Ní Dhuibhne portrays middle-class Irish society as grasping, venal, and pretentious.

Ní Dhuibhne suggests, through the description of Colm's family, that life on the other side of the tracks is not much better because poverty, while not conducive to pretentiousness, exacerbates other middle-class failings, as well as bringing its own problems. In many ways, Colm is the most likeable and admirable of the three principal characters; unlike Ruán, he is not afraid of hard work and is prepared to stand up for himself; unlike Emma, he looks down on no-one and is not concerned with being successful in life. However, Colm is subject to external pressures that limit his choices and curtail his ambitions in ways that Ruán and Emma are incapable of appreciating. Alcohol lubricates social interaction on Ashtree

Avenue, but it destroys lives on the Council estate and Colm's family suffers from his father's unacknowledged alcoholism. Colm, unlike the other two, has to work in a shop in the evenings and at weekends to eke out the family income and, so, has less time to study than they do. Work, however, provides Colm with welcome respite from the ever-present threat of violence that characterises life in the family home (40–41). His mother protects her abusive husband and puts her children at risk, being prepared to incriminate Colm by lying to the police, rather than facing the reality of her domestic situation (62). Colm is a caring, trustworthy, hard-working and honest young man, but these attributes are of little use to him because he is failed by his family and by an inequitable educational system.

Hurlamaboc shows that the Irish educational system benefits middle-class children, like Ruán and Emma, who have space, time and, most importantly, parental encouragement to succeed at their second level studies, go on to third level education, and then take up profitable, professional employment. The system fails Colm because he occupies a liminal position within Irish society and his needs and expectations are different from those of young people whose family background is comfortably middle-class. One of his teachers tells him that he might do well enough in the Leaving Certificate to go on to a third level college, but as Colm sees it, that is never going to be an option because his father will not allow it and it would be impossible to go to university while working full-time to support himself:

> Cén mhaitheas más ea a bhí san Ardteist, do mo leithéidse? Sin freagra nach bhfuair mé riamh ó mhúinteoir ar bith. Dúirt said linn é a dhéanamh, ach ní raibh sé soléir cén fáth. Ní rabhamar ag dul in áit ar bith ina mbéadh cáilíocht den saghas sin úsáideach. (133)

> [What use, then, was the Leaving Cert for the likes of me? That was an answer that I never got from any teacher. They told us to do it, but it wasn't clear why. We weren't going anyplace where that kind of qualification would be any use.]

Educational success is measured by an examination that has little relevance for Colm or for young people like him, and success after school depends on that exam. Ní Dhuibhne suggests that the Irish educational system reflects and perpetuates a middle-class bias that ignores the needs of the socially disadvantaged.

Through Colm's story, Ní Dhuibhne adapts the perennial trope of leaving home to find one's way in the world for the twenty-first-century reader. This trope is common to many folk and fairytales where a youngster undergoes various tests and trials before reaching maturity, acquiring a fortune and finding a mate, usually a beautiful princess. Colm certainly comes in for his fair share of tribulations on his way to maturity, but his story lacks a fairytale ending as he acquires wisdom instead of wealth, and a male friend called Dafydd instead of a princess. In many respects, Colm, the runaway, resembles Holden Caulfield, the hero of the quintessential coming-of-age novel, *The Catcher in the Rye*, but he is stronger and more adaptable than Salinger's narrator. Holden is unable to come to terms with either his own shortcomings or those of society, suffers a breakdown and ends up in a psychiatric institution, from where he hopes to return home. While Holden runs away from life, Colm runs away from home and embraces life as he finds it in Wales. As life in Ireland is geared towards survival of the fittest, Colm will never succeed there, but he can, and does, manage to live successfully elsewhere. Colm survives because he can adapt to changing circumstances. In *Hurlamaboc*, through Colm, but also through Ruán and Emma, Ní Dhuibhne shows that coming-of-age does not mean living happily ever after, but living for the moment, as far as possible on one's own terms, and accepting whatever companionship and happiness life has to offer.

Through the interconnecting stories of Ruán, Colm and Emma, Ní Dhuibhne suggests that behind the veneer of suburban selfishness and superficiality, other, more traditional, communal values lie dormant in Irish society. When Ruán's parents, Lisín and Pól, are killed in an accident in Turkey, where Pól is attending to some business interests before taking a holiday, it is Emma's mother, Eibhlín, who selflessly and unquestioningly helps Ruán cope with the immediate aftermath of the disaster. Her thoughtfulness helps to transform the traumatic upheaval of his parents' death into a liberating experience that enables him to gain a measure of independence. Ruán's maturation is signalled at the end of the novel as he decides to keep Colm's whereabouts in Wales a secret and embarks on a loving relationship with Emma. Within the novel, death functions as a reminder that life is too precious to be wasted and that growing up involves coping with whatever life throws in one's way. Coming-of-age involves coming to terms with oneself and with those around us.

If coming-of-age involves coming to terms with society, it could be argued that *Hurlamaboc* ultimately offers a conservative view of maturation as a process during which young people inevitably learn to live with dominant ideologies. Critics of children's literature have explored the ideological dimensions of the genre's construction of childhood and its approach to maturation and adulthood.[18] Peter Hollingdale, in particular, has drawn attention to the explicit and implicit ways in which ideology permeates fictions created by adults for children so that the young reader becomes susceptible to the ideologies conveyed by the text.[19] John Stephens argues that ideologies are conveyed by the ways in which a story's perceptual point of view privileges one interpretation of events or attitude towards characters over others not explicitly suggested by the text. He concludes that, "implicit authorial control is a characteristic marker of the discourse of children's fiction".[20] While fiction addressed to young adults has received less critical attention than that addressed to younger and older readers, it is undoubtedly a genre which reflects the influences of authorial control and dominant social ideologies. Roberta Seelinger Trites observes that young adult fictions "tend to convey to adolescents that they are better served by accepting than by rejecting the social institutions with which they must live. In that sense, the underlying agenda of many YA [Young Adult] novels is to indoctrinate adolescents into a measure of social acceptance".[21] By applying these critical insights to *Hurlamaboc*, it becomes apparent that, while Ní Dhuibhne advocates a measure of social acceptance, the narrative style of the novel enables her to resist the indoctrination of her young readers into thoughtless compliance with dominant ideologies.

The action of *Hurlamaboc* reflects the experiences of the three principal characters in a generally sequential way, so that the first four chapters deal with Ruán, the next two with Colm and the next with Emma. However, Emma appears in the sequence dealing with Ruán and his family, Ruán appears in the sequence dealing with Colm, and Ruán and Colm's mothers appear in Emma's sequence. Furthermore, the action is not strictly chronological because events are mentioned in more than one sequence as the three principal characters anticipate them and reflect on them at various stages of the unfolding action. These techniques enable Ní Dhuibhne to present interlinking narratives that offer differing perspectives on events and characters. It is no coincidence that a film, *Gone with the Wind*, provides Ní Dhuibhne with another device that facilitates her experimentation with narrative style. The film is broadcast on television at a pivotal juncture in the development of the plot: Ruán watches it on the evening after his parents have left for Istanbul and he is waiting for a large group of friends to arrive (35); it is playing in the background as Colm's drunken father attacks his mother (56–57); Emma leaves the sitting room, rather than watch the film in Greg's company (77). The narrative style of *Hurlamaboc* is cinematic, as it resembles a montage of film shot from different points of view and assembled to present complementary, but by no means identical, perspectives on interlinking characters and events.

The stylistic complexity of the novel is enhanced by a narrative voice that veers from third- to first-person with varying degrees of omniscience, irony, reliability, partiality and objectivity. The unpredictability of the narrative voice means that the point of view is constantly shifting and, thereby, becomes resistant to implicit ideological indoctrination. *Hurlamaboc* opens with what is ostensibly an objective omniscient third-person narrative voice announcing the "ócáid iontach" [wonderful occasion] of the forthcoming party to celebrate the twentieth anniversary of the marriage of Lisín and Pól (5). The irony suggested by the epithet 'wonderful' is confirmed by the way in which the narrative voice focuses, throughout the rest of the chapter, on what Lisín sees as her perfections, but what the reader may see as imperfections – her glamorous appearance, her lack of a job, her manipulation of her husband and children, and her avowed interest in cultural activities (5–9). The chapter ends:

Ní raibh sí riamh díomhaoin agus ba bhean spéisiúil í, a d'fhéadfadh labhairt ar aon ábhar faoin ngrian. Dáiríre. (9)

[She was never idle and she was an interesting woman, who could speak on any topic under the sun. Really.]

As the final qualifier totally undermines the credibility of the preceding depiction of Lisín's apparent perfections, this chapter reveals Ní Dhuibhne's use of third-person free indirect discourse to present an ostensibly flattering portrait of a self-deluding character. As the novel progresses, the third-person narrative voice becomes increasingly sympathetic to Ruán and to Colm. In the chapters devoted to these two young male characters, the narrator sees events and judges characters through their eyes, while the chapters devoted to Emma are written in the first-person, and directly reflect her thought processes. Events and characters are consistently judged from an adolescent, not an adult, perspective, but as the three adolescents differ, the reader is not coerced into simple judgements or into identification with any one point of view. As no one perspective is privileged over another, the reader is encouraged to resist implicit authorial control and to search for meaning by comparing conflicting interpretations of events and characters. In other words, the reader, like the three young principal characters, is confronted with the necessity to make one's own decisions and become as independent an agent as it is possible to be when one is not completely in control of what happens.

Ni Dhuibhne's mix of documentary realism and fantasy adds to the stylistic complexity and interpretative ambiguity of

Hurlamaboc. The majority of the novel is written in a realistic mode, but Chapters 12 and 14, in which the ghost of Lisín appears to Ruán, introduce a disruptive element to the narrative. She first appears after the funeral when Ruán is considering opting out of the Leaving Certificate examination (116–126). Each night, until the exam is over, Lisín knocks at the door, Ruán lets her in, and she cleans and tidies while he sleeps in preparation for the next day's ordeal. As a result of her efforts, Ruán does well in the exam and the social worker is so impressed with the state of the house that his younger brother is allowed to stay in his care. Lisín stops coming when Ruán defies her and applies to study Film instead of Business at third level but, by that time, her appearances have ensured that her two sons will survive the trauma of her death (135–140). The reader is unsure as to whether or not Lisín's intervention is a figment of Ruán's imagination. She appears when he is under great stress; no one else sees her, and ghosts are uncommon in twenty-first-century suburban Dublin. As against that, Ruán is aware that what is happening is scarcely credible; he is sufficiently in possession of his faculties to undertake a taxing examination and to impress a social worker, and Emma observes that his house is so tidy that one would think Lisín was still looking after it (141). As the reader hesitates between believing that Lisín's appearances are illusory, or accepting that they are evidence that there are unseen forces in operation in the real world, they belong to the realm of the fantastic, as defined by Tzvetan Todorov.[22] Lisín's ghostly appearances enable Ruán to cast off her repressive, limiting influence over his life. This irruption of the fantastic in a realistic novel leads to the "dissolution of an order experienced as oppressive and insufficient", a characteristic marker of subversive fantasy literature, as defined by Rosemary Jackson.[23] Ní Dhuibhne's use of fantasy underlines her insistence throughout *Hurlamaboc* that one is never fully in control of one's destiny, so that coming-of-age involves coming to terms with the unforeseen, irrational upheavals that life throws in one's path.

Ní Dhuibhne's recourse to the fantastic in the novel is rooted in the Irish folk tradition. The author recalls that she first heard the word 'hurlamaboc' from Cáit (An Bhab) Feirtéar, a traditional Irish storyteller, in Dunquin, and that when she heard it again on a tape-recording of the now deceased Kerry storyteller, she determined to put it to good use.[24] Despite its contemporary suburban setting and its cinematic mode of narration, the spirit of the traditional Gaelic storyteller infuses *Hurlamaboc*. Lisín's fantastic intervention recalls a feature of a traditional legend about a woman whose untidy home is invaded by witches, collected from Cáit Feirtéar, on which Ní Dhuibhne based her 1995 play, *Dún na mBan Trí Thine*. In Feirtéar's version of the legend, a spirit, who is the woman's mother, helps get rid of the unwelcome visitors. She appears at night, advises her daughter to shout out that the witches' home is on fire and then to tidy the house so that they will be unable to come in again. The daughter follows this advice and regains possession of her house.[25] Lisín's ghostly appearances in *Hurlamaboc* reflect the legend's suggestion that a mother can reach from beyond the grave to put a house in order and to help a child in trouble. However, as Ruán refuses to take his ghostly mother's advice to do a Business course and, thus, ensure his financial future, *Hurlamaboc* departs from its traditional source to suggest that the living must learn to cope for themselves. Folklorist Áine O'Neill points out that the legend "validates the culture of traditional society in more than one way".[26] Ní Dhuibhne adapts the Irish folk tradition to criticise the materialistic culture of contemporary Irish society and to enhance the narrative complexity of *Hurlamaboc*.

The triadic patterning associated with the folktale is evident not only in the focus on three young characters, but also in the three knocks on the door, which each come at a significant time in Ruán's life. The first such chapter – 'Cnag ar an doras' ['A knock on the door'] – includes the disclosure that his parents have been killed; the second – 'Cnag eile ar an doras' ['Another knock at the door'] – signals the reappearance of ghostly Lisín; and in the third and final chapter of the novel – 'An tríú cnag' ['The third knock'] – Emma thinks she hears a knock at the door while Ruán kisses her, but he assures her that it is only the wind. He has grown up enough to leave his mother and the past behind and to seize the chance of present happiness with Emma. Other chapters take their titles directly from Irish language proverbs and traditional songs.[27] Ní Dhuibhne's persistent, but unobtrusive, recourse to Irish folk traditions in a coming-of-age novel set in 'Celtic Tiger' Ireland is imaginative and invigorating. By extension, *Hurlamaboc* suggests that Irish society will come of age by combining tradition with innovation. Ní Dhuibhne's coming-of-age novel for older teenage readers is a valuable contribution to the continuing development not only of Irish children's literature and literature in the Irish language, but also of Irish literature in general.

NOTES

1   All translations are by the author.

2   Writing under the pseudonym Elizabeth O'Hara, Ní Dhuibhne won the 1994–1995 Children's Books Ireland Bisto Book of the Year award for *Blaeberry Sunday* and a 1993–1994 Bisto Merit award for *The Hiring Fair*. Writing as Éilís Ní Dhuibhne, she was short-listed for both the 1990–1991 Bisto awards for *The Uncommon Cormorant*, and the Orange Prize for Fiction 2000 for her English language novel, *The Dancers Dancing*, while her first novel in Irish, *Dúnmharú sa Daingean*, won the principal Oireachtas literary prize the same year.

3   See, for example, Ní Dhuibhne, *Hugo and the Sunshine Girl* (Dublin: Poolbeg, 1992); *Cailíní beaga Ghleann na mBláth* (Baile Átha Cliath: Cois Life, 2003).

4   The Irish-language works of Ré O Laighléis, which were short-listed in 2004–2005, 1996–1997, 1995–1996 and 1994–1995, are exceptions to this general trend.

5   Robert Dunbar, 'My Top 50 Irish Children's Novels'. *Inis*, 10 (Winter 2004: 24–28).

6   See Cat Yampbell, 'Judging a Book by its Cover: Publishing Trends in Young Adult Literature'. *The Lion and the Unicorn*, 29.3 (2005: 348–372), for a discussion on the commodification of young adult fiction,

particularly in terms of increasing recourse to striking covers and one-word titles.

7   Ní Dhuibhne, 'Why Would Anyone Write in Irish?' in Ciarán Mac Murchaidh, ed., *'Who Needs Irish': Reflections on the Importance of the Irish Language Today* (Dublin: Veritas Publications, 2004), 70–82.

8   For figures of students taking Irish for the Leaving Certificate, see the *Irish Times*, 7 June 2005, 1; in a radio interview broadcast on 'Blas', BBC Northern Ireland (3 Feb. 2006), Ní Dhuibhne acknowledged that *Hurlamaboc* may be studied in preparation for the Leaving Certificate at some stage in the future, but confirmed that this possibility was not on her mind when writing the book.

9   Louise Holden, 'The Rise of the Gaelscoil'. *Irish Times*, 17 Apr. 2007: 15.

10 Philip O'Leary, 'The Irish Renaissance, 1880–1940: Literature in Irish' in *The Cambridge History of Irish Literature*. Vol. 2. Margaret Kelleher and Philip O'Leary, eds. (Cambridge: Cambridge University Press, 2006: 226–269), 236–250.

11 Máirín Nic Eoin, 'Contemporary Prose and Drama in Irish' in *ibid.*, 298.

12 Maria Nikolajeva, *Children's Literature Comes of Age: Towards a New Aesthetic* (New York: Garland, 1996), 8; Roberta Seelinger Trites, *Disturbing the Universe* (Iowa: University of Iowa Press, 2000), 9.

13 Both Ní Dhuibhne and Ó Súilleabháin take their titles from an Irish proverb that describes the process of growing up and growing old: fiche bliain ag fás, fiche bliain faoi bhláth, fiche bliain ag cromadh, fiche bliain gur cuma ann nó as [twenty years growing, twenty years in bloom, twenty years stooping, twenty years when no matter whether you are there or not].

14 Ní Dhuibhne, *Hurlamaboc* (Baile Átha Cliath: Cois Life, 2006). Further references to *H* are in parentheses in the text.

15 Ciarán Mac Murchaidh, 'Raic agus Rírá'. *The Irish Book Review*, (Summer 2006), 11.

16 DART is the acronym for the Dublin Area Rapid Transit, the rail line running along the coast of Dublin, from Malahide and Howth southwards as far as Greystones in County Wicklow.

17 Pádraic Ó Conaire, *Scothscéalta*. ed. by Tomás de Bhaldraithe (Dublin, 1956), 148.

18 See, for example, Jacqueline Rose, *The Case of Peter Pan: Or, The Impossibility of Children's Fiction* (London: Macmillan, 1984), 8–9, who argues that children's fiction has consistently constructed the child it purports to address. This constructed, innocent child, who has direct and unproblematic access to language and the world,

reassures adults who feel challenged by the uncertainties that characterise their own relationship with both.

19 Peter Hollingdale, 'Ideology and the Children's Book' in *Literature for Children: Contemporary Criticism*. Peter Hunt, ed. (London: Routledge, 1992: 19–40), 27.

20 John Stephens, *Language and Ideology in Children's Fiction* (London: Longman, 1992), 27.

21 Seelinger Trites, *Disturbing the Universe*, 27.

22 Tsvetan Todorov, *The Fantastic: A Structural Approach to a Literary Genre* (New York: Cornell University Press, 1973), 25.

23 Rosemary Jackson, *Fantasy and the Literature of Subversion* (London: Methuen, 1981), 180.

24 Ní Dhuibhne in conversation with Eamonn Ó Dónaill, *Beo: Internet magazine for Irish speakers in Ireland and worldwide* (58), Feb. 2006, http://www.beo.ie/index.php?page=archive_content&archive_id=17 43

25 The text of Feirtéar's version of the legend is given in *Béaloideas*, 59 (1991), 258–263.

26 Áine O'Neill, '"The Fairy Hill is on Fire" (MLSIT 6071): A Panorama of Multiple Functions'. *Béaloideas*, 59 (1991: 189–196), 194.

27 For example, 'Trasna na dtonnta' ['Across the waves'] and 'Thugamar féin an samhradh linn' [We took the summer with us] are two traditional songs that function as chapter titles, while the chapter entitled 'Ar scath a chéile' is based on the proverb, 'ar scath a chéile a mhaireann na daoine' ['people exist in each other's shelter'.]

Éilís Ní Dhuibhne:
Is Minic Ciúin Athchruthaithe

BRIAN Ó CONCHUBHAIR

"You learn much more than Irish at Irish college".[1]

Sainghné de phrós Éilís Ní Dhuibhne is ea saibhreas samhlaíochta as an ngnáth a chrúitear ó sheantéascanna. Is minic ina saothar idir ghearrscéalta, úrscéalta agus dhrámaí, go ndéantar athléamh ar théacs seanbhunaithe – idir théacsanna ón mbéaloideas nó dírbheathaisnéisí cáiliúla ó aimsir an tSaorstáit. As an athléamh seo tugtar léargas úr dúshlánach, ní hamháin ar an mbuntéacs féin ach ar an saol, ar na himeachtaí agus ar na carachtair. Is fíor é seo go háirithe maidir leis na mioncharachtair a thugann sí chun beatha agus a mbronnann sí dínit agus gradam as an nua orthu. Sainghné leis is ea a leithéid de chleachtadh ag an scríbhneoir feimineach agus ag an scríbhneoir iarchoilíneach mar a mhínítear sa lámhleabhar cáiliúil iarchoilíneachta, *The Empire Writes Back*:

> Feminist and post-colonialist discourses both seek to reinstate the marginalized in the face of the dominant, and early feminist theory, like early nationalist post-colonial criticism, sought to invert the structures of domination, substituting, for instance, a female tradition or traditions, in place of a male-dominated canon. But like post-colonial criticism, feminist criticism has now turned away from such simple inversions towards a questioning of forms and modes, to unmasking the assumptions upon which such canonical constructions are founded, moving first to make their cryptic bases visible and then to destabilize them ... In addition, both feminist and post-colonial critics have reread the classical

texts, demonstrating clearly that a canon is produced by the intersection of a number of readings and reading assumptions legitimized in the privileging hierarchy of a patriarchal or metropolitan concept of literature.[2]

Is minic sa chur chuige seo, más athinsint, athscríobh nó aistriúchán liteartha atá i gceist, go leagtar béim iomlán nua as an bpíosa ar mhioncharachtar ón bpríomhscéal bunaidh. Leagtar fócas ar charachtar áirithe a aithnítear ón mbunscéal, ach nár caitheadh mórán ama ná aird air/uirthi ann. Ach sa saol roghnach samhlaíochta agus sa chruinne mhalartach a chruthaíonn Ní Dhuibhne, is nós léi an dream a fágadh ar an imeall tráth a thabhairt go lár an aonaigh anois. Díríonn sí aird iomlán an léitheora ar shaol an charachtair seo agus is minic a bhronntar tábhacht ar eachtra nach raibh inti ach fo-eachtra roimhe seo. Caitheann Ní Dhuibhne am agus dua leis na mionsonraí sa phríomhleagan den scéal, fiosraíonn sí an leid is luath, go minic an leid nach ndeirtear ach a thuigtear agus ar nós an bhleachtaire, leanann sí uirthi go dtí go nochtann sí saol eile agus taobh eile ar fad den bhunscéal. Sa phróiseas seo tugann sí faoi "unmasking the assumptions upon which such canonical constructions are founded, moving first to make their cryptic bases visible and then to destabilize them".[3] Baineann sí an sprioc sin amach trí amhras a chaitheamh ar an stair údarásach agus trí scéalta idir dhrámaí, ghearrscéalta agus úrscéalta a sholáthar a thugann béaloideas, miotas agus ficsean le chéile – "writing combines folklore and myth 'intertextually' with fiction".[4]

Feictear é seo go soiléir sa ghearrscéal a bhfuil an teideal céanna aige leis an gcnuasach as a dtógtar é, *The Pale Gold of Alaska*, teideal a shíolraíonn ón ndírbheathaisnéis Ultach, *Rotha Mór an tSaoil* le Micí Mac Gabhann.[5] Ní haon iontas é go dtarraingeodh údar a bhfuil bá aici leis an nGaeilge agus le Dún na nGall ach go háirithe leis an saothar seo, saothar a áirítear ar cheann de na dírbheathaisnéisí is mó sa réigiún úd i dteannta le *Mo Bhealach Féin* (Seosamh Mac Grianna),[6] *Nuair a Bhí mé Óg* (Séamus Ó Grianna) agus *Saoghal Corrach* (Séamus Ó Grianna).[7] Cainteoir dúchais Gaeilge as Gleann Bhairr, Gaeltacht bheag i dtuaisceart Dhún na nGall ab ea athair an údair.[8] Tugtar le fios in agallamh dá cuid nach raibh Gaeilge ag a máthair ach ba mhinic a labhraíodh a hathair a theanga dhúchais lena chlann agus iad ag éirí aníos cé go rabhadarsan den tuairim go raibh a chanúint 'an-saoithiúil ar fad'.

Bhíodh m'athair ag caint ina Ghaeilge Chonallach, a bhí éagsúil ar fad leis an nGaeilge a chuala mé i Scoil Bhríde, an scoil náisiúnta ar fhreastail mé uirthi. Bhí cuid Gaeilge m'athar cosúil le teanga eile i gcomparáid leis an nGaeilge sin. Bhí saghas drochmheasa againn, déarfainn, ar Ghaeilge m'athar toisc go rabhamar i gcónaí ag plé le múinteoirí ó Chiarraí agus ó Ghaillimh agus mar sin de. Níor chuala mé aon duine eile riamh ag labhairt Gaeilge ó Dhún na nGall i mBaile Átha Cliath. Ní raibh Gaeilge Dhún na nGall le clos sna scoileanna; is dócha go raibh na daoine ó Thír Chonaill in Albain – ní raibh siad sna scoileanna i mBaile Átha Cliath.[9]

Ní haon iontas ach chomh beag é go léadh Ní Dhuibhne *Rotha Mór an tSaoil*. Scoláire béaloidis í a bhain dochtúireacht san ábhar amach ó Ollscoil Náisiúnta na hÉireann sa bhliain 1982 ar thráchtas a dhein iniúchadh ar an scéal idirnáisiúnta béaloidis ar a dtugann scoláirí an Bhéarla 'With His Whole Heart'.[10] Tá raidhse alt agus aistí foilsithe aici in irisí léannta in Éirinn agus thar lear, agus chaith sí seal ag déanamh staidéir in Ollscoil Chóbanhávan sa Danmhairg, taithí ar bhain sí adhmad as ina húrscéal *The Bray House*. Cé go raibh an Ghaeilge ina fochair agus í ag fás aníos agus gur fhreastail sí ar scoileanna lán-Ghaeilge, is léir nárbh ionann a taithí agus an taithí a gcuirtear síos air i gcuimhní cinn iomráiteach Hugo Hamilton dar teideal, *The Speckled People*. Go deimhin is pointe é sin a dhéantar go tréan san agallamh a luadh thuas:

Ba ghnáthdhuine ón nGaeltacht é m'athair. Ba shiúinéir, níor Ghaeilgeoir é. Labhair sé an Ghaeilge mar gurbh shin an teanga a bhí aige. Ní raibh aon chosúlacht idir é agus athair Hugo Hamilton, a bhí saghas as a mheabhair – de réir an leabhair, pé scéal é ... Taitníonn leabhar Hamilton go mór liom ach ceapaim go bhfuil sé saghas dainséarach, ar bhealach, do chúis na Gaeilge, mar tá saghas steiréitíopa i gceist le fáil go forleathan i measc daoine atá i gcoinne na Gaeilge.[11]

Sa dírbheathaisnéis úd a breacadh ar shaol Mhicí Mhic Gabhann, cuirtear síos ar a shaol i Meiriceá. I measc na n-eachtraí a bhain leis, thit eachtra amach in Butte, baile mianadóireachta siar ó thuaidh ó Pháirc Phoiblí Yellowstone, i Stát Montana, nuair a d'fhuadaigh scata dúchasach bean gheal de chuid na mianadóirí lá. De réir an scéil, eagraíodh meitheal tána ar an bpointe agus sábháladh an bhean gheal ón uafás a bhí, gan dabht, i ndán di dá bhfágfaí faoi chúram na 'n-amhas' í. Sa ghearrscéal seo dar teideal 'The Pale Gold of Alaska' dírítear isteach ar an mionscéal seo agus insítear arís as an nua é ach ó thaobh na mná an t-am seo. Sa ghníomh samhailteach athchruthaitheach seo, tugtar saol agus beatha don bhean gan ainm i *Rotha Mór an tSaoil* agus tugtar ar an léitheoir an ciúnas agus an neamhshuim a deineadh den bhean seo sa bhunscéal a dhiancheistiú. Tá a cur chuige anseo ag teacht ní hamháin lena ndúirt Ashcroft in *The Empire Writes Back*, ach lena gcreideann Schulte i dtaobh na léitheoireachta cúramaí ina leabhar *The Geography of Translation and Interpretation: Traveling Between Languages*:

> Readers are left with various options that they can interpret within the context of that atmosphere. At every step of their work, readers/translators reestablish the inherent uncertainty of each word, both as isolated phenomenon and as semiotic possibility of a sentence, paragraph, or the context of the entire work. The rediscovery of that uncertainty in each word constitutes the initial attitude of the translator. Reading becomes the making of meaning and not the description of already-fixed meanings. As the imaginative text does not offer readers a new comfortable reality but rather places them between several realities among which they have to choose, the words in the text emanate a feeling of uncertainty.[12]

Agus is sa ghníomh sin atá cuid lárnach de bhua Ní Dhuibhne mar scríbhneoir le sonrú go sainiúil. Is é sin an iallach a chuireann a saothar ar an léitheoir dul siar agus athmhachnamh a dhéanamh ar an mbunscéal más mian leis an léitheoir saibhreas iomlán an scéil a bhlaiseadh. Cruthaítear riachtanas ina saothar chun go dtabharfaí aitheantas don fhocal, don abairt, don rud nár dúradh, nó don scread nár chualathas. Ní foláir don léitheoir an nod a aimsiú agus a thuiscint chun blas iomlán a bhaint as an scéal, bíodh an nod sin préamhaithe sa bhéaloideas, sa litríocht bhéil, in imeachtaí ár linne féin nó sa litríocht chlóbhuailte. Is minic go gcaitear amhras ina saothar ar an scéal oifigiúil nó ar an leagan údaraithe, agus ar an insint fhaofa den stair: bá Juliette in *Cailíní Beaga Ghleann na mBláth*, nó iompar na mbuachaillí i ndeisceart Bhleá Cliath in *Hurlamaboc*. Ní ghéilleann prós Ní Dhuibhne don dubh ná don bhán. Scríobhann sí sa chlapsholas agus caitear scáth agus go deimhin scáil ar an tuiscint agus ar an eolas deimhneach a thugann an léitheoir chuig an scéal. Is minic ar chríochnú scéil di, go bhfágtar an léitheoir in amhras faoi údarás an eolais. Fágtar an léitheoir, sna scéalta is fearr, leis an tuiscint nach féidir muinín a bheith ag duine riamh as aon leagan den scéal agus gurb fhearr i gcónaí a bheith in amhras mar a dúirt Pleny, mar gurb í an éiginnteacht an t-aon chinnteacht atá ann. B'fhéidir gur cothaíodh féith an amhrais san údar i dtaobh aon leagan údarásach agus í ina dalta óg scoile:

Ar Scoil Bhríde, bhí b'fhéidir cuid de sin ann agus bhí an saghas meoin ann go raibh an Ghaeilge níb fhearr ar gach aon bhealach ná an Béarla, go raibh tú go maith dá mba rud é gur labhair tú Gaeilge agus go raibh rud éigin mícheart leis an mBéarla. Bhí sé sin go láidir ann agus bhí an náisiúnachas, an Ghaeilge agus an Caitliceachas go léir measctha suas le chéile. Bhíodh siad ag rá, 'Is í an Ghaeilge teanga na n-aingeal ar neamh. Ní labhraíonn an diabhal í'. Is cuimhin liom é sin go maith.[13]

Cá bhfios nach as an díspeagadh a deineadh ní hamháin ar an mBéarla ach ar chanúint Ghaeilge a hathar nárbh iad canúintí oifigiúla na scoile iad a spreagadh spéis Ní Dhuibhne san imeall agus sa chuid sin den saol a mhaireann ar an gciumhais, más ciumhais na sochaí, imeall an náisiúin, nó teorainn an scéil féin é? Is féidir an beag is fiú a deineadh de chanúint a hathar sa chóras oideachais a thuiscint mar mheafar do thionscnamh liteartha Ní Dhuibhne chun aitheantas a thabhairt agus guth a bhronnadh ar an mionlach a bhrúitear faoi chois go minic. Feictear é seo go soiléir má scrúdaítear a leagan den eachtra úd in *Rotha Mór an tSaoil*. Seo an leagan atá in *Rotha Mór an tSaoil*:

Bhí fear as Cloich Cheannfhaola – fear de na Dálaigh – amuigh ansiud san am a raibh mise ann agus bhí bean bhreá dhóighiúil leis. Cha raibh siad i bhfad san áit agus cha raibh smaointiú acu ar chontúirt ar bith. D'imigh sé féin amach i gcionn a ghnoithe lá amháin agus d'fhág sé a bhean sa chábán ina dhiaidh. Is cosúil go bhfuair fear de na boic dhearga a shúil uirthise in am ínteacht agus gur luigh sé thart i bhfolach go bhfaca sé an fear ag imeacht. Nuair a fuair sé ar shiúl é tháinig sé chun cinn agus thug leis ise. Bhí scaifte dá chuid féin ag fuireachas air amuigh ar imeall na coilleadh a bhí in aice an bhaile; chaith siadsan ar dhruim beathaigh í agus thug leo as go brách síos chun an ghleanna í.

Nuair a phill an fear tráthnóna cha raibh tásc ná tuairisc le fáil ar a mhnaoi, ná cosúlacht ar bith ar an chábhán go dearnadh banachas tí ar bith ann ó mhaidin. Bhí an duine bocht san fhaopach ansin, agus nuair a chuaigh sé a chur a tuairisce fríd chábháin eile an bhaile bhig bhí a fhios ag na seanfhundúirí a bhí ansin gur dhuine de na fir dhearga a rinne a fuadach. Théigh fá dtaobh díobh ansin, chruinnigh iomlán fhir na háite le chéile, thug leo a gcuid gunnaí agus tharraing síos chun an ghleanna ar a lorg. Bhí rún acu troid agus cogadh a chur ar an mhuintir dhearga mura bhfaigheadh siad í.

Ádhmharach go leor, cha raibh troid ar bith ann. Nuair a shoichigh siad campa na nIndiach chonaic siad an bhean a raibh siad ar a lorg ina suí i measc scaifte acu ag doras ceann dá gcuid cábhán, agus comh luath agus a chonaic na hIndiaigh an bhaicle mhór seo ag tarraingt orthu fána gcuid arm, theith siad mar bheadh coiníní ann agus d'fhág siad ise ina ndiaidh. Fuair a fear féin ar ais í agus thug leis í chun an chábhán s'acu féin. Bhí an créatúr comh scanraithe agus nach ligfeadh sí a fear amach a dh'obair ní ba mhó agus cha sásódh a dhath í ach iad an dúiche sin a fhágáil ar fad amach. Chuidigh mianadóirí na háite go fial leo fhad agus bhí siad ag fanacht le himeacht. Rinne siad bailiúchán airgid dóibh agus d'imigh an bheirt acu isteach ar ais go sibhialtacht Mheiriceá. Mar sin féin, cha dearn an bhean sin maith go ndeachaigh sí i dtalamh. Bhí an croí scanraithe amach aisti, cé nach dearn na hIndiaigh díobháil ar bith di.[14]

Baineann an téacs seo le seánra faoi leith i gcanóin na litríochta Gaeilge, na dírbheathaisnéisí. Is seánra é a spreagadh cainteoirí dúchais le scríobh le linn bhlianta tosaigh an tSaorstáit ar an gcúis gur chuir siad eiseamláir ar fáil den saoránach agus den saol náisiúnta idéalach ar fáil. Mar a deir an criticeoir Anne McClintock, "the entry into autobiography, particularly, is seen as the entry into the political authority of self-representation".[15] Ba chuid d'fheachtas an Stáit iad na dírbheathaisnéisí seo chun athshamhlú a dhéanamh ar an tír agus ar an gcultúr. Ach ní hionann diúltú do leagan amháin den stair agus teacht slán ón éagóir dar le McClintock:

The production of oral history is a technology of power under contest and as such cannot be isolated from the context of power from which it emerges ... No oral history is innocent of selection, bias, evasion and interpretation. Very real imbalances of power remain in current contexts. Oral histories frequently perpetuate the hierarchy of mental and manual labor of the societies from which they emerge: the hierarchy that ranks those who work and speak differently from those who think and write.[16]

Nocht Ní Dhuibhne a hamhras féin faoin tsochaí a cruthaíodh in Éirinn tar éis chogadh na Saoirse. Bhí tionchar faoi leith, dar léi, ag an náisiúnachas ar shochaí na hÉireann nach raibh fóntúil ná sláintiúil:

What one would be aware of historically is that Irish nationalism constitutes a backlash against everything that's British, but has produced a terribly rigidly Catholic, censorial, punitive society which evolved after independence and which most people now would have enormous problems with. We have a legacy of a rigid, illiberal, punishing society which kept women and children down and was frightened of every sexual impulse and of writing. One of the legacies is constant reaction and constant change. Stability can't happen in any society, but it's impossible for a postcolonial society to have cultural stability. Many reactions have to occur before Ireland is a place where a constant, stable identity can be established.[17]

Sna dírbheathaisnéisí a cumadh, a scríobhadh agus a foilsíodh sa Ghaeilge, bhí tuiscint an-chinnte, an-soiléir, an-chúng ar an iompar, ar an gcultúr, ar an gcleachtas poiblí a rabhthas ag tnúth leo ó shaoránaigh an Stáit óig. An 'bhean bhreá dhóighiúil' seo nach dtugtar a hainm féin di le linn na hinsinte anseo, baintear gach údarás a bhí aici di díreach mar a tharla i gcás chanúint athair Ní Dhuibhne. Is ann di mar thug an Dálach ann í, agus is 'leis' a bhí sí. 'Fágtar' í, 'leagtar súil' uirthi agus 'tugtar' leis í. Easpa oibre a thugann le fios nach ann di agus tuigtear do na seanfhondúirí ar an bpointe gur fuadaíodh í. Ní bheadh i gceist go deo go n-imeodh sí as a stuaim féin, ná go mbeartódh sí gníomhú ar a bonn féin. Ní bheadh an cumas ná an indibhidiúlacht sin inti mar bhean, de réir thuiscint an scéil. Níl inti ach típ a sheasann do gach bean, díreach mar a sheasann an té dúchasach dá phobal ar fad. Mar a dúirt Edward W. Said: "When photographs or texts are used merely to establish identity and presence – to give us merely representative images of the Woman, or the Indian – they enter what Berger call a control sysem".[18] Is é atá mar sprioc ag an gcóras seo ná ionad na mban, ról na bhfear agus imeallú na ndúchasach a léiriú go soiléir. I saothair áirithe, ar nós shaothar Ní Dhuibhne, áfach, tugtar aghaidh ar an éagóir seo agus "those people compelled by the system to play subordinate or imprisoning roles within it emerge as conscious antagonists, disrupting it, proposing claims, advancing arguments that dispute the totalitarian compulsions".[19]

Aimsítear an bhean seo i measc na ndúchasach agus beirtear abhaile í. Neach gan chumas, gan phearsantacht, gan smacht ar bith aici ar a saol ná ar a cinniúint sa scéal seo is ea í. Léiríonn an sliocht seo argóint de chuid Nuala Ní Dhomhnaill gurb ionann cás na mban agus cás na Gaeilge go minic:

Cuireadh faoi chois sinn araon, cuireadh lasmuigh de struchtúr sóisialta, creidimh agus cumhachta an Stáit sinn. D'fhanamair faoi cheilt, gan ainm gan aibítear, ár spiorad beo inár gcuid cainte ach scoite amach ón litríocht agus fiú ón litearthacht. D'fhan an t-anam baineann beo i measc na ngnáthdhaoine nach raibh aon tóir acu ar rachmas ná ar mheas an tsaoil ná aon fháil acu orthu fiú dá mbeadh an tóir dhéin ann. Mar sin urlabhra seo ar mheon na mban agus tá deilbh agus cruth na teanga fíoroiriúnach do litríocht ban.[20]

Roghnaíonn Ní Dhuibhne an fothscéal seo ó *Rotha Mór an tSaoil* agus athshlamhlaíonn sí é ionas go mbronntar dínit agus cumhacht ar an mbean. Deintear duine di le neamhspleáchas, le dúil agus le mothúcháin. Tagann an cur chuige seo leis an léamh feimineach a dtagraíonn Elke D'hoker dó ina halt ar shaothar Ní Dhuibhne: "Ní Dhuibhne's feminist rewriting of the traditional folktale and her retranslation of it in several other stories set in contemporary Ireland, has the effect of investing an otherwise ancient story with new life".[21] Déantar athnuachan ar an mbunscéal agus gintear "new relevance as an interpretation of choices and problems women are still faced with".[22] Ní haon ionadh go mbeadh bean de ghlúin Ní

Dhuibhne tógtha leis an bhfeimineachas agus le cothrom na Féinne a bhronnadh ar na mná a díbríodh ó ardán an tsaoil rompu. Is féidir meon na seascaidí i leith na mban agus ionad na mban sa tsochaí a bhlaiseadh ó chur síos Maeve Flanagan ina cuimhní cinn dar teideal *Dev, Lady Chatterley and Me: A 60s Suburban Childhood*, leabhar a chuireann síos ar shaol mná ag teacht in aois i mbruachbhaile Bhaile Átha Cliath sna seascaidí:

All through school we learned in Irish classes about what happened the day Mammy got sick. We learned the necessary vocabulary and then we wrote our own accounts of what happened in our own homes when our mothers got sick. These books operated on the premise that when a mammy got sick a replacement was needed on the domestic front; in those texts Mammy was always replaced by another female. Depending on our given linguistics proficiency, we wrote what we do, what we did, or what we might do; there was no escaping this particular scenario. It was always a Máire or a Síle who scuabed the *urlár* and prepared a *dinnéar breá blasta* for a *Daidí*, a Diarmuid and a few Pádraigs. A series of wan little Cinderellas dragged hoovers across ugly schoolbook livingrooms; they carted trays up to their *Maimís* in their *leabas*; they beamed in gratitude when Daddy and the lads thanked them for the lovely dinners.

I was sick and tired of it all: our home, the rows and this nonsense in the Irish books, 'Glug, glug, glug'. I sucked a full barrel of ink into my fountain pen and I began. I couldn't have cared less about good or bad marks. I wanted to have my say, for once and for all, and with no repercussions. The anonymity of the public exam system was too good an opportunity to miss. I called for more paper; my friend glanced across at me in horror. 'Glug, glug, glug'; I filled another barrel of ink; there was no stopping me! As long as my *briathra neamhrialta* held out I would be fine. I had lived with Mary Kenny, the *Irish Press* and my parents; a few *briathra neamhrialta* were nothing to an old battle-scarred campaigner![23]

Treisíodh ról neodrach neamhghníomhach spleách na mban trí théacsanna ar nós *Rotha Mór an tSaoil* agus na dtéacsanna scoile agus is sa chomhthéacs cultúrtha sochtheangeolaíochta seo is cóir agus is cuí saothar agus togra scríbhneoireachta Ní Dhuibhne a mheas.

Ba é *Dúnmharú sa Daingean* – 'Part Bridget Jones and part Miss Marple' a bhain duais an Oireachtais 2000 sa chatagóir

'Úrscéal don Phobal' – an chéad úrscéal Gaeilge a d'fhoilsigh Ní Dhuibhne. Ba í breith Phóil Uí Mhuirí san *Irish Times* air ná:

an enjoyable read that won't stretch the reader's Irish or imagination too much. The opening chapters on the vacuity of life in the Temple Bar art scene and traveling on the DART are perceptive and there's a wry sense of humour and light touch throughout. That said, there are narrative weaknesses – in one ungracious moment, Saoirse mentally criticises a recently murdered acquaintance for holding up her development as an artist! – and some very nasty literal translations from English – 'rás na bhFrancach', being one particularly painful example.[24]

Is fíor don léirmheastóir gur 'beautifully produced volume' é ach ina ainneoin sin, áfach, tá laigí sa phlota. Braitear easpa teannais tríd an scéal ar fad, goilleann an chríoch lag éigcinnte ar an léitheoir agus is steiréitíopaí iad go leor de na carachtair ann.

Is úrscéal do dhéagóirí é *Hurlamaboc*, an tríú húrscéal uaithi, agus is teistiméireacht é go bhfuil glúin na ngaelscoileanna ag teacht aníos agus úrscéalta de dhíth orthu agus nach leor na clasaicigh liteartha ná na beathaisnéisí cáiliúla dóibh. Cé gur úrscéal é atá dírithe ar dhéagóirí, is fíor go n-oirfeadh sé d'fhoghlaimeoirí fásta leis. Tá plota maith anseo agus moladh dá réir tuillte ag an úrscéal seo. D'fhógair Ciarán Mac Murchaidh an méid seo a leanas:

Tá leibhéal na teanga éasca go leor agus níor chóir go gcuirfeadh sé stró rómhór ar léitheoirí óga an leabhar a láimhseáil. Mar sin féin, beidh caighdeán measartha maith Gaeilge de dhíth ar léitheoir chun an scéal a léamh ar a shuaimhneas. Taitneoidh an úsáid fhorleathan a bhaintear as gnáth-theanga dhéagóirí an lae inniu le léitheoirí óga – na téarmaí sin atá ag an aos óg ón teilifís nó as a measc féin, *cool, No way!, bogger, scobie, creep* agus a leithéid.[25]

Ar nós *Dúnmharú sa Daingean*, tá móitíf an aistir lárnach in *Hurlamaboc* a bhain 'Gradam Feabhais BISTO' sa bhliain 2007.[26] Más soir go dtí an Bhreatain Bheag a théann Ruán in *Hurlamaboc*, is siar ó dheas go Ciarraí a shireann Saoirse chun éalú ó chaidreamh briste nuair a chailleann sí a post i ndámhlann ardchathrach in *Dúnmharú sa Daingean*.

Admhaíonn Ní Dhuibhne gur d'aon ghnó a fheictear an mhóitíf áirithe seo ina saothar:

Seift a mbainim úsáid aisti go minic i mo shaothar ficsin, idir ghearrscéalta agus úrscéalta, agus ar bhaineas leas aisti freisin sa dráma *Milseog an tSamhraidh*, ná an t-aistear, go háirithe aistear ina mbíonn athrú nó aistriú ó réigiún teanga amháin go réigiún eile i gceist. Mar shampla, in *The Dancers Dancing*, téann Orla agus a cairde ó Bhaile Átha Cliath go dtí an Ghaeltacht i nDún na nGall. Turas den saghas céanna a dhéanann Saoirse in *Dúnmharú sa Daingean*, nuair a fhágann sí an phríomhchathair le cur fúithi i nGaeltacht Chiarraí ar feadh tréimhse, agus a dhéanann Máire in *Cailíní Beaga Ghleann na mBláth*. Sna gearrscéalta 'Gweedore Girl', 'The Pale Gold of Alaska', agus sa dráma *Milseog an tSamhraidh* (a thosaigh amach mar ghearrscéal, 'Summer Pudding') is sa treo eile a théann na carachtair, ón nGaeltacht go dtí an Ghalltacht, nó i gcás *Milseog an tSamhraidh* trasna na farraige go dtí an Bhreatain Bheag agus i gcás 'The Pale Gold of Alaska' ó Thír Chonaill go Philadelphia agus ansin as sin go Klondike (an turas a dhein Micí Mac Gabhann in *Rotha Mór an tSaoil*), a spreag mé chun an scéal áirithe sin a scríobh.[27]

Sonraítear móitíf an aistir in *Cailíní Beaga Ghleann na mBláth* [28] an tarna húrscéal Gaeilge uaithi ach amháin nach aistear fisiciúil amháin atá i gceist ach filleadh meafarach ar an óige, turas siar ar imní agus ar uafás na hóige. Ní foláir don phríomhcharachtar cuairt a thabhairt ar *trauma* agus ar ionad an *trauma* a scanraigh í agus í óg. Is ar turas a chailltear a fear céile le linn an scéil agus is gá galar a hiníne a leigheas má tá sise le tabhairt faoina saol féin a chaitheamh, turas ann féin. Agus Máire, príomhcharachtar an úrscéil ina luí ina leaba agus í náirithe ag Juliet os comhair an tsaoil de bharr í a bheith bocht, feictear í "ina bunc, ina dúiseacht, bóithríní fada dorcha na náire á dtaisteal go neirbhíseach aici" (*CB* 121). Críochnaíonn an scéal agus Máire ag tabhairt faoin aistear a dhein sí i dteannta le muintir Juliette – Mrs. Smith agus Mr. Mac Gabhann – na blianta fada roimhe sin. Ach mar a thuigtear di, ní féidir filleadh; ní hann don áit ná don am sin a thuilleadh. Níl ann ach a leagan pearsanta den stair agus a leagan féin den scéal, scéal a chum sí agus a leanann sí uirthi á chumadh. Mar a deir sí féin: "Níl aici ach a cuimhne féin agus na hargóintí a mhaireann fós inti, na hiarsmaí sin a tháinig slán ó stoirmeacha an tsaoil" (180). In ainneoin gur éirigh léi snámh a fhoghlaim le linn an chúrsa sa choláiste Gaeilge agus gur ghlac sí páirt sna cluichí Oilimpeach a d'Éirinn ina dhiaidh sin, níor éirigh léi riamh imeachtaí an tsamhraidh sin a chur di. Leanann na heachtraí agus tionchar na n-eachtraí í ar feadh a saoil go dtí oíche amháin, i lár stoirme, go gcuirtear iachall uirthi aghaidh a thabhairt ar an scéal agus ar a saol an athuair.

Is fearr i bhfad *Cailíní Beaga Ghleann na mBláth* ná ceachtar den dá úrscéal eile. Dar le Ó Muirí "Is é cuspóir an fhiontair seo an léitheoir a choinneáil ag léamh agus éiríonn le Ní Dhuibhne sin a dhéanamh i dteanga thar a bheith bunúsach. X-ghathú den teanga atá déanta aici – is léir cnámha an choirp ach níl feoil ar bith air. Ní peaca ar bith é sin. Léitheoireacht liteartha seachas litríocht atá i gceist".[29] Ba mholtaí Alan Titley faoin leabhar agus is é atá ann, dar leis, ná "novel of memory and guilt":

The narrative is split complementary between the past and the present, illuminating both. This deceptively simple story is a pleasure to read. The writing is clear, plain, lucid and stylish. The artistry on the surface goes a long way down. Everyday emotions are invested with a charge that becomes more clear when people talk to one another. Éilís Ní Dhuibhne is equally accomplished in dealing with the worry of a mother whose child has emotionally departed and with the pain of a young girl meeting her own age in an environment of freedom for the first time. The petty jealousies, the backbiting and the bitchiness are truly terrifying, just as the small successes are hugely uplifting. In some ways, this is the story of a generation that went to a certain kind of Irish college, and of another generation that has lots of words for the ailments of modern living but no more wisdom than before. While the story is compulsive and drives the novel along, we are being invited to think about other things as well. Even the most organised of lives can be overtaken by events, and irrational beasts lurk in the undergrowth of the suburban garden. Small ticks of personality can turn the world upside down. The past can be revisited, but it is never the same place. Éilís Ní Dhuibhne has shown in her Irish and English fiction that she is a readers' writer. They deserve this.[30]

Ní hí an chéad scríbhneoir comhaimseartha chun leas a bhaint as an institiúid áirithe seo mar shuíomh ná mar théama; bhain an drámadóir Antaine Ó Flatharta ceol as cheana ina dhráma iontach *Gaeilgeoirí* (1986). Go deimhin tá ceol bainte ag Ní Dhuibhne as ábhar agus as suíomh an choláiste Gaeilge ní hamháin ina saothar Gaeilge ach ina saothar Béarla leis. Lonnaíodh a húrscéal *The Dancers Dancing* – "her linguistically innovative novel … captures the complex bilingual experience of life"[31] – sa Ghaeltacht agus is fearr é mar shaothar dar le Pádraigín Riggs and Norman Vance, ná *Cailíní Beaga Ghleann na mBláth*:

> Two of her novels, *The Dancers Dancing* (1999) and *Cailíní Beaga Ghleann na mBláth/The Little Girls of Gleann na mBláth* (2003), each of which could be described as a Bildungsroman, document the experiences of young girls attending an Irish language summer course. Although set in an Irish-speaking environment, both novels are narrated from an English-speaking perspective. Ní Dhuibhne's English-medium novel is, however, more stylistically assured and more convincing than her novel in Irish.[32]

Aithníonn formhór an phobail léitheoireachta in Éirinn an suíomh seo – an coláiste samhraidh Gaeilge. Gné choitianta is ea a leithéid i go leor leor tíortha ar fud na cruinne agus is dlúthchuid de ghnáththaithí mheánaicme na hÉireann í. Bhunaigh Conradh na Gaeilge na coláistí samhraidh sa bhliain 1904, mar thoradh ar scéim Thomáis Uí Dhónaill, feisire na Sasana do Chiarraí Theas. Bunaíodh iad chun oiliúint a chur ar mhúinteoirí scoile a bhí ag tabhairt faoi mhúineadh na Gaeilge mar chuid den scéim dhátheangach.[33] Mar a deir Caitríona Ó Torna ina leabhar *Cruthú na Gaeltachta 1893–1922: Samhlú agus Buanú Chonstráid na Gaeltachta i rith na hAthbheochana*: "Bealach ab ea na scoileanna agus coláistí Gaeilge a bunaíodh sna ceantair Ghaeltachta le struchtúr a chur ar an líon ard daoine a raibh fonn orthu an teanga a fhoghlaim agus a chleachtadh i gcroílár phobal na teanga beo".[34] Ba i mBéal Átha an Ghaorthaidh i gContae Chorcaí, faoi stiúir an Chonartha, a bunaíodh Coláiste na Mumhan, an chéad choláiste Gaeilge. Níorbh fhada gur scaip an coincheap agus bunaíodh coláistí Gaeilge ar fud na tíre. Tuairiscíonn Ó Torna:

> Faoi cheann dhá bhliain, bhí sé choláiste oiliúna ann – Coláiste Chonnacht i dTuar Mhic Éadaigh, Iolscoil na Mumhan sa Rinn,

Coláiste Chomhghaill i mBéal Feirste, Ardscoil Cholmchille i gCloich Cheann Fhaolaidh agus Coláiste Laighean i mBaile Átha Cliath. Coláistí cathrach ab iad na coláistí geimhridh, Coláiste Chomhghaill agus Coláiste Laighean, seachas coláistí á reáchtáil sa samhradh mar a bhí i gceist leis na coláistí sna ceantair Ghaeltachta.[35]

Tháinig fás agus forbairt ar na coláistí úd ó shin i leith agus is cuid lárnach anois iad de thaithí dhéagóirí meánaicmeacha na hÉireann. Sa réamhrá a chuir an t-úrscéalaí Rose Doyle le cnuasach litreacha a scríobh mic léinn le linn dóibh a bheith 'sa Ghaeltacht', d'fhógair sí an méid seo a leanas:

Other cultures have camps, schools and activity centres for their young to play and grow up in during the summer months. We have the Gaeltacht ... Unique and wholly homegrown, the Gaeltacht colleges have been a rite of passage for hundreds of thousands of Irish youngsters since the state itself was a stripling. The Gaeltacht is where girls meet boys and boys girls for the first time away from their parents. The agonies of homesickness strike first at the Gaeltacht and it's also where, recovered from homesickness, youngsters enjoy their first, heady savourings of freedom and independence. Friends are made for life at the Gaeltacht, hearts are broken, the value of money is first appreciated and young palates begin to discover that hunger is good sauce. And it all, of course, happens as Gaeilge.[36]

Is féidir togra athscríobh Ní Dhuibhne a shonrú anseo arís. Bréagnaíonn úrscéal Ní Dhuibhne an íomhá rómánsúil útóipeach seo den choláiste samhraidh. Ní cairde saoil atá ag Máire i ndiaidh an choláiste, ach a mhalairt ar fad. Múnlaíodh dearcadh Mháire i leith na teanga agus i leith an Bhéarla ach go háirithe le linn di a bheith ar an gcoláiste. Mar a deir Máirín Nic Eoin: "tá íoróin bhunúsach ag roinnt le léiriú an Bhéarla i suíomh an choláiste samhraidh, cé gurbh é sin an suíomh sóisialta is coitianta a nglactar le Béarla ann i bhficsean agus i ndrámaíocht na Gaeilge ...".[37] B'ann a tuigeadh di go raibh canúintí éagsúla ann, go raibh ord agus eagar ar aicmí sóisialta agus feictear an fhorbairt sin sna litreacha a scríobhann sí abhaile, go háirithe sna beannachtaí agus sna leaganacha a thugann sí ar a máthair. Seoltar don champa í chun Gaeilge a fhoghlaim ach is ann a thuigtear di go bhfuil canúintí áirithe

Béarla ann agus go bhfuil fochultúr agus tuiscint aicmeach laistiar díobh. Tuigeann Máire go dteastaíonn uaithi dul chun cinn a dhéanamh sa saol agus tosaíonn sí ag tóraíocht saol sona foirfe a chuireann iachall uirthi gnéithe áirithe dá saol agus dá canúint a dhíbirt. Ba dhlúthchuid é an taithí seo, dar leis an úrscéalaí Joseph O'Connor, den phróiseas a mhúnlaigh aos óg na cathrach, agus a bhaist i dtobar an náisiúnachais iad: "Many a 1970s Dublin suburban teenager was sent there in the summers to learn to speak Irish and to experience the purported authenticity that life in Ireland's housing estates did not provide ... you returned, ruddily celticised, to the modernising country where the BBC and Marc Bolan were your cultural touchstones".[38] Leagann an fuirseoir Des Bishop, fear nár fhoghlaim an Ghaeilge le linn dó a bheith ar scoil in Éirinn de bharr go raibh díolúine ó scrúdú aige, a mhéar ar thábhacht na gcoláistí i múnlú an náisiúin. Goilleann sé air nár ghlac sé páirt sa taithí lárnach seo de chuid na hÉireann: "I thought I knew everything about Ireland, yet there's this Irish-speaking culture that's been here the whole time I've been here, and I know nothing about it. As someone who claims to be an observer of Irish society, it's a pretty big hole if you know nothing about this Irish-speaking culture".[39] Seo mar a chuir Ní Dhuibhne féin síos ar an nGaeltacht in agallamh a cuireadh uirthi agus í ag freagairt ceiste faoi *The Dancers Dancing:*

> The setting of the novel in the Gaeltacht, the Irish speaking region of Ireland, is something I experienced, but the characters are not based on real people, to any extent. The novel is, to put it simply, about some Dublin teenage girls who go to the west of Ireland to learn Irish at an institution known as 'Irish College'. I think this particular institution is a very interesting one, unique, and quite central to the experience of many Irish adolescents. In reality, as in the novel, it tends to be a rite of passage experience. Often it is the first time that Irish children are separated from their parents for any length of time. (We don't have a very strong boarding-school tradition.) But although 'going to the Gaeltacht' is such a seminal teenage experience here, it has seldom, if ever, been described in any depth in literature. So I thought it would be a good idea to do that. I also wanted to explore various issues relating to Irish language and cultural identity, and used the novel for this purpose. Finally, I wanted to write about the wildness of young girls on the

brink of adulthood, on their attraction to risk and danger, and about their affinity with the natural world.[40]

San úrscéal atá idir chamáin anseo, *Cailíní Beaga Ghleann na mBláth*, is coláiste Gaeilge nó coláiste samhraidh atá lonnaithe sa Ghalltacht i gCúige Mumhan atá i gceist, "cé nach sa Ghaeltacht atá Gleann na mBláth in aon chor, ach i gceartlár na Galltachta, ceantar atá níos Gallda, más mian leat an téarma sin a úsáid, ná an áit atá siad a fhágáil ina ndiaidh. Coláiste Samhraidh … Capsúl Gaelach i gceartlár ceantair nach bhfuil ann ach Béarla" (*CB* 34). Is léir nach bhfuiltear ródhian ar riail na Gaeilge sa choláiste seo – "Níl siad dáiríre faoi riail ar bith ann. An aidhm atá acu ná go mbeadh saoire dheas ag na cailíní, agus má éiríonn leo cúpla focal Gaeilge a fhoghlaim, bhuel is buntáiste breise é sin. Áit shibhialta shuaimhneach is ea é" (77). Tagraítear do bhéaloideas na gcoláistí éagsúla in imeacht an scéil:

Ní hamhlaidh do na coláistí ar fad. Tá cuid acu an-righin, cuireann siad abhaile thú má bheireann siad ort ag agus trí fhocal Béarla á rá agat as a chéile. Tá cara ag Úna – 'Well, more of an acquaintance actually' – agus thit sé den rothar agus ghortaigh sé a cheann agus dúirt, gan smaoineamh, 'Oh! My God!' Bhí an phian go huafásach. Ach bhí múinteoir ag éisteacht agus cuireadh abhaile é ar an gcéad traein eile. Trí fhocal Béarla. 'Oh! My! God!' (Agus conas a chruthaíodar gur focal Béarla é 'Oh!'? Ar litrigh sé é? (77–8)

Cuid den bhéaloideas comhaimseartha is ea an mac léinn a dhíbrítear abhaile ón gcoláiste Gaeilge as ráiteas neamh-chomhfhiosach Béarla agus a insítear chun déine na hinstitiúide a léiriú agus míréasúntacht na dteagascóirí Gaeilge a chruthú. Ach ní hé seo an t-aon leas a bhaintear as an mbéaloideas comhaimseartha sa saothar seo. Is nós le léirmheastóirí béim a chur ar an leas a bhaineann Ní Dhuibhne as an mbéaloideas ina saothar. Is iondúil, áfach, go samhlaítear an teagmháil seo mar phróiseas aontreo, go mbaintear leas as béaloideas agus as oidhreacht bhéil na Gaeilge chun ábhar a sholáthar do scéal comhaimseartha an Bhéarla. Ach aithneoidh an té a léigh 'Death by Landscape'[41] le Margaret Atwood cosúlachtaí idir é agus *Cailíní Beaga Ghleann na mBláth* agus an gearrscéal Béarla 'The Day Elvis Presley Died'.[42] Dar le léirmheastóir amháin:

Tá dhá scéal á insint anseo faoin duine céanna, Máire Ní Bhraonáin, cailín beag naoi mbliana d'aois, agus bean leathchéad bliain d'aois. Ar bhealach éigin tá an dá scéal fite fuaite ina chéile ach ní thagann na snáthanna uile le chéile go dtí go dtarlaíonn stoirm mhillteanach a chuireann aláram an tí ag bualadh i lár na hoíche de dheasca gearradh cumhachta.[43]

Ar leibhéal amháin, tagann Máire slán. Tugann sí an snámh léi. Leanann sí uirthi ag snámh agus téann sí san iomaíocht sna cluichí Oilimpeacha ar son na hÉireann. Ach ní insítear riamh an fhírinne faoinar thit amach ag an gcampa an samhradh áirithe sin agus fiú ag deireadh an úrscéil níltear iomlán cinnte an timpiste a bhain de Juliet, nó ar mharaigh Diarmuid – an múinteoir óg – í, nó arbh í Máire féin a dhein é mar dhíoltas. I gcomparáid leis na scéalta a pléadh ag tús na haiste seo, baineann an t-úrscéal seo le bean a roghnaigh gan labhairt seachas bean nár tugadh cead ná deis cainte di. Filleann an feall ar an bhfeallaire agus an bhean nár inis an fhírinne agus í ina páiste, níl sí in ann cumarsáid ar bith a dhéanamh lena hiníon féin anois. Is soiléir an fadhb chumarsáide ó thús. Chlis ar Mháire an fhírinne faoinar thit amach do Juliet i nGleann na mBláth a nochtadh agus tá an easpa cumarsáide sin fillte mar fheall uirthi agus ar a clann, nach clann iad ach "daoine a roinneann a teach léi: Muiris, a fear céile, Dara, a mac, agus Emma, a hiníon" (CB 3). Tá easpa cainte agus easpa comhrá le sonrú sa teach. "Ciúnas. Tá an seomra trom le ciúnas, tá an ciúnas ina luí air mar a bheadh ainmhí mór gránna ina luí ar leanbh óg, á thachtadh" (18). Is mór idir an ciúnas seo agus an cogar mogar leanúnach a bhí le braistint sa champa samhraidh agus a bhfuil a scéal fite fuaite le scéal Mháire agus a clainne sa lá atá inniu ann. Is beag caidreamh atá aici lena mac, Muiris: "Ní labhraíonn sé go hoscailte le Máire riamh, agus is beag a bhíonn le rá aige lena athair, cé go mbíonn sé cainteach go leor ar an nguthán agus a chairde féin ar an líne" (5). Ach is measa ar fad cás a hiníne, Emma a bhfuil galar gan ainm uirthi.

Tuigtear go forleathan an leas a bhaintear as athrá sa litríocht bhéil agus is minic san úrscéal go bhfeictear athrá ag leibhéal na teanga agus ag leibhéal an phlota. Tá comparáid le déanamh idir an pionós a ghearrtar ar Juliet sa champa nuair a ghoideann sí cruas milseán Choncepta. Nuair a dhiúltaítear labhairt léi: "Níl ach an t-aon phionós amháin ar fáil dóibh, mar chailíní, mar dhaoine baineanna: gan caint léi" (126). Is ionann a taithí agus taithí Emma cé gurbh í féin a roghnaíonn gan labhairt le haon duine eile. Ach sa dá chás, feictear Máire agus náire uirthi faoina bhfuil ag titim amach. Go minic sa leabhar feictear an eachtra chéanna á cleachtadh faoi dhó – tús chaibidil a hocht mar a bhfuil an triúr ag déanamh neamhshuime de Juliet agus Emma ag tabhairt neamhairde ar a muintir. Feictear Máire ar imeall an chomhluadair sa leabhar nuair atá cogarnaíl ar bun: "Agus tá Máire lasmuigh den tsiosarnach sin ar fad. Tá sí uaigneach, ina haonar, ag spaisteoireacht timpeall ag iarraidh duine éigin, duine ar bith, a aimsiú, duine a tharraingeoidh isteach sa chiorcal draíochta í, ciorcal na gcailíní" (80). Feictear an t-athrá struchtúrtha céanna sa tsiopadóireacht a dhéanann Máire le hEmma sula dtéann sí chun na Fraince agus an t-ullmhúchán a dhein a máthair féin le cabhair Mrs. Smith sular chuaigh sí go Gleann na mBláth (69–70). Feictear arís é nuair a chuireann Máire an turas ó Bhleá Cliath trí Chill Dara agus trí Chaiseal na Mumhan go Gleann na mBláth an athuair tar éis dá fear céile bás a fháil i dtionóisc gluaisteáin. Is í an athimirt is spéisiúla ar fad áfach ná nuair atá Máire ag tabhairt faoi dhul ag snámh sa linn den chéad uair riamh. Tugtar poc sa droim di – Juliet is dócha – agus caitear san uisce í. "Glug glug. Téann sí faoi uisce, tarraingíonn anáil, líonann a scamhóga le huisce. Glug glug glug, tá eagla an domhain uirthi, tá sí á bá, ní thig léi aer a fháil, tá sí i gcruachás … Croitheann sí a ceann, is cuma léi faoi rud ar bith ach an t-uisce sin a dhoirteach amach as a corp" (61). Ar theacht slán di, feiceann sí Juliet "ar imeall na linne, ag briseadh a croí ag gáirí" (61):

> Tá na cailíní eile i bhfeighil a gcúraimí féin. De réir dealraimh níor thug duine ar bith faoi deara cad a tharla, é sin nó is cuma leo. Ceapann Juliet gur greann a bhí ann, cleas beag greannmhar. Ní fiú aon rud a rá. Ní féidir aon rud a rá, tá Juliet lasmuigh agus tá sise istigh, tá glór na gcailíní chomh hard sin nach gcloisfidh Juliet ag

gearán í fiú dá ndéanfadh sí gearán. (Tá an glór cosúil le glór leathmhilliún gainéad ag screadaíl ar charraig.) (62)

Is é an suíomh céanna atá le sonrú ag buaicphointe an scéil nuair a thagann Máire ar Juliet tar éis d'fhear éigin ionsaí, b'fhéidir, a dhéanamh ar Juliet a fhágann i gcruachás ar an trá í le cos agus easna bhriste. Le caoineadh na bhfaoileán agus séideadh na gaoithe isteach agus amach sna góilíní agus na scoilteanna, ní chloistear guth Juliet agus filleann Máire ar an gcampa. "Níl le cloisteáil anois ach an fharraige agus an ghaoth agus an fhearthainn agus na faoileáin. Siansa feargach aoibhinn" (178). Fuarthas Juliet caite i ngóilín idir charraigeacha ar an trá úd trí lá tar éis do na cailíní sa *chalet* na múinteoirí a chur ar an eolas nár fhill sí abhaile an lá sin. Tagtar uirthi faoi dheireadh gan aithne gan urlabhra, a cromán briste agus a cuid easnacha briste. Cailltear tar éis tamaill san ospidéal í.

Ar bhuanna an úrscéil ná an éiginnteacht a bhaineann leis an gclabhsúr seo. Ní fios arbh é an fear úd "ag siúl go tapa, nach mór ag rith, a cheann cromtha cé go bhfuil sé ag siúl leis an ngaoth, *anorak* dúghorm air agus cochall á chlúdach" (176) a bhí "ag siúl sa treo eile, ní ar an gcosán ach ar an bhféar, ar ais ón trá i dtreo an choláiste" (175–6) a dhein an drochghníomh. Tá deis ag Máire teacht i dtír ar a compánach scoile nuair a chloiseann sí í ag glaoch agus ag impí uirthi ach tugann Máire droim láimhe di de bharr an masla a caitheadh léi faoina hathair agus faoi na táillí. Níl ag an léitheoir ag an deireadh ach leagan den scéal. Mar a deirtear san úrscéal: "Sa leagan den scéal a insíonn sí anois, níl sise ar an trá in aon chor in éineacht le Juliet. Sa leagan seo, téann Juliet síos ina haonar, titeann san fharraige agus báitear í. D'aimsigh iascairí a corp roinnt laethanta ina dhiaidh sin" (158).

Tagann Máire slán as an eachtra agus as an gcampa. Leanann sí uirthi leis an snámh agus is ball d'fhoireann na hÉireann sna cluichí Oilimpeacha sa bhliain 1974 í in ainneoin nach mbuann sí bonn. Ach ní féidir éalú ón stair ná ón eachtra lárnach seo. Is ionann í go pointe agus an bhean nár ainmníodh i scéal Mhicí Mhic Gabhann: "Mar sin féin, cha dearn an bhean sin maith go ndeachaigh sí i dtalamh. Bhí an croí scanraithe amach aisti, cé nach dearn na hIndiaigh díobháil ar bith di".[44] Is saothar in aisce go minic é in úrscéalta Ní Dhuibhne an tóir ar an sonas buan.

Ag deireadh an scéil, filleann sí ar Ghleann na mBláth agus is cúis díomá di go bhfuil an seanteach leagtha agus óstán nua tógtha ina áit. An rud nár "éirigh leis na Buachaillí Bána ná le hArm na Poblachta ná fiú amháin le Diarmuid Ó Súilleabháin é a scrios … d'éirigh leis an dream seo, lucht an rachmais, ar leo óstáin ar fud na cruinne, d'éirigh leo é a leagan, agus teach úrnua a thógáil ina áit; teach úrnua ar dhéanamh seantí, ach gan é cosúil le Gleann na mBláth" (172). Cé gur "cosúla an áit anois leis an bhfís a bhí ag Máire sular leag sí súil riamh ar Ghleann na mBláth … Is deise é ná an fhís sin a bhíodh aici, fiú amháin. Is iontach na rudaí deasa is féidir leis an airgead a chur ar fáil" (173). Seachas "giotaí beaga de na colúin a bhíodh ag tabhairt tacaíochta don phóirse Dórach, píosa beag de cholún briste i gcúinne plásóige, giota beag eile greamaithe isteach i mballa nua … níl iarsma ar bith eile san áit de Ghleann na mBláth mar a bhíodh, go bhfeictear di" (173–4). Ach nuair a dhruideann sí i leith, "áit a raibh fothain ón ngrian agus ó sholas geal an deiscirt, áit a raibh cúinní rúnda ina bhféadfaí rud ar bith a cheilt" (174) buaileann faitíos í agus filleann sí ar an trá. Is féidir an tagairt dhébhríoch seo a thuiscint mar nod do thimpiste Juliet nó do chumas na haigne eolas agus stair a cheilt.

Téama coitianta ag sníomh tríd an úrscéal ar fad is ea an 'sonas' agus cad is brí leis nó cad a chiallaíonn an téarma úd. Tá dhá shainmhíniú foclóra ag tús an leabhair agus ardaítear an cheist go luath sa tarna caibidil:

Agus tá cumhacht thar cuimse ag na focail sin, 'chalet', 'private swimming pool', agus 'boating'. Cad a chiallaíonn na focail sin nuair a shuimíonn tú le chéile iad ach 'Aoibhneas' nó 'Sonas'? An rud atá Máire ag iarraidh a bhaint amach di féin, sonas foirfe, agus tá anois le fáil ach greim a fháil ar na híomhánna iontacha sin atá á dtairiscint ag an duine a scríobh an paimfléad sin faoi Ghleann na mBláth. (24)

Tá Máire, an príomhcharachtar, sa tóir ar an sonas foirfe de shíor. Is é an tóir seo i ndiaidh an tsonais fhoirfe a stiúrann agus, i ndeireadh na dála, a loiteann a saol. Ina ainneoin seo, áfach, ní hionann an fhís agus an fhírinne. Samhlaíodh di ar léamh na bpaimfléad ón gcampa samhraidh go mbeadh saol foirfe ann, ach ní hamhlaidh: "*The girls will live in individual chalets. The girls will live in a disused concentration camp, in need of some modernization.* Ba chóngaraí sin don fhírinne" (42). Is ionann an scéal dá saol féin agus í nuaphósta nuair a shantaigh sí post maith nó páiste:

> Bhí sí míshásta an uair sin leis an tslí bheatha a bhí aici, agus bhí sí míshásta freisin toisc nach raibh leanbh aici. Shíl sí dá mbeadh deis aici obair a bheith aici a bhain leis an rud ab ansa léi, cúrsaí spóirt, agus dá n-éireodh léi leanbh a ghiniúint agus a shaolú, shíl sí go mbeadh saol foirfe aici, go mbeadh sí sona sásta. Bheadh sí sona sásta go deo na ndeor agus ní bheadh aon ní de dhíth uirthi. Níorbh aon ghearrcach í ag an am sin ach an oiread, ach bhí sí fós óg go leor chun a chreidiúint go raibh an fhoirfeacht agus an sonas gan mháchail ann, áit éigin, ag feitheamh léi, dá bhféadfadh sí breith orthu, dá ndéanfaí athrú nó dhó ar chúrsaí. (2)

Mar bhean mheánaosta le beirt pháistí agus post mar leaseagarthóir ar rannóg spóirt an nuachtáin a n-oibríonn sí dó a chastar orainn í ag tús an scéil ach in ainneoin na físe a shantaigh sí agus í níos óige, tá sí fós sa tóir ar an saol foirfe. Fíorófar an aisling sin an lá arna mhárach dar léi nuair a bhronnfar torthaí na hardteistiméireachta ar a hiníon, Emma. Taibhsíodh an radharc go minic di, an chlann ag ceiliúradh sa chúlghairdín agus iad ar fad ag ól *champagne* sula ngléasfadh Emma í féin suas "agus rachadh sí amach le cairde deasa ciallmhara chun béile a ithe, b'fhéidir, agus dul ar rince ar feadh uair an chloig i gclub deas sibhialta" (16). Ina ainneoin sin, tá an galar dubh ar Emma, teipeann uirthi sa scrúdú agus ní labhraíonn sí lena máthair ná lena hathair:

> Fanann sí ina haonar ina seomra, ag léamh, ag éisteacht le ceol, ag féachaint ar an teilifís, ag útamáil leis an ríomhaire. Bíonn sí ar an idirlíon. Bíonn sí i dteagmháil leis na ceithre hairde ach ní bhíonn teagmháil phearsanta ar bith aici le haon duine, fiú amháin leo sin atá in aon teach léi, fiú amháin a máthair agus a hathair féin. (8)

Is úrscéal Gaeilge é *Cailíní Beaga Ghleann na mBláth* a roinneann téama agus plota leis an úrscéal Béarla *The Dancers Dancing* agus an gearrscéal Béarla 'The Day Elvis Presley Died'. I dtéarmaí na Gaeilge is é an t-úrscéal is fearr dá bhfuil scríofa ag Éilís Ní Dhuibhne go dtí seo. Is úrscéal é atá soléite, ilghnéitheach agus dea-scríofa ó thaobh plota agus forbairt scéil de. Is úrscéal é atá éasca le léamh agus taitneamhach seachas éadrom agus neamhdhúshlánach. Cé go bhfuil Ó Muirí ródhian air, b'fhéidir, nuair a deir sé gur léitheoireacht liteartha seachas litríocht atá i gceist, tá géarghá lena leithéid sa Ghaeilge agus éiríonn leis an úrscéal seo scéal a chur ar fáil a fhreastalaíonn ar an dá thrá.[45] Seachas go leor de na hiarrachtaí a fhoilsítear sa teanga seachnaítear an ardlitearthacht agus cuirtear scéal dea-chumtha, cliste, dúshlánach ar fáil. D'aimsigh sí ábhar a bhfuil cur amach ag pobal na hÉireann air agus chum sí scéal arbh fhéidir dul i ngleic leis ar leibhéil éagsúla – agus is dea-theist é sin ar shaothar ar bith.[46] Mar a deir sí féin agus í i mbun léirmheasa don Irish Times: "Sometimes the jackpot is what is going on right under their nose. ... And suddenly it looks fascinating, brand new, gleaming".[47] Tá scéal scríofa aici atá lonnaithe i suíomh cathrach, atá comhaimseartha agus inchreidte agus a thugann aghaidh ar Éirinn an Tíogair Cheiltigh. Tá iarracht fhónta chumasach neamhghnách curtha di ag Éilís Ní Dhuibhne san iarracht seo. Tá sé ar cheann de na húrscéalta is fearr dár foilsíodh sa Ghaeilge le blianta beaga anuas agus ba chóir go mbeadh súil ag léitheoirí go mbeidh a thuilleadh den chaighdeán céanna nó níos fearr le teacht amach anseo. Agus é ag déanamh léirmheasa ar Hurlamaboc, an leabhar Gaeilge is déanaí ó pheann Ní Dhuibhne, bhí an méid seo le rá ag an Ó Muirí:

Readers of a certain age may well remember the novels of Séamus Ó Grianna and his depiction of poverty and the mores of Donegal at the beginning of the last century. Ní Dhuibhne has replaced the peasants of rural Donegal with the patricians of urban Dublin. Her language lacks the rich idiom of Ó Grianna but she writes clearly, authentically and has a sharp eye for the small moments of doubt and fear which beset us all. She has, in her own quiet way, brought the novel in Irish into the 21st century.[48]

Bhain Ó Grianna le blianta an ghanntanais, mar a deir Ó Muirí féin, "Ó Grianna (or 'Máire', to use his pen-name) spent his summers, as did many from that region, as an economic migrant in Scotland harvesting and navvying. (The Romanians of their time?)".[49] Baineann Ní Dhuibhne, áfach, leis an Tíogar Ceilteach, baineann sí le hÉire an rachmais agus an léiríonn sí an saol sin go sonrach ina saothar agus na fadhbanna a chothaíonn sé. Dála scéalta Uí Ghrianna, áfach, feictear carachtair ag filleadh abhaile tar éis na mblianta fada le fís den saol agus den áit, ach gan rompu ach an brón agus an tragóid. Má thosaigh úrscéal an fichiú haois, le Stephen Dedalus ag éalú ó líonta an náisiúnachais, an chreidimh, agus na teanga, is féidir argóint a dhéanamh go bhfuil Ní Dhuibhne ag éalú ó chuing an chanúnachais, an choir chainte, na hollinsinte agus na frithinsinte traidisiúnta Gaeilge. Trína húrscéal a lonnú i gcoláiste Gaeilge agus trí úsáid chiallmhar ealaíonta a bhaint as canúintí éagsúla agus as réimsí éagsúla an Bhéarla agus na Gaeilge, éiríonn léi gnéithe de na húrscéalta traidisiúnta Gaeilge a shníomh le chéile le gnéithe den saol comhaimseartha gan titim isteach sna gnáthlaigí a smálaíonn go leor úrscéalta Gaeilge. Ní fheadar an múnla é seo do scríbhneoirí eile ach mar théacs a shnaidhmeann déchinéalachas, is eiseamláir de shaothar atá soléite, tarraingteach agus fónta, an rud is mó a bhfuil éileamh air faoi láthair, seachas iarracht thriallach iarnua-aoiseach eile nach léifear.

NÓTAÍ

1   Róisín Ingle, 'That First Kiss' in *Pieces of Me: A Life-in-Progress* (Dublin: Hodder Headline, 2005), 131.

2   Bill Ashcroft, Helen Tiffin agus Gareth Griffiths, *The Empire Writes Back* (London; Routledge, 1998), 175–76.

3   *ibid.*, 176.

4   Caitriona Moloney agus Helen Thompson, eag. *Irish Women Writers Speak Out: Voices from the Field* (New York: Syracuse University Press, 1003: 101–115), 103.

5   Eilís Ní Dhuibhne, "Saibhreas nó Daibhreas? An Scríbhneoir Dátheangach" in Aisling Ní Dhonnchadha, eag. *An Prós Comhaimseartha. Léachtaí Cholm Cille* XXXVI. (Maigh Nuad: An Sagart, 2006: 139–154), 148.

6   Léirítear bá an údair leis na bochtáin agus leis an daoscarshlua go soiléir sa bheathaisnéis chruthaitheach seo.

7   Tá téama an oideachais lárnach sa dá shaothar le Ó Grianna agus in *Cailíní Beaga Ghleann na mBláth.*

8   'Agallamh Beo', *Beo!* Uimhir 58, Feabhra 2006. [http://beo.ie/index. php?page=archive_content&archive_id=1743]

9   *ibid.*

10 *ibid.* D'fhreastail sí ar Scoil Bhríde a bhí lonnaithe ar Earlsfort Terrace an t-am úd; St Mary's, Bóthar Haddington agus Scoil Chaitríona, Sráid Eccles ina dhiaidh sin. Do bhain sí duais an Bhéarla sa bhliain 1971 agus thosaigh ar an gColáiste Ollscoile, Baile Átha Cliath, áit ar bhain sí bunchéim amach sa Bhéarla sa bhliain 1974 agus máistreacht ina dhiaidh sin i Léann na Meán-Aoiseanna.

11 *Beo!* Uimhir 58, Feabhra 2006.

12 Rainer Schulte, *The Geography of Translation and Interpretation: Traveling Between Languages* (Lampeter: The Edwin Mellen Press, 2001), 50.

13 *Beo!* Uimhir 58, Feabhra, 2006.

14 Micí Mac Gabhann, *Rotha Mór an tSaoil* (BÁC: Foilseacháin Náisiúnta, 1959), 103–4.

15 Anne McClintock, *Imperial Leather* (London: Routledge, 1995), 300–01.

16 *ibid.*, 311.

17 Caitriona Moloney and Helen Thompson, eag. *Irish Women Writers Speak Out: Voices from the Field* (New York: Syracuse University Press, 1003: 101–115), 115.

18 Edward W. Said, *Culture & Imperialism* (London: Chatto and Windus, 1993), 405.

19 *ibid.*

20 Nuala Ní Dhomhnaill, 'An Fhilíocht á Cumadh: Ceardlann Filíochta'. *Léachtaí Cholm Cille*, XVII (1986), 168.

21 Elke D'hoker, 'The Postmodern Folktales of Éilís Ní Dhuibhne'. *Revista da Associação Brasileira de Estudos Irlandeses*, Iml. 6, 2004, 137.

22 *ibid.*

23 Maeve Flanagan, *Dev, Lady Chatterley and Me: A 60s Suburban Childhood* (Dublin: Marino Books, 1998), 68–9.

24 Pól Ó Muirí, 'Self-discovery in Dingle'. *Irish Times*, 9 Meán Fómhair 2000.

25 Ciarán Mac Murchaidh, 'Hurlamaboc'. *The Irish Book Review*, Summer 2006, gan leathanach.

26 Chruthaigh sé go maith sna comórtais liteartha idir Bhéarla agus Ghaeilge agus bhain sé Gradam Feabhais BISTO (2007), Duais an Oireachtais (2006) agus ainmníodh ar Ghearrliosta Ghradam Uí Shúilleabháin (leabhar Gaeilge na bliana) (2006). D'aistrigh Beathag Mhoireasdan as Uig na hAlban an t-úrscéal seo go Gaidhlig na hAlban agus foilsíodh é faoin teideal *Ùpraid* sa bhliain 2006. Cuid d'iarracht ab ea é seo chun litríocht na Gaidhlige a neartú mar a mhínigh an t-údar Albanach Martin MacIntyre in agallamh dá chuid. Feic *Scottish Corpus of Texts and Speech*. Document 1575, Interview 19, Martin MacIntyre

27 Ní Dhuibhne, "Saibhreas nó Daibhreas? An Scríbhneoir Dátheangach" *Léachtaí Cholm Cille* XXXVI: 148.

28 Ní Dhuibhne, *Cailíní Beaga Ghleann na mBláth* (Baile Átha Cliath: Cois Life, 2003). Baintear leas as *CB* idir lúibíní ina dhiaidh seo chun tagairt a dhéanamh do *Cailíní Beaga Ghleann na mBláth*.

29 Pól Ó Muirí, 'Tost million go leith Gaeilgeoir sa Stát'. *Irish Times*, 25 Meitheamh 2003.

30 Alan Titley, 'Anarchy, artistry, ailments'. *Irish Times*, 4 Deireadh Fómhair 2003.

31 Pádraigín Riggs and Norman Vance, 'Irish Prose Fiction' in *The Cambridge Companion to Modern Irish Culture* (Cambridge: Cambridge University Press, 2005), 263.

32 *ibid.*, 252.

33 Feic Caitríona Ó Torna, *Cruthú na Gaeltachta 1893–1922* (Baile Átha Cliath: Cois Life, 2005), 87–95. Feic Mairéad Ní Mhurchú, *Coláiste na Mumhan 1904–2004: comóradh an chéid: céad bliain ag fás, céad bliain faoi bhláth* (Corcaigh: Coláiste na Mumhan, 2004).

34 *ibid.*, 87–8.

35 *ibid.*, 92.

36 *Letters from Irish College*, eag. Rose Doyle (Dublin: Marion Books, 1996), 11.

37 Máirín Nic Eoin, *Trén bhFearann Breac* (Baile Átha Cliath: Cois Life, 2005), 400.

38 Joseph O'Connor, 'Where the Stones Sing'. *The Guardian*, 7 Deireadh Fómhair 2006.

39 Davin Dwyer, 'How's your fadá?' *Irish Times*, 25 Lúnasa 2007.

40 Nicola Warwick, 'Interview with Éilís Ní Dhuibhne'. *One Woman's Writing Retreat* http://www.prairieden.com/front_porch/visiting_authors/dhuibhne.html (2001).

41   Margaret Atwood, 'Death by Landscape'. *Contemporary Fiction: 50 Short Stories since 1970.* Lex Williford and Michael Martone, eag. (New York: Simon and Schuster, 1999), 31–45.

42   'The Day Elvis Presley Died' in *The Pale Gold of Alaska* (Belfast: Blackstaff Press, 2000: 40–86).

43   *Lá,* 30 Iúil 2003.

44   Micí Mac Gabhann, *Rotha Mór an tSaoil* (BÁC: Foilseacháin Náisiúnta, 1959), 104.

45   Pól Ó Muirí, 'Tost million go leith Gaeilgeoir sa Stát'. *Irish Times,* 25 Meitheamh 2003.

46   Níor dhein an aiste seo aon scagadh ar cheist na dteangacha ná na gcanúintí éagsúla idir Bhéarla agus Ghaeilge san úrscéal seo ach is ábhar é ab fhiú go mór a fhiosrú.

47   Ní Dhuibhne, 'Prayers of the Faithful'. *Irish Times,* 7 Iúil 2007.

48   Pól Ó Muirí, 'The Noise of a New Generation'. *Irish Times,* 14 Iúil 2007. Ní foláir *Ag altóir an diabhail: striptease spioradálta Bheartla B* le Tomás Mac Síomóin (2003), *Fontenoy* le Liam Mac Cóil (2005), *An Cléireach* le Darach Ó Scolaí (2007) agus *Cúpla Focal* le hAnna Heusaff (2007) a chur san áireamh mar shaothair a thug úrscéal na Gaeilge isteach san aois nua.

49   Pól Ó Muirí, 'An Irishman's Diary'. *Irish Times,* 6 Deireadh Fómhair 1998.

'Beidh sé crap':
Bilingualism and Pidginisation in Éilís Ní Dhuibhne's
Irish Language Writings[1]

PÁDRAIG Ó SIADHAIL

Éilís Ní Dhuibhne had established her reputation as an English language author before she began writing also in Irish in the mid-1990s. Since then, Ní Dhuibhne has published a substantial body of Irish language material, primarily plays and novels, which have won literary awards and, within a small readership market, have been quite successful commercially. Her first novel in Irish, *Dúnmharú sa Daingean*, has sold over 3000 copies,[2] whereas most works in Irish have sales figures in the low hundreds.[3]

Though Ní Dhuibhne's pre-university education was through Irish and her father was a native Irish speaker, English was the language spoken at home and, as Ní Dhuibhne has noted, when she began writing, the possibility of choosing to write in Irish never occurred to her.[4] Ní Dhuibhne's entry into the field of Irish language writing was by way of accepting an invitation, in the 1990s, to write a play for Amharclann de hÍde, the Dublin-based Irish language theatre project. Most, if not all, of her subsequent work in Irish has resulted from similar commissions.

Commenting on the challenges facing her as she turned to writing in Irish, Ní Dhuibhne has stated: "I have not found it easy to embrace Irish as a literary language. As I write, I learn, and that has ... been an incentive to continue".[5] She has, of course, been able to draw on her experience and technical skills, honed in English. Moreover, she has transferred another ingredient from her writing in English: "I have found that my voice as an author is the same ... when I write fiction, whether it be in English or in Irish, something which surprises me".[6]

Belonging to that relatively small group of creative writers who have a significant body of work both in Irish and English – any respectable list must include Eoghan Ó Tuairisc and Michael Hartnett – it is clear that Ní Dhuibhne recognises that modern Ireland presents an opportunity not just to write in two languages, but to examine the relationship between Irish and English. On the surface a monoglot Anglophone society, Ireland includes communities of native Irish speakers, networks of secondary bilinguals and a large pool of people who have some knowledge of Irish (not to mention new immigrants from a wide range of linguistic backgrounds). Ní Dhuibhne has stated that, "in novels such as *The Dancers Dancing*, or *Dúnmharú sa Daingean* or *Cailíní Beaga Ghleann na mBláth*, I look at (or explore, perhaps I should say) the connections between English- and Irish-speaking Ireland. This bilingual zone is one which I have always inhabited and it happens to be a particularly interesting territory for a writer".[7] The primary setting of each of these novels is one where the Irish language occupies a central role: the Donegal Gaeltacht in *The Dancers Dancing*, Corca Dhuibhne in West Kerry in *Dúnmharú sa Daingean*, and a self-contained Irish language summer college (though in an unnamed, non-Gaeltacht area) in *Cailíní Beaga Ghleann na mBláth*. Yet the majority of Ní Dhuibhne's characters are people whose first language is English.

One can be enthralled by, say, Alan Titley's Irish language novel, *Méirscrí na Treibhe*,[8] set in Zanidia, a fictional sub-Saharan country, without wondering why the cast of black Africans sounds like a conventicle of Irish-speaking Cork hurlers-on-the-ditch in Croke Park on the first Sunday of September, such are the nature, the conventions, and the ultimate power of fiction to create its own terms of reference.

However, in her work in Irish, Ní Dhuibhne purposely draws the reader's attention to the question of language, on occasion by explicitly mentioning that a character is speaking a certain language. Frequently, it is by putting a mixture of Irish and English in a character's mouth, for example, statements such as "Beidh sé crap" [It will be crap] in this essay's title.[9] Most commonly, Ní Dhuibhne drops implicit textual hints that, though she is writing in Irish, her characters are really speaking to each other in English.

In her work in Irish, Ní Dhuibhne appears to mix and match Irish and English in a random way. Yet recent comments by her about the artistic potential and practical difficulties associated with writing a heteroglossial text, in which each language would have equal status, confirm that it is a subject on which she has an abiding interest and strong views.[10] Furthermore, the choices that Ní Dhuibhne has made as she has handled Irish and English in her Irish language works to date raise interesting questions about the current position and future direction of Irish language literature and fit into a larger debate in Irish language circles about the increasing divergence between spoken Irish and the written language and declining standards of literacy in Irish.[11] Thus, in this essay, I wish to pose and address several inter-related questions. In what situations and contexts in her work in Irish does Ní Dhuibhne choose to use English rather than Irish? When does she write a standard form of Irish? In what situations does she prefer pidgin Irish (accepting Wardhaugh's definition of pidgin as a "'reduced' variety of a 'normal' language" and as one that has no native speakers)?[12] And, finally, is her use of English and pidgin Irish an example of dumbing-down to cater to a readership that is unable to deal with literary Irish or cruachaint na Gaeltachta, the rich textured language of the good native Irish Gaeltacht speaker?

Different Approaches in Use of English
The Dancers Dancing[13] is set in a Gaeltacht community, but centres on the Irish language summer college, that rite of

passage from childhood to adolescence for tens of thousands of Irish teenagers over the years. On one level, the choice of English to write about an Irish language setting may seem unusual, but is unremarkable since the novel's focus is largely on the visiting students for whom English remains their language of choice when outside the control and earshot of the college authorities. Nevertheless, the decision to write the novel in English, while opening up a potentially large readership for Ní Dhuibhne, ensures that she must provide background information for readers unfamiliar with the world of the summer college. In the light of the potential target readership in English, it is worth wondering how some readers have handled various scraps of Irish that Ní Dhuibhne leaves untranslated in the novel. For example, as the main character, Orla, considers differences between Conamara and Ulster Irish greetings and vocabulary: "Caidé mar atá tú instead of Conas atá tú. Falsa instead of leisciúil. Fosta instead of freisin. Geafta instead of geata" (*DD* 34); or, as a teacher rebukes students for speaking English: "'Ná bígí ag labhairt Béarla!' warns Killer Jack, carelessly, patrolling the outside of the line. Monica smirks at him and says, 'Nílimid ag labhairt Béarla, a mháistir! An mbeidh tú ag an chéilí anocht?'" [We're not speaking English, sir! Will you be at the céilí tonight?] (149). Whatever authorial and/or editorial considerations went into examples such as these – Ní Dhuibhne has stated recently that readers without Irish would understand this material from the context[14] – the most noteworthy acknowledgement of Irish by Ní Dhuibhne is a scene early in the novel once the students are assigned to their classes. Though writing in what appears to be pidgin English, Ní Dhuibhne draws attention to her characters' use of Irish. As illustrated by this excerpt, she highlights the difference between basic constructions in Irish and English, especially the syntax of Irish (VSO) and English (SVO):

> Hear they Bean Uí Luing under bottom the curtain.
> Sentences a-teaches she.
> I am in sixth class at school.
> I am four years teen of age.
> Better to me tea than coffee.

Hurler good is my brother.
Footballer good is my brother.
There is a cat white to me.
There is a dog black to me.
It is lovely with me my dog black.
Repeat the pupils the sentences after her, and then learn they them
by clean mind. And they learning by clean mind it is able with you
to hear their brains working, like to a machine a-humming, even
only over the curtain. Pleasant, comforting sound it is. (36)

Overall, beyond the achievements that are the novel's plot and
strong portrayal of a range of characters, it is no small feat that
Ní Dhuibhne succeeds in writing convincingly about the
Gaeltacht and the Irish summer college without actually
having much Irish in the novel.

In her first play in Irish, *Dún na mBan Trí Thine*,[15] Ní
Dhuibhne draws on folk culture as she explores the life of a
contemporary urban woman. Ní Dhuibhne's Irish throughout
is a mixture of *An Caighdeán Oifigiúil*, the Official Standard for
written Irish, and Munster Irish, and she demonstrates a sure
grasp of the language and its idiom. Ní Dhuibhne uses little
English in the play, the sole major exception being an excerpt
from a self-help guide, *How to be Happy*, which may merely
reflect an inclination towards a realistic rendering of the
current state of publishing in English, which the Irish language
publishing industry has managed to avoid to date. In her
second play in Irish, *Milseog an tSamhraidh*,[16] a reworking of her
story 'Summer Pudding' from '*The Inland Ice' and Other Stories*,
Ní Dhuibhne interweaves the story of Irish famine refugees in
Wales in 1848 with the relationship of an elderly upper-class
couple, Lady Eleanor Butler and Miss Sarah, characters based
on the real-life 'Ladies of Llangollen', Eleanor Butler (1745–
1829) and her cousin, Sarah Ponsonby (1755–1831), recluses
and celebrities in the Britain of their time. While the local
servant girl in *Milseog an tSamhraidh* speaks Welsh, and the
fleeing Irish are Irish speakers with varying degrees of
elementary English to their credit, Ní Dhuibhne uses English
extensively in the second act of the play, once the famine
survivors arrive at the home of Lady Eleanor. From that point

on, the play is really a bilingual play until the final scene, which features the Irish-speaking refugees.

As with the example of the self-help guide in *Dún na mBan Trí Thine*, Ní Dhuibhne's decision to use English in *Milseog an tSamhraidh* mirrors the linguistic reality that one would not expect to find upper-class Irish speakers outside Ireland in 1848. It stems from a contemporary fact of life too, namely, that Irish speakers and readers also speak and read English. Most contemporary Irish language writers adhere to the conventions that one finds in Titley's *Méirscrí na Treibhe*, allowing the suspense of disbelief that is intrinsic in art to overcome the urge towards realism and, one suspects, enjoying the challenge that comes with dealing in Irish with situations and locations not usually associated with the language. However, Ní Dhuibhne's use of English in *Milseog an tSamhraidh* is not an exception in contemporary literature in Irish. For example, in *Scread Mhaidne* and *Lámh Láidir*, award-winning and best-selling novels by the Conamara Gaeltacht writer and actor, Joe Steve Ó Neachtain,[17] the dialogue between characters from whom one would not anticipate hearing Irish – foreigners and non-Gaeltacht people alike – is in English. While such choices are still unusual in Irish, they may point towards a future trend in literature in Irish. Whatever the merits of going that route in search of greater realism, these treatments also serve another purpose: easing the burden on readers who might feel intimidated by literature in Irish, a point to which I will return presently.

Interestingly, in her other published work in Irish, Ní Dhuibhne does not follow the example of *Milseog an tSamhraidh*. However, just as the influence of the English language is all-pervasive in Ireland, the English language remains a dominant force in her work. In her one published Irish language story to date, 'Luachra', *(pages 319–324)*[18] Fiach, a Dublin teenager who is visiting Kerry with his parents, one of whom is collecting folklore from former Blasket Islandmen, learns the skill of fashioning a St. Brigid's Cross from an aged Islandman. Separated from the elderly Blasketman by several generations and by wildly different lifestyles, the young Dubliner acquires some of the cultural richness and heritage of the old tradition bearer. Central to the story, however, is the vast gap between the linguistic richness possessed by the Blasketmen and the Irish, heavily laden with English vocabulary and syntax and skewed Irish grammar, that Fiach speaks, for example: "Tá mé freezing", "Tá an féar seo cosúil le sponge","Tá mo trainers ag sinkáil", "Cén fáth atá tú ag gathering na rushes anyway? Is féidir leat faigh iad sin gach áit", "Tá mé bored", "'Bhfuil cead agam faigh coke?" ('Luachra' 96).

Fiach's Irish corresponds to the process of pidginisation, which Wardhaugh defines as involving:

> some sort of 'simplification' of a language, e.g., reduction in morphology (word structure) and syntax (grammatical structure), tolerance of considerable phonological variation (pronunciation), reduction in the number of functions for which the pidgin is used (e.g., you usually do not attempt to write novels in a pidgin), and extensive borrowing of words from local mother-tongues.[19]

More specifically, it is an example of the phenomenon that is known in Irish language circles as 'Gaelscoilis', the variety of Irish highly impacted by English syntax and vocabulary that is spoken by students, mainly non-native Irish speakers, who are being educated in Gaelscoileanna, Irish medium schools.[20] While accepting Wardhaugh's point that one usually doesn't write a novel in a pidgin, it is the case that Ní Dhuibhne's deliberate use of pidgin Irish to highlight the huge gulf between the forms of Irish spoken by the Blasket Islanders and Fiach mirrors its use by other writers, such as Liam Ó Muirthile,[21] who have drawn on Gaelscoilis, not just to differentiate levels of language capability, but generational issues as well.

In contrast to its clear signposting in 'Luachra', the question of language seems merely to form part of the backdrop to the plots in Ní Dhuibhne's Irish language novels. Yet, on closer examination, one sees that Ní Dhuibhne adopts different strategies to deal with the treatment of Irish and English in each novel. Moreover, there is a significant evolution in her handling of the issue from her first Irish language novel, *Dúnmharú sa Daingean* (2000), through *Cailíní Beaga Ghleann na mBláth* (2003) and *Hurlamaboc* (2006), a novel aimed at the teenage market, to *Dún an Airgid*, her most recent novel in Irish. While Ní Dhuibhne uses English with certain abandonment in *Dúnmharú sa Daingean*, ironically, it is in *Dún an Airgid*, a sequel to *Dúnmharú sa Daingean*, that one finds the least amount of English in Ní Dhuibhne's novels.

Dúnmharú sa Daingean[22] is a murder mystery set in the Kerry Gaeltacht, west of An Daingean (the town formerly known as Dingle). Keen for a break from the routine that is her shallow existence in middle-class Dublin after losing her flat, her job and her boyfriend, the ironically named Saoirse (freedom) seeks refuge in the Gaeltacht. "Bheadh orm Gaeilge a labhairt" [I would have to speak Irish] Saoirse says to Mairéad, a friend who has arranged a rented house in Kerry for her (*Dúnmharú* 46). This statement implies that Saoirse does not usually speak Irish, and that all her dealings and conversations in Dublin, including her relationship with Marcas, her boyfriend, and this particular conversation with Mairéad, have been in English. Saoirse's Irish consists of what she recalls from her school days, a point that is supported by her listing the opportunity to improve her Irish – "Chuirfeadh sí feabhas ar a cuid Gaeilge leis" (61) – as one of the reasons to head south-west. On the first full morning after Saoirse's arrival in the Gaeltacht, Méiní, who owns the local public house, and whom Saoirse had met the previous evening, visits her: "Gaeilge a bhí á labhairt acu inniu, ar chúis éigin. Bhí Saoirse sásta triail a bhaint as ach go háirithe" [They were speaking Irish today, for some reason. Saoirse in particular was happy to have a go at it] (66). Again, the implication is that when the two women spoke previously, they communicated in English, even though Ní Dhuibhne presents the conversation in Irish. We are told that Seán, Méiní's husband, speaks in Irish to Saoirse, and can deduce from a thought attributed to Saoirse after meeting a local couple, Jason and Jessica, that she would call them chancers – "Dá mbeadh focal Gaeilge aici ar 'chancers'" [If she had the Irish word for 'chancers'] (79) – that she and Méiní now communicate in Irish when they are alone. From textual hints, it appears that Saoirse and Máirtín Ó Flaithearta, the local

Garda, also talk to each other in Irish when alone. Though the lack of reference to a shift in language when Máirtín arrives at Saoirse's house while Marcas, her ex-boyfriend, is visiting (208) suggests that they have been speaking English, this may be due to the author neglecting to tidy up this detail or choosing to ignore it. When Ní Dhuibhne has Máirtín using English words or phrases – "Have I got news for you!" he declares to Saoirse (226), for example – this may be nothing more than a reflection of the linguistic reality that is the present-day Gaeltacht, where there is no escape from English, whether in vocabulary, expressions or syntax. In fact, on close inspection, a fairly clear pattern emerges in *Dúnmharú sa Daingean*. Except where Ní Dhuibhne specifically informs us that her characters are talking Irish – primarily Saoirse speaking to the Gaeltacht character, Méiní, to Seán, a secondary bilingual who chooses to speak Irish, to Máirtín as well as other minor local characters – the characters speak English to each other, even though Ní Dhuibhne presents the dialogue in Irish.

In *Dúnmharú sa Daingean*, Ní Dhuibhne plays on the cultural nuances that separate Irish and English and, in turn, provides clues about language choice. For example, Seán refers to Saoirse as a 'cailín' [girl]:

'Tá tú óg fós, a chailín,' a dúirt sé.

Bhuail croí Saoirse níos tapúla. Ar chúis éigin cheap sí go raibh an nath cainte 'a chailín' corraitheach, ar shlí dheas — ar aon nós, nuair is fear cosúil le Seán a bhain úsáid as. Níor cheart do bhean óg feimineach glacadh leis an teideal 'a chailín' mar mholadh ná mar fhocal ina raibh cion de shaghas éigin intuigthe. Ach mhothaigh sí go raibh cion le brath san fhocal féin, cé gur thuig sí go nglacfadh sí mar mhasla é dá n-aistreofaí go Béarla é. (68)

['You're young yet, girl,' he said.

Saoirse's heart beat faster. For some reason she thought that the expression 'girl' was exciting in a nice way – at any rate, when it's a man like Seán who was using it. A young feminist woman shouldn't accept the title 'girl' as praise or as a word in which affection of any sort was understood. But she felt that there was affection implicit in the word itself, although she understood that she would take it as an insult if it were translated into English.]

Interestingly, Máirtín refers to Saoirse as a 'bean' [woman]: "'Maith an bhean!' arsa Máirtín" ['Good woman!' said Máirtín], which, as Saoirse noted: "Aisteach nár dhein an focal 'bean' aon rud di" [Strange that the word 'woman' didn't do any thing for her] (*Dúnmharú* 145), before he redeems himself at the end of the novel: "'A chailín,' a dúirt sé. 'A chailín! A chailín! A chailín!'" (235).

In another situation, Ní Dhuibhne plays on her readers' understanding of English. Mischievously, she substitutes the place name 'Baile an Rabbitéaraigh' for Baile an Fheirtéirigh, a real-life location in the Corca Dhuibhne Gaeltacht named after the Feiritéar/Ferriter family, punning on similarities between 'Rabbit' and 'Ferret.' This is not the only occasion where Ní Dhuibhne engages in linguistic games. Before heading for Kerry, Saoirse's friend, Mairéad, has reported that life down the country is more exciting than in Dublin:

> 'Tá níos mó ar siúl ansin ná atá anseo, de réir Philib,' arsa Mairéad. 'Drugaí, affaires, fir phósta ag rith i ndiaidh na mban pósta, mná pósta ag rith i ndiaidh na bhfear pósta.'
> 'Wonderful!'
> 'Homaighnéasachas, S and M, transvestitism ... Níl deireadh leis. (47)

> ['There's more happening there than here, according to Pilib [the absent house owner in Kerry],' says Mairéad. 'Drugs, affairs, married men running after married women, married women running after married men.'
> 'Wonderful!'
> 'Homosexuality, S and M, transvestitism ... There's no end to it.']

When we hear about Jessica and Jason, who live in 'Caisleán na bhFuipíní', a large house on an old estate, this seems to be the ideal location for some of the afore-mentioned S and M, since one translation of 'Caisleán na bhFuipíní' is 'Castle of the Small Whips.' In fact, Caisleán na bhFuipíní is a "Saghas resort" [a kind of resort] (74), which promotes a mixture of mundane educational and new-age programmes and likely gets its name from the Irish word, 'fuipín' [puffin]. Having raised the reader's expectation about where Saoirse and we are heading and what we will encounter in the Gaeltacht, we have to be content with a prosaic murder or two.

The extract from Saoirse and Mairéad's conversation above gives a sense of the ways in which Ní Dhuibhne uses English in *Dúnmharú sa Daingean*. Though one can separate its use into major categories, there remains a certain arbitrariness and inconsistency in Ní Dhuibhne's adherence to the following categories: [23]

A: Representing the creole – described by Wardhaugh as "often defined as a pidgin that has become the first language of a new generation of speakers"[24] – that one encounters increasingly amongst Gaeltacht Irish speakers, as reflected in some of Máirtín's utterances or by comments from a minor character such as Mossy Fitz: "Níl an t-infra structure suas chun dáta" [The infrastructure isn't up to date] (87). Talking about his attempts to portray the conversation of young Gaeltacht Irish speakers, the contemporary writer, Micheál Ó Conghaile, has suggested that:

> that might mean mixing some words or phrases in English in through the Irish. There are times when the word in English is a lot stronger than the word in Irish. It can hit a lot harder. If the English word is used in the Gaeltacht it has a stronger register for me as a reader and a writer than the English translation, which might not normally be used and might only be found in dictionaries or among learners of the language.[25]

It is, of course, an irony that 'caint na ndaoine', the language of the Gaeltacht Irish speaker, promoted in the early years of the twentieth century as the ideal medium for modern Irish literature, is now contributing to the undermining of the language.[26]

B: Reflecting the dominance of English as the language of public discourse in Ireland: for example, in the media (1, 33, 232–233). Similarly, reflecting the actual position of English as the first language of Ireland: for example, Dubliners talking on the Dart (7, 9); a minister's eulogy (161–62); or Marcas's greeting on his voice-mail (10). However, the letter from Saoirse's Dublin landlady, informing Saoirse that she is about to be evicted, is in Irish (35).

C: Repeated use of the word 'wonderful' to satirise the vacuous world and consumerist values of young Dublin middle-class professionals (6, 12).

D: Words where the Irish forms might not be well-known by the average reader or Irish speaker: for example, "immersion" (as in water-heater) (10); "AIDS" (24); "take away" (35); "Unfair Dismissals Act" (37); "self-help" (as in books, though Ní Dhuibhne gives the titles in Irish) (41); "osteoporosis" (61); "breathalyzer" (175); "retrospective" (as in art exhibition) (204); and "alibi" (224). As seen above, however, Ní Dhuibhne gives the Irish form "Homaighnéachachas" (47), but not 'S and M' and 'transvestitism'.

E: Words and expressions for which there are well-accepted and widely-used equivalents in Irish: for example, "jeans" (19); "boss" (25); "fiasco" (25); "bug" (27); "niche" (38); "model" (40); "bored" (47); "omelette" (76); "eyesore" (90); "Póg a d'fhág stunned í ar feadh soicind" [A kiss that left her stunned for a second] (105); "serial killer" (129); "close range" (132); "bureaucracy" (143); "so called bleachtairí" [so called detectives] (144); "breakthrough" (175); "outfit" (178); and "punk" (213). It is evident that at least for some of these examples, Ní Dhuibhne uses the English words for effect.

F: Forms that convey a meaning different from their literal meaning: for example, "Post-mortem" (23), an inquest on what has gone wrong.

G: Clichés: "'Keep a low profile!'" (41). Ní Dhuibhne also translates English language clichés into Irish: "An buachaill a ghlaoigh 'Mac tíre'!" [The boy who cried 'wolf'!] (96); and "chun an leac oighir a bhriseadh" [to break the ice, i.e. in social situations] (103–04).

H: Copious curses/exclamations: for example, 'So', 'Right', 'Jesus!', 'God', and 'Gosh'.

I: Examples that could be described as linguistic laziness on the part of the author: "in imeachtaí an European Cup nó an World Cup nó an FAI cup" [in the activities of ... or ... or] (188). Though place names, including foreign ones, are generally in Irish, there is an example such as "Brittas Bay" (202).

J: Forms that are merely English dressed up as Irish: for example, "ag chugáil" [as in a tractor chugging down the road] (115); "zonkáilte" (131) [zonked]; and "Trá Lí a bhypassáil" [to bypass Tralee] (51). As in Category A, one finds this amongst Irish speakers, both Gaeltacht and non-Gaeltacht.

One device that Ní Dhuibhne favours is to have dialogue in which complete sentences in Irish alternate with full sentences in English, for example: "'Oh, jeepers!' arsa Mairéad. 'Ná tosaigh ag gol. He's not worth it. Gheobhaidh mé deoch eile duit?'" [Don't start crying ... I'll get you another drink?] (47). More frequently still, one finds a mixture of Irish and English in one sentence, for example: "'Over my dead body a thógfaidh sé a dhiabhal holiday cottages!' a dúirt Patsy" [Over my dead body he'll build his bloody holiday cottages! said Patsy] (96); or "Yeah. Boring old drugaí. Cad eile?" [What else?] (169).

One can argue that a number of the categories above merely represent examples of colloquial Gaeltacht Irish in its most impoverished form and Gaelscoilis. However, collectively, these categories support the argument that the majority of the characters in *Dúnmharú sa Daingean* only speak English, irrespective of the language in which their comments are presented. More problematically, even if one seeks to explain the pattern of use of English as an attempt by Ní Dhuibhne to represent Irish as it is spoken by various groups, or as a striving for effect, or as a laudable attempt to write a popular work that would get readers hooked on literature in Irish – Ní Dhuibhne has noted the paucity of such material during her childhood[27] – there is a sense that Ní Dhuibhne is too indiscriminate in her use of English in *Dúnmharú sa Daingean* and is not adhering to any clearly thought-out strategy. An examination of her handling of English in her later novels supports this judgement. There is in them a consistency and a method in Ní Dhuibhne's approach to the use of English that is missing in *Dúnmharú sa Daingean*. Indeed, one can view her treatment of this issue in these later works, especially in the sequel, *Dún an Airgid*, as a corrective to the situation in her first novel.

Cailíní Beaga Ghleann na mBláth[28] features two parallel narratives: one contemporary, focussing on the slowly deteriorating family life of a successful middle-aged, middle-class Dublin woman, Máire; the other recreating the summer many years previously when the nine-year-old Máire's stay in 'Gleann na mBláth' Irish college ended in tragedy. In the contemporary narrative, the dialogue is in Irish, but we are informed early in the novel that Máire the Elder hasn't much sympathy for Irish – "Ní raibh mórán bá ag Máire leis an nGaeilge" (*CB* 12) – implying that Máire's world is an English-speaking one. Later, Ní Dhuibhne signals this even more clearly when Emma, Máire's daughter, who is suffering a depression of sorts, finally utters a word:

'A Dhia!' a deir Emma.
Ní mórán é. Focal amháin. 'God' a dúirt sí, ar ndóigh, ní 'Dia'. (158)

['God!' says Emma.
It's not much. One word. 'God' she said, of course, not 'Dia'.]

Unlike *Dúnmharú sa Daingean*, Ní Dhuibhne eschews the use of English in situations where realistically one might expect to hear it, for example, from the family doctor (123–124). We do have an extract from a TV programme featuring a Texas psychologist in English (140), otherwise there is just the occasional word or phrase in English. As such, in those parts of *Cailíní Beaga Ghleann na mBláth* dealing with Máire's contemporary life, Ní Dhuibhne's use of Irish is close to the mainstream variety of the language that one finds in her first play, *Dún na mBan Trí Thine*.

However, in the narrative that focusses on the young Máire's experiences, Ní Dhuibhne adopts a different tack. Much of the dialogue there is in English, and it is evident that Ní Dhuibhne has Juliet, Máire's fellow schoolmate, speak English, not just to reflect the reality that she comes from an English-speaking background, but as part of her portrayal of the spoilt loud brat: "'This food is crap,' a deir Juliet. 'It's a terrible hotel. I don't know how it stays in business serving crappy food like this, so I don't'" (36). Máire's letters home to her mother are in English. Even when the college girls' conversation is given in Irish, they are really talking in English, with few exceptions, such as when the girls are in the proximity of college teachers (47). As in *Dúnmharú sa Daingean*, it is not unusual to have one line of conversation in Irish followed by one in English, for example, "'We had a bit of fun,' a deir Yvonne. 'Tá Juliet fós ansin. Beidh sí ar ais sula i bhfad, bí cinnte de'" [Juliet is there still. She'll be back before long, you can bet] (81). Therefore, apart from short conversations involving the teachers, English, once again, is the main language spoken by the characters in *Cailíní Beaga Ghleann na mBláth*, even when the dialogue is given in Irish. The main differences between *Dúnmharú sa Daingean* and *Cailíní Beaga Ghleann na mBláth* relate both to the significant decrease in the amount and range of actual English in the text from the former to the latter and to the sense that Ní Dhuibhne was much more cautious about inserting English into *Cailíní Beaga Ghleann na mBláth* in contrast to its widespread use in *Dúnmharú sa Daingean*. One could speculate that Ní Dhuibhne's publishers, Cois Life, have exercised tighter editorial control over Ní Dhuibhne in this regard. I would contend, however, that it is a sign of Ní Dhuibhne's development and self-confidence as an Irish language writer, as well as her increased understanding of her responsibility to the language and its tradition, that she has moved towards the methods of most contemporary Irish language writers in seeking to present the world in Irish, even when that world is not an Irish-speaking one, indeed, even when it is specifically an English-speaking environment.

Thus, in *Hurlamaboc*, a novel populated by Dublin English-speakers (and the odd Welsh one), Ní Dhuibhne uses English more sparingly than in the earlier novels. Apart from two public notices – a 'job wanted' advertisement (in Wales), and fragments of dialogue from *Gone with the Wind* – there are scarcely a dozen full sentences in English in the novel. However, there are quite a few English words and expressions sprinkled throughout. Not surprisingly in a novel about the lives of three south-Dublin teenagers, Ní Dhuibhne attempts to capture their use of language by inserting forms such: "Beidh sé cool" (5); "popular" (50); "coolie" (67) (i.e., a cool person), "nerdanna" (67), and "creep" (69). Similarly, Ní Dhuibhne uses English words: "mini-marathon" (31), "a domestic situation" (63) (especially to reflect middle-class suburbia), "four-wheel drive" (45). But also for effect, "toyboy" (71); "stay at home housewives", "career girl", "knacker" (72) and "chick lit" (77). Occasionally, however, it is not clear why Ní Dhuibhne uses English forms, for example, "shopping centre" and "burgers" (99) or "UCD" (12), rather than accepted Irish forms.

If *Hurlamaboc* centres round an English-speaking world, there is also acknowledgement of the existence of Irish. Though we don't meet him in person, Seán, the father of Emma, one of the teenagers, is an Irish language poet. Emma's recollection of a conversation with her father may well be a situation where Irish is actually spoken (74–77). The other is a delightful example of what used to be known in Ireland, in its pre-Celtic Tiger-days, as the 'Torremolinos Syndrome' – referring less to a specific place than to the situation of Irish people abroad who, on holiday and confronted by various foreign languages, and keen to distinguish themselves from English vacationers, suddenly rediscover Irish. In this instance, Emma and a friend end up in a public house in Wales:

> Thosaigh cúpla buachaill ag caint linn, daoine ón áit, Breatnaigh. Thaitin an chanúint a bhí acu linn ach thosaigh siad ag rá rudaí i dteanga iasachta, Breatnais, agus níor thaitin sé sin linn. So, thosaíomarna ag rá rudaí i nGaeilge agus dúirt siad 'Hey what's that?' Agus dúramar leo. Agus ar siad, 'That's cool that you guys have another language too.' Mhúineamar cúpla focal dóibh, Póg Mo Thóin agus na gnáthrudaí, agus mhúin siadsan cúpla focal dúinne. (143–144)

> [A few boys began talking to us, people from the place, Welsh. We liked their accents but they started saying things in a foreign language, Welsh, and we didn't like that. So, we began saying things in Irish and they said, 'Hey what's that?' And we told them. And they said, 'That's cool that you guys have another language too.' We taught them a few words, 'Póg Mo Thóin' and the usual things, and they taught us a few words.]

However, it is Ní Dhuibhne's most recent novel in Irish, *Dún an Airgid*,[29] which best demonstrates her conversion to and espousal of the linguistic conventions that exist in most contemporary Irish language literature. The novel reintroduces us to Saoirse and Máirtín from *Dúnmharú sa Daingean*. Having endured a three year long-distance romance, the couple are now sharing an apartment in *Dún an Airgid*, a fictional Irish town that appears, on the surface, to be a modern model community occupied by HiCos, the Irish tribe who, according to David McWilliams' take on present-day Ireland, appreciate and strive for the best that both the local and the international can offer.[30] The emergence of a serial killer, whose motivation partly stems from his bitterness at the way in which genuine historical sites and cultural artifacts of the area have been destroyed in the name of progress, blows away any suggestion that *Dún an Airgid* is a Utopian location and poses a deadly challenge for Máirtín, now a Garda Inspector, and Saoirse, a painter and part-time teacher. The novel suffers from a shaky plot line. For example, would Máirtín really risk the success of the case and his own position by allowing Saoirse to do the work of a professional in accessing and reading the e-mails of one of the victims? But, in the context of the focus of this essay, the most telling aspect of the novel relates to Ní Dhuibhne's handling of the question of language.

There is no suggestion that *Dún an Airgid* is a Gaeltacht community, yet all the characters speak Irish to each other. There is the usual series of English words in Ní Dhuibhne's Irish language novels, from exclamations to expressions such as "Obsessive-compulsive" (*Airgid* 46), "brownie point" (87), "affordable housing" (103), and to occasional items such as "sitcom" (33) and "croc" (107) (referring to the brand of sandals), but there is barely one full sentence in English in the novel: "O my gosh!" (237). Moreover, in *Dúnmharú sa Daingean*, Ní Dhuibhne uses English when presenting material from the media, but, in *Dún an Airgid*, the newspaper report is in Irish (194–5). In fact, Joe Duffy's RTÉ Radio One 'Liveline' show has been linguistically colonised and renamed 'An Líne Bheo' (36)!

There are two small examples where Ní Dhuibhne chooses to refer to language issues. In the first, Máirtín is contemplating 'Googling' wedding proposal formulae:

B'fhéidir go raibh treoir éigin ar an idirlíon faoi sin freisin? Conas an cheist a chur. Ní bheadh sé i nGaeilge ar ndóigh. How to Propose without Making an Eeejit of Yourself. How to make a successful Proposal. Bheadh air an abairt a aistriú go Gaeilge é féin. (167) [Perhaps there was some guide on the Internet about it too? How to pop the question. It wouldn't be in Irish, of course ... He himself would have to translate it into Irish.]

In the second example, Ní Dhuibhne appears to have been concerned that readers would not recognise that one meaning of the word 'bráthair' (usually a religious brother) is 'monkfish.' Thus, while Saoirse and Máirtín are dining: "Bhí an bráthair, an t-iasc sin ar a dtugtar iasc an mhanaigh i mBéarla ... á ithe acu" [They were eating monkfish, that fish called 'monkfish' in English] (259). But, apart from these examples, Ní Dhuibhne is content simply to present, without comment or subversion, her fictional town of *Dún an Airgid* as one where people speak Irish, and to accept that this artistic and literary decision needs no justification or explanation. Ní Dhuibhne has travelled a long and winding road linguistically from *an Daingean* to *Dún an Airgid*.

Language, Literacy – and Bestsellers

One can approach Ní Dhuibhne's use of English in her Irish language works from the perspectives of both writer and reader. Ní Dhuibhne is a writer who is learning to expand her range in Irish and is gradually becoming more comfortable writing in the language. She is also a person who writes in two languages. Though Ní Dhuibhne has commented on the potential and challenge for the bilingual writer in Irish to write for a readership that can handle works that combine Irish and English, she has lamented the absence of such works and the resistance to such bilingualism from Irish language readers:

Tá scríbhneoirí dátheangacha againn agus tá léitheoirí dátheangacha againn in Éirinn. Ach, lasmuigh de shaothar nó dhó, an rud atá in easnamh orainn ná leabhair dhátheangacha. Is ait an scéal é![31]

214

[We have bilingual writers and we have bilingual readers in Ireland. But, apart from one or two works, the thing that we lack is bilingual books. It's a strange situation.]

Ironically, in light of her comments about hostility towards bilingual works – Ní Dhuibhne may really be talking about Irish language *literati*, critics and academics, amongst whom one senses a certain uneasiness about her handling of Irish in *Dúnmharú sa Daingean* – it is evident that there is a market for the types of novels written by Ní Dhuibhne. Caoilfhionn Nic Pháidín, a co-director of Cois Life, the publishing company that has issued Ní Dhuibhne's Irish language books, has argued that the Irish language publishing industry must strive to cater to ordinary readers:

Má tá rún againn dáiríre an gnáthphobal a chur ag léamh, ní ar an ardlitríocht go príomha ba chóir an bhéim a leagan. Ní mór seánraí nua a shaothrú, ficsean bog, eachtraíocht, agus bleachtaireacht, na cineálacha leabhar is coitianta a léitear in aon teanga.

Tá cuid mhór *litríochta* á foilsiú le blianta agus gan mórán éilimh uirthi, go háirithe na saothair nach mbaineann ionad amach ar chúrsaí ollscoile. Sa mhéid go leanann an seó ar aghaidh beag beann ar an margadh agus tost criticiúil mórthimpeall ar an mórchuid de, táimid ag séanadh freagrachta i luacháil na saothar sin, agus is beag an cúnamh é sin do chothú na léitheoireachta.[32]

[If we are serious about getting ordinary people reading, the emphasis should not primarily be on highbrow literature. It is necessary to cultivate new genres: light fiction, adventure and detective material, the sorts of books most commonly read in any language.

A lot of *literature* has been published over the years for which there has been little demand, especially in the case of works that have not found themselves on university courses. To the extent that the show goes on regardless of the market and largely with a critical silence about what is happening, we are denying responsibility for the evaluation of these works. That is not much help in promoting reading.]

It is interesting that Nic Pháidín has framed her critique in the context of the increasing gap between spoken Irish and the written language, since it is tempting to see a connection between the commercial success of *Dúnmharú sa Daingean* and its accessibility linguistically. It brings to mind the comment by Robert Welch about Brian Friel's *Translations* where, though the play is largely in English, the audience accepts the convention that they are, in fact, listening to Irish. The audience, states Welch, "are engaged in a translation game where they have all the pleasure and none of the effort".[33] So, too, with *Dúnmharú sa Daingean*, a pleasurable read that requires little linguistic effort from the Irish reader.

Undoubtedly, seeing a connection between *Dúnmharú sa Daingean*'s commercial success and its Irish-lite style ignores other potentially important factors. The novel is an enjoyable read. As Ní Dhuibhne notes, sales of the book may have benefited from the publicity garnered by *The Dancers Dancing*.[34] We have no comparative sales figures for the other Irish novels. However, it is likely that much of *Dúnmharú sa Daingean*'s 3000–plus sales have been by university students who are studying Irish as part of their undergraduate degrees. Poet and scholar, Louis de Paor, has commented recently that the centenary commemorations and celebration associated with the birth of Máirtín Ó Cadhain (1906–1970), the major prose writer in Irish in the twentieth century, do not necessarily mean that more people are reading his work. Specifically, de Paor states that, in most Irish universities and third level colleges, one can earn an undergraduate degree in Irish without reading any of Ó Cadhain's work since he is viewed as a difficult writer whose language is too challenging for students. But, as de Paor notes, Ó Cadhain is not the only writer who has been neglected by readers:

> Tríd is tríd, tá glactha againn leis, is cosúil, nár cheart do scríbhneoirí Gaeilge an léitheoir a chur thar a fhulaingt le caint chrua ná le haon ní eile, ó thaobh teicníochta nó foirme, a chuirfeadh ó dhoras í/é.[35]
>
> [In general, we apparently have accepted that Irish language writers should not task the reader with difficult language or anything else, technique- or form-wise that would put him or her off.]

When one adds to this an acknowledgement by Cois Life co-directors, Seán Ó Cearnaigh and Caoilfhionn Nic Pháidín, that commercial success rarely accrues to works that don't use a limited and superficial level of language ["is annamh a bhíonn rath sa mhargadh ar shaothair nach gcleachtaíonn teanga thanaí theoranta"][36] one senses that Ní Dhuibhne's success is due, not just to filling a gap in the Irish language market with books that are readable and enjoyable as works of fiction, but also because her work *Dúnmharú sa Daingean*, in particular, does not tax the limited linguistic resources of much of her readership.

In *Dún an Airgid*, Ní Dhuibhne has, on one level, merely returned to the form and handling of Irish that we found in her play, *Dún na mBan Trí Thine*. Yet, in correcting so comprehensively her approach in her bestseller *Dúnmharú sa Daingean*, Ní Dhuibhne has signalled that she has a fresh awareness of the choices and challenges that she faces as she matures as an Irish language writer. To date, she has made a worthy contribution to literature in Irish. There is no reason to doubt that she will continue to enrich the tradition as she moves forward. However, it will be interesting to see how well she succeeds in bringing her readers along with her on the journey ahead.

NOTES

1 All translations are by the author. I am indebted to Jerry White and Christine St. Peter for their valuable feedback on an early version of this essay.

2 Christine St. Peter, 'Negotiating the Boundaries: An Interview with Éilís Ní Dhuibhne'. *Canadian Journal of Irish Studies*, 32. 1 (Spring 2006: 68–75), 69.

3 Róisín Ní Mhianáin, ed. *Idir Lúibíní. Aistí ar an Léitheoireacht agus ar an Litearthacht* (Baile Átha Cliath: Cois Life, 2003), 15.

4 Ní Dhuibhne, 'Why Would Anyone Write in Irish?' in Ciarán Mac Murchaidh, ed., *'Who Needs Irish': Reflections on the Importance of the Irish Language Today* (Dublin: Veritas Publications, 2004: 70–82), 77.

5 *ibid.*, 80.

6 *ibid.*, 81.

7 St. Peter, 'Negotiating the Boundaries', 68.

8   Alan Titley, *Méirscrí na Treibhe* (Baile Átha Cliath: An Clóchomhar, 1978).

9   Ní Dhuibhne, *Hurlamaboc* (Baile Átha Cliath: Cois Life, 2006), 15. Further references to *H* are in parentheses in the text.

10   Ní Dhuibhne, "Saibhreas nó Daibhreas? An Scríbhneoir Dátheangach" in Aisling Ní Dhonnchadha, ed. *An Prós Comhaimseartha. Léachtaí Cholm Cille* XXXVI. (Maigh Nuad: An Sagart, 2006: 139–154), 152; St. Peter, 'Negotiating the Boundaries, 69.

11   Máirín Nic Eoin, *Trén bhFearann Breac. An Díláithriú Cultúir agus Nualitríocht na Gaeilge* (Baile Átha Cliath: Cois Life, 2005); Caoilfhionn Nic Pháidín, "'Cén Fáth Nach?'- Ó Chanúint Go Críól" in Róisín Ní Mhianáin, ed. *Idir Lúibíní. Aistí ar an Léitheoireacht agus ar an Litearthacht* (Baile Átha Cliath: Cois Life, 2003: 113–130), 123–26.

12   Ronald Wardhaugh, *An Introduction to Sociolinguistics*. 4th ed. (Malden, Massachusetts: Blackwell Publishing, 2002), 60.

13   Ní Dhuibhne, *The Dancers Dancing* (Belfast: Blackstaff Press, 1999). Further references to *DD* are in parentheses in the text.

14   Ní Dhuibhne in Ní Dhonnchadha, 'Saibhreas nó Daibhreas?', 149.

15   Ní Dhuibhne, *Milseog an tSamhraidh* agus *Dún na mBan Trí Thine* (Baile Átha Cliath: Cois Life, 1997), 87–88. Further references to *Dún* are in parentheses in the text.

16   *ibid.* Further references to *Milseog* are in parentheses in the text.

17   Joe Steve Ó Neachtain, *Scread Mhaidne* (Indreabhán: Cló Iar-Chonnachta, 2003); *Lámh Láidir* (Indreabhán: Cló Iar-Chonnachta, 2005).

18   Ní Dhuibhne, 'Luachra' in Cathal Póirtéir, ed. *Scéalta san Aer* (Baile Átha Cliath: Coiscéim, 2000: 96–102). Further references to 'Luachra' are in parentheses in the text.

19   Wardhaugh, *An Introduction to Sociolinguistics*, 62.

20   Caoilfhionn Nic Pháidín in Ní Mhianáin, ed. "'Cén Fáth Nach?', 123.

21   Liam Ó Muirthile, 'Ó, Lucky muid', 'Á, Poor iad', 'Madraí na Nollag', 'Óró Anró'. *Ar an bPeann* (Baile Átha Cliath: Cois Life, 2006: 187–203).

22   Ní Dhuibhne, *Dúnmharú sa Daingean* (Baile Átha Cliath: Cois Life, 2000). Further references to *Dúnmharú* are in parentheses in the text.

23   All page numbers provided in parentheses in sections A – J are from Ní Dhuibhne, *Dúnmharú sa Daingean* (2000).

24   Wardhaugh, *An Introduction to Sociolinguistics*, 61.

25   Micheál Ó Conghaile, 'An Fear Aniar. An Interview with Micheál Ó Conghaile'. *Canadian Journal of Irish Studies*, 31. 2 (Fall 2005: 54–59), 56.

26   Pádraig Ó Siadhail, 'Contemporary Irish Language Literature: A Parasite's Delight (Or Súgáin, Sougawns, and Straw Ropes)'. *The Nashwaak Review*, 10. 1 (Fall 2001: 106–122), 114.

27   Ní Dhuibhne in Mac Murchaidh, ed. 'Why Would Anyone Write in Irish?', 77.

28   Ní Dhuibhne, *Cailíní Beaga Ghleann na mBláth* (Baile Átha Cliath: Cois Life, 2003). Further references to *CB* are in parentheses in the text.

29   Ní Dhuibhne, *Dún an Airgid* (Baile Átha Cliath: Coise Life, 2008). Further references to *Airgid* are in parentheses in the text.

30   David McWilliams, *The Pope's Children. Ireland's New Elite* (Dublin: Gill & Macmillan, 2006), 146–7.

31   Ní Dhuibhne in Ní Dhonnchadha, ed. 'Saibhreas nó Daibhreas?', 153.

32   Nic Pháidín, '"Cén Fáth Nach?', 129.

33   Robert Welch, '"Isn't This Your Job? – To Translate?" Brian Friel's Languages' in Alan J. Peacock, ed. *The Achievement of Brian Friel* (Gerrards Cross: Colin Smythe, 1993:   134–48), 144.

34   St. Peter, 'Negotiating the Boundaries', 69.

35   Louis de Paor, 'Ceist, cé léifeadh Máirtín Ó Cadhain'. *Comhar*, (Samhain) [November] (2006: 7–9), 9.

36   Seán Ó Cearnaigh and Caoilfhionn Nic Pháidín, 'Pláinéad Uaigneach – Prós na Gaeilge' in Aisling Ní Dhonnchadha, ed. *An Prós Comhaimseartha. Léachtaí Cholm Cille XXXVI.* Maigh Nuad: An Sagart, 2006: 7–24), 10.

Indirection in Éilís Ní Dhuibhne's Re-telling of 'The Search for the Lost Husband' and 'Midwife to the Fairies'

JACQUELINE FULMER

A prize-winning writer, a postmodern feminist, and a folklorist walk into a bar. The punch line, if one existed, is that these three are all the same person. Opening with a reference to a common western oral tradition – the bar joke – seems an appropriate way to address the work of an author who regularly carries the qualities of oral art into written art (albeit in a more entertaining manner than I have just now). In an apparent contradiction, Éilís Ní Dhuibhne's fiction brings together an offbeat postmodern feminist sensibility with Irish oral tradition. To clarify my use of the term, I refer to Jean-François Lyotard's description of the postmodern as that "incredulity toward metanarratives", a condition of the late twentieth- early twenty-first-century in which western audiences do not readily agree on common overarching narratives, which may have previously unified a social group or may have previously given a basis for authority to a group of leaders.[1] Increasingly in this time period, audiences – and social critics – hesitate to accept the existence of one "great hero", or even one "great goal", in common.[2] Contemporary Irish culture falls under this description, as neither the accounts of national emergence nor assertions of the Catholic Church carry the same level of influence as they did in previous generations. Yet, if oral tradition represents the passing of enduring stories from one member of a generation to the next, how can Ní Dhuibhne's stories fall under both 'postmodern' and 'traditional' categories? For that matter, how does her humorous fiction reconcile any ideas of the 'traditional' and the 'feminist', especially if one were to interpret the multiple forms of feminism as rejecting many of the traditions that have confronted women through the centuries? The answer is that Ní Dhuibhne brings together the 'postmodern' and the 'traditional' with exacting detail, in a rhetorical approach that reflects the strengths of both subjects. Upon examination, via folkloristics (the study of folklore) and feminist literary criticism (with a special nod to humour studies) one finds, ultimately, no division between Ní Dhuibhne's folkloric, feminist, and postmodern sensibilities. As conjoined in what I refer to elsewhere as "strategies of indirection",[3] the influences of oral tradition and the postmodern flow into a stream that runs throughout Ní Dhuibhne's work. By way of example here, I will draw on two of Ní Dhuibhne's most 'folkloric' short stories: 'The Search for the Lost Husband' and 'Midwife to the Fairies'.

The primary term of this essay – strategies of indirection – does not refer to the linguistic use of free indirect style, such as when the authorial point of view in a story blends into that of a character's. Rather, the term refers to when writers or orators wish to delay or obstruct their audience's comprehension of their position on a subject, which may contradict that of the audience. Skilled authors and speakers manipulate the stages of the audience's understanding to slow or obscure its comprehension of the story's main points. These are rhetorical situations where the rhetor, that is, the speaker or writer, risks losing her audience's good-will, or more, if she approaches a controversial subject directly. To understand what rhetorical indirection is, and how its strategies operate, it is important to first take into account why it must exist at all. That is, we must understand the conditions for rhetorical indirection.

In certain social settings, if too many members of the audience understand too much of the message at too early a point, the rhetor may face grave consequences ranging from censorship and shunning through, even, to death. Indirection, as a term, therefore, represents any communicative strategy designed to smuggle meaning past such obstacles to expression. Different rhetors in different eras produce their own strategies and terms tailored to their communicative context. Ultimately, the thread connecting these gulfs of time, location, and culture is that each rhetor in each situation must not reveal all. The speaker or writer may be trying to communicate within his or her cultural group, to an outside group, or to both at the same time. Different elements of a story may be intended for different factions of the audience. Elements of the story's meaning may, for that matter, be held back from either outside or inside audience members. If indirection stands for the general approach to such rhetorical practice, then 'strategies of indirection' here will refer to the endlessly inventive methods of artists, working in oral or print media, to express themselves under social pressure.

The strategies that grow out of conditions that limit communication include strategies that arise out of oral tradition and other forms of folkloric expression. The relationship between indirection and folklore, then, in Ní Dhuibhne's work, actually propels the postmodern and feminist tendencies in her stories. Folklore, as it forms both the medium and the material for many indirect communications, possesses a unique resistance to censorship, since it can pass from person to person in ways no state or media can effectively control.[4] Folklore's ability to alter itself according to social context, combined with the ability to exist 'under the radar', gives it and its subset of oral tradition a built-in subversive potential. A folktale may contain a point, a moral to the story, or it may leave its point obscured. Ní Dhuibhne, then, utilises folklore's built-in qualities of ambiguity to leave her readers with images and ideas they might have rejected if presented in a direct fashion. Because the storytelling tradition separates the teller and the listener from their immediate surroundings, it lifts the discourse out of the tensions of the present moment. The charm of a 'little story' can disarm an audience out of its vigilance against new or challenging ideas.

Since most storytelling and other folk traditions operate outside the mainstream of a culture's mass media, whether ostensibly free market or state-controlled, the potentially disruptive qualities of those traditions make them unusually appropriate for postmodern critical projects that seek out such creative disruption. The study of folklore, as it appears in literature, assists in postmodern analyses of how various influences shape identity in a society. When uncovering how culture-as-hegemony shapes citizen-subjects, in David Lloyd's example, criticism "depends increasingly on the attempt to recover subterranean or marginalized practices which have been understood variously, as aberrant, pre-modern and residual, or incoherent".[5] Oral and other folk traditions, because they are spread from person to person rather than via 'official' media, have themselves been viewed as "aberrant, pre-modern and residual, or incoherent"[6] epithets often assigned also to groups who have been cut out of mainstream dialogues.

However, Irish authors of the early-twenty-first century, like Ní Dhuibhne, bring the disruptive qualities of oral tradition to mainstream readers. Christina Hunt Mahoney includes Ní Dhuibhne in her critical review *Contemporary Irish Literature: Transforming Tradition,* and she draws a generalisation about Ní Dhuibhne's generation of writers, suggesting that the ancient storytelling tradition is "largely responsible for the magical or revelatory tales recent Irish novelists and other prose writers have been telling us".[7] Mahoney includes Ní Dhuibhne's writing as part of a larger movement in literature, as well as part of an Irish tradition that encourages artists to leave behind linear narrative and "blur the historically sacred boundaries between the real and the imagined".[8] What she distinguishes as 'Irish', in her critical reception of Ní Dhuibhne's body of work, leads back into oral tradition, which, for Mahoney, has never left the culture.[9] With the old comes the new, as Mahoney, in examining the title story of Ní Dhuibhne's *Eating Women Is Not Recommended* (1991), describes Ní Dhuibhne's writing as erupting "into full-scale resentment of the imposition of traditional female roles" and questioning the "strictures imposed upon married women and the expectations society has of them".[10] Consciousness-raising accompanies consciousness of tradition in Ní Dhuibhne's works.

If Mahoney sees feminism joining oral tradition in Ní Dhuibhne's works, then Cristina Bacchilega, in *Postmodern Fairy Tales: Gender and Narrative Strategies*, joins oral tradition and feminism to the postmodern in a way that also reflects upon Ní Dhuibhne's writing. Bacchilega reads similar "postmodern transformations of the fairy tale" as "doubling and double: both affirmative and questioning, without necessarily being recuperative or politically subversive".[11] She clarifies her point by stating that, "in every case, though, these postmodern transformations do not exploit the fairytale's magic simply to make the spell work, but rather to unmake some of its workings", that only those rewritings that "expose or upset the paradigms of authority inherent in the texts they appropriate" are "disobedient".[12]

Adding humor to the 'disobedience' disarms the recalcitrant reader too. The distancing and seduction of storytelling creates a communal space for the audience. In that space, ambiguity is welcomed, and so, therefore, may be the audience members who might otherwise feel alienated by off-putting subject matter. The performative aspects of folklore also create a space for audience members to participate in making the meaning of the tale. Ní Dhuibhne particularly relies on this aspect of folklore in her writing. As the recognition of some of those aspects depends on a shared Irish cultural history, it does help to have a guide to folkloric allusions. This is where noting parallel examples taken from tale type or folklore motif indices may help readers unfamiliar with a certain culturally-specific detail in a story. Regardless, attentive audience members can still spot out-of-the-ordinary moments in fiction where slippage between this world and the Otherworld may exist. Those ambiguous moments allow the rhetor in question, Ní Dhuibhne, to destabilise an audience member's assumptions. With a temporary suspension of 'real world' expectations, the suspension of disbelief allows her readers to entertain different ideas about topics they might not otherwise consider.

While the Censorship Board in Ireland does not operate with the broad reach it once did, it still exists and, as recently as the early 1990s, banned pornography, materials advocating abortion, materials that give "an unduly large proportion of space to matters relating to crime", and without explicitly stating so, materials addressing homosexuality.[13] In asking Ní Dhuibhne herself what topics she considers difficult to broach with an Irish audience, she answered that, "abortion is difficult. Anything which seems to be critical, even mildly, of Irish communities, of their values and mores, can easily cause offence within those communities. Irish language issues. You always stub some sensitive toe. And sex".[14] In spite of the late twentieth-, early-twenty-first- century atmosphere of increased openness on sexuality, greatly reduced censorship, and a still-developing women's movement, Ní Dhuibhne's tales still use 'strategies of indirection', via folklore, to smuggle ideas into the minds of a sometimes recalcitrant audience.

In her re-telling of 'The Search for the Lost Husband' and 'Midwife to the Fairies', Ní Dhuibhne reveals the potential of folklore to pleasurably subvert audience expectations. In addition, her 'folkloric' fiction indirectly expresses views that question the status of women in Ireland. In both stories, young women find themselves caught between the demands of their social positions, their own needs (the acknowledgement of which is seemingly suppressed), and the subtle, but thorough, control their partners exert over them. In this bind, female characters appear either unnaturally silent or faced with a taboo against speaking out on certain subjects. Both stories also feature mothers engaged in life-giving or life-denying actions (depending on the reader's point of view), which transgress the moral code of their fictional worlds. To carry such delicate subjects home to her readers, Ní Dhuibhne employs strategies of indirection, such as folkloric expression and humour. Via indirection, she attracts and holds the attention of a broad audience to the still-volatile subjects of inequality between men and women, and the strains of motherhood.

The thoroughness of the ties between the stories and documented examples of Irish oral tradition may be seen in the easily-traced references to tale types, migratory legend, and motifs found in folklore. An enormous number of Ní Dhuibhne's references may be located in: folklore studies, such as those by Séan Ó Súilleabháin (Sean O'Sullivan); the indices of types of tales and the motifs found in them, such as those collected by Antti Aarne and Stith Thompson; and legends analysed in folklore journals, such as *Béaloideas*.[15] Folklorists, since the mid-nineteenth century, have developed such collections and indices, along with various explanatory theories, because certain plotlines, images, actions, character types, and distinctive objects repeat themselves so often in stories passed from person to person. Researchers have long been drawn to folklore as a subject because of its lasting power to shape identities, peoples, families, and individuals, and because of folklore's lasting influence over every aspect of culture, including literature.[16] Yet the authenticity of her stories' ties to oral tradition does not hold them back from demonstrating the qualities of postmodern fiction. Rather, her thorough grounding in folkloristics enables such questioning and reversals to take place in her fiction. Her expertise in creative writing and folklore seems to give her the ability to complicate and enrich the audience's expectations of both disciplines. As my analysis will show, this is only a contradiction on the surface.

Ní Dhuibhne's interpretation of folklore is no glib restaging of the watered-down princess tales found so often in mass media, and it would be a misconception to assume that folklore offers too old a reference for her contemporary themes. Folklorist Alan Dundes has written that the 'folk' refers "to any group of people whatsoever who share at least one common factor", and that 'lore' refers to those "traditions which [the group] calls its own", often orally-passed customs, stories, songs, sayings, and more.[17] If this is so, then all of us engage at some point in our lives with folklore, regardless of our time period, social position, or locale. In addition, feminist folklorists have been quick to note that oral traditions can operate as "subversive, pluralist, unruly, and potentially revolutionary expressions of a subaltern class", as Angela

Bourke restates some of Antonio Gramsci's ideas on oral tradition.[18] Therefore, even in the midst of the 'traditional', a storyteller can insert elements that question other narratives, as they have been received from more powerful sources in a society. So, in addition to the celebration of culture found in the folkloric references of Ní Dhuibhne's fiction, she employs her cultural understanding to express herself in ways that are sometimes limited by authoritative influences in Irish society. Thus, one of her most prominent rhetorical techniques, her use of indirection, brings all the streams of influence together at once.

Using some of the 'unmaking' and 'disobedience' that Bacchilega and Nancy A. Walker identify in feminist and postmodern fiction, Ní Dhuibhne radically alters two traditional tales that appear in Ireland and elsewhere: the folktale AT Tale Type 425 'The Search for the Lost Husband',[19] and the legend 'Midwife to the Fairies'.[20] In her stories, however, Ní Dhuibhne makes some amusing, yet critical, changes to the original tales.

For example, in most versions of 'The Search for the Lost Husband', such as the one Ní Dhuibhne herself translated for *The Field Day Anthology,* Máire Ruiséal's recitation of 'The Story of the Little White Goat', the wife and the lost husband reunite.[21] But Ní Dhuibhne changes the ending in her version. This 'unmaking' appears in Ní Dhuibhne's 'The Search for the Lost Husband', [22] when the woman searches for the husand "up hill and down dale" only to reject him in the end, stating that, "It's time for me to try another kind of love. I'm tired of all that fairytale stuff" ('Search' 262). In Ní Dhuibhne's translation of the recorded telling of 'The Story of the Little White Goat', Ruiséal ends the tale with, among many blessings, 'they lived happily ever after, and in comfort'.

In a similar way, whereas most versions of the legend 'Midwife to the Fairies' set the tale in an indefinite 'long ago', Ní Dhuibhne gives her version a detailed, late-twentieth-century setting. Yet the two stories bear strong resemblances to the oral tales as described in studies such as the Aarne-Thompson (AT) index, *The Types of the Folktale: A Classification and Bibliography*, and the journal *Béaloideas*, even down to the use of titles common to many of the folk versions of the stories.

Ní Dhuibhne's restaging of the tale 'The Search for the Lost Husband' appears in short increments before, between, and after Ní Dhuibhne's other stories in *'The Inland Ice' and Other Stories*. Her segmented short story contains recognisably exact details, such as one would find in folklorists' analyses of orally-circulated versions of the story. For example, Ní Dhuibhne's story features a transformation of a man to a 'little white goat' who charms a farmer's daughter, which exemplifies Thompson motif B651, 'Marriage to beast in human form'.[23] Thompson motif D621.1, 'Animal by day; man by night' appears when the husband changes from goat to human.[24] Motif D700, 'person disenchanted', appears when, after many travails, the beleaguered wife in the story succeeds in relieving the goat-husband of his curse.[25] More tellingly, motif C31, 'Tabu: offending supernatural wife', mirrors those moments in the written story when Ní Dhuibhne's fictional wife offends her animal husband; in her case, the offense comes when she dares to speak of her grief in losing a child.[26] Even the folktale motifs D1472.1.7, 'Magic table [here, a magic table cloth] supplies food and drink', and D1652.1, 'Inexhaustible food', appear in the short story as part of the wife's adventures.[27] In other words, where many writers may draw upon bits of the oral tradition, Ní Dhuibhne's advantage is her extensive knowledge of where those stories come from and how they can vary in place and time. With that knowledge she constructs a familiar, but rhetorically challenging, short story that consciously draws on – and amplifies – undercurrents of tension in the oral tales.

In a similar vein, Christina Hunt Mahoney sees the interspersing of the fourteen sections of the short story 'The Search for the Lost Husband' throughout the book as replicating the performance and experience of a "nightly storytelling" and giving "an authentically folkloric ring to this tale":[28]

> The alternation between Ní Dhuibhne's more contemporary and topical tales, which frequently feature professional women who find themselves far from home for career reasons ... and the

simplicity of 'The Search for the Lost Husband', suggests a day-and-night rhythm. The latter, interrupted tale is thus placed in the *seanachaí* tradition of fireside stories, often told serially at night ... Her trenchant social commentary is delivered with humor and a sprinkle of magic, and can be devastatingly on target. It is a sustained and highly imaginative voice that is all the more distinctive in that, while answering a feminist imperative, it is not constrained by contemporary feminist fashion or critical *dicta*. [29]

Even though the commentary that appears between the lines does answer a 'feminist imperative' of a sort, as Mahoney notes, Ní Dhuibhne begins the short story 'The Search for the Lost Husband' with a formulaic opening taken from the oldest forms of oral performance: "Long long ago there was a farmer ...". ('Search' 1). Every day the little white goat comes to the door of the farmer's daughter and, eventually, she falls in love with it: "After a year or so the goat stopped coming ... an old woman told her that he had gone over the road to the east. When the girl heard that, she set off after him" (1). Thus begins this latter-day fictionalisation. The qualities, however, that would include this version in Bacchilega's category of the postmodern would also include it among examples of folkloric expression and humour as strategies of indirection, as it refers obliquely to tensions between men and women, power struggles, and mothers lacking support. While innocuous on the first page, the phrase, "after a year or so the goat stopped coming", grows to take on the overtones of an on-again-off-again affair of contemporary times. In the second installment of the story, the un-named farmer's daughter sets up "home in a big fine house. And he was a goat by day and a man by night" (27). 'Well and good', as some Irish storytellers might say, but then the goat of the story sets certain taboos on the young woman. Upon the birth of their baby, he decrees that, "if anything happened", if she were to "shed a tear", "she would lose him, her husband" (43). All three babies are snatched from her, with the goat watching her closely to make sure she does not show her emotions: "haven't you me for company?" is his shallow reply. The narrator of the story ends this segment with the formulaic phrase, "that's how it was" (43).

At this point, not only do the formulaic punctuating phrases, generic setting, and magic of the short story seem familiar, so too do the reactions of some of the story's characters to the situation. Only these do not take their familiarity from the world of folklore, but from something closer to home: the restrictions women hear sometimes from the lips of lovers and husbands. The threat of a husband's leaving held over the young mother's head recalls folk motif F833.2, 'Sword of Damocles. Sword hung on thin thread above person', a motif one actually does see in variants of the legend and the short story version of 'Midwife to the Fairies'.[30] The sword, in 'The Search for the Lost Husband' hovers over the admission of any emotion displeasing to the goat-husband, a common enough occurrence in non-folkloric fiction.

The wording begins to emphasise, more and more directly, aspects more familiar from late-twentieth-century relationship stories than from tales passed orally over generations. This shift shows up most prominently after the young mother sheds one tear after her third baby is "taken away from her" (77). The dialogue of the goat-husband in the short story becomes noticeably ruder to the young mother and deviates from the generic quality of dialogue as encountered in some transcripts of traditional tales. Over many of the short story's segments, interspersed throughout the book, the goat-husband berates the woman for crying over the loss of her children, telling her she has "no sense," and calling her mission to win him back "a fool's errand" (77–78, 138, 124). From another perspective, his language takes on the idiosyncratic qualities that a storyteller might infuse in the character during performance, or that a fiction writer would use to construct a unique character. Such specific details about a relationship's balance of power rarely appears in folktale dialogue to the degree that it does here, as with the goat-husband's language of coercion. In folktales, relationship details will more likely appear in condensed form as imagery and action. Looking at the category of 'Tales of Magic' in Seán O'Súilleabháin's *A Handbook of Irish Folklore*, one is hard pressed to find long arguments over separation listed among the summaries of tales involving marriage.[31] But in Ní

Dhuibhne's story, attention is paid to the goat-husband's alienating comments to his wife, all the while surrounded by documented folk motifs of enchanted persons and magical objects. The extent of the conversations, with their explicit implications of the power the goat-husband holds over his wife, may not show up in that level of detail in transcripts of oral versions of 'The Search for the Lost Husband' (such as in Máire Ruiséal's performance of 'The Story of the Little White Goat'), but folktales such as this one have traditionally provided an outlet for tellers and listeners to contemplate inequitable relations between men and women.

In another example of a much-told tale, one that Ní Dhuibhne has also retold in short story form, 'The Mermaid Legend' consistently carries the theme of a female's capture by a man into domesticity and in which captivity and escape are repeated throughout the many variations of the folktale. The tale's longevity draws attention to the possibilities raised by Maureen Murphy, Bo Almqvist, and Angela Bourke, separately, that the folk versions may have operated as a mask for women storytellers to contemplate "layer upon layer of attitudes and approaches to the problems involved" in male-female relationships[32], as well as to contemplate escape from marriage in a time and place where that could not happen.[33] Just as the tensions and power struggles repeat themselves in the mermaid tale, so do the tensions and power struggles in Ní Dhuibhne's versions of 'The Search for the Lost Husband' and 'Midwife to the Fairies'. However, her more detailed contemporary dialogue brings out these tensions in ways that mere transcription may have muted over past decades of folklore research.

In Ní Dhuibhne's story, the goat-husband delivers his ultimate, verbal blow to the female protagonist. These lines reveal the element of control the enchanted spouses of oral tradition may have held over the spouse in pursuit, depending on the performer's level of emphasis:

> If she shed one tear, he would abandon her, "Now", he said. "I won't stay with you for one more day. You can't keep your eyes dry", he said, "so you can't have me. I warned you", he said. "You

can cry away as much as you like now, but I won't be here to comfort you. I'm leaving you now, and you will never see me again ... you haven't got a chance of getting me back". ('Search' 77–78)

Much of the dialogue in this segment still reflects oral tradition. The rhythm and syntax of the characters' speech sound like the Hiberno-English of Irish folktales, and the narrator repeats the formulaic "that's how it was" (77). Meanwhile, the parallel structure of "you can't keep your eyes dry/you can't have me", and the repetition of "he said" punctuate the lines. All these items reflect traditional oral storytelling style, but the increasingly emotional threats of the goat-husband speak of a more recent vintage. One might find such individualised details of a failed relationship as "you can't keep your eyes dry" in a contemporary novel or short story. Normally, one does not find such specific comments on a couple's relationship in folktales, at least not as they are usually recorded in print. Here, Ní Dhuibhne illustrates Bacchilega's disobedient-to-perceived-tradition, tongue-in-cheek 'shaping' that exposes not only "the paradigms of authority inherent" in the folktale in which the woman goes over hill and dale, unquestioningly, to pursue the lost husband, but also the paradigm of authority inherent in many women's affairs, in which a woman must squelch her emotions to keep from 'scaring off', as it were, a none-too-committed lover.[34]

This may point, too, to Ní Dhuibhne's sense of the performative in storytelling, the individual storyteller's own infusion of personality in the use of character detail and embellishment. The commentary on the power of utterance, and the denial of utterance, where the scale of influence has tipped on one side or the other, strikes me as an example where strategies of indirection – folkloric expression and humour – can broach a still-delicate subject. One could imagine a woman in such a situation leaving the innocuous-looking 'folktale' out on a table for her partner, much like one hears of people leaving out something as public and seemingly neutral as a newspaper advice column. The public nature of folklore, with its popular image as something for children, as non-political, unbiased, non-threatening, in this case works to slip in some 'questioning', as Bacchilega describes, about the nature of power in romantic relationships. Yet this story stays in the realm of the 'affirmative' pleasures of a folklore-influenced example of short fiction. A directly critical approach, as other feminist authors might write for an audience of like-minded readers, would not likely be read by a broader audience, one that might include men who perhaps bear some resemblance to the little white goat.

In addition, the irony of the statement, "you can cry away as much as you like now, but I won't be here to comfort you" (78), lies in a sense of layering between the author, the narration, the character himself in the tale, and the reader. The character does not sense the irony that he was never there to 'comfort' her at any other time, nor that the first clause of the sentence automatically cancels out any possibility of the second clause being true. The dialogue in the narrative appears as a knowing wink to the reader, much as it would to an audience of listeners, that, in this incident, the woman is blameless.

The final 'disobedience' of Ní Dhuibhne's story is found in its ending. After tracking down the husband, losing him, tracking him again, trading magic scissors, a magic comb, and a "food-producing cloth", lifting the curse, and getting her children back, Ní Dhuibhne's story alters the plot, as it has been usually passed down, by having her woman protagonist tell her husband:

> I think I've had enough of you ... Goodbye to you now ... And maybe I will find another husband, who will be kind to me and my children, and who will look after all of us and not lead us around in circles. Because it's time for me to try another kind of love. I'm tired of all that fairytale stuff. (262)

Like the goat-husband's break-up speech, this too carries more nuances of contemporary informal discourse than transcribed folktales usually do. The irony of a fairytale-like character commenting that she herself is tired of "fairytale stuff", and her subversion of the ending – she leaves him – indicates a reversal emblematic of Regina Barreca's feminist humor: "Women's comedy is 'dangerous' because it refuses to accept the givens and because it refuses to stop at the point where comedy loses its integrative function. This comedy by women is about de-centering, dis-locating and de-stabilising the world".[35] As mentioned before, in the Máire Ruiséal recitation of 'The Story of the Little White Goat', the wife and the husband stay together. In that oral version, the most common plotline for this folktale conforms to social expectations of prior generations: that unless enchanted, mortal husbands and wives stay together until death. In Ní Dhuibhne's written version, the wife transgresses that pattern by leaving the no-longer-enchanted husband who, though apologetic, seems too quick to use his previous condition as an excuse for the pain he put her through. Even her leaving is shot through with humour, and the wife enjoys a happy ending of a different kind: a kinder (second) husband. Here, the feminist emphasis on bettering the condition of a woman who has been silenced, held back as a mother, and otherwise 'worn and torn' by her marriage to the goat-husband, meets up with the postmodern emphasis on questioning received narratives.

Ní Dhuibhne ends with this concluding formula: "That is my story. And if there is a lie in it, it was not I who made it up. All I got for my story was butter boots and paper hats. And a white dog came and ate the boots and tore the hats. But what matter? What matters but the good of the story?" (262). When I asked Ní Dhuibhne about the formulaic phrasing, including the meaning of "butter boots and paper hats", she responded with, "nonsense, I think, the message being that the storyteller got nothing at all (ie, no material gain) for the story".[36] In this way, Ní Dhuibhne ends her reinterpretation of both Tale Type 425 and modern break-up stories with humour, folk tradition, and graceful absurdity.

In Bacchilega's terms, this rewriting of a tale 'unmakes' some of the 'workings' inherent in many stories of power struggles between men and women. Likewise, in 'Midwife to the Fairies',[37] Ní Dhuibhne combines short fiction that draws on a news story – that of two dead newborns found within one year in the same rural area in Ireland – and on another example of Irish folklore, Reidar Th. Christiansen's migratory legend type ML 5070. [38] Ní Dhuibhne's story of the same name first appeared in her collection *Blood and Water*, but in a different form from that of 'The Search for the Lost Husband'. Whereas 'Search' appears in short segments between other stories in the book, 'Midwife' appears as one continuous story. However, short italicised segments of the 'Midwife' legend plot, do appear throughout the story, creating a narrative form that more closely resembles versions from oral tradition, but which are embedded in a contemporary story of a late-twentieth-century midwife. The latter-day first-person narrative of Mary the midwife and her frightening encounters with a strange family, whom she suspects of allowing a newborn to die, alternate with a third-person narrative of a midwife from an unidentifiable past.

Ní Dhuibhne admits that she has "counterpointed" the tale of 'Midwife' with "a contemporary story in the news in Ireland", the Joanne Hayes baby case, which she refers to as "a story of infanticide which was very common in Ireland".[39] In April 1984, Joanne Hayes, a 24-year-old woman from Abbeydorney, County Kerry, was accused of double infanticide. She gave birth to a boy in a field behind her family's house, and left the baby, dead, in a pool there. The state pathologist testified that there was no way to be certain whether the Hayes baby had survived independently of the womb, as the child's lungs did not fully inflate.[40] Suspicion was eventually thrown on Hayes after she was treated for heavy bleeding at a local hospital, showing evidence, though she denied it, of having given birth. The authorities also believed that she had given birth to and killed another recent newborn found in the area, despite biological evidence which made the investigators' theory seem far-fetched.

The silences surrounding taboo subjects, such as sex outside of marriage, abortion, contraception, and single motherhood, were broken by these and similar events. Feminist writers such as Nell McCafferty (1985 and 1987), Ailbhe Smyth (1992), and Moira J. Maguire (2001) wrote directly against the abuses they saw in the government's approach to reproductive issues.[41] But, as Maguire points out, what used to be taboo, once brought into the open, now divides people into vehemently opposing sides. Subjects that have become open, but polarised, still remain difficult to discuss.

Taking a completely different approach from others writing on the subject, Ní Dhuibhne wraps the topics of crisis pregnancy and infanticide in gentle humour and detailed references to oral tradition. She recasts the 'Midwife' tale in a chatty, colloquial tone, showing the tale from the point of view of the midwife, only this time a thoroughly contemporary midwife who doesn't like having her 'Late Late Show' interrupted ('Midwife' 29). One of the first signs that Ní Dhuibhne 'disobeys' how the tale may have told before, besides mentioning TV shows, is that, as Críostóir Mac Cárthaigh notes in *Béaloideas*, "the legend is seldom, if ever, bound up with the personal experiences of any one storyteller".[42] From within the deeper memory of folkloric storytelling, Ní Dhuibhne can entice readers with the comfort of the familiar, make them laugh with anachronistic juxtapositions, and unseat their preconceptions with the resulting indirect argument of the short story.

Instead of using the narrative beginning, punctuating, and ending formulas of the 'Search' storyteller, here Ní Dhuibhne inserts a less performative text at different points of the story. She contrasts details of the contemporary midwife missing her 'Late Late Show', a banged up car ("old Cortina"), the investigations on the "telly" of babies found in "rubbish dumps", and slightly silly, exaggerated speeches such as, "and I'm telling no lie when I say I was on my way to the doctor for a prescription for Valium", with the more timeless images of "the rider", "the mare", and the "fair", where the story, as it appears in folktale transcripts, usually ends with the midwife's eye being poked out by the fairy husband.[43] In a potent reversal, Mary the midwife doesn't get her eye poked out. Instead, she finally sees a side of human suffering from which she had previously averted her gaze.

But despite those major differences with the midwife of oral tradition, and of the italicised excerpts, Mary does hold strong ties to oral tradition. Mary states that her mother was also a midwife, "and her mother before her" (28). That is, the protagonist of Ní Dhuibhne's story is herself a woman whose personal history stretches back into the time of exclusively oral, person-to-person transmission of knowledge, which is how a midwife then would have learned her calling.

In addition to the humour of the anachronistic details of Cortinas, chat shows, and Valium as contrasted against horses, riders, and fairs, Ní Dhuibhne juxtaposes eerie references to the fairy folk, in the italicised segments taken from oral tradition, with humorous references to eerie settings from popular culture, such as television shows and horror films. Here is the oral tradition style as it appears in the segments Ní Dhuibhne intersperses between Mary's contemporary segments:

> After a while they came to a steep hill. A door opened in the side of the hill and they went in. They rode until they came to a big house and inside there were lots of people, eating and drinking. In a corner of the house there lay a woman in labour. (30)

The manner of narration shifts from Mary's twentieth-century Hiberno-English to a less culturally specific form of storytelling. Mary, the contemporary narrator, describes the scene in more detail:

> It was a big place, comfortable enough, really ... A big room it was, with an old black range and a huge big dresser, painted red and filled with all kinds of delph and crockery and stuff. Oh you name it! And about half a dozen people were sitting around the room, or maybe more than that. All watching the telly ... And they were glued to it, the whole lot of them, what looked like the mother and father and whole family of big grown men and women. His family or hers I didn't bother my head asking. And they weren't giving out information for nothing either. It was a funny set up, I could see that as clear as daylight, such a big crowd of them, all living together. For all the world like in 'Dallas.' (30)

Mary the midwife's description appears with contemporary Hiberno-English touches, such as "a big room it was", and colloquialisms such as "telly" and "a funny set up" (30). After the italicised section, she tells the events of the birth and further describes the family as "sitting like zombies looking at the late-night film", who give her "the creeps" (31). What we think of as contemporary, juxtaposed with what we think of as ancient, may lead readers to see beyond the artifice erected around the fairytale in modern times. The contrast of language directs us to the timelessness inherent in the contemporary side of the story. Perhaps the questioning of the contrast may also be seen as further evidence of the postmodern qualities of Ní Dhuibhne's re-telling.

The 'questioning' that this strategy of indirection allows Ní Dhuibhne appears in hints, such as when the midwife wants to 'scream' when the eerily still people make no move to take the underweight child to the doctor; when Mary wonders whether to go to the Gardai after the child is found dead; when the father then threatens her with a knife, "like a gangster in 'Hill Street Blues'" (31); and when she sighs, "Well, I'd had my lesson", says "nothing" (33), and ends the story thinking of the baby: "She might have had a chance, in intensive care. But who am I to judge?" (34). The common criminality of the teen 'fairy' father, as well as Mary's efforts to bury her niggling conscience, transgress the boundary of the older story to bring in the new of the real-life cases of infant death, forcing the reader to examine his or her own reactions to similar cases (32). In a story such as this one, anything that might appear critical of secular or religious authority, while not as much of a danger to a writer in recent years as it was in an earlier time, might receive a less open reception from some readers in a country still engaged in dialogues on religious differences and issues of authority. Questions regarding how much control the fairy husband's wife or her contemporary counterpart, the teenage wife, may have had over their conditions as mothers, lead to questions regarding the availability of opportunities for young women in Ireland. These questions may be raised more smoothly in this blend of tradition and popular culture, fantasy and grim reality, tragic circumstances and broad humour. Ní Dhuibhne's humour and, again, the public, trivial, cozy images of folklore, enable her to successfully approach an audience with subjects that have remained volatile in late twentieth-early twenty-first-century Ireland.

Due to the nature of the Hayes, or 'Kerry Babies', news story, as with others like it in the United States, enticing readers to examine their own values regarding these issues would have been harder to do with a realistic portrayal. Pulling the readers closer with details of verisimilitude, then pulling them back, Ní Dhuibhne unsettles her audience's assumptions in ways that realism alone may not, allowing them to access the potentially painful, final questioning of Mary the midwife: "who am I to judge?" (34).

Just as the young mother in 'The Search for the Lost Husband', so Mary the midwife and the teenage mother of 'Midwife to the Fairies' face male characters who silence their objections. While the teenage mother of the story contributes little to the dialogue, Mary recounts details that may indicate an unnatural silence, perhaps rooted in despair, such as the girl's smoking immediately after giving birth and her lack of emotion. While Mary does not witness the teen 'fairy' husband of the story threaten the teenage mother, he does threaten to harm Mary if she speaks. The uneasy silence of the young mother, in that atmosphere of dread, may have been influenced by the thuggish young husband, as well.

While the threats to Mary the midwife, and perhaps the teenage mother, encompass physical violence, the threats made by the goat-husband to the young mother in 'The Search for the Lost Husband' are emotional, yet result in her becoming physically worn from the exertions of her search. In each story, Ní Dhuibhne uses indirection, in the lure of the comforts of oral tradition and an occasional joking tone, to infiltrate the minds of readers, leaving behind vivid images of endangered mothers, emotionally abandoned partners, devalued infants, and a seeming void of social concern over these conditions. When, in 'Search', the young wife leaves her former goat-husband, or when the eerily silent teenage mother of 'Midwife' seems to have cut herself off emotionally from her newborn, Ní Dhuibhne may be soliciting shock from her readers, but only in the service of soliciting deeper inquiry into why the characters respond as they do. When even Mary's husband, Joe, initially forbids her to go out in the late night to help deliver the doomed baby, readers may notice the questioning of male authority in Ní Dhuibhne's stories. Such questioning can be maintained for readers all the way to the end of the stories because of the flexibility of the oral tradition. A tale type may be widespread, with numerous recorded variations, but its familiarity lends each storyteller the freedom to emphasise different elements of the tale. Likewise, Ní Dhuibhne's fiction gently tugs at oral tradition's already malleable shape so that readers find themselves happily caught in this nexus of fantasy, wit, realism, and social inquiry.

When it comes to this interrelationship of author, narrator, audience, real life, and history, Ní Dhuibhne has her own critique. In an essay she wrote for *Béaloideas*, on "the craft of the storyteller and the writer", she states that:

> Fiction and folklore are free countries, I suppose, and there is no moral issue at stake. But as a folklorist, one tends to take a critical stance and to look askance at writers who continue to reinterpret and mystify folklore with scant regard for the attitudes of the folk who originally created it.[44]

Judging from Ní Dhuibhne's shorter works, she has made great strides in bringing the two 'countries' together in ways that better respect the uniqueness of each.

Out of her expertise with both old and new forms of narrative, Ní Dhuibhne's different take on postmodern feminism allows a broad audience to see with new eyes the narratives propagated by those who have power over women. In 'The Search for the Lost Husband' and 'Midwife to the Fairies', funny and appealing female characters express themselves on tension-filled topics, even when some characters inside and outside the world of make-believe do not want to hear them. These two stories show how adept Ní Dhuibhne is with folklore, postmodern fiction, feminist humour, and strategies of indirection that hold the attention of readers who might otherwise be averse to such elements in literature. Beyond Ní Dhuibhne's success here, and the successful continuation of Irish oral tradition, strategies of rhetorical indirection will surface wherever humans struggle to ask questions about where power resides.

NOTES

1   Jean-François Lyotard, *The Postmodern Condition: A Report on Knowledge*. (Minneapolis: University of Minnesota Press, [1984] 1997), xxiv.

2   *ibid*.

3   For a more extensive discussion of oral tradition and indirection in Ní Dhuibhne, see Jacqueline Fulmer, *Folk Women and Indirection in Morrison, Ní Dhuibhne, Hurston, and Lavin* (London: Ashgate, 2007).

4   Alan Dundes, *Motherwit from the Laughing Barrel* (Jackson, Mississippi: University of Mississippi Press, 1990), 2.

5. David Lloyd, *Anomalous States: Irish Writing and the Postcolonial Moment* (Durham: Duke University Press, 1993), 7.

6. *ibid*.

7. Christina Hunt Mahoney, *Contemporary Irish Literature: Transforming Tradition* (New York: St. Martin's Press, 1998), 25.

8. *ibid.*, 25.

9. *ibid*.

10. *ibid.*, 260.

11. Cristina Bacchilega, *Postmodern Fairy Tales: Gender and Narrative Strategies* (Philadelphia: University of Pennsylvania Press, 1997), 20-21, 22.

12. *ibid*. 23 (Bacchilega quoting Nancy A. Walker).

13. Julia Carlson, *Banned in Ireland: Censorship and the Irish Writer* (Athens, GA: University of Georgia Press, 1990), 2.

14. Correspondence with author, 11 Dec. 2001.

15. The use of the word 'motif' in folkloristics differs somewhat from its use in the arts, as a motif in folklore represents "a unit of the narrative capable of independent traditional life, as for example, the acquisition of a magic sword". Kenneth and Mary Clarke, *A Concise Dictionary of Folklore* (Bowling Green, KY: Kentucky Folklore Series, No. 1, 1965), 24; see also, Stith Thompson and Antti Aarne, *The Types of the Folktale: A Classification and Bibliography* (Helsinki: Folklore Fellows Communications [FFC], No. 184, 1961). For motifs, see Stith Thompson, *Motif-Index of Folk-Literature*, 6 Vols. rev. ed. (Helsinki: Folklore Fellows Communications [FFC], Nos. 106–109, 116, 117, 1932–1936).

16. The unusually high level of folkloric detail in Ní Dhuibhne's fiction makes sense when one discovers that she has worked for many years as a curator of manuscripts in the National Library of Ireland and holds a doctorate in folkloristic studies.

17. Alan Dundes, *The Study of Folklore* (Englewood Cliffs, NJ: Prentice-Hall, Inc., 1965), 2–3.

18   Angela Bourke, General Introduction, 'Oral Traditions'. *Field Day Anthology of Irish Writing, Volume IV: Irish Women's Writing and Traditions*. Ed. Angela Bourke, *et al*. (New York: New York University Press, 2002), 1193.

19   Séan Ó Súilleabháin (Sean O'Sullivan), ed. *Folktales of Ireland* citing from the Aarne-Thompson Type Index (Chicago: University of Chicago Press, 1966), 267. Ó Súilleabháin points out that Type 425 also encompasses the tale of Cupid and Psyche, familiar to many. Also see Séan Ó Súilleabháin and Reidar Th. Christiansen, *The Types of the Irish Folktale* (Helsinki: Folklore Fellows Communications [FFC] 78, no. 188, 1963), 90. Also, a range of AT Tale Types, 400–459, cover 'Supernatural or Enchanted Husband (Wife) or Other Relatives', Stith Thompson, *The Folktale* (Berkeley: University of California Press, 1977), 483. A range of Thompson motif index nos., B600–B699, cover 'Marriage of Person to Animal', Stith Thompson, *The Folktale* (Berkeley: University of California Press, 1977), 490.

20   Thompson motif no. F372.1 'Fairies take human midwife to attend fairy woman'. Stith Thompson, *The Folktale*, 492. A variation is listed under the tale 'The Fairy Frog' in Séan Ó Súilleabháin, (Sean O'Sullivan), ed. *Folktales of Ireland*, 169–171, 271–272, 301. Also see Críostóir MacCárthaigh, 'Midwife to the Fairies', *Béaloideas: The Journal of the Folklore of Ireland Society*, 59, No. 1991 (1991): 133, 142; and Peter Narváez, ed. *The Good People: New Fairylore Essays* (Lexington: University of Kentucky Press, 1991), 53.

21   Ní Dhuibhne, trans., 'The Story of the Little White Goat' as told by Máire Ruiséal, *Field Day Anthology of Irish Writing, Volume IV: Irish Women's Writing and Traditions* (New York: New York University Press, 2002), 1219–1232.

22   Ní Dhuibhne, 'The Search for the Lost Husband' in *'The Inland Ice' and Other Stories* (Belfast: Blackstaff Press, 1997). Further references to 'Search' are in parentheses in the text.

23   Stith Thompson, *The Folktale* (Berkeley: University of California Press, 1977), 490.

24   *ibid.*

25   *ibid.*

26   *ibid.*

27   *ibid.*, 491.

28   Hunt Mahoney, *Contemporary Irish Literature*, 260.

29   *ibid.*, 261.

30   Mac Cárthaigh, 'Midwife to the Fairies', 133, 142 138.

31   Seán O'Súilleabháin, 'Tales of Magic', *A Handbook of Irish Folklore* (Wexford: The Educational Company of Ireland for The Folklore of Ireland Society, 1942), 611–628.

32   Maureen Murphy, 'Siren or Victim: The Mermaid in Irish Legend and Poetry' in *More Than Reality: The Fantastic in Irish Literature and the Arts*. Donald E. Morse and Csilla Bertha, eds. (New York: Greenwood Press, 1991), 38.

33   Bo Almqvist, 'Of Mermaids and Marriages. Seamus Heaney's "Maighdean Mara" and Nuala Ní Dhomhnaill's "An Mhaighdean Mhara" in the Light of Folk Tradition'. *Béaloideas: the Journal of the Folklore of Ireland Society*, 58 (1990), 40; Angela Bourke, *The Burning of Bridget Cleary: A True Story* (New York: Viking, 1999), 43.

34   Bacchilega, *Postmodern Fairy Tales*, 23.

35   Regina Barreca, ed. *Last Laughs: Perspectives on Women and Comedy*. Studies in Gender and Culture, Vol. 2. (New York: Gordon and Breach Science Publishers, 1988), 15.

36   Correspondence with author, 5 Dec. 2001.

37   Ní Dhuibhne, 'Midwife to the Fairies' in *Blood and Water*, 25–34. Further references to 'Midwife' are in parentheses in the text.

38   Mac Cárthaigh, 'Midwife to the Fairies', 133.

39   Caitriona Moloney and Helen Thompson, eds. *Irish Women Writers Speak Out: Voices from the Field* (New York: Syracuse University Press, 1003: 101–115), 108.

40   Joanne Hayes, *My Story* (excerpt) (1985), *Field Day Anthology of Irish Writing, Volume V: Irish Women's Writing and Traditions* (New York: New York University Press, 2002), 1442.

41   Nell McCafferty, *A Woman To Blame: The Kerry Babies Case*, (Dublin: Attic Press, 1985) and *Goodnight Sisters* (Dublin: Attic Press, 1987); Ailbhe Smyth, *The Abortion Papers, Ireland* (Dublin: Attic Press, 1992); Moira J. Maguire, 'The Changing Face of Catholic Ireland: Conservatism and Liberalism in the Ann Lovett and Kerry Babies Scandals'. *Feminist Studies*, 27.2 (Summer 2001: 335–58).

42   Mac Cárthaigh, 'Midwife to the Fairies', 140.

43   *ibid*. 133. Mac Cárthaigh also cites Thompson as designating the traditional tale's plotline specifically as motif F235.4.1(a): "Mortal midwife or nurse gets some of the fairy ointment in her eye as she anoints the eye of the child. She is able to see the fairies as they are. Later, woman sees fairies, often at a fair. She speaks to one. He asks which eye she sees him with and blinds the seeing eye" (quoting Thompson).

44   Ní Dhuibhne-Almqvist, 'Legends of the Supernatural in Anglo-Irish Literature'. *Béaloideas*, 60–1. No. 1992–3 (1992: 145–150), 149.

'Ethnografiction':
Irish Relations in the Writing of Éilís Ní Dhuibhne[1]

HELENA WULFF

Irish relations, particularly from a female perspective, are at the heart of Éilís Ní Dhuibhne's writings. In addition, Ní Dhuibhne conveys these relations as they unfold in a nation going through major social and economic transformations, in particular, Ireland's 'Celtic Tiger' economy and its aftermath. As Anne Fogarty has remarked, Ní Dhuibhne:

> more than any other contemporary Irish writer ... explores the gaps between decades of the late twentieth century that appear to be contiguous and shows how the tensions between competing timeframes and value systems are at the basis of the moral and emotional dilemma of her characters. The uncanny familiarity and oddity of the past are central preoccupations of many of her stories.[2]

Trained in Irish folklore, Ní Dhuibhne has an acute awareness of ethnographic detail that makes her portraits of people and their relations revealing of human life beyond the specific contexts of her fiction. In anthropology, the term ethnography refers, on the one hand, to 'fieldwork', the method for collecting data mainly through so-called participant observation, which entails hanging around with the people one is studying on a long term basis. On the other hand, the term ethnography refers to writing, to a type of text.[3] In this article, I will use ethnography in both senses, as Ní Dhuibhne can be said to make observations, just like an ethnographer, while participating in life around her: "I'm not a sociologist, but I think I have an interest in Ireland and its part in the world", she told me in an interview, and also that "I care about very specific Irish experiences".[4] By focussing on girls and women in Ní Dhuibhne's writings, I hope to contribute to a discussion on the discipline of anthropology with its ethnographic method and fiction, a genre I am going to call 'ethnografiction'.

In Marilyn Strathern's inaugural lecture at the University of Cambridge, entitled 'The Relation', she looked back to the sixteenth and seventeenth centuries, when the concept of relations was "applied to connections via kinship".[5] Moving to the twentieth century, Strathern says that, "it was a creative appropriation of The Relation, at once the abstract construct and the concrete person, that lay behind some of the dramatic development of anthropology in the middle years of this century",[6] and she specifies:

> Routing relations through persons became the substance of anthropological empiricism. Whether the relations were intellectual or social, made in fantasy or acted out in daily life, their source in people's interactions was made significant.[7]

Relations are understood by Strathern as "principles of social organization" or as "interactions between persons". The notion that "classification of relatives" could reveal larger, more general social principles, produced the proposition that "persons are classifiable by their relations to one another".[8]

One of the dramatic developments of anthropology in the middle years of the twentieth century was the appearance of feminist studies, as formulated in such groundbreaking publications as Shirley Ardener's *Perceiving Women*, and Judith Okely's *Simone de Beauvoir: A Rereading*, the latter also being informed by the impact of autobiography on anthropology.[9]

To my own autobiography belongs the fact that I was in love with literature and studied comparative literature as an undergraduate, before I discovered anthropology. Having just completed an anthropological study of dance, memory and mobility in Ireland,[10] I am now conducting an anthropological study of Irish literature. I was drawn in this direction already during my research on dance, but it was only when I discovered Ní Dhuibhne's novel *The Dancers Dancing* that I began making active use of Irish fiction as ethnography in my writings. This was, however, nothing new. As postgraduate students in the Stockholm Anthropology Department, we were encouraged to read fiction from our fields, as one way to learn about the places and people we were studying. But this raises a number of questions, not least, what exactly is it that an anthropologist can learn through fiction and what is the relationship between ethnography and fiction? For my study on dance in Ireland, I found exquisite descriptions of Irish relations in Ní Dhuibhne's work, especially those of mother-daughter, as well as relationships and friendships between teenage girls and sisters, descriptions that extended my findings about tightly-knit family networks. But it also added new ideas, such as the particular position of women who are under pressure to conform to contradictory ideals from previous times as well as the present. This I could follow up through interviews and observations, something I continue doing in my present study, as this is anthropology of literature, which depends on complementary data from interviews and participant observation with writers in their cultural contexts.

The Dancers Dancing[11] is a rhythmical rendering of a group of adolescent girls who spend the summer of 1972 learning Irish in the Gaeltacht. Just like the Irish language movement set up by the Gaelic League almost a century earlier, these classes in the Irish language are combined with learning to dance at a céilí, a dance gathering. Fogarty notes that *The Dancers Dancing* is a *Bildungsroman*, "at once an ethnographic fiction and a celebratory tale of sexual and emotional awakening".[12] But if "going to the Gaeltacht" is a "seminal teenage experience" in Ireland,[13] then adolescence is a universal one. The following scene captures closeness as well as tensions between tradition and transformation in Ireland: Orla, the protagonist of the novel, who comes from Dublin, is expected to visit her Auntie Annie who lives in the vicinity of the Irish College. But Orla is embarrassed by her aunt's odd appearance and old-fashioned house where her father grew up, and so keeps postponing her visit. Then, one day towards the end of the stay, Orla summons her courage and tells two of her friends, a girl and a boy, that she is going to see her aunt. To Orla's horror, they want to come with her and "Orla feels something break inside her head, like the shell of an egg. Her big secret is disintegrating" (*DD* 221–223). Nevertheless, the three of them:

> troop across the yard and into the house. It's dark inside, as in all the old, small-windowed houses. And, despite the lack of sunshine, it's hot in the kitchen, where the range is burning brightly. (221)

There they find Aunt Annie, as well as two of their teachers who, it seems, have visited before. The woman teacher says, "isn't this the lovely cosy house?" (221) and:

> Orla looks at the ticking sunray clock, the uneven rocky floor, the painted dresser stocked with blue plates and an odd assortment of ornaments ... She looks at the bare bulb dangling from a twisted wire in the middle of the ceiling ... Who could find a single thing to praise in this gloomy, old-fashioned ridiculous house? A house that Orla has often wished would burn to the ground and be forgotten for all time. (221)

Aunt Annie greets Orla warmly, and soon they all have tea:

> They eat and drink chatting softly. The warmth of the room increases and the clock ticks loudly on the mantelpiece. Orla finds her sense of well-being burgeoning. The room encloses her like a cradle, warm and old and dark and comfortable. Peace seeps into her soul from the mellow walls, the rocky bed of the floor. Flames flicker in the range, spoons clink against plates, voices rise and fall in meaningless chatter: it is a tune that has been played in this kitchen often before. For hundreds of years. Right in this room. (223)

The male teacher "changes the tune. 'Time to do some work!' he says, depositing his cup on the table and plugging a tape recorder into the socket" (223). Turning to Orla, he explains that, "Annie is going to tell me some stories" (223), and Orla realises, with a sudden sense of pride, that her odd aunt is recognised as an authority on local folklore. The tension that Orla has been haunted by, between tradition and modernity, is thus happily resolved here. This turn of events can be analysed as one aspect of the way tradition is incorporated in modern life in Ireland, and lives on in partly new forms. It is important as an indicator of how Irish modernity is constituted.

Ní Dhuibhne's story, 'Midwife to the Fairies',[14] also brings out tensions in Ireland's contemporary historical moment, illustrated through a woman's perspective. Here, Ní Dhuibhne weaves a legend into a modern story set in Dublin, which, Fogarty says, "in fact, transposes and retells it".[15] The story is about a Dublin midwife who is called late one night to a woman in labour. The woman gives birth to a small, unwanted baby, and the midwife informs the new mother that the baby needs to be in an incubator, after which she leaves and tries to forget about the whole thing. But, shortly afterwards, she learns from a newspaper article that the baby had been found "dead in a shoebox, in a kind of rubbish dump" ('Midwife' 28). This story could be interpreted as a straightforward critique of the laws against abortion, which exist in the Republic of Ireland while, at the same time, the interpolated sections from the legend create historical depth. For an anthropologist, this is an example of how traces of traditional beliefs can be found in modern thought and life, not only in Ireland, which admittedly has a strong folkloric tradition, but in other societies as well.

In discussing how she composes her characters and their lives, Ní Dhuibhne has said that they are often based on two or three real people and events, mixed with one spoonful of fantasy, and an imaginative rendering of plot as a potential of what could happen.[16] Time and place can be moved around freely in fiction while ethnography remains a kind of reporting of what has, in fact, happened, including accurate accounts of places and times, from a certain theoretical perspective. The crux of the matter is that Ní Dhuibhne's fiction conforms to realist conventions: with the possible exception of the fairies, her stories could have happened – some actually have happened – and the relations she draws on are realistic ones. In the volume *True Fiction*, Dutch anthropologist Peter Kloos considers similarities and differences between fiction and anthropology:[17] "Is anthropology a science or is it an art?" he asks rhetorically in the opening line of his introductory chapter. His reply is "that it is both":

After all, any science is a combination of creative imagination, primarily associated with the artist, and methodological rigour, usually believed to be the trademark of the scientist.[18]

Separating the texts of science and art in different genres, sorting literary texts in one category consisting of "the novel, the short story, the poem, the essay", Kloos puts anthropology in "monographic account or ethnography, the theoretical treatise, the specialized article, the introductory text, and again the essay".[19] He argues that the novel and the ethnographic account are not easily divided into different genres, as "boundaries between the two are ambiguous".[20] It is likely that, from an artistic perspective, most ethnographies are dull, as Kloos claims, and that, from a scientific perspective, novels are considered problematic when it comes to reliability since they do not offer a report on the research process. Kloos points to the fact that not only novels but, indeed, ethnographic accounts tend to lack "independent replications". Comparing artistic and scientific representations of reality, Kloos suggests three outcomes: in the first one, the two representations convey the same piece of information; in the second, they diverge leaving the scientist rejecting the artistic representation as incorrect; and in the third outcome, which is also one of differences, the artistic rendering displays data that has eluded the scientist. According to Kloos, "novelists have something to offer that is often sadly absent in scholarly work: a sensitivity to important currents and values in actual life ... why is it that scholars often fail to notice these things?" The scientist, on the other hand, provides "systematic and explicit description ... and explanation ... general statements that explain what can be observed: theories, if you like". It is a curious circumstance, Kloos concludes, that, "an artistic description often rests on what is not said at all!" [21]

According to Ní Dhuibhne, it was the experience of writing a dissertation, as part of her M.Phil degree, on the history of Chaucer's 'The Friar's Tale', that inspired her dark novel about fear of nuclear disaster, *The Bray House*. The novel features a Swedish woman archaeologist who comes to Ireland "with the purpose of reconstructing its culture by carrying out a dig in a countryside devastated by nuclear meltdown",[22] but fails to find the true story of it. This is fiction as science fiction, including a meticulous account of a scholarly method of collecting archeological data and steeped in a chilling thriller format. The novel also engages with one of Ní Dhuibhne's central concerns: where is the true story – in fiction or in scholarship?

In the article 'Ethnography and Fiction: Where Is the Border?', Kirin Narayan makes clear that the border is fuzzy in many ways, but that there are differences between these two writing styles when it comes to disclosure of process, generalisation, representations of subjectivity, and accountability.[23] Writing about the place of fiction in anthropological scholarship and analysis, Eduardo Archetti distinguishes between three types of fiction:

> the realistic historical novel that attempts to 'reconstruct' a given period in a given society; the totally imagined story set in a historical period; and the essays devoted to an interpretation of a nation, its characteristics and creed.[24]

As Archetti argues, "some kind of historical and sociological knowledge is important in fiction",[25] which makes the task of writing fiction similar to that of writing anthropology. This is in accordance with how Ní Dhuibhne describes how she works:

> short stories come at the spur of the moment, they're not planned. A novel has to be planned, it takes longer, it requires doing research.[26]

Archetti makes the case for the possibility that a novelist unintentionally brings out certain cultural topics. This is fiction as "ethnographic raw material, not as authoritative statements about, or interpretations of, a particular society".[27] Still, there is, again, fiction by writers who were trained as academics. It is common that key interlocutors in anthropological research are intellectuals, with or without training, who may have an intellectual inclination that provides the anthropologist with insightful analyses of the society they are studying. Archetti's suggestion that, "a literary product is not only a substantive part of the real world but also a key element in the configuration of the world itself",[28] is important for the anthropologist to keep in mind.

This affair between anthropology and literature has a long history, and can be discerned in the repertory of quite a number of Euro-American anthropologists, mostly men: Victor Turner argues that African ritual and western literature were "mutually elucidating"[29]; Clifford Geertz explores the anthropologist as author (more precisely Malinowski, Benedict, Evans-Pritchard, Lévi-Strauss),[30] and there was a substantial writing culture debate at the end of the twentieth century.[31] Handler and Segal discuss Jane Austen as ethnographer of kinship and marriage in her time and class in England, which allowed them to uncover diverse social realities within this culture,[32] and in Nigel Rapport's research on the village Wanet in England, E.M. Forster became a fellow ethnographer, as Rapport juxtaposed Forster's writings to his own findings about the village.[33]

In Ireland, the nationalist cultural revival, undertaken by the Gaelic League at the end of the nineteenth century, saw the inclusion and promotion of literature as crucial. Headed by Yeats, the literary movement turned into a major force in the political process towards national independence.[34] In his influential study, *Inventing Ireland*, Declan Kiberd argues that it was during the literary revival that Ireland became a modern nation.[35] More recently, Kiberd has discussed the impact of exile on Irish writers and of the diaspora on Ireland, and identified not only political conflict but also connections between Irish and English culture through literature, Ireland's increasing presence in the European Union, as well as the question of postcoloniality.[36]

The fact that "Ireland has produced some of the most illustrious writers in the English language over the past two centuries" is observed by Patrick Duffy, and his interest extends to the role of place and landscape in literature and art in relation to "constructs of Irishness"[37] in Ireland as well as abroad. Duffy suggests that "literary texts can be regarded as signifying practices, which interact with social, economic and political institutions".[38] Citing Barnes and Duncan, Duffy endorses the view that literary texts "are read, not passively, but, as it were, rewritten as they are read".[39] Rather than merely reflecting social reality they, in fact, negotiate multivocal meanings that keep changing.

In his comprehensive *Reader on Irish Writing in the Twentieth Century*, David Pierce presents four main topics of Irish writing: 'history, politics and religion'; 'the city and the country'; 'culture and identity', which includes 'colonialism/postcolonialism', 'Irish language', 'folklore and folk tales', 'women writers', as well as 'humour'; and, finally, 'the Irish diaspora', and 'return' to Ireland. Pierce ponders the relationship between gender and modern Irish writing and lists such issues as the representation of Ireland as female, rites of passage in male autobiographical writing, guilt, the body, male violence, domesticity, sexuality and desire, gay sexuality, history and evasion, and censorship, as factors in defining that relationship.[40]

With some exceptions, notably Lady Augusta Gregory (who, among many other accomplishments, worked with Yeats in establishing a national Irish theatre), the literary tradition in Ireland tends to be presented as predominantly male, while, in fact, there were a number of women who wrote poems, plays, and fiction during the literary revival in the late nineteenth century, something that is revealed in the anthology *Voices on the Wind*, edited by Ní Dhuibhne. These early women writers shared an engagement with Irish culture, and "like many other writers of the period, their mission, conscious or unconscious, was to transmit the primary literature and folklore of Gaelic Ireland to their readers in a diluted form".[41] This was the time of the cult of the Celt, which entailed certain sentiments that Ní Dhuibhne finds exaggerated. It is interesting to learn that it was "thoroughly acceptable for women to write" and that many men "encouraged and admired their female colleagues"[42] who were then able to publish with the leading publishing houses and take part in the literary establishment. Ní Dhuibhne attributes this upsurge in women's writing, around the year 1900, to the existence of a lively cultural climate in Ireland consisting both of international literary and intellectual currents, such as women's suffrage and a search for Irish identity. It did not last very long, however, and it would take until the 1960s and 70s for the second literary revival of Irish women writers to emerge.

In 2002 the encyclopaedic *Field Day Anthology of Irish Women's Writing and Traditions: Volumes IV and V* were published. They include more than seven hundred and fifty Irish women writers, as they reach back to the year 600 AD and forward to the year 2000. These two volumes were preceded by three Field Day volumes on Ireland's literary history that contained very few women writers, a circumstance that led to debate in the Irish literary world and, eventually, the publication of the women's volumes. It took eleven years for them to appear and they have done little to shift the dominant notion of literary history in Ireland as belonging to men. Nevertheless, *The Field Day Anthologies* on Irish women writers indicates women's existence, as do a substantial number of other publications ranging from *Woman's Part* edited by Janet Madden-Simpson (1984), *The Female Line* edited by Ruth Hooley (1985), and *Wildish Things* edited by Ailbhe Smyth (1989), to *Two Irelands: Literary Feminisms North and South* by Rebecca Pelan (2005) and *Opening the Field* edited by Patricia Boyle Haberstroh and Christine St. Peter (2007).[43]

"My impression was that Irish women hadn't had a voice", Ní Dhuibhne told me in an interview, and explains that this is why she started and still writes short stories and novels about women's lives.[44] The idea for her story 'The Flowering'[45] came from an anecdote about a gifted woman embroideress who was prevented from doing her art when her father died and she had to help support the family. Missing her lace-making made her wither away, go mad and finally die. Ní Dhuibhne's story ends with a reflection about similarities between the craftsmanship of fiction and scholarship, embroidering and writing. The story seems to convey an urgent message that women writers who have found fulfillment in writing should be given every opportunity to write. If their inner drive to write is thwarted, their lives will be thwarted also.

Building on autobiographical experiences, Ní Dhuibne's writing depicts her Ireland, which often unfolds against a backdrop of Dublin working-class life, such as when the Dublin girls in *The Dancers Dancing* go to Irish language class in the Gaeltacht. This accentuates "the relationship between the Irish language and the English language – the cultural schizophrenia – we experience at moments like that" she explains.[46]

But, of the relations Ní Dhuibhne creates, I think the ones between mothers and daughters are especially well-crafted. These are usually narrated through the daughter's perspective, and tend to tell of the type of motherly love that warms the daughter when she is away and homesick, which happens now and then to Orla in *The Dancers Dancing* during her summer at the Irish College. Like any close bond, this mother-daughter relationship has many dimensions, even of shared mischief: in an entertaining episode, Orla and her mother dress up and have afternoon tea in a fancy hotel, mocking the snobbery of the place. In 'The Catechism Examination', which is about a teacher who harasses a slow girl, the narrating girl avoids this distress because, "Mummy tests me every night, in front of the fire, before she reads *Alice in Wonderland*".[47] But some of the women are also daughters in alienated relationships, such as the successful professional woman archaeologist in *The Bray House*[48] who has not seen her mother for many years and who states, at the time of her mother's death that, "I'd lost contact with her. For the simple reason that I didn't like her. And the feeling was mutual" (*BH* 41). Yet, despite their alienation, the mother is constantly on the adult daughter's mind and she admits that the holidays her mother took her on had been crucial since, "the seeds of my anthropological zeal were undoubtedly sown by her, during those many trips to so many different and fascinating lands" (46). At first, there is a sense that the narrator resembles her mother in coldness of character and careerism. As a student, the woman sets out on a brilliant academic career, supported by an older male mentor, but when he retires, the woman announces that she is applying for his job, which he does not approve of, on the grounds that she is a woman. Ultimately, a less qualified man is appointed. Here the feminist message about unequal career opportunities for women and men is clear.

To what extent siblings can be real friends is disputed in anthropological kinship studies, one relation being ascribed, the other achieved and voluntary, but there is no doubt that siblings, especially as children, can be close. Ní Dhuibhne's story 'Wuff Wuff Wuff for de Valera',[49] which is a play on the Irish children's rhyme, 'Vote vote vote for de Valera', reminds the woman narrator of a skipping game and happy playtime with her twin sister in the working-class street where they grew up. Having married well, into housewifery, the narrator can afford an ironic attitude, looking down as she is looking back: "We had one of those quaint working-class childhoods Irish writers are always going on about: scruffy corner shops, luke warm baths once a week, disastrous clothes" ('Wuff' 3). Her sister, however, did not have time for that kind of irony, becoming, instead, a single parent as a teenager and "that's why she sort of didn't make it" (4), according to the narrator, who concludes that her sister ended up working as a civil servant without being promoted. Despite this difference in class and comfort, a sense of competition between the sisters comes through, even in the childhood memory. The fact that children – sisters, brothers, cousins, friends, classmates – have competitive relationships that they carry with them into adulthood is yet another observation in Ní Dhuibhne's writings.

But Ní Dhuibhne has also published well-crafted academic articles, such as one on 'The Irish', where she identifies loquacity as a central characteristic of the Irish, and that:

> A high opinion of the Irish gift for writing and talking is shared by many, especially the Irish themselves. That the Irish are verbally gifted is a sine qua non of the image we sell to tourists, but it is probably based on truth. Ireland has produced a high proportion of internationally renowned writers, such as the verbally generous James Joyce and the verbally frugal Samuel Beckett. It is commonly believed that there are more writers per capita in Ireland than in other countries.[50]

Ní Dhuibhne also notes that a talent for writing appears in every historical ethnic group: the four Irish authors who have been awarded the Nobel Prize in literature are Shaw, Yeats and Beckett who were Dublin Protestants, and Heaney who is a Northern Irish Catholic, and, of course, she points out that Joyce, surely "the most well-known and influential of all Irish writers", was not a Nobel laureate. Ní Dhuibhne also reminds us of the absence of Irish women writers in this category.[51]

In a country where creative wit is highly regarded, Ní Dhuibhne tells us that, not only writers of literature or drama, but Irish people on the whole "are talkative".[52] Again, though, there is a gender boundary here, according to Ní Dhuibhne, since Irish men are considered to be wittier than Irish women: Irish men tell more jokes, and their conversation is full of funny comments and anecdotes. The Irish like to make fun of other people, says Ní Dhuibhne, for speaking and behaving in a different, exaggerated way, by boasting especially. This ridicule is not presented to a person's face, but are typically "laughed at behind their backs". Yet Ní Dhuibhne is eager to add the crucial piece of information that, "the Irish like to laugh at themselves, at their sorrows".[53]

So far, I have discussed Ní Dhuibhne's writings in terms of 'ethnografiction' as she builds her fiction on what can be seen as ethnographic observations of social life and lore in Ireland. This has accentuated the real side of fiction. It was through Ní Dhuibhne's work that I first realised the predicament of women in this contemporary moment of sudden social and economic change in Ireland. Even if there is now something of an economic down-turn, the 'Celtic Tiger' economy that existed over the last few years brought prosperity, which produced a new cultural confidence. At the same time, the expansion of the economy also put a lot of pressure on women in the sense that many of them are now expected to have both modern careers and traditional families with husband and children. Many of Ní Dhuibhne's characters are struggling to combine contradictory ideals of what a woman should be: traditional wife or successful professional, mother or mistress. There does not seem to be any real reconciliation between the different demands. In Ní Dhuibhne's recent novel, *Fox, Swallow, Scarecrow*, which is a social satire of contemporary Ireland, she writes:

> Divorce was available in Ireland these days, but it had arrived, strangely enough, at the same time as the big increase in house prices. When people could afford to divorce, it wasn't available, and then when it became available, it became unaffordable. Almost overnight. The free market economy was doing what the Church had done for centuries.[54]

On a stylistic note, many of Ní Dhuibhne's stories work so well, in my opinion, because of the first-person woman narrator who speaks to the reader, as confidante. Yet not all her readers are women, and prominent male writers and critics, such as Declan Kiberd and Derek Hand,[55] have reviewed her work in highly appreciative ways.

Ethnography is often said to be about everyday life, the mundane, and this is probably one reason why I first took to Ní Dhuibhne's writings; by feeling an affinity. As Ní Dhuibhne herself says:

> Stories come to me. People tell me stories. The world is choc-a-bloc with them. I think I have what might seem to some people an inflated sense of the significance of what we call ordinary life. It doesn't seem at all ordinary to me. People's mundane experiences fascinate me.[56]

So, this is finally how ethnography and fiction fuses into the 'ethnografiction' of Ní Dhuibhne's work. It is a perceptive, witty and learned woman's writing about contemporary Irish relations from a female perspective.

NOTES

1   An earlier version of this article was first presented as The Phyllis Kaberry Commemorative Lecture, International Gender Studies Centre, University of Oxford, May 2006.
2   Anne Fogarty, 'Preface' to Ní Dhuibhne, *Midwife to the Fairies* (Cork: Attic Press, 2003), xii.

3   See Thomas Hylland Eriksen, *Small Places, Large Issues: An Introduction to Social and Cultural Anthropology* (London: Pluto Press, 1995), and Clifford Geertz, *Works and Lives: The Anthropologist as Author* (Stanford: Stanford University Press, 1988). Ethnology, or European Ethnology as it is often termed nowadays, is a different discipline than anthropology, even though there are many connections between the two of them, not least when it comes to the ethnographic method for collecting data. As the term indicates, European Ethnologists tend to do research in Europe, in their own countries, while anthropologists also go abroad, traditionally to other continents such as Africa and Asia for their research. In Ireland, the designation folklore has been more common than ethnology. See Diarmuid Ó Giolláin, *Locating Irish Folklore: Tradition, Modernity, Identity* (Cork: Cork University Press, 2000).

4   Interview with author, 29th March 2006.

5   Marilyn Strathern, *The Relation: Issues in Complexity and Scale. Inaugural Lecture 1994 by the William Wyse Professor of Social Anthropology* (Cambridge: Prickly Pear Press, 1995), 9.

6   *ibid.*, 10.

7   *ibid.*, 12.

8   *ibid.*, 14.

9   Shirley Ardener, ed. *Perceiving Women* (London: Malaby Press, 1975); Judith Okely, *Simone de Beauvoir: A Rereading* (London: Virago Press, 1986); Judith M. Okely and Helen Calloway, eds. *Anthropology and Autobiography: Participatory Experience and Embodied Knowledge* (London: Routldge, 1992).

10   Helena Wulff, *Dancing at the Crossroads: Memory and Mobility in Ireland* (Oxford: Berghahn Books, 2007).

11   Ní Dhuibhne, *The Dancers Dancing* (Belfast: Blackstaff Press, 1999). Further references to *DD* are in parentheses in the text.

12   Fogarty, 'Preface' to *Midwife to the Fairies*, xiii.

13   Nicola Warwick, 'Interview with Éilís Ní Dhuibhne'. *One Woman's Writing Retreat* http://www.prairieden.com/front_porch/visiting_authors/dhuibhne.html (2001).

14   Ní Dhuibhne, 'Midwife to the Fairies' in *Midwife to the Fairies*, 22–30. Further references to 'Midwife' are in parentheses in the text.

15   Fogarty, 'Preface' to *Midwife to the Fairies*, xi.

16   Interview with author, 29th March 2006.

17   Peter Kloos, ed. *True Fiction: Artistic and Scientific Representations of Reality* (Amsterdam: Vrije Universiteit Press, 1990a).

18   Peter Kloos, 'Reality and its Representations' in *ibid.*, 1.

19   *ibid.*

20   *ibid.*, 2

21   *ibid.*, 5

22   Fogarty, 'Preface' to *Midwife to the Fairies*, xi.

23   Kirin Narayan, 'Ethnography and Fiction: Where Is the Border?' *Anthropology and Humanism*, 24(2): 134–147.

24   Eduardo P. Archetti, 'Introduction' in *Exploring the Written: Anthropology and the Multiplicity of Writing* (Oslo: Scandinavian University Press, 1994), 16.

25   *ibid.*

26   Interview with author, 29th March 2006.

27   Archetti, 'Introduction', 17.

28   *ibid.*, 13.

29   Victor Turner, 'African Ritual and Western Literature: Is a Comparative Symbology Possible?' in Angus Fletcher, ed. *The Literature of Fact*. English Institute Series (New York: Columbia University Press, 1976), 77–78.

30   Clifford Geertz, *Works and Lives: The Anthropologist as Author* (Stanford: Stanford University Press, 1988).

31   James Clifford and George E. Marcus, eds. *Writing Culture: The Poetics and Politics of Ethnography* (Berkeley: University of California Press, 1986).

32   Richard Handler and Daniel Segal, *Jane Austen and the Fiction of Culture: An Essay on the Narration of Social Realities* (Tucson: University of Arizona Press, 1990).

33   Nigel Rapport, *The Prose and the Passion: Anthropology, Literature and the Writing of E.M. Forster* (Manchester: Manchester University Press, 1994).

34   Diarmuid Ó Giolláin, *Locating Irish Folklore: Tradition, Modernity, Identity* (Cork: Cork University Press, 2000).

35   Declan Kiberd, *Inventing Ireland: The Literature of the Modern Nation* (London: Vintage, 1996).

36   Declan Kiberd, *The Irish Writer and the World* (Cambridge: Cambridge University Press, 2005).

37   Patrick J Duffy, 'Writing Ireland: Literature and Art in the Representation of Irish Place' in Brian Graham, ed. *In Search of Ireland* (London: Routledge, 1997), 65.

38   *ibid.*

39   *ibid.* Duffy's citation is from Trevor J. Barnes and James S. Duncan, *Writing Worlds: Discourse, Text and Metaphor in the Representation of Landscape* (London: Routledge, 1992), 5–6.

40   David Pierce, *Irish Writing in the Twentieth Century: A Reader* (Cork: Cork University Press, 2000), 1267–1281.

41   Ní Dhuibhne, 'Introduction' to *Voices on the Wind: Women Poets of the Celtic Twilight* (Dublin: New Island Books, 1995), 11.

42   *ibid.*, 13

43   Janet Madden-Simpson, ed. *Woman's Part: An Anthology of Short Fiction By and About Irish Women 1890–1960* (Dublin: Arlen House, 1984); Ruth Hooley, ed. *The Female Line: Northern Irish Women Writers* (Belfast: Northern Ireland Women's Rights Movement, 1985); Ailbhe Smyth, ed. *Wildish Things: An Anthology of New Irish Women's Writing* (Dublin: Attic Press, 1990); Rebecca Pelan, *Two Irelands: Literary Feminisms North and South* (New York: Syracuse University Press, 2005); Patricia Boyle Haberstroh and Christine St. Peter, eds. *Opening the Field: Irish Women, Texts and Contexts* (Cork: Cork University Press, 2007).

44   Interview with author, 29th March 2006.

45   Ní Dhuibhne, 'The Flowering' in *Midwife to the Fairies*, 9–21). Further references to 'Flowering' are in parentheses in the text. This story was inspired by an anecdote in Elizabeth Boyle, *The Irish Flowerers*. Ulster Folk Museum, Queen's University Belfast. Institute of Irish Studies. (Cultra Manor, Holywood, Co. Down, 1971).

46   Interview with author, 29th March 2006.

47   Ní Dhuibhne, 'The Catechism Examination' in *Midwife to the Fairies*, 48.

48   Ní Dhuibhne, *The Bray House* (Dublin: Attic Press, 1990). Further references to *BH* are in parentheses in the text.

49   Ní Dhuibhne, 'Wuff Wuff Wuff for de Valera' in *Midwife to the Fairies*, 1–8. Further references to 'Wuff' are in parentheses in the text.

50   Ní Dhuibhne, 'The Irish' in *Europeans: Essays on Culture and Identity*. Åke Daun and Sören Jansson, eds. (Lund: Nordic Academic Press, 1999: 47–66), 53.

51   *ibid.*

52   *ibid.*

53   *ibid.*, 54

54   Ní Dhuibhne, *Fox, Swallow, Scarecrow* (Belfast: Blackstaff Press, 2007), 45.

55   Declan Kiberd wrote a new essay for the 2007 edition of *The Dancers Dancing;* Derek Hand, 'Being Ordinary – Ireland from Elsewhere'; *Irish University Review*, Special Issue: Irish Contemporary Fiction, 3. Anthony Roche. ed. Spring/Summer, (2000) 30: 103–116.

56   Warwick, 'Interview with Éilís Ní Dhuibhne'. *One Woman's Writing Retreat*   http://www.prairieden.com/front_porch/visiting_authors/dhuibhne.html (2001).

With Her Whole Heart:
Éilís Ní Dhuibhne and Irish Folklore[1]

ANNE O'CONNOR

Éilís Ní Dhuibhne is not only one of Ireland's foremost writers, she is also an internationally-recognised folklorist and academic researcher, collector, editor and writer. This paper traces Ní Dhuibhne's development as an academic folklorist and recognises the central place the Irish oral tradition holds in Ní Dhuibhne's life and work. The writer's familiarity with different forms or genres of oral narrative and her own written expression, in both the Irish and English languages, are explored, as are the ways in which this passion for Irish oral culture may be seen to be reflected in her writing.

Folklore in Ireland
UNESCO defines folklore as follows:

> Folklore (or traditional and popular culture) is the totality of tradition-based creations of a cultural community, expressed by a group or individuals and recognized as reflecting the expectations of a community in so far as they reflect its cultural and social identity; its standards and values are transmitted orally, by imitation or by other means. It[s] forms include, among others, language, literature, music, dance, games, mythology, rituals, customs, handicrafts, architecture and other arts.[2]

Irish folklore has long been the serious subject of study by a myriad of Irish and international scholars.[3] Coined by William Thoms in 1846, folklore is a word used to describe the oral, inherited, popular wisdom and customs of generations of people in a particular place or cultural area.[4] Often used pejoratively, the original meaning of the word was simply an antiquarian's attempt to define a body of popular culture not easily recorded or analysed by strictly constrained disciplines in arts and the social sciences. Folklore, therefore, is oral, traditional, anonymous and variational: it is dynamic and changes in transmission from one person, group and generation to another. While folklore is expressed by individuals, it comprises a substantive body of collective and shared belief and custom, as against singular or individual experience on its own, which amounts to an easily recognisable body of popular belief and tradition. In many ways, the Irish word 'béaloideas' describes this concept beautifully: oral wisdom or knowledge.[5] Seán Ó Súilleabháin's *A Handbook of Irish Folklore* is generally acknowledged by Irish folklorists as comprising the extent and depth of the subject.[6]

As part of her Bachelor of Arts Honours degree in Pure English at University College Dublin (UCD) in 1973, Ní Dhuibhne took a special course entitled 'The Folktale and Medieval Literature' presented by Professor Bo Almqvist, the recently-appointed Professor of Irish Folklore at the (then) Department of Irish Folklore, or Roinn Bhéaloideas Éireann, at UCD. This department was created in 1971, incorporating Coimisiún Béaloideasa Éireann (the Irish Folklore Commission), which had been founded in 1935, and which itself had developed from the Irish Folklore Institute or Institiúid Bhéaloideas Éireann,[7] founded in 1930.

The new department, therefore, inherited all the staff and holdings, comprising archive materials and special library collections, of the Irish Folklore Commission, and was committed to continuing its work. Dr Séamus Ó Duilearga (James Hamilton Delargy) had been the Commission's Director, and he later became Professor of Irish Folklore at University College Dublin. Strong links with Scandinavia had been created: the Irish folklore archives were initially modelled on those of Swedish archives in Uppsala. The new Professor of Irish Folklore in 1972 was Bo Almqvist, a Swede who had himself been instructed by Professor Ó Duilearga, Dr Seán Ó Súilleabháin and Dr Caoimhín Ó Danachair (Kevin Danaher). Since the foundation of the Irish Folklore Commission to date, over two million pages of transcribed text has been collected, together with thousands of hours of sound recordings, thousands of photographs, hundreds of video tapes, and many more thousands of, as yet, untranscribed text. Since its inception, the Irish folklore archives are closely related to Scandinavian archives in their layout and design.[8] The Department of Irish Folklore at UCD has, since 2005, been renamed as the UCD Delargy Centre for Folklore Research and the National Folklore Collection (Lárionad Uí Dhuilearga do Bhéaloideas na hÉireann agus Cnuasach Bhéaloideas Éireann), which is situated in the UCD School of Irish, Celtic Studies, Irish Folklore and Linguistics. The National Folklore Collection, therefore, constitutes the primary source for all scholarship on aspects of Irish folklore, and is also augmented by new and other collections such as those of the National Library, the National Archives, Radio Telefís Éireann (RTÉ), the Irish Traditional Music Archive, Comhaltas Ceoltóirí Éireann and University College Cork.

A detailed discussion of folkloristic method and contemporary approaches to folklore are beyond the scope of this paper, however, in order to situate Ní Dhuibhne's scholarship, I believe it important to present a brief outline. The Irish school at UCD, originally under the direction of Professor Séamus Ó Duilearga in the first instance, and continued by Professor Bo Almqvist, has largely followed the Finnish historical-geographical method in its approach to folklore and ethnology. As the name suggests, the focus in this approach is about gaining an understanding of how and where a story or tale is likely to have originated and how it is likely to have been disseminated over time and space. The structural components of the tale and the various episodes or actions are carefully analysed and, in this way, various redactions can be identified. The social functions of the tale are also investigated and attention to linguistic- or performance-related variances are noted.

Over the last twenty years, however, different methods and approaches have become prevalent, with varying degrees of emphasis, from structuralism to post-structuralism, and with a now universally-acknowledged focus upon folklore as performance and process. Thus, the context, text and texture of narrative are examined with the insights to be gained from an understanding of how individuals interact in social communities, and where storytellers are, above all, consciously artistic performers engaging with their various audiences. At present, methods from postmodernist theory and cultural studies have come to the fore, and these are currently employed by folklorists worldwide.

Within the discipline of folklore studies, or folkloristics, genre analysis and terminology definition is a fundamental framework for classification and interpretation of items of folklore. Function, content and form are examined to elucidate structure and meaning in 'oral narrative', itself a much-disputed term, while genre analysis examines style, structure, function, age and dissemination, and has been used to internationally classify tale and legend types by folklorists, for whom a 'folktale' is a multi-episodic narrative, usually long, imaginary, not believed, internationally-represented and undetermined in time and place,[9] while a 'legend', by contrast, is a single-episodic, shorter narrative, which is often believed, localised and determined in time and place. The fundamental building block of any genre of oral literature is the 'motif'[10] – a single, identifiable element of a narrative.

In international folk narrative, the 'legend' comprises a range of genres: belief legends, international or migratory legends, and memorates.[11] Essentially, the distinction focuses on the degree of representation, in terms of evidence of a widespread and collective tradition. Like international folktales, international migratory legends[12] have been classified and are easily recognised. Finally, the 'memorate'[13] is understood as the statement by an individual reflecting a more commonly held belief.[14] The word 'lore', in Irish 'seanchas', is often used to refer to material that encapsulates much of folk belief and practice through belief statements rather than through structured narrative. The debate continues with regard to genre analysis, and Irish folklore scholars have contributed greatly to international scholarship in this area, specifically under the leadership of Professor Bo Almqvist.[15] In particular, the systematic studying of Irish folktale and legend types has been profoundly important for international oral narrative studies. Folklore scholarship in Ireland today continues primarily in UCD and University College Cork, as well as being part of Irish studies in Ireland and elsewhere.

Éilís Ní Dhuibhne and Folklore

In 1976, Ní Dhuibhne submitted a dissertation entitled 'Chaucer's Use of Popular Material in "The Friar's Tale"' as the major part of her M.Phil degree. Her minor subject was Old Irish and for her thesis Ní Dhuibhne was awarded a first-class honours degree. This was followed by her PhD thesis in Irish Folklore, submitted in 1982, entitled 'With His Whole Heart: A Study of an International Folktale in Oral and Literary Sources'. Ní Dhuibhne's prowess in the analysis of folklore text and medieval literary sources was exemplified in this research and several academic publications resulted.[16]

In 1978, Ní Dhuibhne received a Danish Government Postgraduate Research Scholarship, which allowed her to spend a year at the University of Copenhagen where the developing folkloristic debates were at a height at that time. Ní Dhuibhne learned to read and speak Danish, collected some folklore in Copenhagen, and also attended classes at the Folklore Institute, where she was present when the great Danish folklorist Bengt Holbek presented a seminar on the meaning of folktales. Holbek's interpretation of the symbols of fairytales was to have a far-reaching effect on Ní Dhuibhne's creative writing.

At this time, in the late 1970s, the Department of Irish Folklore at UCD was a vibrant and exciting place: Professor Almqvist and the other staff members of the Department were passionate about their subject and about the need to collect, preserve, publish and publicise the richness of the Irish folklore heritage. In addition to Irish and English, Swedish, Icelandic and Finnish were regularly heard in the corridors and rooms of the department, and students there felt themselves to be part of an exciting international centre of research as well as custodians of a singular folklore archive.[17] Students were encouraged to avail themselves of the various scholarships being offered by European governments at that time, which was long before Erasmus and similar schemes came into operation. Many graduate students of the Department of Irish Folklore at that time spent a year studying in a European country, particularly the Scandinavian countries, where folklore studies were prominent.[18]

In-between completing the M.Phil thesis and the submission of her doctoral thesis, Ní Dhuibhne was engaged by the Department of Irish Folklore at UCD as a supervisor in the pioneering Urban Folklore Project, undertaken by the Department from 1979 to 1980. Ní Dhuibhne collected substantial quantities of material in Dublin, and also collected folklore in County Donegal. In 1982, Ní Dhuibhne married Bo Almqvist and from then on wrote under the name of 'Éilís Ní Dhuibhne-Almqvist' in most of her folkloristic writings. As Éilís Ní Dhuibhne-Almqvist she has edited, with UCD Professor Séamas Ó Catháin, a collection dedicated to her husband, Emeritus Professor Bo Almqvist, on the celebration of his sixtieth birthday,[19] and she was a co-writer, with Professor Ó Catháin, of the *festschrift* presented to Bo Almqvist for his seventieth birthday.[20]

Ní Dhuibhne's debut folkloristic article, 'The Brave Storyteller', published in 1980 in *Sinsear, the Folklore Journal*, is a deliberately, ostentatiously and mischievously facetious treatment of an international folktale type, which Éilís herself collected from Joe Mac Eachmhartaigh in County Donegal on two occasions, in April 1978 and September 1979. It is highly entertaining and delightfully light. Ní Dhuibhne uses the metaphor of a mock trial to ascertain the storyteller's prowess. The story, known as 'the brave tailor', or AT 1640 in the Aarne-Thompson international index of folktales, where it is classified as a 'lucky accident', is subjected by Ní Dhuibhne to a typical folkloristic analysis, using the methods of the historical-geographical method, but with a deliberate undercutting and tongue-in-cheek tone. It is worth remembering that when *Sinsear, the Folklore Journal* was founded in 1975, and the present author was the first editor of that journal, the initial aim was to allow students of the Department of Irish Folklore an opportunity to publish their research in a new student publication, but also to allow for a more light-hearted treatment of folklore topics. This, Ní Dhuibhne's first academic folklore publication underlines her already creative and playful approach to writing about folklore topics.

As mentioned, Ní Dhuibhne collected from Joe Mac Eachmharcaigh in 1978 and 1979. Writing about her collecting experience, she has said:

> One of my memories from those days is the excitement of meeting Joe Mac Eachmharcaigh. I went to Donegal for a week in January 1978 to write a seminar paper for the Folklore Department post-graduate seminar – possibly my first seminar paper there. I called in to Seán Ó hEochaidh to say hello and he suggested I visit Joe Mac Eachmharcaigh in Doire Chonaill. It was cold and snowing when I found the place – I walked everywhere, having no car in those days. He was welcoming and charming, in his little warm pre-fabricated cottage, where he lived with his aged aunt. He told me he could tell me a lot of stories. The next day I walked to Falcarragh to buy a cassette recorder, and that night I collected folklore for the first time in my life, and continued to do so all week. It was all magical, plodding along the lane through the mountain in the snow, avoiding the angry dogs, smelling the turf smoke, and then coming into the little over heated house and hearing the stories. He would have told me a version of 'Maighdean an tSolais', one of his favourite stories, on the first night.[21]

Ní Dhuibhne here refers to Seán Ó hEochaidh, full-time collector with the Irish Folklore Commission and, later, the Department of Irish Folklore. In addition to collecting from Joe, Ní Dhuibhne also collected folklore in Dublin during the Urban Folklore Project and from Máire Uí Gaoithín, in Dún Chaoin (Dunquin), County Kerry.

The international folktale, 'With His Whole Heart' (AT 1186), is the basis for Chaucer's 'Friar's Tale' from *The*

Canterbury Tales. This is an international folktale which is classified as follows:

> With his Whole Heart. The judge carried off. (The Devil and the Advocate). The devil refuses to take things not offered him with the whole heart. He hears the judge (advocate) cursed for fraud with such sincerity that he carries him off.[22]

While only three Irish sources are referenced in the Aarne-Thompson index, the *Types of the Irish Folktale* list many references, including those classified as AT 813 'A Careless Word summons the Devil'.[23] Indeed, in her doctoral research, Ní Dhuibhne had to seek out these various versions to ascertain which were 'true' versions of AT 1186, and she uncovered some hitherto unknown versions during the course of her work. In the Irish versions of the story, we are told how a man – usually a member of the legal profession such as a lawyer, judge or a bailiff – meets the devil one day. The devil refuses to take anything offered to him unless it is given 'with the whole heart'. The bailiff is then cursed with such sincerity that his soul is damned and the devil can take the man's soul as a result.

Ní Dhuibhne published a lengthy article on her doctoral thesis in *Béaloideas* in 1980,[24] in which she says she is 'testing' the historical-geographical method as to its value for contemporary folkloristic inquiry, a 'test' that she possibly felt necessary in light of the attitude of certain Danish folklorists who had advised her to give up her study. In this work, Ní Dhuibhne focuses very clearly on the structure, function, motifs and regional distribution of the Irish variants, examined within the overall context of the interplay between literary and oral sources of international folktales. In her conclusion, Ní Dhuibhne suggests that the historical-geographical method, as practised by Irish folklorists, can be viewed in a 'positive' way. This folktale is a 'satire' concluded Ní Dhuibhne, and it manifests social protest.

In her article in *Northern Lights* in 2001, Ní Dhuibhne 'revisits' the tale and her PhD thesis, stating that:

> I began work on 'With His Whole Heart' in 1974, for my M. Phil thesis, and as a story it did not much appeal to me. I thought it was

dry, and lacking in complexity. My supervisor, Bo Almqvist, however, insisted that it was a brilliant story. I could not see why, but there were practical reasons for working on it: I was a student of Old and Middle English, with an interest in Chaucer, who wanted to write a folkloristic thesis. 'With His Whole Heart' was a story which neatly bridged the gap between the Department of Middle English and the Department of Irish Folklore, meaning I could register with one and work in the other. A scholarly consideration was that while a few articles on analogues to Chaucer's tale in oral tradition had been written, no exhaustive study had been carried out. The Irish analogues, which were rather close to Chaucer's version, had never been examined by anyone, Chaucerian or folklorist. So I proceeded to work on this little tale for several years, completing my doctorate, which examined all the available versions, in 1982.[25]

Ní Dhuibhne goes on to reassess the core message of the story as 'sincerity vanquishes evil' and observes that the 'brilliance' of the story is more apparent to her now that she has grown more mature. In this revisiting of her earlier work, Ní Dhuibhne asks new questions of this folktale, such as, what does an exhaustive investigation of a single tale type teach us about the process of literary creation, about literature and about the narrative imagination,[26] and what does a study of a tale like this tell us about the nature of narrative creativity?[27] Ní Dhuibhne tells us that Chaucer's version of the tale is the best literary version, but it is "flawed at the dramatic level" as "the pace is too slow to be entirely effective in an oral rendering".[28] Ní Dhuibhne explores these questions, finally observing that "literary and narrative creativity has little to do with the invention of plot, and everything to do with how you tell the tale". She concludes:

> The writers and narrators who engaged most seriously and energetically with the text they had heard produced the most satisfactory, intelligent, and coherent narratives. In the corpus of versions, their work is thrown into relief, their skill and imagination highlighted. The comparison of treatments reveals some of the secrets of excellent narrative composition.[29]

There can be little doubt that Ní Dhuibhne's writing has, itself, been greatly influenced by her engagement with Irish and international folklore, most especially storytelling and the folkloristic genres of folktales and legends. Her deepening understanding of the nature of narrative creativity is apparent in her analysis of the 'With His Whole Heart' tale type in her 2001 article where, as a more mature woman, she revisits her earlier thesis and discovers and sees much more about storytelling as a result.

Other academic articles by Ní Dhuibhne include her published work from the Dublin Urban Folklore Project (UFP) 1978–1980. The UFP features in the article Ní Dhuibhne published in *Béaloideas* in 2006 and, earlier, her tale type index of Urban Legends was published in *Béaloideas* (1983) under the title 'Dublin Modern Legends: An Intermediate Type-list'.[30] In her 1982–83 article in *Sinsear, the Folklore Journal*, entitled 'Old English Metre and Children's Street Rhymes', Ní Dhuibhne examines Dublin street rhymes and finds parallels with old English metre.[31]

In her UFP article, entitled '"They made me tea and gave me a lift home"; Urban Folklore Collecting 1979–1980',[32] Ní Dhuibhne retraces her collecting experience, presenting some of her diary entries and sharing her memories of "that unique and wonderful year".[33] During this year, Ní Dhuibhne says, people were "almost angelically co-operative" and "they let you record them and told you great stories".[34] As the title suggests, they then 'gave you a cup of tea and a lift home.' It is apparent that Ní Dhuibhne learned a great deal about Dublin and its people, their stories, speech and traditions during that collecting year.

In her article 'The Old Woman as Hare: Structure and Meaning in an Irish legend', in *Folklore* (1993), Ní Dhuibhne presents a scholarly analysis of an international legend, namely, 'The Old Woman as Hare', which is an Irish redaction of the international legend type 'The Witch that was Hurt' classified by Reidar Christiansen as ML 3055,[35] and classified as Irish legend type MLSIT 3056 in Bo Almqvist's *Crossing the Border* preliminary Irish legend index.[36] Ní Dhuibhne examines the Irish versions of this international legend where the 'hag-as-hare' motif is blended with the 'milk-stealing witch' motif, and compares this legend type with contemporary oral narrative and, specifically, with modern versions of the legend collected in Dublin.

Ní Dhuibhne's knowledge of Anglo-Irish literature and the interaction between Irish folklore and literary work is also seen in her analysis of J. M. Synge's use of popular material in *The Shadow of the Glen*.[37] The self-conscious use or re-use of folkloric motif and narrative structures by Synge and the other proponents of the Anglo-Irish literary revival are manifest in this work. Ní Dhuibhne-Almqvist investigated the Irish folklore archives to see if she could find the origin of 'Pat Dirane's story'. The source quoted by Synge himself, in a letter published in the *United Irishmen* on 11th February 1905, was that of a story he heard 'from an old man' on Inis Meán in 1898. In her essay on the subject, Ní Dhuibhne conducts a forensic analysis and asks herself "the questions a folklorist must ask concerning this play".[38] The essay is intriguing in both its content and analysis since Ní Dhuibhne deconstructs the original story as recorded and reveals rich layers of interpretation as a result. Indeed, Ní Dhuibhne states, referring to J. M. Synge, that, "scholarly and creative skills are not necessarily mutually exclusive",[39] something that, of course, may also be applied to Ní Dhuibhne herself. Ultimately, Ní Dhuibhne traces the story complex back to Irish versions of the international folktale classified as AT 1350, 'The Loving Wife', which is summarised as follows:

> The Loving Wife. The man feigns death. The wife is immediately ready to take as husband the man who brings her the news.[40]

In Ireland, the story is more often called 'The Man Who Pretended to be Dead',[41] and would seem to have been widely known, especially in the north and north-west. Ní Dhuibhne explains that she is not conducting a "comprehensive historical-geographical analysis" of this story, but concludes that this is "a man's story" since:

> Women are not likely to have invented or to have been given to telling stories of this misogynistic nature, and in fact the majority of variants were told by men and have men playing the role of witness.[42]

Given Scottish analogues, Ní Dhuibhne suggests that the story originated in Scotland and travelled to Donegal, and from there to Connaught and Munster. Ní Dhuibhne shows that Pat Dirane's version of the story is a typical example of the variant most commonly attested in Galway and Conamara, and she asserts that Synge heard this story in English from Pat Dirane, and indicates how Synge, "did not invent or import this particular mixture of the burlesque and the tragic; rather he took it, consciously we must presume, lock stock and barrel from oral tradition".[43]

Finally, Ní Dhuibhne pays tribute to Synge as a collector of folklore, saying that:

> His utilisation of the story in his play is, necessarily, to some extent subjective, but in the main respectful of the original material. In changing so little, in being receptive to the peculiar tone and texture of the oral story, which happened to be foreign to literature and to drama, he demonstrated unusual insight and literary courage. And as a reward, as it were, by changing so little he created something which was wholly novel, a landmark in Irish and world drama. A less modest, more egotistical, less pure artist than Synge could not have achieved this.[44]

In 'The Cow that Ate the Pedlar in Kerry and Wyoming' (1999),[45] Ní Dhuibhne-Almqvist examines a collection of short stories by Annie Proulx where one story, 'The Blood Bay', is revealed to be a version of an international tale, which is, according to Ní Dhuibhne:

> A version of an international tale, confusingly and unnecessarily classified twice in the Aarne-Thompson index, both under the number AT 1281A Getting Rid of the Man-eating Calf, and the number AT 1537*, Corpse's Legs Left.[46]

In a short survey of Irish analogues, Ní Dhuibhne-Almqvist highlights the "delicate relationship between fantasy and reality which characterizes this folk story",[47] and publishes a version collected by Bo Almqvist on 20 December 1975 from Cáit 'An Bhab' Feiritéar, the renowned storyteller from Dún Chaoin, County Kerry. A final folkloristic article to mention is 'The Land of Cokaygne': A Middle English Source for Irish Food Historians', published in *Ulster Folklife* (1988), where, again, Ní Dhuibhne's Middle English interests blend with the ethnological.

In summary, therefore, Ní Dhuibhne's academic work has mainly focused on oral narrative, storytelling, folklore collecting (primarily urban material but also some Gaeltacht collecting), and the interplay of folklore and literature – and these areas of interest are clearly reflected in Ní Dhuibhne's literary work also.

Influence of Folklore on Ní Dhuibhne's Literary Works

Influence of Folklore on Ní Dhuibhne's Literary Works

Ní Dhuibhne herself has often stated that her work has been "influenced by folklore".[48] In her introduction to the *Midwife to the Fairies* collection (2003), Anne Fogarty suggests that:

> Ní Dhuibhne's doctoral study of the many oral and literary versions of a common European narrative, used most memorably by Geoffrey Chaucer in *The Friar's Tale*, attests to her fascination, not just with the content but also with the variegated shapes assumed by stories ... Drawing upon her academic interests, Ní Dhuibhne frequently incorporates folklore into her fiction and uses it to explore the divergences and continuities between tradition and modernity in Irish society. In 'Midwife to the Fairies,' a folk tale is interpolated into a contemporary story that, in fact, transposes and retells it. The double-levelled structure makes us aware of the different modes of narration that typify the oral composition and its modern analogue ...
>
> A more elaborate variant on this technique of interweaving oral material with postmodern perspectives may be found in *The Inland Ice*. Here, instalments of a folk tale, 'The Search for the Lost Husband', are interspersed between the stories in the collection ...[49]

In an interview with Christine St. Peter, Ní Dhuibhne has said of herself:

> How do I use folklore in my writing? I allude to old stories. I counterpoint my own stories, set in the now, with oral stories, set in the past, or, more accurately, set in the never never or the always always. I feel, and hope, that this enhances my ordinary stories, gives them a depth and a mythic quality which, on their own, they would find it hard to achieve. It puts them in a large context – not only an Irish context, since the first thing one learns about oral narrative is its international nature.

Also – this is important also … I know that oral stories have survived because they are good stories. Very, very good stories – tightly plotted, packed with symbol, nuance and meaning. If you base a story, however loosely, on an ancient oral tale you will find it hard to go wrong. They are dramatic, they are intelligent. J.M. Synge found this out when he wrote his plays – he seldom strays far from his source.[50]

This interview reveals much of Ní Dhuibhne's own attitudes as to influences in her writing and traces her development as a writer through this discussion. The interplay of folklore and literature,[51] which is a constant, dynamic process, continues, and is inherent in Ní Dhuibhne's creativity.

Significantly, in one of her short stories, 'The Flowering',[52] Ní Dhuibhne's protagonist, Lennie, says:

Archaeology, history, folklore. Linguistics, genealogy. They tell you about society, not about individuals. It takes literature to do that … The oral tradition. What oral tradition? It went away, with their language when the schools started … Slowly they are finding a new tradition. They are inventing a new tradition. Transform, adopt or disappear. (12)

This is also echoed in the St Peter interview where Ní Dhuibhne explains why writing is so important for her.[53]

In her radio drama, *Casadh an Tape Recorder*,[54] Ní Dhuibhne reveals a particular interest in Irish and international folklore. The drama is a marvellous re-construction of a folklore collecting session, in which the ardent student from Dublin arrives in the Gaeltacht to record the folkloric gems from the old people of the area. It is a wonderful send-up on the whole process, and one can hear Ní Dhuibhne laughing both with and at the endeavours of the play's young female protagonist.

Similarly, in her play, *Dún na mBan trí Thine*,[55] a plethora of folkloric characters are represented, as the author deftly switches between present reality and times past. The title of the drama itself is reminiscent of the well-known Irish folklore story called 'The Fairy Hill is on Fire!', an international migratory legend that is particularly well represented in Ireland.[56] In this way, folklore themes, beliefs and narratives are referenced, all of which add to the mystery and meaning of the dramatic action. Mná na Leasa (the women of the Lios or fairy fort) are primary characters, whose presence and message is threatening (*'Dún'* 74). They act as a chorus, similar to that in T.S. Eliot's *Murder in the Cathedral*. But, in addition, Ní Dhuibhne includes a variety of characters and themes from Irish folklore, for instance: a child believed to be an iarlais, or changeling, who is thrown into the fire, the traditional method of banishing the creature (80, 84–45); while fishing, Eoin encounters 'An Mhaighdean Mhara', or the mermaid who needs her cloak in order to be able to return to the sea (90); reference is made to the belief that an unmarried woman should not walk out alone at night as she would be particularly vulnerable to the fairies (105); and to the belief that a woman could take the form of a hare (95), namely the story of the witch-stealing hare, as discussed above; reference is made to the belief that women who die in childbirth are unhappy souls (110); and to well-known Irish legends, such as the 'midwife to the fairies' (127); 'Petticoat Loose' (128); [57] and 'An Bhean Sí', the Banshee (128).

Ní Dhuibhne has acknowledged that the Irish language – a "threatened language" [58] – is important for her. In her article *'Saibhreas nó Daibhreas. An Scríbhneoir Dátheangach'*, she suggests, particularly in relation to her novel *The Dancers Dancing*, that:

Dhein mé iarracht i gcaibidil amháin rithimí agus comhréir na Gaeilge a chur in iúl trí mhéain an Bhéarla.[59]

[I made an effort in one chapter to present the rhythms and the syntax of Irish through the medium of English.]

Ní Dhuibhne considers the issue of Irish identity and how bilingualism contributes to or takes away from this concept: she seems to conclude that most Irish-speaking people would consider bilingualism as a threat, and she quotes from Jerry White in this context.[60] Ní Dhuibhne talks about the value of using a journey as a literary device, thus:

Seift a mbainim úsáid aisti go minic i mo shaother ficsin, idir ghearrscéalta agus úrscéaltaa, agus ar bhaineas leas aisti freisin sa dráma Milseog an tSamhraidh, ná an t-asitear, go háirithe aistear ina mbíonn athrú nó aistriú ó réagúin teanga amháin go réigiún eile i gceist ...

Cuid den scéal, cuid thábhachtach, i ngach saothar díobh seo ná an malartú ó theanga amháin go teanga eile agus an tionchar a bhíonn ag an athrú seo ar mheon agus ar shaol na gcarachter.[61]

[A device I often use in my fiction, in both short stories and novels, and which I also used in my drama *Milseog an tSamhraidh* is the journey, especially where there is a journey or a change from one linguistic area to another.

Part of the story, an important part, in all these works, is the change from one language to another and the influence of that change on the outlook and the lives of the characters.]

In many ways, Ní Dhuibhne's essay entitled 'The Irish',[62] indicates much of her own opinion and perspectives on Irish identity, again addressing the issue of the Irish language, the Gaeltacht, and the place it holds in the contemporary Irish psyche. In this characteristically honest and wry paper, Ní Dhuibhne casts a critical eye on 'the Irish', considering their many gifts, flaws and foibles. In her interview with Christine St Peter, Ní Dhuibhne said that:

It is in particularity, T.S. Eliot said, writing about Yeats, that the universal is best expressed – or words to that effect. When people talk, as they do, about the necessity to "globalize" modern Irish literature, or to desist from navel gazing, they ignore the wisdom of these words. The best literature is local, and specific, and in that specificity – that historicity, if you like – the universal is expressed.[63]

In her writing, Ní Dhuibhne is, thus, consciously "documenting the way people feel at this juncture in history and in this place".[64] There are, therefore, recurring themes in both her folkloristic academic research and her literary works and, indeed, aspects of her own life and experience, evident in her writing.

Feminism and Folklore

In her 'Introduction' to the 'International Folktales' section of the *Field Day Anthology, Volumes IV and V*, Ní Dhuibhne discusses the representation of women and gender in Irish folklore scholarship, more or less concluding that it would be difficult to ascertain any bias. Speaking of Professor James Delargy, Ní Dhuibhne asks:

> What of Delargy's general impression, that the majority of storytellers telling the large, public genres, were men, while women had a relatively 'passive' knowledge of complex forms such as the fairytale and hero tale, but were active tellers of legends and other kinds of lore which were told in smaller and more private situations than the long stories? [65]

Ní Dhuibhne continues, saying that, "when the tradition was in decline" women might have been allowed the opportunity to tell their stories in a way which might not have been possible "when storytelling was a living tradition", and suggests that:

> It is not difficult to imagine that it would have been much easier for a woman to tell stories to a folklore collector on a one-to-one basis, than to sit in front of a gathering of twenty or thirty neighbours, and do the same thing. The difference is between public performance and private chat. It is probably no exaggeration to say that for most Irishwomen the latter has been, and to some extent still is, the more agreeable context for performance of any kind. In any case, women in country households were so occupied with house and farm work that they had limited opportunities for any kind of leisure activity. Collectors' memories and diaries indicate that it was difficult to collect from women: they were always jumping up to do something in the kitchen. [66]

Ní Dhuibhne then introduces stories from five women storytellers, chosen for inclusion in the anthology. Significantly, in terms of Ní Dhuibhne's fiction, one of these chosen stories is an Irish version of the international folktale known as 'The Search for the Lost Husband' classified as AT 425 in the Aarne-Thompson index, and which features in Ní Dhuibhne's collection, 'The Inland Ice' and Other Stories. [67]

In her discussion of the burning of Bridget Cleary in County Tipperary in 1895, Angela Bourke proposed that "postcolonial and feminist scholarship has re-examined received narratives, asking by whom they have been constructed and what is revealed by their logic and silences", [68] which suggests that new questions may now be asked of traditional oral narratives. Folkloristics in Ireland has changed, and over the last thirty years or so, postmodern, postcolonial, post-structuralist and feminist scholarship and methodologies have brought about different readings of material held sacred for so long. Through the telling of certain stories, and through the remembering of certain events and happenings, people, consciously or unconsciously, create or construct meaning in their lives, and folklore, in its exploration of oral communications between people, seeks to understand and interpret that meaning. New and revived ways of seeing, imagining, and representing life and lore are increasingly thrust upon us. The study of Irish folklore today continues amidst a dynamic and stimulating analysis of the nature of Irish cultural identity, and the legacy of Ireland's rich cultural heritage, particularly in terms of the creative and imaginative storytelling tradition.

Éilís Ní Dhuibhne as folklorist, therefore, has already made a considerable contribution to the study of Irish and international folk narrative. Her work on folktales and legends, and especially the linkages between oral and literary texts, is exemplary. In addition, Ní Dhuibhne's use of folklore and folkloric motif in her literary works brings this wonderful material to new audiences, as well as situating Ní Dhuibhne's writing in the particularity of Irish life and experience at this time. In many ways, Ní Dhuibhne's literary work both embodies and manifests a new, *and* a revival of, interest in the 'Irish tradition'.

NOTES

1   All translations are by the author. I have known Éilís for nearly thirty years as friends and *alumni* of folklore studies at UCD. This personal connection is important and should be understood as informing my approach to this paper.

2   UNESCO website and documents regarding 'intangible cultural heritage'. See http://www.unesco.org/culture/heritage/intangible/ html eng/ index_en.shtml; See also: the website of the American Folklore Society (www.afsnet.org) for discussion regarding the definition of 'folklore'; Diarmuid Ó Giolláin, *Locating Irish Folklore: Tradition,Modernity, Identity* (Cork UP, 2000; 180); Anne O'Connor,

The Blessed and the Damned, Sinful Women and Unbaptised Children in Irish Folklore (London: Peter Lang, 2005), 13ff.

3   See O'Connor, *The Blessed and the Damned*, for an overview of the development of Irish folklore studies.

4   William Thoms, *The Atheneum*, (22 August 1846) and quoted in full in Alan Dundes, *The Study of Folklore* (University of California at Berkeley, 1965), 4–5.

5   See Dáithí Ó hÓgáin, 'Béaloideas – Notes on the History of a Word'. *Béaloideas*, 70 (2002): 83–98, for a comprehensive history of this word.

6   Seán Ó Súilleabháin, *A Handbook of Irish Folklore* (1942) is accepted as the definition of folklore in Ireland, and forms the basis for the indexing system of the Irish Folklore Collections.

7   Séamas Ó Catháin 'Institiúid Bhéaloideas Éireann'. *Béaloideas*, (2005): 85–110.

8   See Bo Almqvist, *The Irish Folklore Commission: Achievement and Legacy* (Dublin: Folklore of Ireland Society, 1979); Gerard O'Brien, *Irish Governments and the Guardianship of Historical Records, 1922–72* (Dublin: Four Courts Press, 2004); Department of Irish Folklore UCD website, http://www.ucd.ie/folklore

9   Cf. Stith Thompson, *The Folktale* (Los Angeles: University of California Press, 1946). [Reprinted 1977] and Thompson, *Motif-Index of Folk Literature*, Folklore Fellows Communications, FFC Series No. 106, I–VI, (Revised; Copenhagen, 1955–1958) for the international motif index of folk literature; see Antti Aarne, and Stith Thompson, *The Types of the Folktale*, Folklore Fellows Communications, FFC Series No. 184 (Helsinki: Suomalainen Tiedeakatemia, Academia Scientiarum Fennica, 1964) (hereafter AT), for international folktale classifications AT numbers correlate with those listed in Seán Ó Súilleabháin, and Reidar Th. Christiansen, *The Types of the Irish Folktale*, Folklore Fellows Communications, FFC Series No. 188 (Helsinki: Suomalainen Tiedeakatemia, Academia Scientiarum Fennica, 1967) (hereafter TIF); see also Bengt Holbek's *Interpretation of Fairy Tales: Danish Folklore in a European Perspective*, Folklore Fellows Communications, FFC Series No. 239 (Helsinki: Suomalainen Tiedeakatemia, Academia Scientiarum Fennica, 1987); cf. Dan Ben-Amos, ed. *Folklore Genres* (Austin: University of Texas Press, 1976); cf. Axel Olrik, 'Epic Laws of Folk Narrative', in Alan Dundes, ed. *The Study of Folklore* (Berkely: University of California at Berkeley, 1965), 129–141.

10 Stith Thompson, *Motif-Index of Folk Literature*.

11 See Carl W.Von Sydow, *Selected Papers on Folklore* (Copenhagen: Rosenkilde and Bagger, 1948).

12   Reidar Th. Christiansen, *The Migratory Legends*, Folklore Fellows Communications, FFC Series No. 175 (Helsinki: Suomalainen Tiedeakatemia, Academia Scientiarum Fennica, 1958).

13   Carl W. Von Sydow, *Selected Papers on Folklore*; Lauri Honko 'Memorates and the Study of Folk Belief'. *Journal of the Folklore Institute*, 1–2, 1964, 5–19; L. Dégh and A. Vaszonyi 'Legend and Belief.' *Genre*, 4, (Sept.) 2, 1971, 281–403.

14   See, for example, Bo Almqvist and Patricia Lysaght, 'The Banshee Questionnaire', *Béaloideas*, 42–44, (1974–1976), 88–119.

15   See Bo Almqvist 'Irish Migratory Legends on the Supernatural: Sources, Studies and Problems', *The Fairy Hill is on Fire!* Proceedings of the Symposium on the Supernatural in Irish and Scottish Migratory Legends, Dublin 7–8 October 1988. *Béaloideas*, 59, (1991), 55–66, and 'Crossing the Border, A Sampler of Irish Migratory Legends about the Supernatural,' *The Fairy Hill is on Fire!*, 210–324 (MLSIT), and 'Crossing the Border' a type list of Irish migratory legend; *Béaloideas*, (1992–1993), (1994–1995), international colloquia, such as Bo Almqvist, Séamas Ó Catháin, and Pádraig Ó Héalaí, eds., *The Heroic Process. Form, Function and Fantasy in Folk Epic*, Proceedings of the International Folk Epic conference, UCD, 2–6 Sept. 1985 (Dublin: Glendale Press, 1987); *Béaloideas* (1991): *The Fairy Hill is on Fire!*, and Patricia Lysaght, Séamas Ó Catháin, and Dáithí Ó hÓgáin, eds., *Islanders and Water-Dwellers*, Proceedings of the Celtic-Nordic-Baltic Symposium held at University College Dublin, 16–19 June 1996 (Dublin: DBA, 1999), and see various articles published in *Béaloideas* and *Sinsear, the Folklore Journal* and in other international academic journals.

16   See, especially, Ní Dhuibhne, 'The Brave Storyteller' in *Sinsear, the Folklore Journal*, 1980: 84–91 and 'Ex Corde: At 1186 in Irish tradition' in *Béaloideas*, 1980: 86–134.

17   See *Sinsear, the Folklore Journal*, 2005, which is a special commemorative volume of the student journal originally started in 1975, for some personal reminiscences of that time in the Department of Irish Folklore: see also Anne O'Connor, 'A Personal Reflection of the Influence of Irish Folklore' in *Sinsear, the Folklore Journal*, 2005:7–8.

18   Including the author who was awarded a Norwegian Government Scholarship in 1980.

19   Ní Dhuibhne-Almqvist and Séamas Ó Catháin, eds., *Viking Ale, Studies on Folklore Contacts Between the Northern and Western Worlds* (Aberystwyth: Boethius Press, 1991).

20   Ní Dhuibhne and Séamas Ó Catháin, 'Introduction', *Northern Lights, Following Folklore in North-Western Europe, Essays in Honour of Bo Almqvist* (Dublin: University College Dublin Press, 2001).

21   Communication with author, 27th Sept. 2006.

22   AT, 372.

23   TIF, 220–221.

24   'Ex Corde: AT 1186 in Irish Tradition'. *Béaloideas*, 1980: 86–134.

25   Ní Dhuibhne 'Fer in the North Contree: With His Whole Heart Revisited' in Séamas Ó Catháin, ed, *Northern Lights* (202–214), 203.

26   *ibid.*, 204.

27   *ibid.*, 212.

28   *ibid.*

29   *ibid.*, 213

30   'Dublin Modern Legends: An Intermediate Type-list'. *Béaloideas*, 1983: 55–69.

31   Ní Dhuibhne, *Sinsear, the Folklore Journal*, 1982–1983: 76–82.

32   Ní Dhuibhne, '"They made me tea and gave me a lift home"; Urban Folklore Collecting 1979–1980' *Béaloideas*, 2006b: 63–84.

33   *ibid.*, 67.

34   *ibid.*, 83.

35   Reidar Th. Christiansen, *The Migratory Legends*, XX.

36   'Crossing the Border, A Sampler of Irish Migratory Legends about the Supernatural,' *The Fairy Hill is on Fire!*.

37   Ní Dhuibhne, '"The Loving Wife": Synge's Use of Popular Material in *The Shadow of the Glen*' *Béaloideas*, 1990: 141–180.

38   *ibid.*, 144.

39   *ibid.*, 144.

40   Aarne-Thompson, *The Types of the Folktale*, 400.

41   TIF, 239–240.

42   Ní Dhuibhne, '"The Loving Wife": Synge's Use of Popular Material in *The Shadow of the Glen*' *Béaloideas*, 1990: 141–180, 152.

43   *ibid.*, 165.

44   *ibid.*, 167.

45   Ní Dhuibhne, 'The Cow that Ate the Pedlar in Kerry and Wyoming'. *Béaloideas*, 1999: 125–134.

46   *ibid.*, 125.

47   *ibid.*, 127.

48   Including in communication to the author, 27 Sept. 2006.

49   Fogarty, 'Preface' to *Midwife to the Fairies*, x–xi.

50   St. Peter, 'Negotiating the Boundaries', 73.

51   Cf. Bo Almqvist *An Béaloideas agus an Litríocht* (Baile Átha Cliath: An Cumann le Béaloideas Éireann, 1977).

52 Ní Dhuibhne 'The Flowering' in *Midwife to the Fairies* (Cork: Attic Press, 2003).

53 Christine St. Peter, 'Negotiating the Boundaries: An Interview with Éilís Ní Dhuibhne'. *Canadian Journal of Irish Studies*, 32. 1 (Spring 2006: 68–75).

54 RTÉ Radio 1 drama first broadcast on 17th Oct. 2003.

55 Ní Dhuibhne, *Milseog an tSamhraidh and Dún na mBan trí Thine* (BÁC 1997, 73–134). Further references to *Dún* are in parentheses in the text.

56 This is classified as Irish legend type MLSIT 6071 in Bo Almqvist's *Crossing the Border* preliminary Irish legend index.

57 See O'Connor, *The Blessed and the Damned* (2005).

58 St. Peter, 'Negotiating the Boundaries', 3.

59 Eilís Ní Dhuibhne, "Saibhreas nó Daibhreas? An Scríbhneoir Dátheangach" in Aisling Ní Dhonnchadha, ed. *An Prós Comhaimseartha. Léachtaí Cholm Cille* XXXVI. (Maigh Nuad: An Sagart, 2006: 139–154).

60 *ibid.*, 151.

61 *ibid.* 148

62 'The Irish', in Åke Daun and Soren Jansson, ed., *Europeans. Essays on Culture and Identity* (Lund, Nordic Academic Press, 1999: 47–66).

63 St. Peter, 'Negotiating the Boundaries', 5–6.

64 *ibid.*, 6.

65 'Women and Irish Narrative Tradition' (essay on women storytellers, with examples of international folktales told by Irish women), Supplement to the *Field Day Anthology of Irish Writing. Vols. IV and V* (Cork: Cork University Press, 2002).

66 *ibid.*, 1217–1218. The contention of Séamus Ó Duilearga that women were indeed 'passive' while men were 'active' bearers of tradition, as evidenced in Ó Duilearga's *The Gaelic Storyteller* (London: John Rhŷs Memorial Lecture, Proceedings of the British Academy, Vol. XXXI, 1945), is one that has been subject to some critical evaluation in recent years.

67 Ní Dhuibhne, *'The Inland Ice' and Other Stories* (Belfast: Blackstaff Press, 1997).

68 Angela Bourke 'The Burning of Bridget Cleary: Newspapers and Oral Tradition,' *Tipperary Historical Journal*, (1998): 112–127.

Appendices

The Man Who Had No Story

ÉILÍS NÍ DHUIBHNE

Finn O'Keefe is driving along the M50. He's on his way to the
country. It's bucketing down as usual and the motorway is like
an obstacle course. For most of it you have to drive at sixty
kilometres an hour, steering on a narrow track between rows of
yellow cones, a good few knocked over and rolling around: an
extra little challenge for the weary driver. You'd be quicker
going through town, in all probability. But you never know,
and at least it's all moving along now, at this in-between time.
Four o'clock. Sunday. Not many people leave town so late, and
the great return from the country has not yet started.

Grainne, Finn's wife, is in the summer house they've rented
for July and half of August, at a high enough price, down there
in the west. They 'moved down' – he liked saying that, even to
himself – three weeks ago. The plan was that they would relax,
go for walks in the green hills and swim in the bracing ocean,
eat good little things bought in the local town. He was going to
write. He's a teacher – so is she – he writes in the summer, is
the theory, and Grainne chills. But it hasn't worked. Not after
the first few days, when he wound down by reading a travel
book about Tuscany called *Bella Tuscany*, which was so good
that he started writing a similar sort of thing, except about the
west of Ireland. *Bella Kerry* – a working title obviously. He got
right into it and when you thought about it this place *had*
plenty in common with Tuscany. The sweet smell of the clover,
the wild flowers all over the place. Cute little shops and

287

restaurants in the town. The organic butcher. The farmer's market. It hadn't rained the first few days so that had encouraged the comparison. They'd been able to go for long walks up the hill at the back of the house – stunning with gorse and heather, purple and yellow, the exact same colours as the Wexford football jersey as he noted in his writer's notebook, in case the simile would come in handy (how could it? who cared that the mountain where Finn was on holiday reminded him of the Wexford strip? His notebook was full of such useless scraps). Those first days, they let the waves and the wind do their work. Of cleaning out their cobwebbed heads, their sticky hearts.

Then the troubles started. First, the rain. Then Grainne's back acted up. After all the housework before they left home – she had to do it, nobody lifted a finger apart from her, all that – and the long drive. A whole day in the Medical Centre – a country medical centre, ok, he wrote about it in his *Bella Kerry* book – you could include some bad things in that sort of book, as long as you kept them to a minimum.

Next thing their son, Mattie, who is minding the house in Dublin, which to him means putting out food for the cat when the thought strikes him – it could be every two days – phoned. The cat's sick. Doesn't eat anything. Doesn't even move.

Quelle surprise!

But Grainne worried. So back to town they went, the two of them. Three days running to the vet with the sick cat – Pangur Bán she is called, the most common cat name in Ireland thanks to that quirky monk who wrote about his cat in Old Irish high on a mountain in Austria in the eighth century or something. Everyone's favourite poem. Pangur, apparently – their Pangur, the real cat, born in the 20th century but living still in this one, a two century cat – may have Aids, or cancer, or both. She definitely has a heart condition and there's something wrong with her kidneys. And she's dehydrated. Hard to explain that, said the vet, giving Finn a suspicious look. It was Finn's guess that Pangur hadn't been given a drink of water or milk or anything at all in approximately ten days. But he didn't reveal this to the vet, who disapproved of him. As if it was his fault the cat is sick. Which of course it was, in a way. Maybe the owners of ageing cats should not go off down the country to chase words. Or go anywhere, to do anything.

The vet ran tests, cleaned out Pangur's system with a twenty-four hour drip, administered a few injections, all of which Pangur hated. Then he prescribed antibiotics and heart pills, and advised, in that solemn slow voice of his, that they would have to consider things and make a decision. Meaning, Finn supposed, it was soon to be curtains for Pangur. A thousand euros later and now they should consider putting her down. Shouldn't the vet have mentioned that before?

Anyway, after all the medication, Pangur looked ok. Relatively. So Grainne decided they should bring her back with them, down the country. 'Mattie loves Pangur, she's his cat.' Yes. Indeed. He had brought her home one day when he was ten and she was four weeks old, a little cute white kitten with bright blue eyes – he had fair hair then too, falling like flax into his eyes, also blue, sparkling like the sea in sunshine – thirteen years ago. Finn and Grainne had never wanted a cat. Or any pet. 'But I don't think he looks after her properly. It's not fair to expect that of him. She needs a lot of attention and he's got his own life.' Mattie is busy, reading Nietzsche, playing the guitar, and watching television, not necessarily in that order, from mid-day when he gets up until 1am when he hits the sack after his long strenuous days sitting on the sofa.

Pangur isn't keen on long journeys. (Or short journeys. She howls her head off even on the five minute drive to the vet). But she came to Kerry, in her cage, on the back seat of the car. After four hours she stopped howling and dozed off – you couldn't say she slept, as such. It was more that she collapsed into a state of semi-consciousness, like a prisoner whose body just can't take any more torture. They made lots of stops to encourage her to drink a drop of water, nibble some 'treats'. She refused every time, but Grainne kept on trying. Amazingly, Pangur survived the trip and began to recover– the change of scene seemed to do her good. Being away from home worked for her the way it is supposed to work for a human, though often doesn't. This cheered them both up no end. For once they had done the right thing, by the cat. Instead of killing her, as suggested by the vet, they had taken her down the country for a holiday, and she got better.

Then, no sooner was Pangur settled in, eating a mouthful of Treats and a tiny can of gourmet catfood a day than Mattie was on the phone again. He never phoned when things were ok, so Finn smelt a rat as soon as he overheard Grainne talking to him. Mattie always talked to her first; even if Finn answered the phone, he'd ask for his mother.

A mouse. Mattie had seen one, in the conservatory, eating from the cat dish. A dish of catfood that had been left out, even though there wasn't a cat in the house. It didn't bear thinking about. And – troubles don't come singly – the fridge had stopped working.

They'd have to go back to Dublin, to deal with the mouse and the fridge. But somebody had to stay and mind Pangur. It wouldn't be fair to put her through the ordeal of the journey, again. Or Grainne, with her back.

Finn spent a whole week in Dublin, and now he's on the road south for the third time in a few weeks. Maybe his break can start at last. July is nearly over. Before you know it it will be September. Can he write *Bella Kerry* in four weeks? He wonders how long the woman who wrote *Bella Tuscany* spent doing hers, Frances something – he likes her style; he must Google her sometime, see what she looks like. He envisages her as laughing, with shining fair hair. Tall and slender – she mentions, on page fifty, that she has 'long rabbit feet'. Beautiful. A gazelle.

The Red Cow roundabout. It's in transition from being a roundabout to being a cloverleaf junction, and is essentially a complete nightmare – last time he took the wrong lane, found himself at the toll bridge having to pay to cross over, do a U-turn, then pay to get back, losing forty minutes and four euro as punishment for his mistake. But it's a bit easier this time; they've put up signposts. He makes the right choices and soon enough he's out on the N7. From then on, it should be plain sailing down across Ireland to the south west. Apart from some thunderstorms – Laois has descended into a Dantean pit of despair – this turns out to be right.

Bella Kerry. It's easy to do. But he has to write something else. Not a rip off of *Bella Tuscany*, which, he knows quite well, is a waste of time and will never get finished. Basically writing it is an excuse for not writing something else. This happens more and more, he finds. Something else is what he's always writing, never whatever it is he is supposed to be doing. Which is, at the minute, a short story. A short story that will make his name. Again. Or even a short story that he knows in his heart is a good short story, no matter what anyone else thinks.

He used to write them when he was younger. He even published a collection once, ages ago. Retrospectively it seems to him he wrote those stories effortlessly. Some autobiographical, about things that happened to him – mainly women ditching him, him ditching women – this was before he was married, of course. Made up ones about people he saw on the bus or the train, mainly about women ditching them, or them ditching women – these imagined lives bore a close resemblance to his own.

But he can't think of anything to write about. He never thought much of his talent, but looking back he admires his younger self, the self who had the wit, the imagination, the energy, to write any kind of story, even a bad one. How on earth did he do it?

He hasn't the foggiest idea.

He hasn't the foggiest idea, although he is a teacher of creative writing. He tells other people how to do it and encourages them. It always surprises him that they can write anything, and he is even more surprised that plenty of it is good. And how they can write, all those kids! He just tosses them an idea, a topic, an opening line (a trigger, he calls it, he's getting tired of that word, but hasn't come up with a satisfactory alternative) and off they go. Writing for all they're worth. Trouble is, he can't give himself a trigger. Well, that's not true, of course he can – he knows hundreds, literally, enough to get him through a ten-year course with the same class, although no course actually lasts longer than ten weeks. But none of those triggers fire anything, shoot anything, whatever triggers do. None of them hits the target. Because his imagination is dead. Dead as a fox on the motorway (he's passed three of them, squashed like eggs in the frying pan, poor buggers). He used to have loads of imagination. It was his hallmark. But it's gone, like the colour in his hair, and the other things he had when he was younger. Such as? *Joie de vivre.* Passion. Bright dreams.

There's a story he heard. On the radio. There used to be storytellers in the place they are staying, that deep green valley on the edge of the ocean, but not any more that he knows of. It was a recording of a storyteller who used to live down the road from his rented cottage in the same townland, *Baile na hAbha*, the town by the river. The Man Who Had No Story. That was the name of the story and that's what it was about. The man – let's say his name was Dermot, from *Baile na hAbha* – was looked down upon by the people. Everyone was expected to have at least one story they could entertain their neighbours with. Good storytellers knew a few hundred, the professor guy who was commenting on this story said. But Dermot hadn't even one. He was hoping for a free night's lodging but he couldn't sing for his supper, as it were. And it just wouldn't do. The professor says this story indicates how important storytelling was in the Irish community. It was considered an essential skill. Some were better at it than others, but not having anything to say for yourself, not having even one single story, was considered anti-social, very bad manners. Nearly criminal. The man was thrown out of the house, in disgrace. 'Go to the well and fetch a bucket of water,' the woman of the house said, crankily. 'You'd better do something for your keep.' And at the well poor old crestfallen Dermot came across some fairies. And the fairies lifted him up in a blast of wind and swept him through the sky. East and west and north and south they carried him. And he landed in front of a big house. And in the house a wake was going on. As soon as he stepped inside the door a very nice-looking girl with curly black hair asked Dermot to sit beside her. Which he did. Gladly.

And the man of the house said: 'We need a bit of music. Somebody go and find the fiddler.'

The beautiful girl said: 'No need. The best fiddler in Ireland is sitting here beside me. Dermot O'Keefe from *Baile na hAbha*.'

Dermot was gobsmacked. :Who, me? Sure I've never played a tune in my life. He said.

But lo and behold there was a fiddle in one of his hands and a bow in the other, and the next thing he was playing the most beautiful music anyone ever heard.

And then, later, the man said: 'Somebody go and get the priest to say Mass, because we want to get the corpse out of the house before daybreak.'

No need, said the curly haired girl. Isn't the best priest in Ireland right here beside me?

Dermot. Up he stood and said Mass, and all the prayers afterwards, as if he'd been doing it every day of his life.

Then four men took the coffin in their shoulders to carry it to the graveyard. There were three very short men and one very tall man. And the coffin was wobbling all over the place.

'Somebody call the doctor!' said the man of the house. 'So he can shorten the legs of this long fellow, and make the coffin even.'

'Isn't the best doctor in Ireland here at hand!" said the lovely girl. 'Dermot O'Keefe from *Baile na hAbha*.'

And – to his own surprise – Dermot performed the amputation like one of the stars of *ER*. And off they all went to the graveyard. But just before they reached it, a big blast of wind came and swept Dermot off his feet. And he was blown east and blown west and north and south. And when he was finished being blown all over the place, down he fell at the well where he had gone to fetch the water. The bucket was full to the brim with sparkling clean water. He picked it up and brought it into the house.

'Well, now, Dermot,' said the woman of the house. 'Can you tell us a story?'

'I can,' said Dermot, pleased with himself. 'Indeed. I am the man who has a story to tell. You'll never believe what's after happening to me ...'

'This tale seems to tell us that if you just let things happen to you, you can make a story out of them,' said the professor. God, these guys! thinks Finn. So patronizing. As if that isn't obvious to anyone. 'Basically the story is saying, get a life, then tell your story.' 'Yes,' says the interviewer. 'And get confidence in yourself, so you can make things up? Play the fiddle even if you never learnt.' 'It's saying that too,' agrees the learned one, thoughtfully. Because how can you play the fiddle if you haven't learnt, is probably what he's thinking. It's impossible. But the professor says, 'Yes, Dermot has never played the fiddle, and yet, he can play a good tune, when requested.' 'And he has never amputated a person's leg,' says the interviewer. There's a critical edge creeping into his voice, a hint of a sneer. 'That's a bit weird, isn't it? How did your man feel, minus a chunk of his legs? I mean he's not even a corpse he's alive as you and me and whap, off with half his leg!' The interviewer chuckles and so does the professor. Both sound a little uneasy. 'Of course, the fairies have given him the gift,' says the Professor. 'The gift of imagination. What they are telling Dermot is that it doesn't matter if he's a fiddler or a priest or a doctor, he can pretend that he is, in a story. He can make it all up.' 'That's it, I suppose,' says the interviewer. He cheers up. 'It's just fiction! A pack of lies. Blame the fairies for it, folks!' He's nearly singing, the interviewer. 'And now we'll go east and go west and east again – to a commercial break.'

Get a life. *And* use your imagination. It is the sort of thing Finn tells his own students. In fact he could give them this story, as a sort of insight into the history of story in Ireland – they might like that. As for him, well, he's had as much life, interesting life, as he's ever going to get, and he doesn't believe in the fairies. In the old days, the storytelling days, they were always there. To frighten ordinary decent people. And to give the gift of music, or story, or song, to the other ones, to the artists in the community.

The mouse was, as Finn had suspected, a rat. And they usually aren't alone, my friend, said the rat man. He kept addressing Finn as My Friend, which was nice – the kind of thing he might mention in *Bella Kerry*, although the rat and the rat-catcher were in a suburb of Dublin – the pest control company was, in fact, just around the corner from Finn's house, a thing he had never known before, and which he did not find reassuring, even if it was convenient. He could shift everything down south, though, for the purposes of the story. The rat man put plastic bags of poison down various holes. The skirting boards were full of little holes, which Finn had never noticed before. The rat man promised to come back in a week and do another round of poison. We'll get them, my friend, he said. He was a small intelligent looking wiry man, with dark grey hair, and an ironic, cheerful manner. They're everywhere. You're never more than six yards from a rat.

'See you later, my friend,' said the man. Three hundred euro for the basic job. About an hour's work. But who'd want to do it? He was a hero, the rat man, all things considered. These people were the real heroes.

Finn could be a hero too. Especially since he wanted to escape from town and get back to the country and to his writing. He'd help the Pied Piper. He'd back up the bags of poison with traps.

Rat traps: big versions of mouse traps. Like the holes in the skirting, he'd never seen them before, but there they were, in Woodies. Down in the garden section, next to the weed-killer.

Before going to bed, he set two of them near the fridge, where the rat came out, he was pretty sure.

Ten minutes later Mattie came up.

'The mouse is in the trap,' he said, in a thick voice. His blue eyes had darkened since childhood. The colour had not changed, but the light had. They didn't sparkle any more. It was not a thing Finn had noticed before, but he saw it now, and wondered, as he went downstairs, when that had happened.

Death had been instantaneous, Finn guessed – though he didn't care one way or another. Broken neck. Long brown body. Surprised expression in the eyes. He picked up the rat, in its trap, with a plastic bag wrapped around his hand, and dumped the whole thing in the wheelie bin. To his surprise, he felt suddenly queasy, as if he might vomit. But he gritted his teeth and set another trap before going back to bed. He was going to get them.

Three rats in two days.

And he could hear them eating the rat man's poison.

By the third rat, he still felt sick after disposing of them. But by then he was feeling sorry for them too. Their little pointy faces looked so shocked, in the trap – a vicious machine. They just came up from their home under the floorboards for a bite to eat. And snap. Guillotined. He was beginning to know the rats now – their habits, their points of ingress. They'd been under his house for quite a while, was his guess, and they'd eaten lots of things. Mostly cat food, but other stuff too. They loved plastic. He cleaned out the cupboard under the sink, one of those cupboards that gets left, uncleaned, for years and years, and found heaps of shredded plastic bags in at the back behind the old tins of shoe polish and dried up window cleaner. They were also very fond of electric wires – that's what had happened to the fridge. The cable to the dish washer was well gnawed too but was holding out for the minute – apparently they preferred the cyanide to electric cables. Poor things. They'd probably watched their nearest relatives, their mother and dad, their brothers, getting electrocuted. Death Row in the O'Keefe kitchen.

Finn stayed in Dublin for a week. A whole week out of his precious month in the country, his writing summer. The rat man had made a return visit and pronounced himself well pleased. He'd come back in another fortnight. Finn arranged with Mattie, who was sickened at the thought of dead rats (Mattie was a vegetarian, and a sort of Zen Buddhist, some such thing, Finn wasn't sure exactly), to let the rat man in, and only to call him, Finn, back to town if it were absolutely essential. He'd tried to start a conversation with Mattie a few times in the course of the week; he'd seldom been alone in the house with him before. But nothing doing. Mattie got that stony look in his eye and left the room whenever his father tried to talk to him.

Six hours later and he's back in the cottage.

Grainne is sitting in front of the fire in one chair, Pangur in the other.

Pangur miaows when Finn comes in, which is more than Grainne does. She doesn't even turn in her chair.

Finn sighs.

Pangur looks thin. Now that he's been away for a week he sees her with clear eyes. He sees that she's not really getting that much better, even here, in the country. He's been deluding himself.

Also he sees that there's no dinner on the table. He'd been imagining. A nice bit of marinated lamb. Mint sauce. A bottle of Chianti. Candles. Grainne had had no car of course. She could have got the bus, though – there's one on Fridays, bringing the old folk into town to collect their pensions. Anyone can use it if they pay the fare.

'You look tired,' is what she says, in an accusing voice, when she finally looks at him.

That means, you don't look attractive. You look old.

Of course I'm bloody tired, he thinks. I've spent a week catching rats instead of writing my story. I've driven two hundred and forty miles across Ireland in the rain.

He says nothing.

'Rats,' she says, with a sigh.

And then it blows up.

A full scale row.

His selfishness. The rats. The way he never cooks or cleans anything. His fathering. he is bad at it, that's why Mattie is the way he is, which is too closed in, too involved with his own hobbies, just like his father. His stupid writing. His selfishness (this is a refrain, evoked when invention fails). His diary. She'd snooped, she'd read it when he was away. Fantasies about Frances in Tuscany. When he never had sex with her. (not that she wanted it, but of course she conveniently left out bits of the story in this version, the quarrelling version).

It's over.

She wants out.

And on and on.

The rows.

They have them periodically – every few weeks, over a stretch of time. Then months might go by. Half a year, more. They had a spot of rowing, it finished, they struggled on. He believes marriage is like that for a lot of people. But of course how would he know? And does that make it right?

Frances and her second husband in *Bella Tuscany* never seem to have a row. They have candlelit dinners, long walks, holidays. Outings with friends. He wonders what it was like with her first husband? How could a marriage to someone as lovely and charming and pleasant as Frances come to an end?

I want some peace and happiness while there is still time.

That's Grainne.

He's heard the words a hundred times before. He's even said them himself, once or twice, and thought them much more often. Some peace and happiness. How wonderful it would be, how wonderful. But would there be peace and happiness if they split up? He can't imagine life without Grainne. He could hardly say he loves her, not in the old sense, the erotic sense. Eros and Agape. Maybe a bit agape, hardly any eros – infatuation, being in love, lasts for eighteen months, he's read somewhere. It's over before you even marry, apparently. Still, he missed Gráinne when he was in Dublin, catching the rats. Trying to talk to his silent son. *Is fearr an troid ná an t-uaigneas,* he heard on the radio, another day. The fighting is better than the loneliness. They'd a proverb for every situation, the old folks. Finn wonders who made them up, in the first place, and if anyone does that, any more. If he was making one it would be this: Life is a matter of balance. But they have one for that too. You've to take the good with the bad. Only the very young, like Mattie, believe it should be all good and that if not, it's not worth living. But that's wrong. A balance is as good as it gets.

He thinks he should kiss Grainne, now, here in the dark kitchen. That would, he is ninety five percent sure, calm her down, put a stop to the row. But he's afraid to. She's still really angry. So instead he says, I am very tired, which is perfectly true. I'm going to get some sleep. And off he trundles, to bed.

His laptop is on the table in the window, its blue light still on. On standby, which is what he hoped Mattie is on – someday in a year or two he'll switch on and talk again, stop being a Buddhist and climb off the sofa and back into ordinary life. He looks at the laptop, and out the window at the dark blue black sky, milky with stars. He considers writing a few lines, but he's too tired. Tomorrow he'll sit down. He'll stare out the window at the green island and the green ocean and start telling his story.

He gets into bed. The sheets are cool, the room fresh and uncluttered. It's a nice bungalow, this place they've rented for their month in the country. But when he closes his eyes he's back in the messy Dublin kitchen. And the rat is there, in the big trap beside the fridge. Its eyes surprised. Its long rat body, long tail, sticking out behind. Mattie is standing silently by the kitchen door, looking at the rat, his eyes as sad as sad can be.

Nausea grips Finn. His stomach heaves with that queasiness he got when the tossed the dead rats into the dustbin. Even as he lies flat on his back between the fresh cool sheets in the room that looks out on the dark beauty of sea and sky and stars, he is filled with terror.

He makes a supreme effort. He pushes the rat out of his mind. Because dreaming of rats is the worst thing there is.

Near Exit Thirteen, which is where the Dundrum shopping centre is, on one side, and the Dublin Mountains, on the other, he saw from the corner of his eye this thing: a bank of wildflowers. Long golden grass. Buttercups splattered through them, brilliant yellow. And a profusion of poppies. So scarlet, so scarlet. At that very moment the sun broke through the massed grey clouds and drenched the wild flowers of July in its warm summer light. The rock of the mountains appeared on his left then – the very heart of the mountain, which they must have blasted away to make the road. He passed the bank of flowers – you weren't allowed to stop – but tucked the picture away, stored it safely, to take out when he wanted to. Next up was the sign that appeared like magic at odd intervals along the motorway and that always lifted his spirits: In Case of Breakdown, Await Rescue. The only road sign that does not try to frighten you, or nag you and make you feel guilty. The road sign that made him remember his mother, who died two years ago, whom he still missed, especially when he was leaving home to go on a journey.

And then – because the motorway was still slicing through the mountain – came the yellow sign with a picture of a deer on it. A black deer, springing carelessly into the bright air. A deer rampant. Young and lovely. Full of energy and full of joy.

(Thanks to Séamas Ó Catháin, 'An Fear Nach Raibh Sceal Ar Bith Aige', *Bealoideas* XXXV, 51–64).

The Sugar Loaf

ÉILÍS NÍ DHUIBHNE

The woman on the weather forecast says: 'Try to get out and enjoy the good weather tomorrow.' She gives a big motherly smile and points at the little suns which are dotted all over the map. Tonight she is wearing a velvet jacket: a deep mellow plum colour. And earrings. She must be going on to something after the weather forecast – Audrey imagines her at a party, holding a crystal glass of champagne, chatting to elegant people near a roaring log fire. Or maybe eating dinner in some cosy restaurant, the candlelight flickering, the forgiving light making everyone look beautiful.

This woman has been doing the weather for ages. She has always smiled brightly, even when telling the nation to expect more unsettled weather, issuing gale and flood warnings. But she has never before said 'Get out and enjoy it'. Not that Audrey, who has hardly ever in her life missed the nine o'clock news followed by the weather, can recall.

It seems right to take her advice.

It is October. The summer was dreadful. In two weeks the clocks will go back, at the same time the leaves fall thick and heavy from the trees which are now in their autumn beauty.

Sunday morning. Honey coloured sunlight pours into the front room. Get out and enjoy it, the advice rings in her ears like a command from a kindly tyrant. But Audrey can't, not yet.

There is far too much to do. She has to prepare her classes for tomorrow. Audrey has been teaching English in Mulberry Manor for thirty three years, but she still always has to prepare every day. She can never find her notes. Her mother used to raise her eyebrows at her.

'If you spent a few days tidying up you'd save yourself a lot of time in the long run,' she'd say.

"Ah, will you stop annoying me!' Audrey would respond. 'If I had time to tidy up I'd tidy up, but when would I get the time?'

Her mother had no answer to that. But she set her mouth in a straight line like a one inch zip. That was how she expressed disapproval, or dismay, or despair.

The truth was, Audrey really was very very busy. Preparing, correcting copy books. Exams. And she had her busy social life. She did salsa dancing. Drama. Belonged to a choir although she wasn't much of a singer. She had her piano lessons, too, at least until the teacher said she was moving to another country and could no longer take private pupils. Audrey had asked if she could recommend another teacher, but no, she could not.

She drinks her coffee – she can't face the day without a few strong mugs, although the doctor has told her she'd be less anxious if she cut it out altogether, but that's easy for him to say, and she's sceptical about that coffee taboo. Fashions change so often, in health as in everything else. It's not so long ago that doctors were sticking disgusting insects to sick people and bleeding them to death. Doctors differ and patients die, she says to herself, as she drinks her third mug. She is sitting on the only chair in the kitchen which is not piled with newspapers, letters, schoolbooks, essays or exams by pupils, some still in Mulberry Manor and some long gone. Long graduated from university. Two are dead, but their compositions still survive, in the archive of Audrey's kitchen. Audrey never likes to throw anything out. When her mother was alive, she occasionally insisted on doing a blitz, clearing at least one room in the house so they'd have somewhere to sit in comfort, or to place a guest. Not that they often had a guest, apart from Ben, Audrey's brother, who lives in England and used to visit about once a year. (You'd think England was the far side of the moon). As Audrey's mother got older, she wasn't able to do much herself, and no amount of her sulks could get Audrey to tidy up. She just never had the time. That was the long and short of it.

She goes to her desk still wearing her dressing gown. It's fluffy turquoise with a big brown stain on the side. It doesn't look very attractive, but nobody sees her, so what matter? She knows the brown stain is just hair dye. Iced Chocolate. It's a good dye, her hair is always shiny and natural looking – if young shiny hair is the definition of natural – for at least a week. After that it turns the dead black of ink. Or black clay. Her hair was always her crowning glory, the one beautiful thing she had, so she doesn't want to let it go grey before she has to. Iced Chocolate is the answer. It's close to her real colour, that is, the colour she had until she was about forty two or three, which is when it started to fade. (She doesn't know what its real colour is now, because it is always covered with Iced Chocolate). The hairdresser might give a more lasting shine, but it would cost ten times as much as the home stuff. A hundred euros for highlights and blow dry. You can buy six fluffy dressing gowns for a hundred euros. In Penney's. Which begs the question, how much do the women who make the dressing gowns get? Audrey asks this question sometimes, usually of some class in school. But it doesn't stop her buying all her dressing gowns, and most of her other clothes too, in Penney's. She can't really be expected to solve all the problems of the world on her own. She's busy enough solving all the problems of Mulberry Manor.

Tomorrow they'll be doing John McGahern, *Amongst Women*. It's a hard enough novel even for Sixth Years, but they'll have to make the most of it. She'll ask them which characters they find most interesting. And they'll say Rose, or Sheila, or Maggie, or Mark or Michael. They'll all pick a different one. That's what she likes about the novel, that everyone has their own favourite character. Hers is Luke, the son who runs away and stays away. He's intriguing because he is never in the book. And she admires his guts. Anyone can run away, but it takes real courage to stay there.

The sun is around at the back of the house by the time she's even got herself dressed. Hot enough to sit out. The garden looks great in this forgiving light. Nasturtiums climb over everything – the fence, the hedge, the trees, the lawn. They're even creeping over the yard and into the drain, they're incorrigible, they'd grow anywhere, even in a sewer! The yellow dahlias, too, are exuberant. They are a special tough kind of dahlia, those, they'd survive anywhere. Some of them are pushing up the slabs on the patio, so strong are they, and growing through them – the nasturtiums are doing their best to strangle them, but good for the yellow dahlias, they're holding out. So are the nerines, which her mother planted the spring before she died. Their bubble gum pink is a pleasant shock in the autumn palate of dark reds and yellows. Bulbs, they are, which are great in a garden, they just look after themselves. Like weeds, which is what most of the garden is covered with – but weeds is just another name for wild flowers. Audrey's garden, once her mother's pride and joy, has been transformed to a nature reserve. Not appreciated by the neighbours, but beloved of hedgehogs, urban foxes, insects of all kinds. And mice and rats (they have a nice nest in the old compost heap, lovely and warm).

She could easily spend the day here. Enjoying the weather and maybe going so far as to do a bit of gardening. Even for a nature reserve it's getting overgrown. The nettles at the back of the garden make it difficult to get to the big bin tucked away behind the shed where she throws the empty bottles. Her mother had plenty of time to look after the garden and she went on doing that till she had her heart attack. Audrey could get someone in, but why would she? They rip you off and what do you get for it?

The Sugar Loaf she can see from the front garden. It rises from a nest of green hills, the Dublin mountains and the Wicklow mountains, a dramatic peak that looks like a volcano, although it has never been a volcano, she knows, from listening to 'Mooney Goes Wild on One' on the radio. (She used to listen a lot to the radio, before she mislaid it. It must have got thrown out by mistake. Or else it is buried under papers somewhere in the kitchen). Audrey has seen the mountain almost every day for fifty years, ever since they came from a house in the inner city to live in this suburb, when she was four and Ben was two. They moved out of town because their father had got a promotion – that is what people who were doing well did in those days. They said goodbye to the old Victorian terraces, and colonized the new white estates built on the fields and farms all around the edge of the city. Audrey can remember the excitement of all that, how pleased she and Ben and her mother were with the big windows, the bright rooms filled with light. The enormous bare garden.

During that fifty years – her life – she has driven close to the Sugar Loaf dozens of times and seen people walking up the road that winds to its summit. But she has never climbed it. Not even when she was a child. When she and Ben were kids their parents brought them out on a drive almost every Sunday. They would drive to some field or beach. Then they'd eat tomato sandwiches and sweet biscuits, drink sugary orange juice in the back of the car or sitting on a rug spread on the ground at the side of it. There was a flask of hot tea for Mammy and Daddy. They called that a picnic. When it was over they'd turn around and drive back home. They never climbed a mountain or went for a hike or anything like that. They never even went for a swim in the summer because Daddy had a thing about water. (His grandfather, a policeman in the country, had drowned – he had been pushed into the sea by a smuggler he was apprehending. This happened when Daddy was four years old, in 1918. Daddy's earliest memory was of seeing somebody empty the water out of his grandfather's rubber boots. He had never forgotten it).

Audrey had revived the Sunday drives when Daddy died ten years ago. She did it to give her mother a change of scene at the weekends, and to ease the tension that could arise when they were both cooped up together in the house for too long. Of course they never climbed the Sugar Loaf. Her mother couldn't have, at that stage. She was old, she had a weak heart, and arthritis, and various other complaints (as she called them, although she never actually complained but bore her pains in silence).

It is almost three o'clock by the time Audrey gets away. She does not know where the day has gone to. She has managed to get dressed, but she had not managed to finish her preparations for tomorrow's classes. She's slower than usual today. When she opened the McGahern novel her heart sank and her head swam. She couldn't engage with Maggie and Moran and Rose and all of them. All she could see was 6C sitting in their desks, like flowers in a bed of weeds, eager to get space and light, eager to escape from school and get started on life. Their big kohled eyes full of contempt for people like Audrey, locked in the school forever.

She drives out to the main road. As soon as she gets away from her own suburb, the Sugar Loaf disappears from view. After about ten minutes driving it occurs to her that she doesn't actually know where it is. Not in the way you need to know where a mountain is in order to climb it. Audrey often does this – sets off in her car, sure she knows the way to someplace, only to realise en route that she has no more than a general clue as to its whereabouts.

Of course, she knows the mountain can't be far away; otherwise she wouldn't see it from her front garden. She drives along, glancing to the right all the time, to see if she can spot it over the cars and trucks that roar along the motorway. Eyes off the road, she swerves out of her lane twice. A driver honks at her, and another gives her that sign with his fingers that means 'Fuck Off!'. Obviously someone with Road Rage Syndrome. The Sugar Loaf remains elusive.

At Kilmacanogue, on a hunch, she turns right towards Glendalough. Then she does a sensible thing, the sensible thing she should have done at home before she set out. She decides to consult a map.

Parking outside a bungalow, in a little lay-by, she searches for the map of Ireland. There are ten of them at least in the car, on the front seat and in the glove compartment and on the back seat, mixed up with some other things made of paper, and some not (there's an apple butt on the seat, and a packet of liver pate she bought two years ago). She picks up the cleanest one and looks at it. Yes, she seems to be headed in the right direction. In fact, if she is reading the map correctly (she's not all that good at reading maps) she could be half way up the Sugar Loaf already. According to the map this road she is on is on the side of the mountain. She looks out. The bungalow is an ordinary one, with a tiled roof and a little tarred patch of yard in front, two green wheelie bins and an old fridge at the side. Behind it is a slope covered with heather and furze. That could be a mountain side all right.

There is a tiny little thin blue line off this road, and the spot called Sugar Loaf on the map seems to be somewhere between this road that she is actually on, and that little one. The L1031.

To her surprise she finds the L1031 without difficulty.

It's nearly as narrow as the line on the map. Just a track really. There is nothing to indicate that the Sugar Loaf is on it. You'd think there would be a sign at least, but no. They expect you to be divinely inspired as usual. Sugar Loaf. She goes along anyway. She has no choice once she starts – turning back would not be easy on this narrow track. It runs through between flat fields, with sheep in some of them and cows in others, and a bog. That must be Callary Bog. She always liked that name. She doesn't know why.

She has not gone far along the narrow track when she sees cars. Something is happening – some country event. There are lots of cars, parked along the side of the road, which is wide enough for two only. Families stand around their boots, eating sandwiches and drinking tea. It must be a point to point,

Audrey thinks. She's not quite sure what a point to point is. But all these people look as if they are waiting to see horses, or dogs, hunting some animal across the bog. They don't look as if they came to the side of this narrow road just to eat their sandwiches and then go home. To Audrey, other families have always seem purposeful, in control of their lives, on their Sunday afternoons.

She drives carefully along the free side of the road. After half a mile or so there is gap in the line of cars. And suddenly out of the blue the mountain appears. That familiar sandy peak. The Sugar Loaf – unless there is some other mountain around here. The Little Sugar Loaf? Or that one with the name that sounds like Juice? Funny name for a mountain. Though it sort of goes with Sugar Loaf.

Whatever it is, the peak is close to the road, and not high. I'll be up that and down again in less than half an hour, Audrey thinks, as she starts to plod across the springy turf. The sun shines in a clear sky, but she's wrapped up in her warm green cardigan, and she put on her green parka too. Just in case the temperature is lower at the top. (On Mount Etna, where she was in the summer, there was snow). The landscape is exhilarating – the hill, fields with cattle and sheep spread behind. Hundreds of people are walking up and down the hill. Half of Dublin is here. On its crest there is a line of things that look like burned spruce trees. Or crucifixes.

She overtakes a family: a mother and father, with two small children in tow. 'Are we there yet?' the little boy says, whining. They have hardly left the carpark. He looks to be about three, so he may not know it's a cliche. Though children are so precocious now, it's possible that he does and is being ironic. 'Not yet,' his mother says, patiently. His father looks at the boy in exasperation. 'We're going up there,' he points to the peak. 'See where those people are? Up there.' He points at the crucifixes and utters the words with slow, exaggerated patience.

'All the way up there?' the boys whines. 'Will you give me a carry?'

'That'll be fun for you!' says Audrey, smiling at the father. 'He's no light bundle!'

The father nods, but doesn't say anything. The little boy looks alarmed. He runs back to his mother and takes her hand. The mother gives Audrey a sharp, questioning glance.

She hurries on.

A big group of girls, long haired, mostly blond, clad in light summery clothes blocks the path. They stand right across it so Audrey can't pass. One of them, dressed all in white, comes tentatively towards her, holding out a camera.

'Yes, yes, of course!' says Audrey, without waiting to be asked. Relieved, although she knew nobody could attack her, here, with half of Dublin to witness it.

The white girl goes back and stands with her crowd.

'Smelly Sausages!' says Audrey, and the girls smile, but they don't laugh. So she says it again and takes another one. They don't laugh this time either.

"I should take one more,' Audrey says to the white girl. 'I didn't hear a click.'

'I did,'says the girl.

'Sure I'm half deaf,' says Audrey, and waits for them to laugh. But they don't. They give a little smile and look away.

It takes her an hour to reach the foot of the final peak. It's farther away than it looks. She's sweating by the time she gets there – it's much too hot for the cardigan and the parka. The parka she takes off – she doesn't feel like removing the cardigan; then she'd just have to carry it. Most people are in their t-shirts. She looks up at the peak – a mound of rocks. Scree. Grey stones tumbling down the slope – that's what the sugar is. The peak, which looks like the point of a needle from her village, is about twenty square metres in circumference, at least. It's a little platform at the top of the stony scree.

Audrey feels just a tiny bit light headed, and also a bit queasy. Altitude sickness? The mountain is 500 metres high –

she noticed this when she was looking at the map – but maybe some people can get altitude sickness at that height? She wonders if the Twin Towers were five hundred metres high. Probably about that. You wouldn't get altitude sickness at the top of a building that you worked in every day, even one that a plane could crash into and destroy. It must be her heart.

She sits down to takes a rest.

Maybe she should not go up any farther.

The view from here is good anyway. The cars are a necklace of black diamonds strung gently around the foot of the mountain. There is Powerscourt, nestling in its dark woods. The big hotel at Kilternan in a patchwork of fields. Her landscape – where she has always lived. It's lovely, she thinks, gratefully. Of course she's always known that.

Someone sits beside her. An older woman – older than Audrey.

'Stay here and we'll be down soon,' says someone. She is a comfortable looking person, in a tracksuit. She settles the woman, who is clearly her mother, into a fold up chair.

'I'll be grand,' says the older woman. 'It's lovely here. Take your time, enjoy the view from the top.'

The younger woman kisses the older woman and starts to climb the mountain. She has two children, a boy and a girl, who also kiss the older woman and shout: bye bye granny, bye bye, see you in a while!

Last year, Audrey and her mother had been down there at Powerscourt one Sunday afternoon. An overcast day, it was not looking its best. But her mother had loved it. You go and walk for as long as you like, she said to Audrey. I'll sit here and wait, I'm grand. She sat on an iron seat in the garden, looking down at the steps, the statues, the fountain. The flowers. The Sugar Loaf, soaring over the garden, as if built for it, as a suitable backdrop.

Audrey had walked dutifully through the gardens, looked at a few unusual trees with labels on them, tripped across the tiny bridge in the Japanese gardens. The things everyone does at Powerscourt. But the grey day depressed her. In the pets' graveyard she was overwhelmed with loneliness. A sense of being totally lost, abandoned, although there were people all around. Within ten minutes she was back with her mother. 'I'd love a cup of coffee,' her mother had said. She seldom asked Audrey for anything. She loved having cups of coffee in cafes, but knew Audrey didn't share her taste for this form of amusement and usually refrained from asking. This day was different, for some reason. She hadn't been out of the house for weeks, and she was overjoyed to see something different from the four walls of the messy sitting room. She was overjoyed to see the gardens and the fountain and the great house. To see the Sugar Loaf soaring over all that.

'OK,' said Audrey, gruffly.

They went into the cafe. Of course it was packed, as she knew it would be. Everyone stuffing themselves, escaping from the nasty weather. She put her mother at a table in the corner – lucky to find one – and queued for coffee and cakes.

For about twenty minutes. That's how long it took to get two coffees and one slice of chocolate meringue gateau and cream.

By the time she got back to her mother she was as cross as a bear. She snapped and snapped. But her mother didn't mind. She was used to Audrey's snapping. She no longer heard it – like someone who lives beside a railway track and doesn't hear the trains roaring by every five minutes. She sipped her coffee and ate her chocolate meringue gateau slowly, with great enjoyment. She was happy. Anyone could see it. She glowed. In love with the fields and the flowers and sky. In love, yes, with the chocolate cake.

Audrey didn't hear her own snapping either. While she was doing it, snapping away and drinking her coffee, she was thinking, it's great to see her having such a good time. I must bring her on a holiday somewhere before the end of the summer. Wales say. Somewhere that would be easy to get to, but a different country. They could go over on the ferry, bring the car. Go up to the top of Mount Snowdon on the Mountain

Railway and drink coffee up there, look down over Wales. And Ireland. They say you can see Ireland on a clear day from the top of Snowdon.

Her mother had been finding the summer long and gloomy. The garden was out of bounds most of the time, because of the rain. She had to sit in the house, listening to Audrey snapping at her, eating sandwiches for dinner more often than not – Audrey didn't bother cooking much since Daddy died. The sandwiches were not bad. Ham and cheese, smoked salmon. Crisps on the side and often a bit of salad from a bag. Audrey had her wine to wash it all down, which seemed to make a difference. But her mother didn't like wine. So she had nothing but tea to flavour the sandwiches. It got monotonous.

Audrey did not bring her on a holiday. Because a very strange thing happened last summer. A man in the choir, Brendan, asked Audrey out, and then he asked her to go on a holiday with him, to Sicily. Brendan was fat and had big sticking out ears. Still, he was nice enough. Audrey didn't want to go – she could not leave her mother for so long. But it was her mother who insisted. She phoned Ben and persuaded him to come over to stay for the week Audrey would be away. Audrey was sure everything would go pear-shaped in Ben's incompetent hands. But when she came home the two of them, Ben and Mammy, were sitting in front of a blazing log fire in the front room, which he had cleaned up, listening to nice music, and looking as happy as larks.

The hotel in Sicily was great. Five Star, with a lovely pool surrounded by mature palms, and a view of Mount Etna, conveniently erupting. The food was good, although the wine was a bit expensive, and of course they drank a lot of it. On the second day, after settling in, they went up to the volcano, in a bus. Audrey loved that, even though Brendan shivered when he got out of the bus, and instead of climbing upwards with the other tourists they had to head for the cafe to have a cappuccino, then get the bus back down again. But it was great even half-way up – you could see for miles around, the gorgeous coastline, the deep green interior.

After that day things started to go downhill. Brendan became far too fond of getting massages from the Chinese girls who worked the beaches. They were pests, you couldn't get a minute's peace from them. As soon as you settled into your lounger one of them was over, with her straw hat and little simpering smile, whispering , 'Massage, massage?'

'Go away, go away!' Audrey had said to them, swatting at them with her towel, as if they were flies.

Brendan had laughed at her. At first. Then Audrey started refusing to go to the beach, saying she preferred the pool anyway. She told him the story about her grandfather and the boots. So he had to put up with it – he couldn't force her and he wouldn't go to the beach alone. But it annoyed him. When they came home he never contacted her. He stopped attending choir practice.

That was at the end of August. Her mother had a heart attack on the first of September, the first day of school, and a month later, she died. The Sunday in Powerscourt, it turned out, was her last day out. Ever.

She used to come here as a girl. Audrey's mother. She had often talked about it. With her best friend, Myrtle, who worked with her in a grocer's shop, she would cycle out to Enniskerry on Sundays. They would go to the Powerscourt Waterfall, and stand under it, getting splashed all over with the water that cascaded down the side of the cliff. Then they'd have tea in a cafe in the village, if they had a shilling to spare. Myrtle and Audrey's mother, in their gabardine coats and headscarves, laughed a great deal. There was a black and white snapshot of them on the mantelpiece, them and their bicycles with the Waterfall behind, laughing their heads off. This was in the 1940s, because by 1950 they were both married and no longer worked in the shop or cycled out to the country on their bikes. This place had been on her mother's map, all her life. Just as it is on Audrey's. The place you could go to on a Sunday for a drive or a walk or a climb or a cycle.

Audrey looks up at the top of the mountain. The things that looked like trees or crosses from below are just people, standing on the crest. Happy to have got up there. Now she knows that there is where she has to go.

She says goodbye to the granny, who doesn't answer because she has fallen asleep.

You have to clamber up the rocky slope. It's steep. But Audrey finds this bit easy. She used to love climbing frames when she was small. There was a good one in the park in their suburb, beside the graveyard. You're my little monkey, you're my little monkey, daddy used to say. He used to bring her there to get her out of her mother's hair sometimes. Ben would be playing football. My monkey, he would say, catching her from the top of the frame and swinging her, swinging her, in the crisp bright air so her skirt flew out in the wind and she screamed with delight.

There is a constant stream of people going up and coming down the rockface. They all use the same track. You have to move out of the way all the time, to let someone coming down pass.

She is about a third of the way up, her eyes fixed on the rock face in front of her, when someone bumps into her and nearly knocks her down.

A man.

He apologizes, then stares at her. He is long legged, dressed all in black, like a spider. Dark grey hair. The kind of face that is called distinguished in a man. There is something familiar about him. He must be somebody's father, someone she has met at a Parent Teacher Meeting. They usually recognize her, although she can't possibly be expected to remember all their names and faces.

'It's you,' he says. This is not a thing the students' fathers say to her.

As soon as he speaks she recognizes the voice. She takes a good look at him, as he stands there on the uneven rocks, with the sky all blue behind him. His grey hair turns black before her eyes. His young face emerges from his old face, where it is buried, to be discovered by those who know how to find it.

Padraig. She loved him to distraction, between the ages of eighteen, when she met him at a dance in college, and twenty, when he went to America on a J1 visa for the summer. She was to go too, but at the last minute she got cold feet. Her mother was encouraging but her father had reservations. The US. Anything could happen there. What if Padraig abandoned her? What would she do then?

Ara, couldn't she just catch the plane and come home? said her mother. And he won't abandon her, what would he do that for?

The religion thing was never mentioned. But it was there, nevertheless, unvoiced, like a huge mountain hidden in fog. (They did not know – how would you? – that when the fog cleared the mountain would have disappeared, melted away like sugar in water).

In the end she did not go to America. She just couldn't face being away from home, from her mother and father and the house she had always lived in, for such a long time. She wasn't ready to leave.

During the first weeks Pádraig wrote letters and postcards. There was no question of telephone calls from America in those days. After a month the letters stopped coming. And she never heard from him again.

'Yes,' she says. So she is still recognizable. She wishes, how she wishes, that she looked smarter. She hasn't even bothered to comb her hair. The green cardigan is about twenty years old. The sleeves are black with coal dust, from emptying the ashes, something she noticed yesterday, but she wore it anyway. And the trousers are work trousers, not sporty looking, not feminine. (Padraig preferred skirts on girls). Her hair is a rat's nest. If she'd even stuck a scarf on to cover it up. But how could she have known that half of Dublin would have the same idea as herself? Would heed the weather woman's advice to get out and enjoy the good day? She hadn't thought she'd meet anyone at all on the mountain. Still less this man whom she hasn't bumped into since June 1975.

'How are you?' he asks, in a calmer, kinder tone.

Hs voice had always calmed her down, made her feel all right. He was the only person who could do that for her. Ever. She had loved him much more than her father or her mother or her brother or anyone she met in later life (two other men, including Brendan. You don't meet a lot of men in Mulberry Manor). The realization, which should have come to her that summer, June 1975, is like a light going on in her brain. A light that makes her feel very sick and very well at exactly the same time.

'I'm grand,' is what she says.

'We should meet sometime, in more comfortable circumstances,' he says, smiling. 'Can I give you a call?'

'That would be nice,' she says. 'I'm in the phone book.'

'Under your own name?'

She admits it.

'Yes, my own name. Thompson, Audrey.'

'I can remember that!' he says, grinning. He looks up at the top of the mountain. 'Well, don't let me keep you from your climb. This last bit is hard but it's worth it.'

'I'm sure it is,' she says.

After forty years he does not want to keep her from her climb.

She wants to scream, stay, stay. She wants to grab him by the black anorak and keep him here on the side of the scree.

Already he has started to go down the slope, facing away from her this time. Even though there are several people trying to get past her, she stands for a full minute watching at him retreat. The back of his head. His trim body in its black jeans and anorak. A woman is coming towards her now, down the sugary slope. Something tells her this is Padraig's wife. Younger than him. And good looking. Lots of women who are not good-looking have husbands. But not husbands like him, successful and presentable and talkative. They always get pretty wives and if you're not pretty you just won't do.

Audrey never said this to herself before. It's simple when you realize it.

Someone should tell the girls at school.

Or maybe they know that. They know so much. And so much has changed. Nobody cares whether you're Catholic or Protestant. Nobody cares whether you're married or single either. (Though the girls paint their eyes and diet and care dreadfully about clothes. So they do care about something, although it's not quite clear what, or why).

Audrey reaches the top. And there are the twelve German girls, in their light, white blouses, their long hair blowing in the wind. They are standing on the crest of the Sugar Loaf in a circle. They must have passed her by when she was taking her rest on the ridge beneath.

On Friday she had 4C for English, last class of the week. It's never easy. They get so giggly and so damned silly. But she knows how to deal with them. Mountains of work if they dare to step out of line, she threatens them with. Not that they bother doing it, that's the trouble. She has to send them to the Principal then. And the Principal is getting fed up of her, but what can she do, it's not her fault. She was late for class on Friday, she'd stayed too long with 1B. They've been in the school for less than two months so they haven't learnt to be brats. She was nearly ten minutes late. The door was closed and there was the usual cacophony of noise inside the room. Bracing herself, she opened it.

Jessica Black was sitting on the teacher's desk. She was draped in a big red coat, which looked just like Audrey's coat, however she'd managed to get her hands on it. Her hair was pulled back into a bun and she had painted a big black moustache on her face.

'Girls, girls, girls! Quiet please girls. You're so bold.'

'Please Miss Byrne where does your big black moustache come from?'

Emma Murphy said. 'Can we shave it off for you?'

'No,' said Jessica Black. 'If you did that I wouldn't be the ugliest woman in the school, would I? Now, open your novel, girls. I hope everyone has read Chapter Five?'

There are clouds in the distance, over Enniskerry and Powerscourt. A few swathes of rain like cobwebs hanging in the valley. But they won't make it here. The woman on the weather promised. All sun and no rain. Those veils of rain will evaporate before they reach this mountain.

She takes off her green cardigan.

The twelve German girls are dancing now on the crest of the mountain, in a ring, their white blouses fluttering, their hair floating on the wind. She knows she should go and offer to take a photo of them, now that they are at the top of the mountain. Before and after. If she were a different sort of person she would do that. It would be easy. It would be a kind and friendly act.

But she doesn't.

She sits down on the heather.

In the clean air the laughter of the German girls sounds like a nice etude by Chopin or John Field. It is the very sound of human delight. On her bare arms, on her bare face, the sun is warm and sweet, like the breath of someone you love dearly.

Below the cars glide noiselessly along the M11 like toys. Then the sea. Bobbing sailboats, and the big white ferry slowly making its way eastwards. Pale blue, dark blue, azure. On the horizon a bumpy grey line, and a triangular peak rising out of the bumps.

It could be some sort of cloud formation. But she knows it's not. It's Wales, and the triangle is Mount Snowdon. They say you can see it, on a really clear day, from the top of the Sugar Loaf. She had always heard that, but she had never really believed it. Who would believe that you can actually see another country from the island of Ireland, which always seems so far away from the rest of the world?

Luachra

ÉILÍS NÍ DHUIBHNE

Tá luachra á bhailiú againn sa pháirc laistiar den tigh tábhairne. Lá Coille. Solas an lae ag sleamhnú ón míntír isteach sa bhfarraige. Dath an amhiarainn ar an uisce. 'Tá mé *freezing*', a deir Fiach, mo mhac, agus pus air. 'Tá an féar seo cosúil le *sponge*'.

'Ní thógfaidh sé ró-fhada', a deirim go fealsúnta. 'Tá mo *trainers* ag *sink*áil'. Is fíor dhó. Tá an chuma ar an bpáirc go bhfuil sé tirim. Ach níl ann ach portach faoi cheilt. 'Cén fáth atá tú ag *gathering* na *rushes anyway?* Is féidir leat faigh iad sin gach áit'.

'*No*', táim cuíosach dearfach, mé ag gearradh dorn luachra go cúramach le siosúr ingne. 'Nuair a théim á lorg sa bhaile, ní aimsím iad'.

'Tá mé *bored*', a deir sé. 'Bhfuil cead agam faigh *coke?*' Tugann sé sracfhéachaint ar an tigh tábhairne.

Buailim cnag ar dhoras thigh Mhíchíl agus Phádraig, 'na *Christian Brothers*' mar a thugann siad orthu féin. Osclaím an laiste agus siúlaim isteach, ar nós Coitín Dearg. Fiach im dhiaidh, beart luachra faoina ascaill aige.

Laistigh: solas agus scáth. Tine mhóna. Mícheál agus Peig Sayers, an cat, ar thaobh amháin den tinteán, Pádraig agus Jim, mo fhear céile, ar an dtaobh eile. Lampa íle ar an mbord. Trí

319

aghaidh ag lonradh sa chlapsholas. Trí ghloine uisce beatha ag lonradh leis. Buí, donn, ór, dubh. Pictiúr deartha ag Rembrandt. Léimeann Pádraig agus tairgíonn deochanna dúinn. Níl fonn orm uisce beatha a ól. Is cuma. Tá Coke aige dos na mná agus dos na leanaí. Fágann Pádraig a chathaoir chompordach fúmsa agus suíonn ag bord na cistine. Suíonn Fiach os a chomhair amach. Ag caint faoin seanshaol ar an mBlascaod atá Mícheál agus Pádraig, mar a bhíonn i gcónaí nuair a thagann Jim ar cuairt orthu.

'Bhímist ag imirt cártaí. Fiche haon. Ceatharcha haon. Ceatharcha haon an cluiche is mó a bhídíst ag imirt. Ó sea! Bhídíst ana-thugtha ar fad dó san, bhídíst'.

Mícheál a dhéanann an chuid is mó den chaint. Fear mór láidir is ea é. Aghaidh chineálta, leathan, gan roc ar bith air. Súile gorma críonna, lán de heagna, ach tá díomá éigin le feiscint iontu. Toisc an t-eolas atá aige ar an tsaol, b'fhéidir? Tá sé os cionn an cheithre scór. Nó b'fhéidir an rud atá ina shúile ná gaois agus imní an té is sine sa chlann. Eisean an seanóir. Tá a dheartháir, atá ina theannta ó rugadh iad, cúpla bliain níos óige ná é. Níl sé ach sna seachtóidí. Agus tá pearsantacht aerach, mheidhreach an deartháir óig aige fós. É éadrom, galánta. Níl mórán cainte aige ach is minic é ag gáirí.

'An mbídíst ag imirt ar son airgid?'

'Ó gan amhras, ar son airgid a bhídís ag imirt. Ar son pinginí'.

'Agus go déanach istoíche?'

'Go dtí a dó nó a trí a chlog ar maidin! Ní bhíodh fonn ar bith orthu dul a chodladh, ní bhíodh!'

Labhrann se go tapaidh, gach abairt ag tosnú ós íseal, ag ardú i lár baill, agus ansin ag titim ar ais arís go ciúnas ionas go mbíonn sé deacair na habairtí a chlos uaireanta. Rithim na dtonn, d'fheadfá a rá. Nó an rithim a bhíonn ag an ngaoth.

Tógann sé tamaillín orm dul i dtaithí ar a chuid cainte, cé go bhfuil sé cloiste go minic cheana agam. Ní thuigeann Fiach focal, gan amhras. Tá an deoch á hól go mall aige, chomh mall agus is féidir. Tá sé ag útamáil leis na luachra atá caite ar an mbord aige.

'Cad a dhéanfaidh tú leis na luachra?' fiafraíonn Padraig dó.

'Cad?' Féachann Fiach ormsa.

Cuireann Pádraig an cheist arís, i nguth ard mall, an saghas a d'usdadfá agus tú ag caint le heachtranach nó duine lagintinneach.

'*St. Bridget's crosses*', a deir Fiach.

'Ó, go maith', cuireann Mícheál a ladhar isteach.

'An mbíodh siad á ndéanamh ar an Oileán?' fiafraíonn Jim.

'Bhíodh', arsa Micheál. 'Ó do bhí. Dheinidís iad agus chrochaidís iad os cionn an bhóithigh agus sa tigh cónaithe leis. Ó do dheinidís iad ceart go leor ar an Oileán'.

'Agus cad eile a dheinidís Lá le Bríde?'

Cuireann Jim a théipthaifeadán ar siúl.

Níl leictreachas sa tigh seo. Tá an chistin mar a bhí sí daichead bliain ó shin, nuair a tháinig na deartháireacha amach ón Oileán den chéad uair. Dath buí ar na fallaí, an dath sin a bhíonn ar thithe san Iodáil nó i ndeisceart na Fraince.

Is mó cistin álainn sa ghleann seo. Cuid acu nua-aimseartha, cuid acu sean. Pearsantacht na ndaoine le brath i ngach cistin acu. Ach tá níos mó ná áilleacht ag an gcistin seo, cistin Phádraig agus Mhíchíl. Tá uaisleacht ann, agus stíl ealaíonta, chlasaiceach na simplíochta. Feidhm ag gach rud atá sa tigh. Sciléad ar crochadh os cionn na tine nach bhfeicfeá de ghnáth ach in iarsmalann, ach bácálann Pádraig arán ann gach maidin, bulóga móra órga. Bhí turcaí a rostadh sa phota sin lá Nollag. Níl aon ornáidí sa tigh néata seo, ach tá gach rud ann thar a bheith ornáideach.

Caomhnóirí na deartháireacha. Níor dheineadar aon athrú ar an tigh, ach níor ligeadar d'aon ní titim as a chéile. Ionas gur féidir leat suí anois ann agus tuiscint conas a mhair daoine céad bliain ó shin. Céad bliain ó shin, cúig mhíle bliain ó shin.

Agus mé im shuí sa leathsholas, mo Coke á ól agam, téim ag taisteal. Siar siar i stair na gcistiní. Braithim ceangail leis na chéad intreabhaigh a tháinig i dtir anseo, leis na manaigh a chuir fúthu sna clocháin. Leis na daoine a chuir fúthu i bpluaiseanna, fiú. Sleamhnaím siar, agus glór Mhíchíl ag cur leis an aisling mar a dhéanadh dreas ceoil le Mozart.

Ach tá rud éigin ag tarlú ag an mbord.

Tá Pádraig ag ohair leis na luachra, á ngearradh agus á lúbadh agus Fiach ag breathnú go géar air.

Tá lámha fada tanaí ag Pádraig, lámha atá cliste chun arán a dhéanamh. Na lámha a bheadh ag fear a bheadh go maith chun pianó a sheinm, nó veidhlín. Oibríonn siad go mall, ionas go dtuigfidh Fiach cad tá ar siúl. Ach mar sin féin ní fada go dtí go mbíonn cros bheag déanta aige, cros Bhríde, cuma an mhuilinn ghaoithe uirthi. An chros nach cros in aon chor í, ach rúndiamhair phágánta an earraigh.

'D'ithimis na fuipíní', tá Mícheál ag rá leis an dtéip. 'Bhídís deas go leor, rostaithe, agus salann orthu, cé go raibh an iomarca íle iontu'.

Tugann Pádraig cúpla luachra d'Fhiach agus déanann comhartha dó triail a bhaint as cros a dhéanamh é féin. Tosnaíonn Fiach ag lúbadh na luachra ach bíonn sé i bponc sar i bhfad. Tógann Pádraig lámh Fhiaigh ina lámha féin, agus oibríonn na ceithre lámh i dteannta a chéile ar feadh tamaillín. Lámha fada tanaí Mhíchíl, agus lámha beaga bána Fhiaigh. Níl focal le clos ó cheachtar acu. Ní thuigeann siad teanga a chéile. Agus ar aon nós níl cead cainte nuair a bhíonn an téip ar siúl.

Nochtaim mo smaointe faoin dtigh do Jim agus muid ag siúl abhaile.

Cuireann sé i gcuimhne dom cad a tharla nuair a thángamar go dtí ár dtigh féin seachtain ó shin. Ní raibh an leictreachas ag obair. Ní raibh uisce sna buacairí. Bhí an teileafón as ord. Mar a bhíonn go minic nuair a thagaimid.

Shuigh mé síos i lár an urláir agus thosaigh mé ag gol. Dúirt mé go raghainn abhaile láithreach. Dúirt mé – scread mé – nach gcaithfinn lá amháin eile san áit dhamanta seo.

'Rachaidh mise le tú', a duirt Fiach. 'Ní féidir mé mo Sega Mega a imirt'.

'Ach mar sin féin', a deirim. Mar sin féin glacaim le seoid luachmhar nuair a chuirtear im lámh é. Tá a fhios agam nach féidir an rud atá cothaithe ag Pádraig agus Mícheál a athchruthú in áit ar bith, cé go dtugtar faoi sin a dhéanamh go minic. Tá an tigh atá acu cosúil le pictiúr le Rembrandt. Tá sé cosúil leis seo, tá sé cosúil leis siúd ach ní hionann é agus rud ar bith eile. Iontas is ea é. Iontas. Tá sé cosúil leis na pirimidí, tá sé cosúil Ie Brú na Bóinne, tá sé cosúil leis na sléibhte, té sé cosúil leis na réalta. Ba mhaith liom an áilleacht iontach sin a cheiliúradh ach conas is féidir é a dhéanamh?

Fillimid ar an mbaile an lá dár gcionn. Baile Átha Cliath. Aimsir fhliuch ainnis. Fliú ar gach éinne. Téimid go dtí an dochtúir, slogaimid *anti-biotics*. Filleann Fiach ar scoil, fillimse ar an oifig. Téann Jim thar leat go dtí leabharlann sa Ghearmáin chun doiciméidí a bhaineann leis an mBlascaod a léamh ann.

Tá na luachra caite ar urlár an gharáiste. Ó am go chéile téann Fiach isteach ann. Sciobann sé leis roinnt des na luachra agus tógann go dtína sheomra codlata iad. Suíonn sé ar a leaba ag breathnú ar *Simpsons* nó ar *Friends*. Bíonn a lámha gnóthach ag obair leis an luachra.

Go hobann tagann lá earraigh. Aimsir mheirbh. Go hobann tá na gairdíní ar fad breactha le spící lusanna na gcromcheann.

Tagann an glaoch gutháin oíche Dhomhnaigh, ag deireadh mhí Eanáir. Cara liom sa ghleann. Tá a fhios agam chomh luath agus a chloisim a guth go bhfuil duine éigin caillte.

Pádraig. Fuair sé slaghdán. Chuaigh sé go dtí an t-ospidéal. Fuair sé bás.

Ní théim go dtí an tsochraid. Táim ró-ghnóthach, níl laethanta saoire ar bith fágtha agam. Cuirim cárta aifrinn sa phost. Smaoiním ar Phádraig.

Lá geal is ea lá na socraide. Tá an ghrian ag taitneamh ar shráideanna na cathrach agus dóchas an earraigh san aer. Ar réamhaisnéis na haimsire ar an dteilifís feicim ar an léarscáil go bhfuil an ghrian ag taitneamh i ngach cuid den tír, fiú amháin i gCorca Dhuibhne. Tá sé ag taitneamh i reilig Dhún Chaoin agus ar an mBlascaod Mór. Tá sé ag doirteadh isteach trí fhuinneoga na gcistiní i nDún Chaoin mar a bheadh mil ag sileadh ó phróca.

Tugann Fiach leathdhosaen Cros Bhríde dom, mar bhronntanas, an lá sin.

'Dhein mé *pile* mór *of them* duit', a deir sé. 'Is féidir leat tabhair iad do do chairde Lá le Bríde'.

Tá siad beag, snasta, foirfe, gach aon chros acu. Cuireann siad mórtas orm, agus áthas. Beartaím cóisir bheag a bheith agam Lá le Bríde. Gloine fíona le roinnt cairde. Beidh *take home bags* acu, i bhfoirm Chros Bhríde, an chros nach cros cheart í ach muileann gaoithe.

Táim idir dhá chomhairle an ceart bás Phádraig a lua le Fiach. Ach insím, i ndeireadh na dála. I ndeireadh na dála, is beag nach n-insím dó.

Níl mórán le rá aige.

'Cé tugfaidh a *catfood* do Pheig Sayers?' a deir sé. Ansin tosnaíonn sé ag ohair leis an gcúpla brobh luachra atá fágtha ar an urlár, luachra nach bhfuil ar aon fhad nó aon dath, an dríodar. Sníonn sé na feaganna buí, donna agus uaine le chéile chun cros eile a dhéanamh. Cros bheag ghreannmhar, ilmhianaigh, ildaite a bheidh ann.

Sin an chros a choinneoimid dár dtigh féin.

BIBLIOGRAPHY

'Agallamh Beo.' *Beo!* Uimhir 58, Feabhra 2006.

Almqvist, Bo. 'Of Mermaids and Marriages. Seamus Heaney's "Maighdean Mara" and Nuala Ní Dhomhnaill's "An Mhaighdean Mhara" in the Light of Folk Tradition.' *Béaloideas: the Journal of the Folklore of Ireland Society* 58 (1990).

Almqvist, Bo. 'Irish Migratory Legends on the Supernatural: Sources, Studies and Problems.' *The Fairy Hill is on Fire!* Proceedings of the Symposium on the Supernatural in Irish and Scottish Migratory Legends. Dublin (7–8 Oct. 1988). *Béaloideas* 59 (1991).

Almqvist, Bo. 'Crossing the Border, A Sampler of Irish Migratory Legends about the Supernatural. *Ibid.*

Almqvist, Bo. *The Irish Folklore Commission: Achievement and Legacy.* Dublin: Folklore of Ireland Society, 1979.

Almqvist, Bo. *An Béaloideas agus an Litríocht.* Baile Átha Cliath: An Cumann le Béaloideas Éireann, 1977.

Almqvist, Bo and Patricia Lysaght. 'The Banshee Questionnaire.' *Béaloideas.* 42–44 (1974–1976).

Anderson, Benedict. 'Exodus'. *Critical Enquiry* 20. 2 (1994): 314–327.

Anzaldúa, Gloria. *Borderlands/La Frontera: The New Mestiza.* San Francisco: Aunt Lute Books, 1987.

Archetti, Eduardo P. 'Introduction.' *Exploring the Written: Anthropology and the Multiplicity of Writing.* Oslo: Scandinavian Uni Press, 1994.

Ardener, Shirley, ed. *Perceiving Women.* London: Malaby Press, 1975.

Arensberg, Conrad M. and Solon T. Kimball. 'Family Transition at Marriage.' *Family and Community in Ireland.* Ennis: Clasp, [1968] 2001.

Ashcroft, Bill *et al. The Empire Writes Back.* London: Routledge, 1998.

Atwood, Margaret. 'Death by Landscape.' *Contemporary Fiction: 50 Short Stories since 1970.* Williford, Lex & Martone, Michael, eds. NY: Simon and Schuster, 1999.

Bacchilega, Cristina. *Postmodern Fairy Tales: Gender and Narrative Strategies.* Philadelphia: University of Pennsylvania Press, 1997.

Bachelard, Gaston. *La Poétique de l'Espace*, 1957; *La Poetica dello Spazio*, Italian Trans. Ettore Catalano. Bari: Dedalo, [1975] 1999.

Banville, John. *Long Lankin.* London: Secker and Warburg, 1970.

Barnes, Trevor J. and James S. Duncan, *Writing Worlds: Discourse, Text and Metaphor in the Representation of Landscape*. London: Routledge, 1992.

Barreca, Regina, ed. *Last Laughs: Perspectives on Women and Comedy*. Studies in Gender and Culture, Vol. 2. NY: Gordon and Breach, 1988.

Beale, Jenny. *Women in Ireland: Voices of Change*. Bloomington, IN: Indiana University Press, 1987.

Ben-Amos, Dan, ed. *Folklore Genres*. Austin: University Texas Press, 1976.

Benjamin, Walter. 'The Storyteller: Observations on the Works of Nikolai Leskov' in *Walter Benjamin Selected Writings: Volume 3 1935–1938*, trans. Edmund Jephcott, Howard Eiland *et al*. Howard Eiland and Michael W. Jennings, eds. Cambridge, Mass.: The Belknap Press of Harvard University Press, 2002: 143–66.

Bhabha Homi. *The Location of Culture*. London: Routledge, 1994.

Bhabha, Homi K. 'DissemiNation: Time, Narrative, and the Margins of the Modern Nation.' *Narration and Nation*. Homi K. Bhabha, ed. London: Routledge, 1990: 291–322.

Boland, Eavan. 'Anna Liffey.' *A Time of Violence*. Manchester: Carcanet, 1994.

Bourke, Angela. General Introduction, 'Oral Traditions'. *Field Day Anthology of Irish Writing, Volume IV: Irish Women's Writing and Traditions*. Angela Bourke, *et al*. NY: New York University Press, 2002.

Bourke, Angela. *The Burning of Bridget Cleary*. NY: Penguin, 1999.

Bourke, Angela. 'The Burning of Bridget Cleary: Newspapers and Oral Tradition.' *Tipperary Historical Journal*. (1998).

Bourke, Angela. 'Language, Stories, Healing.' *Gender and Sexuality in Modern Ireland*. Anthony Bradley and Maryann Gialanella Valiulis, eds. University of Massachusetts Press/Amherst. Published in co-operation with the American Conference for Irish Studies, 1997.

Boyle, Elizabeth. *The Irish Flowerers*. Ulster Folk Museum, Queen's University Belfast. Institute of Irish Studies, 1971.

Boyle Haberstroh, Patricia and Christine St. Peter, eds. *Opening the Field: Irish Women, Texts and Contexts*. Cork: Cork University Press, 2007.

Bridges, Roy. 'Exploration and Travel outside Europe.' *The Cambridge Companion to Travel Writing*. Peter Hulme and Tim Youngs, eds. Cambridge: Cambridge University Press, 2002: 53–69.

Butler Cullingford, Elizabeth. 'Our Nuns Are Not A Nation: Politicizing the Convent in Irish Literature and Film.' *Eire-Ireland*. 41. 1 (2006): 9–39.

Butler, Judith. *Gender Trouble*. New York: Routledge, 1990.

Cairney, Christopher Thomas. 'Éilís Ní Dhuibhne.' *British and Irish Short-Fiction Writers 1945–2000*. Cheryl Malcolm and David Malcolm, eds. Farmington Hill, MI: Thompson Gale Publishers, 2006: 263–269.

Carlson, Julia. *Banned in Ireland: Censorship and the Irish Writer*. Athens, GA: University of Georgia Press, 1990.

Carr, Marina. *Woman and Scarecrow*. Loughcrew: The Gallery Press, 2006.

Christiansen, Reidar Th. *The Migratory Legends*. Folklore Fellows Communications, FFC Series No. 175. Helsinki: Suomalainen Tiedeakatemia, Academia Scientiarum Fennica, 1958.

Clarke, Kenneth and Mary. *A Concise Dictionary of Folklore*. Bowling Green, KY: Kentucky Folklore Series, No. 1, 1965.

Cleary, Joe. 'Toward a Materialist-Formalist History of Twentieth-Century Irish Literature.' *Boundary* 2. 31. 1 (2004), 207–241.

Clifford, James and George E. Marcus, eds. *Writing Culture: The Poetics and Politics of Ethnography*. Berkeley: University of California Press, 1986.

Conrad, Kathryn. *Locked in the Family Cell*. Madison, WI: University of Wisconsin Press, 2004.

Cronin, Michael. *Translating Ireland*. Cork: Cork University Press, 1996.

Dégh, L. and A. Vaszonyi. 'Legend and Belief.' *Genre* 4, (Sept.) 2, (1971): 281–403.

de Certau, Michel. *The Practice of Everyday Life*. [1974] Trans. Steven Randall. Berkeley: University of California Press, 1988.

de Paor, Louis. 'Ceist, cé léifeadh Máirtín Ó Cadhain.' *Comhar* (Samhain) [November] (2006: 7–9).

D'hoker, Elke. 'The Postmodern Folktales of Éilís Ní Dhuibhne.' *ABEI Journal (The Brazilian Journal of Irish Studies)* Iml. 6 (June 2004): 129–39.

Doyle, Roddy. *The Deportees' and Other Stories*. London: Cape, 2007.

Doyle, Rose, ed. *Letters from Irish College*. Dublin: Marion Books, 1996.

Duffy, Patrick J. 'Writing Ireland: Literature and Art in the Representation of Irish Place.' *In Search of Ireland*. Brian Graham, ed. London: Routledge, 1997.

Dunbar, Robert. 'My Top Fifty Irish Children's Novels.' *Inis* 10 (Winter 2004): 24–28.

Dundes, Alan. *Motherwit from the Laughing Barrel*. Jackson, Mississippi: University of Mississippi Press, 1990.

Dundes, Alan. *The Study of Folklore*. Englewood Cliffs, NJ: Prentice-Hall, 1965.

Dwyer, Davin. 'How's your fadá?' *Irish Times* (25 Lúnasa 2007).

Eagleton, Terry. 'Home and Away: Internal Émigrés in the Irish Novel.' *'Crazy John and the Bishop' and Other Essays on Irish Culture*. Notre Dame, IN: Notre Dame University Press, 1998: 212–247.

Ferriter, Diarmaid. *The Transformation of Ireland 1900–2000*. London: Profile, 2004.

Fink, Bruce. 'The Dialectic of Desire' in *A Clinical Introduction to Lacanian Psychoanalysis: Theory and Technique*. Cambridge, Mass.: Harvard University Press, 2000: 50–71.

Finnegan, Frances. *Do Penance or Perish: Magdalen Asylums in Ireland*. Oxford: Oxford University Press, 2001.

Flanagan, Maeve. *Dev, Lady Chatterley and Me: A 60s Suburban Childhood*. Dublin: Marino Books, 1998.

Fogarty, Ann. 'Preface' to Éilís Ní Dhuibhne, *Midwife to the Fairies*. Cork: Attic Press, 2003.

Foucault, Michel. 'Of Other Spaces.' *Diacritics*. 16 (Spring 1986): 22–7.

Friel, Brian. *Translations*. London: Faber and Faber, 1981.

Fulmer, Jacqueline. *Folk Women and Indirection in Morrison, Ní Dhuibhne, Hurston, and Lavin*. London: Ashgate, 2007.

Geertz, Clifford. *Works and Lives: The Anthropologist as Author*. Stanford: Stanford University Press, 1988.

Gibbons, Luke. 'Dialogue Without the Other? A Response to Francis Mulhern.' *Radical Philosophy* 67 (1994).

Gray, Breda. 'Unmasking Irishness: Irish Women, the Irish Nation and the Irish Diaspora.' *Location and Dislocation in Contemporary Irish Society: Emigration and Irish Identities* in Jim MacLaughlin, ed. Notre Dame, IN: Notre Dame University Press, 1997: 209–235.

Gray, Breda and Louise Ryan. 'Dislocating "Woman" and Women in Representations of Irish National Identity.' *Women and Irish Society: A Sociological Reader*. Anne Byrne and Madeleine Leonard, eds. Belfast: Beyond the Pale, 1997: 517–532.

Gregory, Augusta. 'Ireland Real and Ideal.' *Nineteenth Century* 44 (Nov. 1898).

Grosz, Elizabeth. *Volatile Bodies: Toward a Corporeal Feminism.* Bloomington: Indiana University Press, 1994.

Hale, Dorothy J. ed. *The Novel.* Oxford: Blackwell, 2006.

Hand, Derek. 'Being Ordinary. Ireland from Elsewhere: A Reading of Éilís Ní Dhuibhne's *The Bray House.*' *Irish University Review.* (Spring/Summer 2000): 103–16.

Handler, Richard and Daniel Segal, *Jane Austen and the Fiction of Culture: An Essay on the Narration of Social Realities.* Tucson: University of Arizona Press, 1990.

Hanson, Clare. *Short Stories and Short Fictions, 1880–1980.* London: Macmillan, 1985.

Harley, J.B. 'Deconstructing the Map.' *Writing Worlds: Discourse, Text and Metaphor in the Representation of Landscape.* Trevor L. Barns and James S. Duncan, eds. London: Routledge, 1992: 231–247.

Harte, Liam and Michael Parker, eds. *Contemporary Irish Fiction: Themes, Tropes, Theories.* Basingstoke: Macmillan, 2000.

Hirsch, Marianne. 'The Novel of Formation as Genre: Between *Great Expectations* and *Lost Illusions.*' *Genre XII,* 3 (1978): 293–311.

Holbek, Bengt. *Interpretation of Fairy Tales: Danish Folklore in a European Perspective.* Folklore Fellows Communications, FFC Series No. 239. Helsinki: Suomalainen Tiedeakatemia, Academia Scientiarum Fennica, 1987.

Holden, Louise. 'The Rise of the Gaelscoil.' *Irish Times.* (17 Apr. 2007): 15.

Hollingdale, Peter. 'Ideology and the Children's Book.' *Literature for Children: Contemporary Criticism.* Peter Hunt, ed. London: Routledge, 1992: 19–40.

Honko, Lauri. 'Memorates and the Study of Folk Belief.' *Journal of the Folklore Institute,* 1–2, (1964): 5–19.

Hooley, Ruth ed. *The Female Line: Northern Irish Women Writers.* Belfast: Northern Ireland Women's Rights Movement, 1985.

Horowitz, Sara R. *Voicing the Void: Muteness and Memory in Holocaust Fiction.* New York: State University Press of New York, 1997.

Hughes, Linda K. and Michael Lund. *The Victorian Serial.* Charlottesville: University Press of Virginia, 1991.

Hull, Eleanor Hull.'*The Tragical Death of the Sons of Usnach*'. *The Cuchullin Saga in Irish Literature: Being a Collection of Stories Relating to the Hero*

Cuchullin. Translated from the Irish by Various Scholars: Compiled and Edited with Introduction and Notes by Eleanor Hull. London: David Nutt in the Strand, 1898.

Hulme, Peter. 'Travelling to Write (1940–2000).' *The Cambridge Companion to Travel Writing.* Peter Hulme and Tim Youngs, eds. Cambridge: Cambridge University Press, 2002: 87–101.

Hunt Mahony, Christina. *Contemporary Irish Literature: Transforming Tradition.* London: Macmillan, 1998.

Hylland Eriksen, Thomas. *Small Places, Large Issues: An Introduction to Social and Cultural Anthropology.* London: Pluto Press, 1995.

Ingle, Róisín. 'That First Kiss.' *Pieces of Me: A Life-in-Progress.* Dublin: Hodder Headline, 2005.

Jackson, Rosemary. *Fantasy and the Literature of Subversion.* London: Methuen, 1981.

James, Henry. *The Portrait of a Lady.* Harmondsworth: Penguin, 1986.

Jameson, Frederic. *The Political Unconscious: Narrative as a Socially Symbolic Act.* London: Routledge, 1986.

Jeffers, Jennifer M. *The Irish Novel at the End of the Twentieth Century: Gender, Bodies, and Power.* New York: Palgrave, 2002.

Jenkins, Richard. 'Witches and Fairies: Supernatural Aggression and Deviance among the Irish Peasantry.' *Ulster Folklife.* 23 (1977): 50–51.

Joyce, James. *A Portrait of the Artist as a Young Man.* Chester G. Anderson, ed. Harmondsworth: Penguin, 1982.

Kaplan, Caren. *Questions of Travel, Postmodern Discourses of Displacement.* Durham and London: Duke University Press, 1996.

Kaveney, Roz. 'The Science Fictiveness of Women's Science Fiction.' *From my Guy to Sci-Fi. Genre and Women's Writing in the Postmodern World.* Helen Carr, ed. London: Pandora, 1989: 78–97.

Keenan, C. and Mary Shine Thompson, eds. *Studies in Children's Literature.* Dublin: Four Courts Press, 2004.

Keenan, Celia. 'Reflecting a New Confidence: Irish Historical Fiction for Children.' *The Lion and the Unicorn* 21.3 (1997): 369–378.

Keenan, Celia. 'Irish Historical Fiction' in *The Big Guide to Irish Children's Books.* Dublin: Irish Children's Book Trust, 1996.

Kelly, Shirley. 'Fiction is to Take You to Places You Didn't Know.' *Books Ireland.* No. 236 (Dec. 2000).

Kiberd, Declan. *The Irish Writer and the World*. Cambridge: Cambridge University Press, 2005.

Kiberd, Declan. 'Excavating the Present: Irish Writing Now.' Lecture Transcript. Dublin: Irish Writers' Centre and the James Joyce Centre, 2001: 1–23.

Kiberd, Declan. *Inventing Ireland: The Literature of the Modern Nation*. London: Vintage, 1996.

Kiberd, Declan. 'Childhood and Ireland.' *Inventing Ireland*. London: Vintage, 1995: 101–2.

Killfeather, Siobhan. 'Sex and Sensation in the Nineteenth-Century Novel.' *Theorizing Ireland*. Claire Connolly, ed. New York: Palgrave Macmillan, 2003: 105–113.

Kloos, Peter ed. *True Fiction: Artistic and Scientific Representations of Reality*. Amsterdam: Vrije Universiteit Press, 1990.

Kloos, Peter. 'Reality and Its Representations.' *True Fiction*. Peter Kloos, ed. Amsterdam: Vrije Universiteit Press, 1990.

Kreilkamp, Vera. 'Fiction and History.' *The Anglo-Irish Novel and the Big House*. New York: Syracuse University Press, 1998.

Lacan, Jacques. 'The Subversion of the Subject and the Dialectic of Desire in the Freudian Unconscious' in *Écrits: A Selection*, trans. Alan Sheridan. London: Tavistock Publications, 1977), 292–325.

Lawrence, D.H. 'The Fox.' *Four Short Novels of D.H. Lawrence*. New York: Viking Press, 1965.

Lloyd, David. *Anomalous States: Irish Writing and the Postcolonial Moment*. Durham: Duke University Press, 1993.

Lo, Jacqueline. 'Beyond Happy Hybridity: Performing Asian-Australian Identities' in *Alter/Asians*. Ien Ang, Sharon Chambers, Lisa Law and Mandy Thomas, eds. London: Pluto Press, 2000: 152–168.

Luckhurst, Roger. *Science Fiction*. Cambridge: Polity Press, 2005.

Luddy, Maria. 'Moral Rescue and Unmarried Mothers in Ireland in the 1920s.' *Women's Studies* 30. 6 (2001): 797–818.

Luddy, Maria. Rev. of *Do Penance or Perish* by Frances Finnegan. *American Historical Review*. (April 2005), 557.

Luddy, Maria. *Women and Philanthropy in Nineteenth-Century Ireland*. Cambridge: Cambridge University Press, 1995.

Luddy, Maria. 'Prostitution and Rescue Work in Nineteenth-Century Ireland.' *Women Surviving*. Maria Luddy and Cliona Murphy, eds. Dublin: Poolbeg, 1989: 51–84.

Lyotard, Jean-François. *The Postmodern Condition: A Report on Knowledge*. Minneapolis: University of Minnesota Press, [1984] 1997.

MacCárthaigh, Críostóir. 'Midwife to the Fairies.' *Béaloideas: The Journal of the Folklore of Ireland Society*. 59, No. 1991 (1991): 133, 142.

Mac Cumhaill, Fionn. *Na Rosa go Bráthach*. BÁC: Oifig an tSoláthair, 1939.

Mac Gabhann, Micí. [eag. Proinsias Ó Conluain] *Rotha Mór an tSaoil*. Indreabhán: Cló Iar-Chonnachta, 1959/1996.

MacGill, Patrick. *Children of the Dead End*. B. D. Osborne, ed. Edinburgh: Birlinn, 1999.

MacGill, Patrick. *The Rat-Pit*. London: Jenkins, 1915.

MacLaughlin, Jim. 'The New Vanishing Irish: Social Characteristics of "New Wave" Irish Emigration.' *Location and Dislocation in Contemporary Irish Society: Emigration and Irish Identities*. Jim MacLaughlin, ed. Notre Dame, IN: Notre Dame University Press, 1997: 133–155.

Mac Murchaidh, Ciarán. 'Raic agus Rírá.' *The Irish Book Review*. (Summer 2006): 11.

Mac Murchaidh, Ciarán. '*Hurlamaboc*'. *The Irish Book Review*. (Summer 2006).

Mac Murchaidh, Ciarán, ed. '*Who Needs Irish?*' *Reflections on the Importance of the Irish Language Today*. Dublin: Veritas Publications, 2004.

Madden-Simpson, Janet ed. *Woman's Part: An Anthology of Short Fiction By and About Irish Women 1890–1960*. Dublin: Arlen House, 1984.

Magri-Mourgues, Véronique. 'Écrire le Désert.' *Création de l'Espace et Narration Littéraire*. Gérard Laverge, ed. Colloque International Nice-Séville. (6–7–8–mars 1997). Cahier de Narratologie N. 8 (1997): 249–61.

Maguire, Moira J. 'Foreign Adoptions and the Evolution of Irish Adoption Policy, 1945–52.' *Journal of Social History*. 36. 2 (2002): 387–404.

Maguire, Moira J. 'The Changing Face of Catholic Ireland: Conservatism and Liberalism in the Ann Lovett and Kerry Babies Scandals.' *Feminist Studies* 27.2 (Summer 2001): 335–58.

Marquez, Gabriel Garcia. *One Hundred Years of Solitude*. London: Harper Collins, 1997.

Mathews, P.J. *Revival: The Abbey Theatre, Sinn Féin, The Gaelic League and the Co-operative Movement.* Cork: Cork University Press in assoc. with Field Day, 2003.

McCafferty, Nell. *Goodnight Sisters.* Dublin: Attic Press, 1987.

McCafferty, Nell. *A Woman To Blame: The Kerry Babies Case.* Dublin: Attic Press, 1985.

McClintock, Anne. *Imperial Leather.* London: Routledge, 1995.

McGahern, John. *Nightlines.* London: Faber and Faber, 1970.

McGahern, John. *Getting Through.* London: Faber and Faber, 1978.

McGarry, Patsy. 'Renogotiation of Deal with State "Not On" Says Nun.' *Irish Times.* 9 July 2004: 11.

McKillop, James, ed. *A Dictionary of Celtic Mythology.* Oxford University Press, 1998. Oxford Reference Online. Oxford University Press.

McWilliams, David. *The Pope's Children. Ireland's New Elite.* Dublin: Gill & Macmillan, 2006.

Meaney, Gerardine. 'Territories of the Voice: History, Nationality and Sexuality in Kate O'Brien's Fiction.' *Irish Journal of Feminist Studies* 2. 2 (Winter 1997), 100–118.

Midalia, Susan. 'The Contemporary Female *Bildungsroman*: Gender, Genre and the Politics of Optimism.' *Westerly.* 41.1 (Autumn 1996): 89–104.

Minsky, Rosalind, ed. *Psychoanalysis and Gender: An Introductory Reader.* London: Routledge, 1996: 164–76.

Moane, Geraldine. 'Legacies of Colonialism for Irish Women: Oppressive or Empowering?' *Irish Journal of Feminist Studies* 1. 1 (1996), 77–92.

Moloney, Caitriona and Helen Thompson, eds. *Irish Women Writers Speak Out: Voices from the Field.* NY: Syracuse University Press, 2003: 101–115.

Morris, Carol. 'The Bray House: An Irish Critical Utopia. Éilís Ní Dhuibhne.' *Études Irlandaises.* 21–1 (Printemps 1996): 127–140.

Murphy, Maureen. 'Siren or Victim: The Mermaid in Irish Legend and Poetry.' *More Than Reality: The Fantastic in Irish Literature and the Arts.* Donald E. Morse and Csilla Bertha, eds. NY: Greenwood Press, 1991.

Nash, Catherine. 'Remapping and Renaming: New Cartographies of Identity, Gender and Landscape in Ireland.' *Feminist Review.* 44 (Summer 1993): 39–57.

Narayan, Kirin. 'Ethnography and Fiction: Where Is the Border?' *Anthropology and Humanism*. 24(2): 134–147.

Narváez, Peter ed. *The Good People: New Fairylore Essays*. Lexington: University of Kentucky Press, 1991.

Nic Eoin, Máirín. 'Contemporary Prose and Drama in Irish.' *The Cambridge History of Irish Literature*. Vol. 2. Margaret Kelleher and Philip O'Leary, eds. Cambridge: Cambridge U. Press, 2006: 226–269.

Nic Eoin, Máirín. *Trén bhFearann Breac*. Baile Átha Cliath: Cois Life, 2005.

Nic Pháidín, Caoilfhionn. '"Cén Fáth Nach?'– Ó Chanúint Go Criól." *Idir Lúibíní. Aistí ar an Léitheoireacht agus ar an Litearthacht*. Róisín Ní Mhianáin, ed. Baile Átha Cliath: Cois Life, 2003: 113–130.

Ní Dhomhnaill, Nuala. 'An Fhilíocht á Cumadh: Ceardlann Filíochta'. *Léachtaí Cholm Cille*, XVII (1986).

Ní Dhonnchadha, Aisling and Máirín Nic Eoin. *Ar an gCoigríoch: Díolaim Litríochta ar Scéal na hImirce*. Indreabhán: Cló Iar-Chonnachta, 2008.

Ní Dhonnchadha, Aisling, ed. *An Prós Comhaimseartha. Léachtaí Cholm Cille XXXVI*. Maigh Nuad: An Sagart, 2006.

Nikolajeva, Maria. *Children's Literature Comes of Age: Towards a New Aesthetic*. New York: Garland, 1996.

Ní Mhianáin, Róisín ed. *Idir Lúibíní. Aistí ar an Léitheoireacht agus ar an Litearthacht*. Baile Átha Cliath: Cois Life, 2003.

Nolan, Janet. *Ourselves Alone: Women's Emigration from Ireland 1885–1920*. Lexington, KY: University Press of Kentucky, 1989.

O'Brien, Gerard. *Irish Governments and the Guardianship of Historical Records, 1922–72*. Dublin: Four Courts Press, 2004.

O'Casey, Sean. *Drums under the Window*. London: Macmillan, 1945.

Ó Catháin, Séamas. 'Institiúid Bhéaloideas Éireann.' *Béaloideas* (2005): 85–110.

Ó Cearnaigh, Seán and Caoilfhionn Nic Pháidín. 'Pláinéad Uaigneach – Prós na Gaeilge.' *An Prós Comhaimseartha. Léachtaí Cholm Cille XXXVI*. Aisling Ní Dhonnchadha, ed. Maigh Nuad: An Sagart, 2006: 7–24.

Ó Conaire, Pádraic. *Scothscéalta*, Tomás de Bhaldraithe, ed. Dublin, 1956.

Ó Conghaile, Micheál. 'An Fear Aniar. An Interview with Micheál Ó Conghaile.' *Canadian Journal of Irish Studies* 31. 2 (Fall 2005): 54–59.

O'Connor, Anne. *The Blessed and the Damned, Sinful Women and Unbaptised Children in Irish Folklore*. London: Peter Lang, 2005.

O'Connor, Anne. 'A Personal Reflection of the Influence of Irish Folklore.' *Sinsear, the Folklore Journal* (2005): 7–8.

O'Connor, Joseph. 'Where the Stones Sing.' *The Guardian* (7 Deireadh Fómhair 2006).

Ó Giolláin, Diarmuid. *Locating Irish Folklore: Tradition, Modernity, Identity.* Cork: Cork University Press, 2000.

Ó Grianna, Séamus. *Caisleáin Óir.* BÁC: Preas Dún Dealgan, 1924.

Ó hÓgáin, Dáithí. 'Béaloideas – Notes on the History of a Word.' *Béaloideas* 70 (2002): 83–98.

Okely, Judith M. and Helen Calloway, eds. *Anthropology and Autobiography: Participatory Experience and Embodied Knowledge.* London: Routledge, 1992.

Okely, Judith. *Simone de Beauvoir: A Rereading.* London: Virago Press, 1986.

O'Leary, Philip. 'The Irish Renaissance, 1880–1940: Literature in Irish.' *The Cambridge History of Irish Literature.* Vol. 2. Margaret Kelleher and Philip O'Leary, eds. Cambridge: Cambridge U. Press, 2006: 226–269.

Olrik, Axel. 'Epic Laws of Folk Narrative.' *The Study of Folklore.* Alan Dundes, ed. Berkeley: University of California at Berkeley, 1965.

Ó Muirí, Pól. 'The Noise of a New Generation.' *Irish Times.* (14 Iúil 2007).

Ó Muirí, Pól. 'Tost million go leith Gaeilgeoir sa Stát.' *Irish Times.* (25 Meitheamh 2003).

Ó Muirí, Pól. 'Self-discovery in Dingle.' *Irish Times.* (9 Meán Fómhair 2000).

Ó Muirí, Pól. 'An Irishman's Diary.' *Irish Times.* (6 Deireadh Fómhair 1998).

Ó Muirthile, Liam. 'Ó, Lucky muid', 'Á, Poor iad', 'Madraí na Nollag', 'Óró Anró'. *Ar an bPeann.* Baile Átha Cliath: Cois Life, 2006: 187–203.

Ó Neachtain, Joe Steve. *Lámh Láidir.* Indreabhán: CIC, 2005.

Ó Neachtain, Joe Steve. *Scread Mhaidne.* Indreabhán: CIC, 2003.

O'Neill, Áine. '"The Fairy Hill is on Fire" (MLSIT 6071): A Panorama of Multiple Functions.' *Béaloideas* 59 (1991): 189–196.

Ó Siadhail, Pádraig. 'Contemporary Irish Language Literature: A Parasite's Delight (Or Súgáin, Sougawns, and Straw Ropes).' *The Nashwaak Review* 10. 1 (Fall 2001): 106–122.

Ó Súilleabháin, Seán, ed. *Folktales of Ireland.* Chicago: University of Chicago Press, 1966.

Ó Súilleabháin, Séan and Reidar Th. Christiansen. *The Types of the Irish Folktale*. Helsinki: Folklore Fellows Communications [FFC] 78, no. 188, 1963.

O'Súilleabháin, Seán. 'Tales of Magic.' *A Handbook of Irish Folklore*. Wexford: The Educational Company of Ireland for The Folklore of Ireland Society, 1942.

Ó Torna, Caitríona. *Cruthú na Gaeltachta 1893–1922*. BÁC: Cois Life, 2005.

Patten, Eve. *The Cambridge Companion to the Irish Novel*. 14. *Contemporary Irish Fiction*. http://cco.cambridge.org/extract?id=ccol0521861918 _CCOL052186 1918A015

Peach, Linden. *The Contemporary Irish Novel: Critical Readings*. London: Palgrave Macmillan, 2004.

Pelan, Rebecca. *Two Irelands: Literary Feminisms North and South*. New York: Syracuse University Press, 2005.

Perry, Donna. 'Éilís Ní Dhuibhne.' *Backtalk. Women Writers Speak Out*. New Jersey: Rutgers University Press, 1993: 245–60.

Phillips, Richard. 'Writing Travel and Mapping Sexuality. Richard Burton's Sotadic Zone.' James Duncan and Derek Gregory, eds., *Writes of Passage. Reading Travel Writing*. London: Routledge, 1999.

Pierce, David. *Irish Writing in the Twentieth Century: A Reader*. Cork: Cork University Press, 2000.

Raftery, Mary and Eoin O'Sullivan. *Suffer the Little Children: The Inside Story of Ireland's Industrial Schools*. Dublin: New Island, 1999.

Rapport, Nigel. *The Prose and the Passion: Anthropology, Literature and the Writing of E.M. Forster*. Manchester: Manchester U. Press, 1994.

Revie, Linda. 'Nuala Ní Dhomhnaill's "Parthenogenesis": A Bisexual Exchange.' *Poetry in Contemporary Irish Literature*. Micheal Kenneally, ed. Gerrards Cross: Colin Smythe, 1995.

Riggs, Pádraigín and Norman Vance. 'Irish Prose Fiction.' *The Cambridge Companion to Modern Irish Culture*. Cambridge: Cambridge U. Press, 2005.

Roberts, Adam. *Science Fiction*. London: Routledge, 2000.

Roberts Schumake, Jeanette. 'Accepting the Grotesque Body: *Bildungs* by Claire Boylan and Éilís Ní Dhuibhne.' *Estudios irlandeses*. 1 (2006): 103–11.

Roche, Anthony. 'Introduction: Contemporary Irish Fiction.' *Irish University Review* (Spring/Summer 2000): VII–XI.

Rose, Jacqueline. *The Case of Peter Pan: Or, The Impossibility of Children's Fiction*. London: Macmillan, 1984.

Russell, Ruth. *What's the Matter with Ireland?* NY: Devin-Adair, [c1920].

Said, Edward W. *Culture & Imperialism.* London: Chatto & Windus, 1993.

Said, Edward. 'The Mind of Winter.' *Harpers.* 269 (1984): 49–55.

Sax, Boria. *The Serpent and the Swan: The Animal Bride in Folklore and Literature.* Blacksburg, Virginia: McDonald and Woodward, 1998: 21–2.

Schulte, Rainer. *The Geography of Translation and Interpretation: Traveling Between Languages.* Lampeter: The Edwin Mellen Press, 2001.

Seelinger Trites, Roberta. *Disturbing the Universe.* Iowa: U. of Iowa Press, 2000.

Shildrick, Margrit and Janet Price, eds. *Vital Signs: Feminist Reconfigurations of the Bio/logical Body.* Edinburgh: Edinburgh University Press, 1998.

Siegel, Kristi, ed. *Issues in Travel Writing: Empire, Spectacle and Displacement.* New York: Peter Lang, 2002.

Smith, James M. 'The Politics of Sexual Knowledge: The Origins of Ireland's Containment Culture and the Carrigan Report (1931).' *Journal of the History of Sexuality.* 13. 2 (2004), 208–233.

Smyth, Ailbhe. *The Abortion Papers, Ireland.* Dublin: Attic Press, 1992.

Smyth, Ailbhe. 'The Floozie in the Jacuzzi.' *Feminist Studies* 17.1 (1991), 6–29.

Smyth, Ailbhe ed. *Wildish Things: An Anthology of New Irish Women's Writing.* Dublin: Attic Press, 1989.

Smyth, Gerry. *Space and the Irish Cultural Imagination.* Basingstoke: Palgrave, 2001.

Smyth, Gerry. *The Novel and the Nation.* Chicago: Pluto Press, 1997.

Spackman, Barbara. *'inter musam et ursam moritur*: Folengo and the Gaping "Other" Mouth.' *Refiguring Woman: Perspectives on Gender and the Italian Renaissance.* Marilyn Migiel and Juliana Schiesari, eds. Ithaca, NY: Cornell University Press, 1991: 19–34.

Stephens, John. *Language and Ideology in Children's Fiction.* London: Longman, 1992.

Stover, Leon. *Science Fiction from Wells to Heinlein.* North Carolina: McFarland, 2002.

St. Peter, Christine. 'Negotiating the Boundaries: Interview with Éilís Ní Dhuibhne.' *Canadian Journal of Irish Studies,* 32: 1 (Spring 2006), 68–75.

St Peter, Christine. *Changing Ireland: Strategies in Contemporary Irish Women's Fiction.* New York: Palgrave St Martin's, 2000.

Strathern, Marilyn. *The Relation: Issues in Complexity and Scale. Inaugural Lecture 1994 by the William Wyse Professor of Social Anthropology.* Cambridge: Prickly Pear Press, 1995.

Sucher, Laurie. *The Fiction of Ruth Prawer Jhabvala: The Politics of Passion.* New York: Palgrave Macmillan, 1989.

Tatar, Maria ed. *The Classic Fairy Tales.* New York: W.W. Norton and Company, 1999), 25–72.

Tempus Weinrich, Harald. *Besprochene und erzählte Welt.* Stuttgart: Kohlhammer, 1964. Italian translation, Tempus. *Le funzioni dei tempi nel testo.* (Bologna: Il Mulino, [1978], 2004.

Thompson, Stith. *The Folktale.* Berkeley: U. of California Press, 1977.

Thompson, Stith and Antti Aarne. *The Types of the Folktale: A Classification and Bibliography.* Helsinki: Folklore Fellows Communications [FFC], No. 184, 1961.

Thompson, Stith. *Motif-Index of Folk-Literature.* 6 Vols. rev. ed. Helsinki: Folklore Fellows Communications [FFC], Nos. 106–109, 116, 117, 1932–1936.

Titley, Alan. 'Anarchy, artistry, ailments.' *Irish Times* (4 Deireadh Fómhair 2003).

Titley, Alan. *Méirscrí na Treibhe.* Baile Átha Cliath: An Clóchomhar, 1978.

Todorov, Tsvetan. *The Fantastic: A Structural Approach to a Literary Genre.* New York: Cornell University Press, 1973.

Tóibín, Colm. *Walking Along the Border.* London: MacDonald Queen Anne Press, 1987.

Tóibín, Colm. *Mothers and Sons.* London: Picador, 2006.

Tolstoy, Leo. *Anna Karenina* (London: Oxford University Press, 1998.

Turner, Victor. 'African Ritual and Western Literature: Is a Comparative Symbology Possible?' *The Literature of Fact.* Angus Fletcher, ed. English Institute Series. New York: Columbia University Press, 1976.

Ui Cnáimhsí, Pádraig. *Róise Rua.* BÁC: Sáirséal Ó Marcaigh, 1988.

W. Von Sydow, Carl. *Selected Papers on Folklore.* Copenhagen: Rosenkilde and Bagger, 1948.

Wardhaugh, Ronald. *An Introduction to Sociolinguistics.* 4th ed. Malden, Massachusetts: Blackwell Publishing, 2002.

Warner, Marina. *From the Beast to the Blonde: On Fairy Tales and Their Tellers*. London: Vintage, 1995.

Warwick Nicola. 'Interview with Éilís Ní Dhuibhne'. *One Woman's Writing Retreat*. http://www.prairieden.com/front_porch/visiting_authors/dhuibhne.html (2001).

Welch, Robert. '"Isn't This Your Job? – To Translate?" Brian Friel's Languages.' *The Achievement of Brian Friel*. Alan J. Peacock, ed. Gerrards Cross: Colin Smythe, 1993: 134–148.

Wulff, Helena. *Dancing at the Crossroads: Memory and Mobility in Ireland*. Oxford: Berghahn Books, 2007.

Yampbell, Cat. 'Judging a Book by its Cover: Publishing Trends in Young Adult Literature.' *The Lion and the Unicorn* 29.3 (2005): 348–372.

Yeats, W.B. *The Countess Kathleen: And Various Legends and Lyrics*. London: T. Fisher Unwin, 1892.

Novels in English

The Bray House (Dublin: Attic Press, 1990).

Singles (Dublin: Basement Press, 1994).

The Dancers Dancing (Belfast: Blackstaff Press, 1999/2000/2007; London: Hodder Review 2000).

Fox, Swallow, Scarecrow (Belfast: Blackstaff Press, 2007).

Novels in Irish

Dúnmharú sa Daingean (Baile Átha Cliath: Cois Life, 2000).

Cailíní Beaga Ghleann na mBláth (Baile Átha Cliath: Cois Life, 2003).

Dún an Airgid (Baile Átha Cliath: Cois Life, 2008).

Short Story Collections

Blood and Water (Dublin: Attic Press, 1988).

Eating Women Is Not Recommended (Dublin: Attic Press, 1991).

'The Inland Ice' and Other Stories (Belfast: Blackstaff Press, 1997).

'The Pale Gold of Alaska' and Other Stories (Belfast: Blackstaff Press, 2000; London: Hodder Review 2000).

'Midwife to the Fairies': New and Selected Stories (Cork: Attic Press, 2003).

Short Stories in English

'Green Fuse', *Irish Press*, New Irish Writing, February 1974 (published under the pseudonym Elizabeth Dean).

'The Duck-billed Platypus', *Irish Press*, New Irish Writing, 1975 (pseud. Elizabeth Dean).

'A Fairer House', *Irish Press*, New Irish Writing, 1976 (pseud. Elizabeth Dean).

'Prepare a Face', *Irish Press*, New Irish Writing, 1978 (pseud. Elizabeth Dean).

'The Postmen's Strike', *Irish Press*, New Irish Writing, 1979 (pseud. Elizabeth Dean).

'Looking', *Sunday Independent*, 1981.

'The Catechism Examination' *Irish Press*, New Irish Writing, 1982.

'Blood and Water', *Irish Press*, New Irish Writing, 1983.

'A Visit to Newgrange', *Irish Times*, 1985.

'Fulfilment', *Panurge Magazine*, 1986.

'Eating Women Is Not Recommended', *Irish Times*, 1989.

'The Garden of Eden', *Irish Times*, 1990.

'The Makers', in *The Phoenix Book of Irish Short Stories*. Ed. David Marcus. (London: Phoenix, 1998).

'The Master Key', in *Ladies Night at Finbar's Hotel*. Ed. Dermot Bolger. (Dublin: New Island Books/London, Picador, 1999).

'The Moon Shines Clear, the Horseman's Near', in *Phoenix Book of Irish Short Stories*. Ed. David Marcus. (London, Phoenix, 2002).

'It is a Miracle', in *Arrows in Flight: Irish short stories*. Ed. Caroline Walsh, (Dublin/New York: Townhouse, 2002).

'Evelina', first broadcast BBC Radio 4, 2004.

'A Literary Lunch', in *Faber Book of Irish Short Stories 2006*. ed David Marcus, (London, Faber & Faber, 2006).

'The Strange Case of the Scream in the Night', first broadcast BBC Radio 4, 2008.

'Right of Passage', Amnesty Series, *Irish Times*, July 2008.

Short Stories in Irish

'Luachra' in Cathal Póirtéir, eag. *Scéalta san Aer* (Baile Átha Cliath: Coiscéim, 2000: 96–102).

Children's Books

The Uncommon Cormorant (Dublin: Poolbeg, 1990).

Hugo and the Sunshine Girl (Dublin: Poolbeg, 1991).

The Hiring Fair (Dublin: Poolbeg, 1993).

Blaeberry Sunday (Dublin: Poolbeg, 1994).

Penny Farthing Sally (Dublin: Poolbeg, 1996).

The Sparkling Rain (Dublin: Poolbeg, 2003).

Hurlamaboc (Baile Átha Cliath: Cois Life, 2006).

Úpraid (Glasgow: Úr Sgeul, 2006) – Scots Gaelic version of *Hurlamaboc*.

Poetry

'Roots', *Cyphers*, 1983.

'St John's Eve', *Irish Press*, New Irish Writing, 1984.

'Evening at Annaghmakerring', *Irish Press,* New Irish Writing, 1984.

'Cafe Au Lait', *Sunday Tribune*, New Irish Writing, 1985.

'Hair', *Sunday Tribune*, New Irish Writing, 1987.

'The Little Girls', *Poetry Ireland*, c. 1987.

'Lust for Lunch', *Sunday Tribune*, New Irish Writing, 1991.

Mark My Words. Meditations to Accompany Alice Maher's exhibition, 'The Night Garden', Dublin, Royal Hibernian Academy, 2007.

Plays

Dún na mBan Trí Thine, produced by Amharclann de Hide and first performed at the Peacock, Dublin, 1995.

Milseog an tSamhraidh, produced by Amharclann de Hide and first performed at the Samuel Beckett Theatre, Trinity College, 1996.

(Published as *Milseog an tSamhraidh* agus *Dún na mBan Trí Thine* (Baile Átha Cliath: Cois Life, 1998).

The Wild Swans, produced by the Abbey and performed at the Peacock Theatre, Dublin, 1998.

Radio Plays

Casadh an Tape Recorder. RTÉ Radio 1 drama first broadcast on 17 October 2003.

Bábóga, Raidio na Gaeltachta, first broadcast autumn 2008.

Non-Fiction

Editor, *Voices on the Wind: Women Poets of the Celtic Twilight* (Dublin: New Island, 1995).

'The Irish', in Ake Daun and Soren Jansson, ed. *Europeans. Essays on Culture and Identity*. (Lund, Nordic Academic Press, 1999: 47–65).

'Family Values: The Sheehy Skeffington Papers in the National Library of Ireland'. *History Ireland*, (Spring 2000).

'Reader, I Married Him', in *From Newman to New Woman. UCD Women Remember*. Ed Anne Macdona, (Dublin, New Island, 2001: 175–79).

'Narrative Techniques in *The Mai'*, in *The Theatre of Marina Carr*, ed. Cathy Leeney and Anna McMullan, (Dublin: Carysfort Press, 2003: 65–74).

'Why Would Anyone Write in Irish?' in Ciarán Mac Murchaidh, ed., *'Who Needs Irish?': Reflections on the Importance of the Irish Language Today* (Dublin: Veritas Publications, 2004).

'Learning Language Without Words'. *Irish Times*, 5 August 2005.

'Transcending Genre: Sebastian Barry's Juvenile Fiction', in *Out of History: Essays on the Writings of Sebastian Barry*. Ed. Christina Hunt Mahony, (Dublin: Carysfort Press, 2006: 25–36).

WB Yeats, Works and Days. Ed, with James Quin and Ciara McDonnell. (Dublin: National Library, 2006).

"Saibhreas nó Daibhreas? An Scríbhneoir Dátheangach" in Aisling Ní Dhonnchadha, ed. *An Prós Comhaimseartha. Léachtaí Cholm Cille XXXVI*. (Maigh Nuad: An Sagart, 2006: 139–154).

'Prayers of the Faithful'. *Irish Times*, 7 July 2007.

Folklore

'The Brave Tailor'. *Sinsear, the Folklore Journal*, (1980): 84–91.

'Ex Corde: At 1186 in Irish tradition'. *Béaloideas*, (1980): 86–134.

'Old English Metre and Children's Street Rhymes'. *Sinsear, the Folklore Journal*, (1982): 76–82.

'Dublin Modern Legends: An Intermediate Type-List'. *Béaloideas*, (1983): 55–69.

'"The Land of Cokaygne"': A Middle English Source for Irish Food Historians'. *Ulster Folklife*, (1988).

'"The Loving Wife": Synge's Use of Popular Material in *The Shadow of the Glen*'. *Béaloideas*, (1990): 141–180

With Séamas Ó Catháin, eds., *Viking Ale, Studies on Folklore Contacts between the Northern and Western Worlds* (presented to Bo Almqvist on the occasion of his 60th birthday) (Aberystwyth: Boethius Press, 1991).

'Legends of the Supernatural in Anglo-Irish Literature'. *Béaloideas*, 60–1. No. 1992–3 (1992): 145–150.

'The Old Woman as Hare: Structure and Meaning in an Irish Legend'. *Folklore*, Vol. 104 (1993).

'The Irish' in Åke Daun and Sören Jansson, eds. *Europeans: Essays on Culture and Identity* (Lund: Nordic Academic Press, 1999: 47–66).

'The Cow that Ate the Pedlar in Kerry and Wyoming'. *Béaloideas*, (1999), 125–134.

Introduction to Séamas Ó Catháin, ed., *Northern Lights, Following Folklore in North-Western Europe, Essays in Honour of Bo Almqvist* (Dublin: University College Dublin Press, 2001).

'Fer in the North Contree: With His Whole Heart Revisited' in Séamas Ó Catháin, ed, *Northern Lights* (Dublin: University College Dublin Press, 2001: 202–214).

Translator of 'The Story of the Little White Goat' as told by Máire Ruiséal, *Field Day Anthology of Irish Writing, Volume IV: Irish Women's Writing and Traditions.* (New York: New York University Press, 2002: 1219–1232).

'Women and Irish Narrative Tradition'. Supplement to the *Field Day Anthology of Irish Writing: Volumes IV and V* (Cork: Cork University Press, 2002).

'"They made me tea and gave me a lift home": Urban Folklore Collecting 1979–1980'. *Béaloideas*, (2006), 63–84.

Blood and Water (Dublin: Attic Press, 1988).

The Uncommon Cormorant (Dublin: Poolbeg, 1990).

The Bray House (Dublin: Attic Press, 1990).

Hugo and the Sunshine Girl (Dublin: Poolbeg, 1991).

Eating Women Is Not Recommended (Dublin: Attic Press, 1991).

Co-Editor with Séamas Ó Cátháin, *Viking Ale, Studies on Folklore Contacts between the Northern and Western Worlds* (Aberystwyth: Boethius Press, 1991).

The Hiring Fair (Dublin: Poolbeg, 1992).

Blaeberry Sunday (Dublin: Poolbeg, 1993).

Singles (Basement Press, 1994).

Editor, *Voices on the Wind: Women Poets of the Celtic Twilight* (Dublin: New Island Books, 1995).

Penny Farthing Sally (Dublin: Poolbeg, 1996).

'The Inland Ice' and Other Stories (Belfast: Blackstaff Press, 1997).

Milseog an tSamhraidh & *Dún na mBan Trí Thine* (BÁC: Cois Life, 1998).

The Dancers Dancing (Belfast: Blackstaff Press, 1999).

'The Pale Gold of Alaska' and Other Stories (Belfast: Blackstaff Press, 2000).

Dúnmharú sa Daingean (Baile Átha Cliath: Cois Life, 2000).

Cailíní Beaga Ghleann na mBláth (Baile Átha Cliath: Cois Life, 2003).

Midwife to the Fairies: New and Selected Stories (Cork: Attic Press, 2003).

The Sparkling Rain (Dublin: Poolbeg, 2003).

Hurlamaboc (Baile Átha Cliath: Cois Life, 2006).

Co-Editor with James Quin and Ciara McDonnell, *WB Yeats, Works and Days* (Dublin: National Library, 2006).

Fox, Swallow, Scarecrow (Belfast: Blackstaff Press, 2007).

Dún an Airgid (Baile Átha Cliath: Cois Life, 2008).

ANNE FOGARTY is Professor of James Joyce Studies at UCD and President of the International James Joyce Foundation. She is Director of the UCD James Joyce Research Centre and editor of *Irish University Review*. With Luca Crispi, she is editor of the newly-founded *Dublin James Joyce Journal*, co-published with the National Library of Ireland. She has been Academic Director of the Dublin James Joyce Summer School since 1997, and is recipient of the 2008 Charles Fanning Prize in Irish Studies.

JACQUELINE FULMER took her PhD in Rhetoric, with an emphasis in Oral Tradition Studies, from the University of California, Berkeley. She has taught rhetorical theory, Irish literature and culture, African-, Irish-, and Chinese-American literature, women's studies, American cultures studies, and folklore at UC Berkeley and San Francisco State University. She is the author of *Folk Women and Indirection in Morrison, Ní Dhuibhne, Hurston, and Lavin* (Ashgate, 2007).

ANNE MARKEY is a Post-doctoral Fellow in the Centre for Irish-Scottish and Comparative Studies in Trinity College Dublin. Her research interests focus on the intersections between Irish-language traditions and Irish writing in English. She has published widely on this subject and is currently working on a new edition of Joseph Campbell's translations of Patrick Pearse's short stories, to be published by UCD Press in 2009.

CAITRIONA MOLONEY is an Associate Professor in the English Department at Bradley University, where she is the British modernist and also teaches Irish literature. She is co-editor, with Helen Thompson, of *Irish Women Writers Speak Out: Voices from the Field*. Caitriona is currently working on a book on contemporary Irish women fiction writers.

BRIAN Ó CONCHUBHAIR is an Assistant Professor in the Department of Irish Language and Literature and a Fellow of the Keough-Naughton Institute for Irish Studies at the University of Notre Dame. His recent publications include *Gearrscéalta Ár Linne* (CIC, 2006) and *Why Irish? Irish Language and Literature in Academia* (Arlen House, 2008). He is currently completing a manuscript on the Irish language *Fin de siècle*.

ANNE O'CONNOR is passionate about Irish folklore and has been a friend and colleague of Éilís Ní Dhuibhne's since the late 1970s. Anne's major research focuses on the representation of women in Irish religious belief and legend and her book, *The Blessed and the Damned: Sinful Women and Unbaptised Children in Irish Folklore* (Peter Lang, 2005), reassesses the subject of her doctoral thesis in the light of feminist and postmodern perspectives. Anne currently works with Radio Telefís Éireann (RTÉ).

Sarah O'Connor is Assistant Professor of Celtic Studies in St. Michael's College, University of Toronto. A former Government of Ireland HEA Scholar she was also one of the Irish-language researchers working on the Database of Irish Women Writers 1800–2005 funded by the Arts and Humanities Research Council and directed by Professor Gerardine Meaney (UCD) and Professor Maria Luddy (U of Warwick).

Pádraig Ó Siadhail is Associate Professor and holder of the D'Arcy McGee Chair of Irish Studies at Saint Mary's University, Halifax, Nova Scotia. His most recent book is *An Béaslaíoch: Beatha agus Saothar Phiarais Béaslaí, 1881–1965* (2007), a biography of the Liverpool born and bred Irish language writer who played a significant role in the Irish Revolution and was the original biographer of Michael Collins.

Mary Shine Thompson is Dean of Research and Humanities at St Patrick's College, Drumcondra. She is president of the Irish Society for the Study of Children's Literature (ISSCL) and chair of *Poetry Ireland*. In 2006–07, she chaired the Bisto Children's Book of the Year Judging Panel. She has written biographical notes of authors and story-notes for the 20 books in the series of *Irish Independent Great Children's Books* (2006).

Christine St. Peter is Professor of Women's Studies at the University of Victoria, Canada. She has published widely in the areas of Irish and Canadian women's writing, and in women's health issues in Canada. Her monograph, *Changing Ireland: Strategies in Contemporary Women's Fiction* (Macmillan) won a 'Choice' award in 2001. Her most recent publication is a collection of essays co-edited with Patricia Haberstroh, *Opening the Field: Irish Women: Tests and Contexts* (Cork University Press, 2007).

Giovanna Tallone is a graduate in Modern Languages from Università Cattolica del Sacro Cuore, Milan, and holds a PhD in English Studies from the University of Florence. An EFL teacher, she is currently attached to the Department of English at Università Cattolica, Milan. Her main research interests include Irish women writers, contemporary Irish drama, and the remaking of Old Irish legends.

Helena Wulff is Professor of Social Anthropology at Stockholm University. She is author of *Dancing at the Crossroads: Memory and Mobility in Ireland* (2007, Berghahn) and editor of *The Emotions: A Cultural Reader* (2007, Berg). Her most recent research concerns writing and Irish literature as cultural process and form. Geographically, her research has been located in London, Stockholm, New York, Frankfurt-am-Main and, most extensively, in Ireland.

INDEX

Aarne, Antti, 227, 242, 281, 338
Aarne-Thompson Index, 228, 243, 268, 270, 274, 279, 283
Abbey Theatre 136, 148, 333, 342
Almqvist, Bo, 232, 244, 264-5, 267-8, 271-2, 274, 281-4, 325, 243
An Caighdeán Oifigiúil, 130, 154, 201
Annaghmakerrig, 24, 28
Anzaldúa, Gloria, 14, 28, 325
Archetti, Eduardo, 251, 260, 325
Ardener, Shirley, 246, 259, 325
Ashcroft, Bill, 174, 193, 325
Atwood, Margaret, 186, 196, 325
Austen, Jane 55, 252, 260, 329

Bacchilega, Cristina 225, 228, 230, 233-5, 242, 244, 325
Bakhtin, Mikhail 13-4, 27,
Banshee 20, 277, 282, 325
Banville, John 70, 85, 325
Barreca, Regina 234, 244, 326
Bartlett, Richard 31
Beckett, Samuel 256-7
Benjamin, Walter 71, 85, 326
Beauty and the Beast 72, 75, 84
Bhabha, Homi 13, 27, 105, 112, 326
Big House 117-8, 123-4, 128, 331
Bildungsroman/Bildungsreise 5, 25, 29-30, 34, 43, 46, 48-9, 106, 139-41, 155, 183, 247, 333
Binaries 12, 14, 22
Bishop, Des 185
Bisto 145, 151, 153, 168, 180, 195, 346
Bolan, Marc 185
Boland, Eavan 29, 46, 326
Bolger, Dermot 51, 341
Borrow, George 106

Bourke, Angela 105, 112, 116-7, 127, 228, 232, 243-4, 279, 284, 326
Bowen, Elizabeth 26, 113-5, 118, 127
Boyle Haberstroh, Patricia 254, 261, 326
Bronte, Charlotte 141
Brothers Grimm 75
Butler Cullingford, Elizabeth 96, 110, 326

Carr, Marina 23, 28, 327, 342
Catholic 35, 44, 47,.89, 91, 93-5, 97-9, 106, 123-4, 138, 158, 177, 221, 244, 257, 317, 332
Celtic Tiger 12, 45, 89, 102, 156, 168, 245, 257
Census 134
Chaucer, Geoffrey 53-4, 250, 267, 269, 271, 275
Chekhov, Anton 82
Chernobyl 51
'Chick-Lit' 3, 16
children/children's literature 5, 11, 15, 19, 26, 33-5, 45, 55, 69, 74-5, 93-8, 115-6, 118, 120-1, 127, 129, 131-2, 137-8, 144-5, 148-153, 160-1, 163, 165, 168-70, 177, 185, 231, 233-4, 256-7, 272, 281, 308, 310, 327, 329-30, 332-4, 336-7, 341, 343, 345-6
Christiansen, Reidar Th. 235, 243, 272, 281-3, 327, 336
Class 11-2, 31, 33-4, 41, 44-5, 47-9, 96-7, 99-103, 123, 125, 133-4, 140, 156-62, 201-2, 204, 208, 210, 212, 227, 252, 255-6
Cleary, Bridget 112, 244, 279, 284, 326
Cleary, Joe 88, 108, 327

Cois Life 211, 215, 216
coming-of-age 5, 25, 30, 132, 151, 156, 162-3, 166, 168
Communicable Diseases Act 94, 96
Connolly, Claire 50, 66, 110, 112, 331
Conrad, Kathryn 91, 108, 327
Conradh na Gaeilge 130, 134, 148, 183
Cronin, Michael 134, 148, 327

Dean, Elizabeth (pseudonym) 15, 340
Death 18-20, 22, 24, 41, 53, 62, 65, 87-8, 133, 137, 139, 141, 143, 163, 166, 186, 196, 222, 235, 239, 255, 273, 296, 302, 325, 329
Dedalus, Stephen 138, 193
Defoe, Daniel 53, 150
De Paor, Louis 216, 219, 327
D'hoker, Elke 85, 178, 194, 327
Dirane, Pat 273-4
Delargy, James H. 73, 264, 279,
Dénouement 66, 132, 141
Donoghue, Emma 16,
Doyle, Roddy 51, 70, 85
Doyle, Rose 184, 195
Duffy, Patrick 252-3, 260, 327
Dunbar, Robert 145, 149, 152, 168, 327
Dundes, Alan 227, 242, 281, 328
Dwyer, Davin 195, 328
Dylan, Bob 55

Ecocriticism 56
Eliot, T.S. 53, 277-8,
Emigration 87-9, 92-3, 99-100, 102, 107-8, 148-9, 328, 332, 334
Enlightenment 42,
Ethnography 245, 247, 249-51, 258, 260, 327, 334
Exile 5, 26, 87-89, 91, 100-2, 105-8, 111, 136, 139, 142, 147, 252

Fairytales 55, 72-3, 75-6, 116,l 162, 225, 228, 234, 239, 267, 279
feminism/feminist 11, 16, 22, 26-7, 47, 51, 53, 91, 171, 178, 205, 221-3, 225, 227-8, 230, 234-6, 241, 246, 256, 278-80
Ferriter, Diarmaid 137
Field Day Anthology 72, 228, 243-4, 254, 278, 284, 326, 343
Finnegan, Frances 93-5, 97-8, 109-10, 328
Flanagan, Maeve 179,194, 328
Flynn, Dermod 137
Fogarty, Anne 5, 26, 69, 245, 247, 249, 258, 259-60, 275, 283, 328, 345
Folklore 11-2, 15, 18-9, 26-8, 37, 41, 48, 72, 85, 89, 102, 111, 154-5, 172, 202, 222-7, 231-5, 239, 241-5, 248, 253, 259-60, 263-9, 271-83, 325-9, 332, 334-8, 343-5
Folktales 85, 118, 194, 231-4, 243, 266-8, 270, 272, 278, 280, 284, 327, 335
Forster, E.M. 252, 336
Friel, Brian 23, 28, 134, 144, 149, 216, 328, 339
Fulmer, Jacqueline 6, 26, 85, 221, 242, 328, 345

Gaeilgeoiri 134, 183, 195-6, 335
Gaeltacht 30, 34-5, 43-5, 47, 89, 102-4, 113-4, 125, 129-31, 133, 154, 156, 172-3, 181, 183-5, 195, 198-9, 201-2, 204-7, 209, 213, 247, 255, 275-6, 278, 336, 242
Geertz, Clifford 252, 259, 260, 328
Gender 11, 31, 33, 36, 41-3, 45, 47-8, 53, 73, 80, 84-5, 87-9, 92, 102, 108, 127, 150, 225, 242, 244, 253, 257-8, 278, 325-7, 330, 333, 337
Gibbons, Luke 143, 149, 328
Gothic 22, 132
Gray, Breda 91-2, 96, 98-9, 101, 108, 110-1, 328

Gregory, Lady Augusta 136, 148, 253, 328
Grosz, Elizabeth 42, 48, 329

Hamilton, Hugo 173
Hand, Derek 53, 66-7
Handler, Richard 252, 260, 329
Hanson, Clare 85, 329
Harley, J.B. 30, 47, 329
Harte, Liam 146, 150, 329
Hartnett, Michael 198
Hayes, Joanne 236, 239, 244
Henebry, Richard 154
Holbek, Bengt 267, 281, 329
Hooley, Ruth 254, 261, 329
Hopkins, Gerald Manley 30, 37, 40
Horowitz, Sara R. 116-7, 127, 329
Hughes, Linda K. 139, 149, 329
Hunt Mahoney, Christina 224, 229, 242
Hybridity 13-4, 22, 27, 331
Hyde, Douglas 134-5

Identity 144, 146-7, 177-8, 185, 224, 253-4, 259-61, 263, 277-8, 28, 284, 328, 333, 335, 342-3
Indirection 6, 27, 70, 85, 221-3, 226, 228, 230, 233, 239-42, 328, 345
Infanticide 11, 41, 48, 236-7
Intertextuality 12, 51, 53, 72, 84, Irish Free State 93-4, 109
Irish Republican Army 87
Irish language 6, 12, 17-8, 26-7, 35, 48, 89, 102-3, 125, 129, 132, 134-5, 148, 151, 153-5, 168-9, 183, 197-203, 211-17, 219, 226, 247, 253, 255, 277-8, 332, 335, 342, 345

James, Henry 140, 144, 149, 330
Jameson, Frederic 144, 146, 149-50, 330
Jeffers, Jennifer 146, 150, 330
Jouissance 33, 76, 79, 84-5, 142
Joyce, James 9-10, 29, 45-6, 82, 87, 136, 138, 149, 256-7, 330, 345

Jungian Archetype 19, 28

Keenan, Celia 145, 150, 330
Keyes, Marian 16
Kiberd, Declan 46, 126, 128, 252, 258, 260-1, 331
Kilfeather, Siobhan 96
Kreilkamp, Vera 123-4, 128, 331
Kloos, Peter 249-50, 259, 331

Lagerlof, Selma 53-55
Leprince de Beaumont, Jeanne-Marie 75
Lloyd, David 224, 242, 331
Lo, Jacqueline 13, 27, 331
Luddy, Maria 93, 97-8, 109-10, 331-2
Lund, Michael 139, 149, 329
Lyotard, Jean-François 221, 242, 332

Mac Cóil, Liam 196
MacDonagh, Oliver 123, 128
Mac Eachmhartaigh, Joe 268
Mac Gabhainn, Micí 137
MacGill, Patrick 130, 137, 139, 142, 149, 332
Mac Grianna, Seosamh 172
MacIntyre, Martin 195
MacLaughlin, Jim 88, 108, 110-1, 328, 332
Mac Murchaidh, Ciarán 48, 148, 169, 180, 195, 217, 219, 332, 342
MacNamara, Brinsley 159
Mac Síomóin, Tomás 196
Madden-Simpson, Janet 254, 261, 332
Magdalen asylums 93-7, 109-10, 328
Maguire, Moira J. 94-5, 109-10, 236, 244, 332
McCafferty, Nell 236, 244, 333
McClintock, Anne 176-7, 194, 333
McCourt, Frank 139
McCullough, Rose 138

McGahern, John 47, 70, 85, 303, 306, 333
McWilliams, David 213, 219, 333
magic realism 22
Mann, Thomas 53-4
Mansfield, Katherine 82
maps/mapping 25, 29-32, 36-8, 40-2, 44-5, 47, 49-52, 59-61, 64, 66, 68, 301, 307, 310, 313, 329, 333, 336
Markey, Anne 5, 26, 151, 345
Marquez, Gabriel Garcia 22, 28, 332
Meaney, Gerardine 48, 88, 108, 333, 346
Melville, Herman 53
Metafiction 51
Moane, Geraldine 92, 109, 333
Moloney, Caitriona 5, 26, 47-8, 66, 87, 112, 193-4, 244, 333, 345
Morris, Carol 53, 66-8, 333
Morrison, Van 87
Mother Ireland 88
Mothers 21, 34-6, 40-1, 44-5, 49, 51, 55, 63, 70, 74, 85, 89, 91, 93, 97-8, 100-1, 104-5, 109, 114, 122, 124, 129-30, 136, 138, 144, 146, 156-8, 160-2, 164, 167-8, 179, 182, 210, 226, 230-1, 235-40, 247, 249, 255, 257, 290, 296, 299-306, 308-316, 331, 338
Motifs 25, 30, 105, 152, 227, 229, 232, 242, 270
Mulrennan, John Alphonsus 138
Murphy, Maureen 232, 244, 333
Muteness 116-7, 127, 329

Narayan, Kirin 251, 260, 334
Nash, Catherine 31, 47, 333
Nic Eoin, Máirín 149, 154, 169, 184, 195, 218, 334
Ní Dhuibhne, Éilís, publications
Singles (1994) 15-6, 25, 28, 340, 344
Fox, Swallow, Scarecrow (2007) 16-8, 20, 22-3, 25, 28, 69, 258, 261, 340, 344

The Bray House (1990) 5, 25, 49-55, 57-68, 173, 250, 261, 329, 333, 340, 344
The Dancers Dancing (1999) 25, 30, 46, 49-50, 62, 66, 69, 111, 113, 127, 131-2, 168, 181, 183, 185, 191, 198-9, 216, 218, 247, 255, 259, 261, 277, 340, 344
'The Inland Ice' and Other Stories (1997) 26, 69-72, 76, 83-5, 105, 109, 111-2, 201, 229, 243, 275, 279, 284, 340, 344
Cailíní Beaga Ghleann na mBláth (2003) 26, 47, 113, 117, 127-8, 168, 181-2, 186, 191, 196, 204, 210-1, 219, 340, 344
The Hiring Fair (1993) 26, 48, 137, 142, 145, 148, 168, 341, 344
Blaeberry Sunday (1994) 26, 48, 131-6, 142, 145, 148, 168, 341, 344
Penny-farthing Sally (1996) 26, 48, 131-4, 141, 143-4, 148, 341, 344
Hurlamaboc (2006) 5, 26, 131-2, 145, 151-6, 161-4, 166-9, 175, 180, 192, 195, 204, 211-2, 218, 332, 341, 344
Blood and Water (1988) 15, 47-9, 69, 89, 102-4, 110-1, 236, 244, 340, 344
Eating Women is Not Recommended (1991) 69, 111, 224, 340, 341, 344
The Pale Gold of Alaska (2000) 47, 69, 88-9, 91, 100, 108-9, 111, 172, 174, 181, 196, 340, 344
Midwife to the Fairies (2003) 6, 10, 27, 48, 69, 221-2, 226, 228, 231-2, 235, 240-1, 243-4, 249, 258-61, 275, 277, 283-4, 328, 332, 340, 344
The Sparkling Rain (2003) 132, 148, 341, 344
Dúnmharú sa Daingean (2000) 168, 179-81, 197-8, 203-5, 207, 209-11, 213, 215-8, 340, 344
Dún na mBan Trí Thine (1998) 167, 201-2, 210, 217-8, 276, 284, 342, 344
Milseog an tSamhraidh (1998) 181, 201-2, 218, 277-8, 284, 342, 344

Dún an Airgid (2008) 204, 209, 212-4, 217, 219, 340, 344
Casadh an Tape Recorder (2003) 276, 342
Ní Dhuibhne-Almqvist, Éilís 15, 244, 268, 273-4, 282
Ní Dhomhnaill, Nuala 119-20, 128, 178, 194, 244, 325, 334, 336
Nic Pháidín, Caoilfhionn 215-6, 218-9, 334
Nolan, Janet 89, 108, 334
Northern Ireland 33, 116

Ó Cadhain, Máirtín 216, 219, 327
Ó Catháin, Séamus 268, 281-3, 300, 334, 343-4
Ó Cearnaigh, Seán 216, 219, 334
Ó Conaire, Pádraic 159, 169, 334
Ó Conchubhair, Brian 5, 26, 171, 345
Ó Dálaigh, Seosamh 72
Ó Danachair, Caoimhín 265
Ó Duilearga, Séamus 264-5, 284
Ó hEochaidh, Seán 269
Ó Flatharta, Antaine 183
Ó Grianna, Séamus 149, 172, 192-4, 335
Ó Muiri, Pól 182, 192-6, 335
Ó Muirthile, Liam 203, 218, 335
Ó Neachtain, Joe Steve 202, 218, 335
Ó Siadhail, Pádraig 6, 26, 46-7, 197, 219, 335, 346
Ó Súilleabháin, Diarmuid 190
Ó Súilleabháin, Muiris 155, 169
Ó Tuairisc, Eoghan 198
Ó Torna, Caitríona 183, 195, 336
O'Casey, Sean 134, 148, 334
O'Connor, Anne 6, 27, 263, 280-2, 284, 334-5, 345
O'Connor, Joseph 51, 185, 195, 335
O'Connor, Sarah 5, 26, 113, 346
O'Donoghue, Bernard, 146
O'Flaherty, Liam 143

O'Hara, Elizabeth (pseudonym) 15, 28, 48, 148, 168
O'Sullivan, Eoin 137, 149, 336
O'Sullivan, Mark 132
O'Toole, Fintan 101
Okely, Judith 246, 259, 335

Paddy the Cope 137, 148
Parker, Michael 146, 150, 329
Parkinson, Siobhan 132
Patten, Eve 146, 150, 336
Peach, Linden 146-7, 150, 336
Pearse, Padraig 130, 154, 345
Pelan, Rebecca 5, 9, 91, 98, 108, 110, 254, 261, 336
Pierce, David 253, 260, 336
Poe, Edgar Allen 82
Postcolonial 11, 13, 26, 42, 92, 146, 177, 242, 252-3, 279-80, 331
Postmodern 13, 26-7, 67, 70-1, 76, 85, 105, 132, 139, 194, 221-5, 227-8, 230, 235, 239, 241-2, 244, 266, 275, 280, 325, 327, 330, 332, 346
post-structuralist 11, 41, 280
Protestant 35, 47, 123, 158, 257, 317

Raftery, Mary 137, 149, 336
Rapport, Nigel 252, 260, 336
Revie, Linda 120, 128, 336
Richardson, Samuel 53, 55
Riggs, Pádraigín 183, 195, 336
Robinson, Mary 88, 132, 147, 150, 336
Roche, Anthony 67, 145, 150, 261, 336
Ruiséal, Máire 72-3, 75, 228, 232, 235, 242, 343
Ryan, Louise 91, 108, 328

Said, Edward 101, 111, 178, 194, 337
Salinger, J.D. 155, 162
Sax, Boria 75, 85, 337
Sayers, Peig 119, 121, 130, 324
Seanchaí 73
Schulte, Rainer 174, 194, 337

Scotland 106, 193, 274
Seelinger Trites, Roberta 163, 169-70, 337
Segal, Daniel 252, 260, 329
Sellafield 51
Sexuality 26, 33, 41, 43, 68, 70, 76, 79, 87-8, 90-5, 97, 108-9, 121, 127, 226, 253, 326, 333, 336-7
shape-shifting 39
Shaw, George Bernard 257
Shine Thompson, Mary 5, 26, 129, 150, 330, 346
Smyth, Ailbhe 92, 108, 236, 244, 254, 261, 337
Smyth, Gerry 53, 67, 111, 146-7, 150, 337
Stephens, John 163, 170, 337
Stevenson, Robert Louis 55
Stewart, Garrett 144, 149
Strathern, Marilyn 246, 259, 338
St Peter, Christine 5, 25, 29, 111, 276, 337, 346
Synchronic 10, 61
Sucher, Laurie 89, 108, 338
Supernatural 18, 22-4, 28, 128, 229, 243-4, 282-3, 325, 330, 343
swimming 34, 118-22, 190, 283, 343
Synge, John Millington 273-4, 276

Tallone, Giovanna 5, 25, 49, 346
Thompson, Stith 227-9, 242-4, 268, 270, 274, 279, 281, 283, 338
Thompson, George 130
Thoms, William 263, 281
Titley, Alan 182, 195, 198, 202, 218, 338
Todorov, Tzvetan 166, 170, 338
Tóibín, Colm 70, 85, 130, 137, 148-9, 328
Tolstoy, Leo 16-20, 23-5, 28, 338

Uí Gaoithín, Máire 269
Uí Dhónaill, Tomáis 183
Urban Folklore Project 268-9, 272

Utopia 52, 64, 67, 213, 333

Vance, Norman 183, 195, 336

Walker, Nancy A. 228, 242
Wardhaugh, Ronald 199, 203, 207, 218, 338
Warner, Marina 84-5, 339
Warwick, Nicola 28, 127, 148, 195, 259, 261, 339
Wells, H.G. 52
Witches 128, 167, 330
Wulff, Helena 6, 27, 245, 259, 339, 346

Yeats, William Butler 55, 105, 112, 126, 130-1, 135, 144, 149, 252-3, 257, 278, 339, 342, 344
Yellowstone 174